I0729661

Francisco de Goya

and the Art of Critique

Francisco de Goya
and the Art of Critique

Anthony J. Cascardi

ZONE BOOKS · NEW YORK

2022

ZONE BOOKS
633 Vanderbilt Street
Brooklyn, NY 11218

Distributed by Princeton University Press,
Princeton, New Jersey, and Woodstock, United Kingdom

Zone Books series design by Bruce Mau
Typesetting by Meighan Gale
Image placement and production by Julie Fry
Printed and bound by Graphicom S.p.A., Verona

Library of Congress Cataloging-in-Publication Data
Names: Cascardi, Anthony J., 1953– author.
Title: Francisco de Goya : art of critique / Anthony J. Cascardi.
Description: New York : Zone Books, 2022. | Includes bibliographical references and index. | Summary: "The subject of this book is the relationship between the enormous, extraordinary, and sometimes baffling body of Goya's work, and the interconnected issues of modernity, in art, the Enlightenment, and the project of critique" — Provided by publisher.
Identifiers: LCCN 2021048502 (print) | LCCN 2021048503 (ebook) | ISBN 9781942130697 (hardcover) | ISBN 9781942130703 (ebook)
Subjects: LCSH: Goya, Francisco, 1746-1828 — Aesthetics.
Classification: LCC N7113.G68 C27 2022 (print) | LCC N7113.G68 (ebook) | DDC 759.6 — dc23/eng/20211231
LC record available at https://lccn.loc.gov/2021048502
LC ebook record available at https://lccn.loc.gov/2021048503

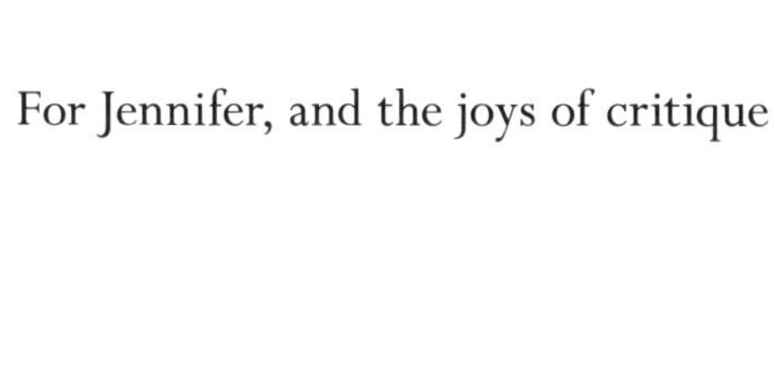

For Jennifer, and the joys of critique

Contents

Introduction 9

I *Secularization and the Aesthetics of Belief* 15

II *A Promise of Happiness?* 55

III *Goya, Modernity, Aesthetic Critique* 89

IV *The Limits of Representation* 137

V *Conflicts of the Faculties: Goya and Kant* 187

VI *Extremities* 229

VII *Freedom and the Face of Darkness* 269

VIII *Beauty and Sympathy* 301

Acknowledgments 329

Notes 331

Index 357

Image Credits 368

Introduction

My subject in this book is the relationship between the enormous, extraordinary, and sometimes baffling body of Francisco de Goya's work and the interconnected issues of modernity, Enlightenment, and critique. This is admittedly a very large topic, but my hope in considering it is that it might help shed some light both on some of the difficulties that Goya's work presents and on the paradoxes of Spanish modernity while establishing that Goya was dedicated throughout his career to the making of art in the service of critique. As for the apparent inconsistencies within Goya's work and its relationship to Enlightened modernity, consider, for example, the fact that *Los desastres de la guerra* (*Disasters of War*) seem to presage the truth-telling function of modern photojournalism, while Spain is often cast as retrograde and reactionary when it comes to a model of modernity that hinges on Enlightenment values. Goya's so-called "Black Paintings" are often thought to represent fearless journeys into regions of the psyche that were charted only much later, by figures such as Ludwig Kirchner and Edvard Munch. The influence of the Black Paintings on the history of modern art is a subject often commented upon by art historians.[1] And yet Goya's portraits of aristocrats are elegantly sedate and mostly conformist, while his colorful and light-filled tapestry "cartoons" seem to portray the leisure activities of a society too happy to be troubled by even the most disturbing domestic and international events.

I take exception to the standard view that relies predominantly on Goya's darkest images to establish his relevance for modernity, and I suggest instead that his work invites us to consider the critical role of art with respect to the modern social and historical worlds, worlds of which it is nonetheless a part. For one thing, the standard views are not altogether coherent, either about Goya or about modernity in art more generally: with respect to Goya, they locate the truth function of art sometimes in a figural literalism (for example, of the *Disasters of War*) and sometimes in fantastical realism (for example, of the Black Paintings), and then with respect to modern art more generally, they simply flatten the curve of these contradictions by telling a story of the eclipse of figuration by abstraction. Yet these very contradictions are among some of the difficulties that the corpus of Goya's work seems to embrace, rather than resolve. They hardly do justice to Goya's oeuvre as a whole, where the inconsistencies are manifest. Indeed, we do well to reckon with the gulf that seems to divide the *Disasters of War* and the Black Paintings, on the one hand, from Goya's scenes of bourgeois life or from the well-mannered portraits of aristocrats, military men, and intellectuals, on the other. What I want to suggest here is that these apparent contradictions themselves offer us the gateway into a vision of the critical function of art within the framework of a modernity that many tend to associate with the dominant Enlightenment values of Germany, England, and France. Call it a vision of aesthetics as critique, one that both identifies itself with and distances itself from what we regard all too broadly and uniformly as "the Enlightenment."

What is "critique"? To the work of criticism, critique adds a self-conscious dimension that incorporates reflection on history, on tradition, on the underlying accepted categories and conditions of knowledge and belief, as well as on the medium through which these are represented. The chapters that follow are meant to illuminate Goya's adherence to this project—a project carried out, perhaps needless to say, within the nondiscursive field of visual art. This affords an alternative to the standard readings of Goya's work, many of which acknowledge the explicit social criticism evident in certain parts of it (for example, the *Caprichos*), but that have little to say about those parts of his work that are not explicitly engaged in the work of social criticism. Indeed, the field of social relations is but one of many with which Goya's project of critique is engaged. In order to convey the diversity of those engagements and to capture Goya's relentless pursuit of the project of critique, the chapters that follow focus on a number of the different fields with which Goya's work is critically engaged: religion and its antitheses (in secularism, on the one hand, and superstition, on the other); society (taking into account the valuation of happiness as associated with the nascent bourgeoisie, as well as the self-deception that social relations can enable); the individual (taking into account the role of portraiture as the form of art in which the dignity of the subject was made canonical, beginning in the Renaissance); history (including the representation of large-scale forces, such as revolution); and the psyche (interpreting questions of desire in the Black Paintings and the depictions of violence and the drive toward death in the bullfight images).

Much of this involves an account of Goya's critical relationship to conventions that had become well established in the visual arts for rendering a truthful likeness of the world. I argue that Goya came relatively early in his career to reflect on the means by which any view of the world, including any view of art as creating a faithful image of the world, is constructed and sustained — "invented," rather than "natural" — and invented in ways that are often concealed by the very conventions that enable it. That recognition, I argue in Chapter 2, was underpinned by a process of secularization that was nonetheless incomplete. It was a process that enabled the creation of images of the world by the use of rational visual perspectives as a means of organizing space (the convention known as "artificial perspective"), but it did not root out all the possible irrational causes of fear, anxiety, and violence that continued to haunt the world. It was also, as Goya makes plain, a wholly artificial process with no inherent claims to truth, albeit one that was made to appear as if it were wholly natural.

There is no doubt that this questioning of the established conventions of secular art — its reliance on the artifice of perspective and certain other elements of scenic composition — is a crucial element in Goya's relationship to modern art. But there is at least one important difference, at least between Goya's work and what is often regarded as the achievement of "high" modern (that is, modernist) art, which is to say, the art that begins roughly with Manet and continues through Cézanne and the avant-gardes all the way to abstract expressionism. This is the gradual, but systematic elimination of figuration, leading to a kind of art that eventually was not "about" anything in the world at all, other than itself and its component elements — for example, color, shape, flatness. Goya's work may sometimes appear to be "subjectless." There are images whose subject matter would be hard to name, and there are others where Goya's involvement in the medium of art (paint, in particular) seems to overwhelm whatever subject the work may be "about." And yet Goya rarely ceases to engage a particular subject of some kind. His relationship to whatever art may be "about," its subject, matters for the execution of the work of critique. But it may be misleading to say that Goya's works are simply "about" the subjects they depict. In the case of Goya, that "aboutness" is hardly a passive relationship; the truth is that his works inevitably have an active, critical relationship to the things they might seem simply to be "about."

There is a parallel relationship between Goya's works and the routes of explanation that have conventionally been invoked in order to explain it. The differences between various segments of Goya's work are sometimes explained by appeal to a number of external factors, all of them in fact quite common in the accounts that are given of the works of many artists. His career as a professional artist in relationship to various official recognitions and commissions is one such factor; his personal history, including his amorous entanglements and his illnesses, is another; national politics is yet another; the state of Spanish society is another; international politics, war, and large-scale historical movements are further factors. All these factors and more have an undeniable bearing on Goya's work. My argument here, however, is that they do not fully explain the work and that to say so is to think centripetally, to move conceptually in interpretation *away* from the work itself. Rather, I argue that while Goya's work is manifestly involved with all the things that might seem to explain it, the work is engaged in an active, critical response to the very things that might be thought of as explaining it. In doing so, it unsettles the conventions on which art criticism and history tend to rely.

Still, one may wonder about the conditions that made such a project possible. How and why was it that Goya was in a position to undertake such a project of critique? Recognizing that there can be no complete answer to this question, I would nonetheless hazard a response that has some basis in the facts and that is borne out in relation to a number of the images to which I refer in the chapters to follow. This has to do with Spain's position in relation to the rest of Europe at the end of the eighteenth century and the beginning of the nineteenth. Goya saw the attractiveness of the "enlightened" cultures of France, England, and Germany, just as he saw the severe limitations of traditional Spanish society and of the Spanish past. But at the same time, he could see — and forcefully showed in the executions in *The Third of May, 1808*, for example — that the Enlightenment could bring its own forms of barbarism. The ethical ideals of Kant and Hegel epitomize the attractions of enlightened thinking and serve as foils to Goya's work at various points in the chapters that follow. Goya's position was one of distance both from the superstitions and backwardness of the Spanish past and from the promises offered by Enlightenment culture. It seems quite plausible that the project of critique that runs throughout his work was informed by the need to maintain a distance from both these alternatives.

CHAPTER ONE

Secularization and the Aesthetics of Belief

A great many accounts of Goya's career begin with an outline of his beginnings as a young painter in Zaragoza under the tutelage of José Luzán, his travels to Italy, and his subsequent return to Spain, where he enjoyed the support of his brother-in-law Francisco Bayeu, in Zaragoza and in Madrid. In Madrid, the neoclassical painter Antón Raphael Mengs, then official court painter, reigned supreme in the world of official art and served as the de facto arbiter of taste. These early years are treated primarily for their biographical interest, and with but a few exceptions (including some surprising images in Goya's Italian Sketchbook that I will have occasion to mention below), there is little reason to regard them otherwise. Goya's career as an artist of consequence begins with his first court commissions — with the paintings he made between 1775 and 1792 as "cartoons" for tapestries that were to hang in various royal residences — once his formidable talent had already gained some recognition. From there, it is common and not entirely mistaken to chart the evolution of a body of work that grows increasingly difficult *and* more modern as it grows increasingly dark.

For one understanding of Goya's work, the tapestry cartoons are indeed a very important place to begin, not least because they model many of the subjects that Goya returns to with a far more critical eye over the course of his later career. But there is more to Goya's work than the story of an artist's darkening view of the world can tell and more also than can be explained in terms of Goya's refusal of the obligatory cheerfulness of his tapestry commissions on occasions when he was free to work as he wished. I say this in full view of Goya's own statements about the importance of "invention" in art, both in his announcement for the *Caprichos* in the *Diario de Madrid* on February 6, 1799 ("inventadas y grabadas al agua fuerte por Don Francisco Goya" — "invented and engraved in aquatint by Don Francisco Goya") and in his earlier speech to the Royal Academy of Fine Arts of San Fernando, where he famously proclaimed that "there are no rules in painting." As he went on to say on that occasion, it is less important to adhere to convention than to recognize talent and to allow it to flourish freely (to "reward and protect he who excels in [the arts]; to hold in esteem the true Artist, to allow free reign to the genius of students who wish to learn them, without oppression, nor imposition of methods.")[1] This statement is largely about Goya's aversion to academic pedagogy and makes sense in the context of the Academy's expressed interest in reform. But there is something beyond the endorsement of raw talent and unstructured learning that needs to be taken into account when gauging Goya's commitment to "invention." To say that the *Caprichos* are invented means of course that Goya did not have prior models for the images. But equally important to grasp is the way in which Goya himself began to confront a series of inherited assumptions regarding the making of images, assumptions crucial to their making. His works often incorporate particular views of the world as part of their thematic content; that is one basis for their critical work, and it is especially important in works that address the social world, including the *Caprichos*. But in addition to this, I want to suggest, Goya came relatively early in his career to reflect on the means by which any view of the world, including any view put forward under the guise of "art," is constructed — invented, rather than natural, and invented in ways that are often concealed.

This awareness may well have been enabled by the fact that eighteenth-century conventions of perspective were not as normalizing as one might assume. Yet it was precisely the invented and constructed nature of the work of art that was largely concealed by the three traditions that provided the most important contexts for Goya's early works: the tradition of religious painting, largely neoclassical in its formalism; the tradition of picturesque naturalism that forms the background for many of the tapestry cartoons; and the tradition of late baroque illusionism, best exemplified by Tiepolo's large-scale frescoes. While deferring a full discussion of Goya's tapestry cartoons to Chapter 2, it is nonetheless important to note that many of them take as their baseline a normative view of the world as it presents itself to the members of established society. The point of departure for the cartoons is the ideal of a transparent gaze, presented as if it were wholly natural, even though it is one that Goya began to question almost from the start. Hence, one prominent Goya scholar, Valeriano Bozal, could write of the picturesque background of these works that "the painter . . . ought to paint as if the image were the direct product of his gaze — an attentive, interested, and pleasant gaze — which, rather than eliminate liveliness, valorizes it."[2] My argument in what follows here suggests that Goya did not take the image space of secular art for granted but in fact understood it as a construction, perhaps even as a fantasy, sustained on painting's side by techniques of sculptural modeling and coloration inherited from the traditions of religious art and baroque illusionism. The contrast between sacred and secular domains, and more importantly, the idea of a passage from one domain to the other, leads to a recognition that there are contradictions *within* secular space, the most important one being the fact that it seems never to be fully demystified.

To understand something about how Goya came to reckon with the constructedness of the image, I want to proceed with a discussion of his religious paintings and with a related body of his works that pose questions about the power of belief, in aesthetics and otherwise. To be sure, the main body of Goya's work belongs to the secular world, but he seems to have understood that secular space had to be won before it could be called into question: it was won through a *process* of secularization that involved, among other things, a recognition of the necessary tensions between aesthetic plausibility and religious belief. With this came a self-consciousness about such things as perspective, composition, and the beholder's standpoint, all of which reveal themselves as inner-worldly *constructions*, not as divinely ordained for nature. Goya seems to have been deeply engaged with such questions in spite of the fact that roughly from Alberti onward, the reigning principles of image making *assumed* the naturalness of a secular point of view. As Norman Bryson pointed out in *Vision and Painting: The Logic of the Gaze*, Albertian perspective served to normativize the set of techniques by which painting could support the fiction of a "natural standpoint."[3] To understand that the "naturalness" of the beholder's standpoint was itself constructed implied something quite different from the acceptance of Albertian principles. In Goya, though certainly not in Goya alone, the representation of a "natural-looking" image carries with it an awareness of the fact that the image was itself a product of invention and that it has a social and material base. It is hardly surprising to see Goya move rapidly away from the picturesque naturalness that informs the tapestry cartoons, since that aesthetic was designed to conceal these very facts. (I will say more about this in the chapter to follow.)

Moreover, the process of secularization is one that seems never to be complete. Various forces that may be associated with the "spirit" seem to persist in many forms, even within an apparently autonomous, fully secular space. The spirit world has a demonic afterlife that invariably throws the secular world off-kilter, reminding it of its own precarious status as a contradictory collection of provisional and sometimes obscure, even irrational practices and beliefs, all yoked together under the guise of "reason" or its proxy terms. As Goya was also quick to recognize, this was something that the members of secular society seemed surprisingly unable to see. The persistence of "official" religion within an increasingly secular world tells only part of the story; equally important is the way in which the winged demons of desire and self-deceit reoccupy the place of pretty angels in his work or in which sublime miracle scenes present themselves as the occasions of bloody horror.

A painting that can provide a particularly insightful point of entry into some of these questions is the fresco ceiling in the church of San Antonio de la Florida in Madrid (Figure 1.1). Goya completed the fresco in 1798, when he was already fifty-two, then deaf for six years, and at quite a high point in his artistic powers and prestige. The date of the work is of interest because it places the fresco as contemporaneous with the *Caprichos*, which were executed in 1797–98 and published in 1799. His success as a painter of cartoons for royal tapestries had earned him a significant reputation. There is speculation that the commission for the work in the church of San Antonio may have been obtained through the intercession of one of Goya's most prominent "enlightened" friends, Gaspar Melchor de Jovellanos, but Goya was by this time sufficiently well established to have secured it on his own. On the central dome of the church, Goya represents the climactic scene from the key miracle in the life of St. Anthony of Padua. The scene as Goya renders it is significant both because it is a secular setting of a miraculous event and because the work poses important questions about perspective, construction, and belief in painting.

According to popular legend and church accounts, including one that had just recently been translated into Spanish,[4] the background story of the miracle is as follows. Anthony of Padua received news that his father, in Lisbon, had been accused of murder. In response, Anthony requested permission to take leave from his monastery in order to intercede on his father's behalf. The story further has it that the future saint made a miraculous flight to Lisbon and, once there, became the central actor in a dramatic courtroom scene. Confronting the trial judge, the saint demanded that the victim's corpse be produced for questioning. Turning then to the corpse, Anthony asked the dead man to say for certain whether or not his father was the murderer. The corpse rose to reply "no" and then sank back into his coffin, while the assembled courtroom crowd was seized with fear and awe

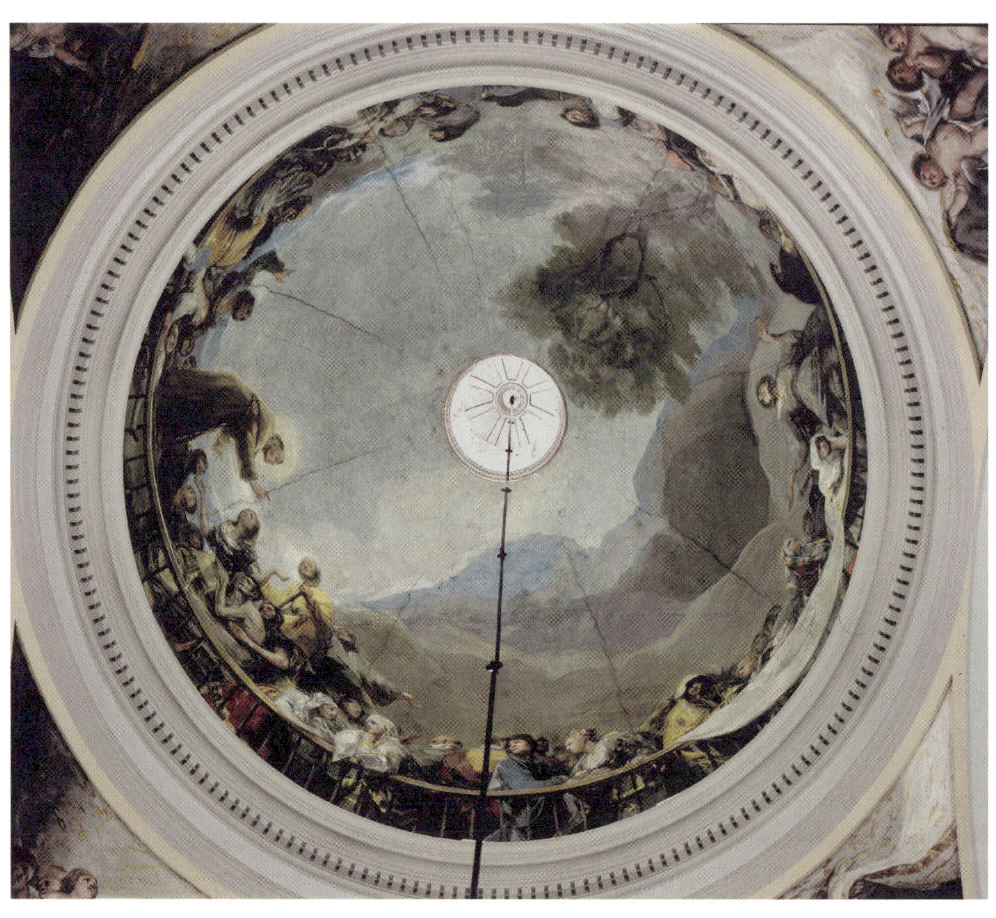

Figure 1.1.
The Miracle of St. Anthony, 1798. Fresco, approx. 7m^2.
Chapel of San Antonio de la Florida, Madrid.

(Figure 1.2). The accused was presumably exonerated. The central dome on which the miracle of St. Anthony is painted (some 5.5 meters in diameter) is only a part of the overall decoration of the church of San Antonio. It is flanked by four spandrels and four archivolts, where Goya painted angels who appear to reveal the miracle scene by retracting curtains (Figure 1.3). But these angels seem incongruous, if not irrelevant, to the way in which Goya handles the image on the central dome. They are not set within an illusionistic version of heavenly space, as conventions of religious painting might have required, but are rather decorative ancillaries to a secular scene. The images inhabit two different aesthetic regimes: the decorative angels in their peripheral, relatively constrained theatrical spheres, and the miracle in a central, open-air space. The two are scarcely in visual dialogue at all; indeed, the angels seem oddly to reveal a terrestrial scene that rises physically *above* them. One of the best commentators on Goya's religious paintings, Fred Licht, remarks that there is something odd about the arrangement, something "sardonically heavy-handed in the way [these] shabby and rather dusty theatre-prop wings are stuck to the shoulder blades of Goya's angels, just as there is something awkwardly prosaic in the fall of the draperies, which no longer flutter as if animated by the free winds of the heavens but fall to the ground like badly hemmed costumes."[5]

Within the central dome itself, the sky above the miracle is left virtually blank. Moreover, the scene of the miracle forms only a part of the large central dome. The greater part of the dome is devoted to a series of figures who form a circle around its perimeter. What is often said about these figures is quite true, as far as it goes: that Goya removed the miracle of St. Anthony from the context of the religious sublime so as to concentrate on a broad cross-section of ordinary Madrid society. This is a work that largely refuses the aesthetics of religious wonder, in spite of the fact that it is a miracle scene. Notwithstanding the dramatic gestures of a few of the figures, which recall the theatricality of baroque imagery, with all its rhetorical emphases, this is a work in which a great many internal spectators

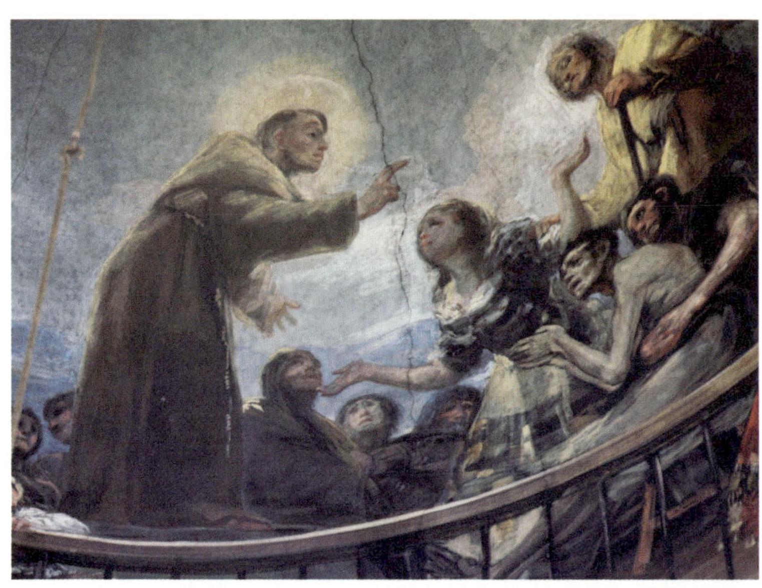

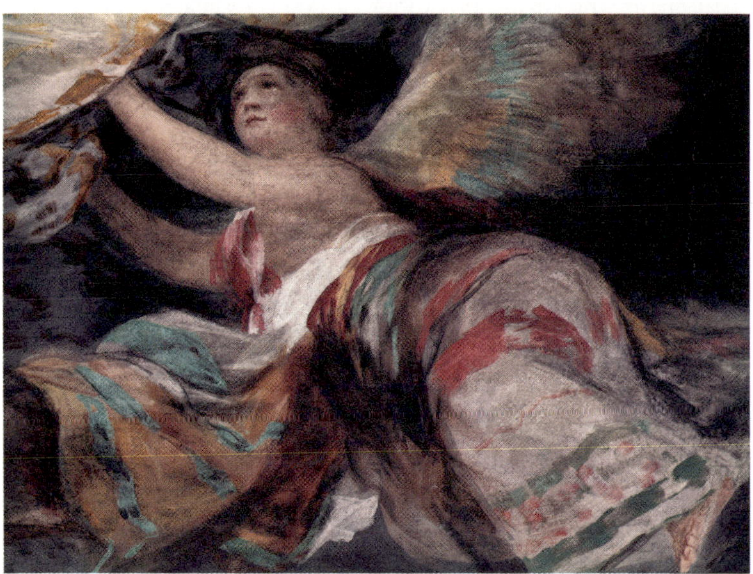

Figures 1.2 and 1.3.
The Miracle of St. Anthony (details), 1798. Fresco.
Chapel of San Antonio de la Florida, Madrid.

seem to pay little attention to the miraculous event. Moreover, the circular composition makes it almost impossible to imagine the image as having a magnetic, visual center. As I will suggest below, all these factors raise questions about the power of belief, both in relation to the implied force of the miracle and in relation to the task of painting.

Given the historical context and situation of the fresco, the incorporation of a group of figures drawn from contemporary society is hardly surprising. The work is secular in this ordinary sense. From its humble beginnings in the sixteenth century as little more than a devotional shrine, the church of San Antonio de la Florida had a history as the people's place of worship. Legend has it that the simple sixteenth-century shrine was frequented by ordinary women who would stop there to pray on their way to the Manzanares River to do the daily washing. Some critics have remarked that women of this type figure directly in Goya's painting; the suggestion is that the work was meant to acknowledge, if not to flatter, the ordinary churchgoers of Goya's era in that district. The late eighteenth-century chapel itself was the result of numerous reconstructions and displacements on the site of a much older shrine. Over time, a second chapel was built, and the amplified structure was elevated to the status of church. Subsequently, the architect José Benito de Churriguera was commissioned to construct a more permanent and elaborate structure out of brick. Then, during the course of various improvements to the city of Madrid under the reign of Charles III, plans were made to improve the route on which that church stood, and so a new one was ordered to be built, still respecting the original place and traditions of worship, even while the structure was conceived on a substantially larger scale. The resulting neoclassical edifice where Goya painted his frescoes was opened in 1798, though not consecrated until 1799, a year after Goya had finished the work. He was working among the people who worshiped there and made the frescoes just after the builders had completed the construction itself.

In his landmark study of the frescoes, Hans Rothe described the scene of the central dome as a "popular gathering" ("festejo popu-lar").[6] More recently, Robert Hughes characterized it as "vernacu-lar."[7] The scene impresses both because of the diversity of the indi-vidual types represented in it and the intensity with which they are rendered. There is remarkable energy in the brushwork and in the handling of the paint itself (a topic to which I will return below), as well as a power of insight into the differences among social types that go well beyond convention. The women who are grouped in constel-lations of twos and threes appear to be young *majas*; a haggard *celes-tina* stands nearby. There is also an older man beside the saint (who some speculate may be the accused man, Anthony's father), as well as a younger woman who attends the miracle scene at close range (the saint's mother, perhaps), a toothless beggar, an aged man with a white beard, shadowy figures fleeing in the background, a blind man with a staff, a boy who straddles the painted railing in *trompe l'oeil* fashion (Figure 1.4), and at a point in the circle directly opposite the saint, a figure who stands up high on a ledge, his hands outstretched and raised as if in wonder or awe or in imitation of a priestly gesture that rhymes with the figure of the woman who faces the saint directly. He has been dubbed the "ecstatic one"; his secular clothing and his mystical posture seem to demonstrate the effects of spiritual forces working at a distance within the secular world.

But other details seem purposefully to avoid spiritual connota-tion. Several critics have compared the white cloth that Goya drapes over the railing to the banners that might be seen hanging over the wall of a bullring (Figure 1.5). And yet there is no attempt to set this scene in any particular location. The central scene and the surround-ing figures are placed neither in Lisbon, where legend has it that the miracle took place, nor in Madrid, where these figures belong socially. (If a bullring is indeed the suggestion, the scene could just as easily be imagined as set in either place.) The background of the image is a landscape with rocks that rise up as bulks of color, verging on sheer abstraction. There is a tree, whose form is vaguely reminis-cent of those in the earlier tapestry cartoons, especially in the way in

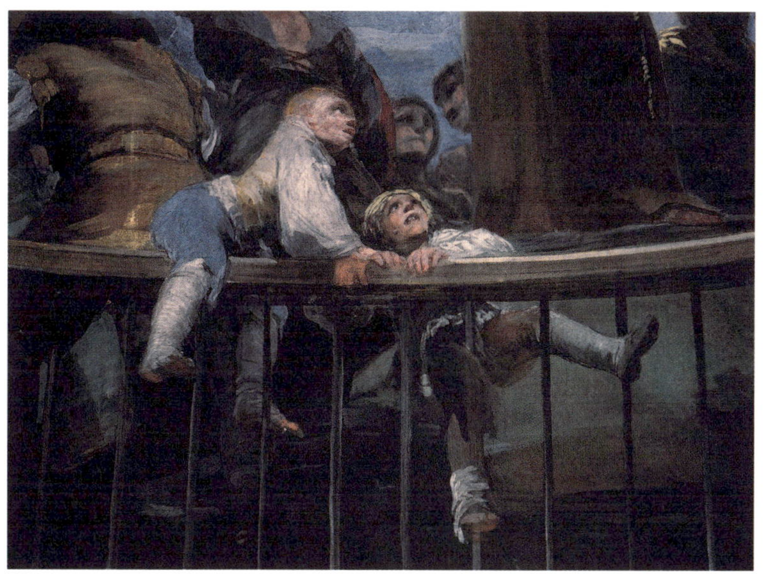

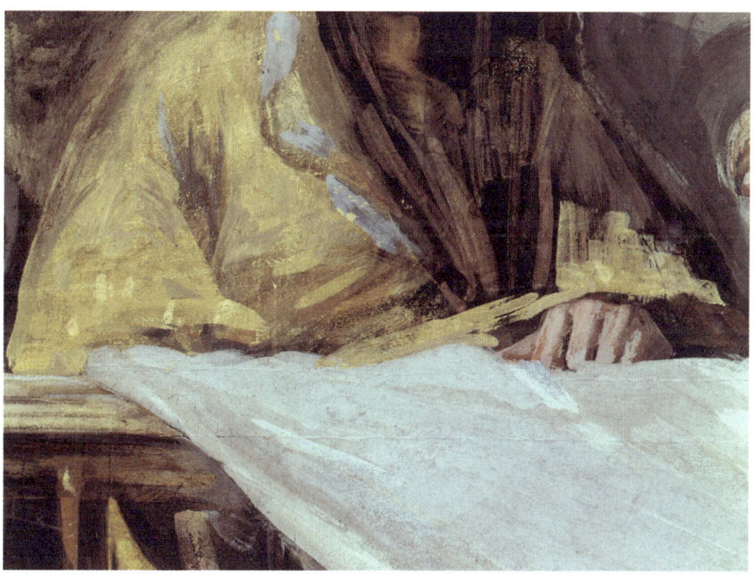

Figures 1.4 and 1.5.
The Miracle of St. Anthony (details), 1798. Fresco.
Chapel of San Antonio de la Florida, Madrid.

which the limbs and leaves are outlined, but this tree bends to cover the curvature of the dome, not with the wind. The sky is vacant of anything heavenly; indeed, the space that rises up to the central cupola is remarkably bereft of allusion of any sort.

The principal element in the foreground of the work is the painted railing, which is set significantly above the lower edge of the dome itself, as if to contain the entire spectacle. But from what, or from whom, are these figures being held back? What space does the railing divide? The effect is theatrical and wholly secular. "Above" and "below" seem to have no spiritual meanings here. Nor is this railing anything like the architectural elements of so many painted baroque ceilings, which help sustain the illusion of a heavenly space, often pictured in the form of a sky with billowy clouds where weightless figures reel and tumble, free of care. Goya invokes, but mostly in order to invert and finally to refuse, the kind of illusionism that would make the painted figures in this fresco appear to defy the laws of gravity by floating in space. The posture of the risen victim suggests that it is gravity, as much as death itself, that the miracle must overcome. This miracle scene is indeed set on a *terrestrial* plane, and yet is paradoxically located *overhead* in relation to the spectator standing in the church. This paradox is confronted directly in the composition of the image. Consider the boy who has climbed on top of the railing and straddles it. One cannot easily say where this boy would land if he were to fall. Indeed, the image as a whole seems to refuse any analysis that would be coherent both with the figures within it and with the beholder's position beneath it. All this goes to say that the narrative of the "secularized" miracle stands in tension with the visual space in which it is constructed and with the standpoint from which it must be viewed. Those, it seems, are among the irreducible aesthetic facts it presents.

As a point of comparison, consider Tiepolo's fresco ceilings. In the course of a relatively recent book, *Tiepolo Pink*, Roberto Calasso described these works as "airy and intoxicating." This is quite true: it is precisely their airiness that makes Tiepolo's frescoes seem so invulnerable to doubt. It is "the sweeping range, the invincible sense of lightness, a coefficient of antigravity,"[8] that makes them part of a visual world that counts on principles of belief that simply do not hold in Goya's work. How else, other than by an aesthetics of belief, might one explain the exotic, allegorical representations of Asia, Africa, America, and Europe in Tiepolo's vast fresco ceiling for the Treppen-haus of the Residenz of the prince-bishops of Würzburg (Figure 1.6)?[9] How else except by an aesthetics of belief might one explain his many images of religious apparitions and secular apotheoses — of the Pisani family, of Aeneas, of the Babaro family and, in the Royal Palace in Madrid, of Spain itself? All these works rely on a form of belief that allows Tiepolo to fashion illusionistic spaces that would be utterly implausible on virtually any other terms.

In painting the frescoes for San Antonio, Goya would certainly have had Tiepolo in mind, not least because Tiepolo had completed what was then the most important fresco in Madrid, the ceiling of the throne room of the Royal Palace (Figure 1.7). Although it may sound surprising to say so, Tiepolo was in many ways both a more secular artist than Goya — secular sometimes to the point of pagan in his adherence to the mythological world — *and* more of a believer, at least in matters aesthetic. Indeed, the grounds of that belief remained surprisingly intact, even among painters who were aware, through Alberti, of the mechanics of perspective. (According to Vasari's *Lives of the Artists*, some, such as Uccello, were so obsessed with perspective that the other dimensions of painting were overlooked.)[10] To the extent that his large frescoes convey a buoyant faith in the subjects they treat — whether allegorical, epic, or religious in nature — that faith finds its aesthetic supports in the way that Tiepolo manages the use of color and natural light. Indeed, there are specific effects of light that depend in crucial ways upon the particular interiors for which his works were created. The seeming naturalness of the light was one way that Tiepolo could manage to render otherwise improbable and exotic subjects with such apparent ease. In his most successful works, the natural light creates a context for the display

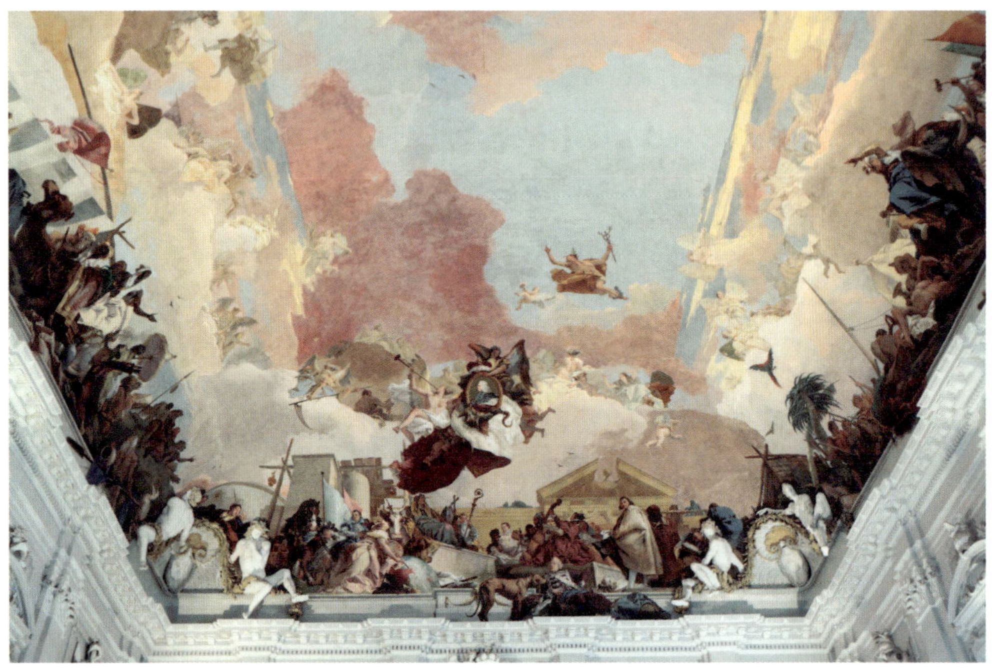

Figure 1.6.
Giovanni Battista Tiepolo, Treppenhaus (staircase) ceiling of the Würzburger Residenz,
1752–53. Fresco, 30.5 × 19 m. Würzburg, Germany.

Figure 1.7.
Giovannni Battista Tiepolo, *Wealth and Benefits of the Spanish Monarchy under Charles III*,
1762–66. Fresco, 27 × 10 m. Throne room ceiling, Royal Palace, Madrid.

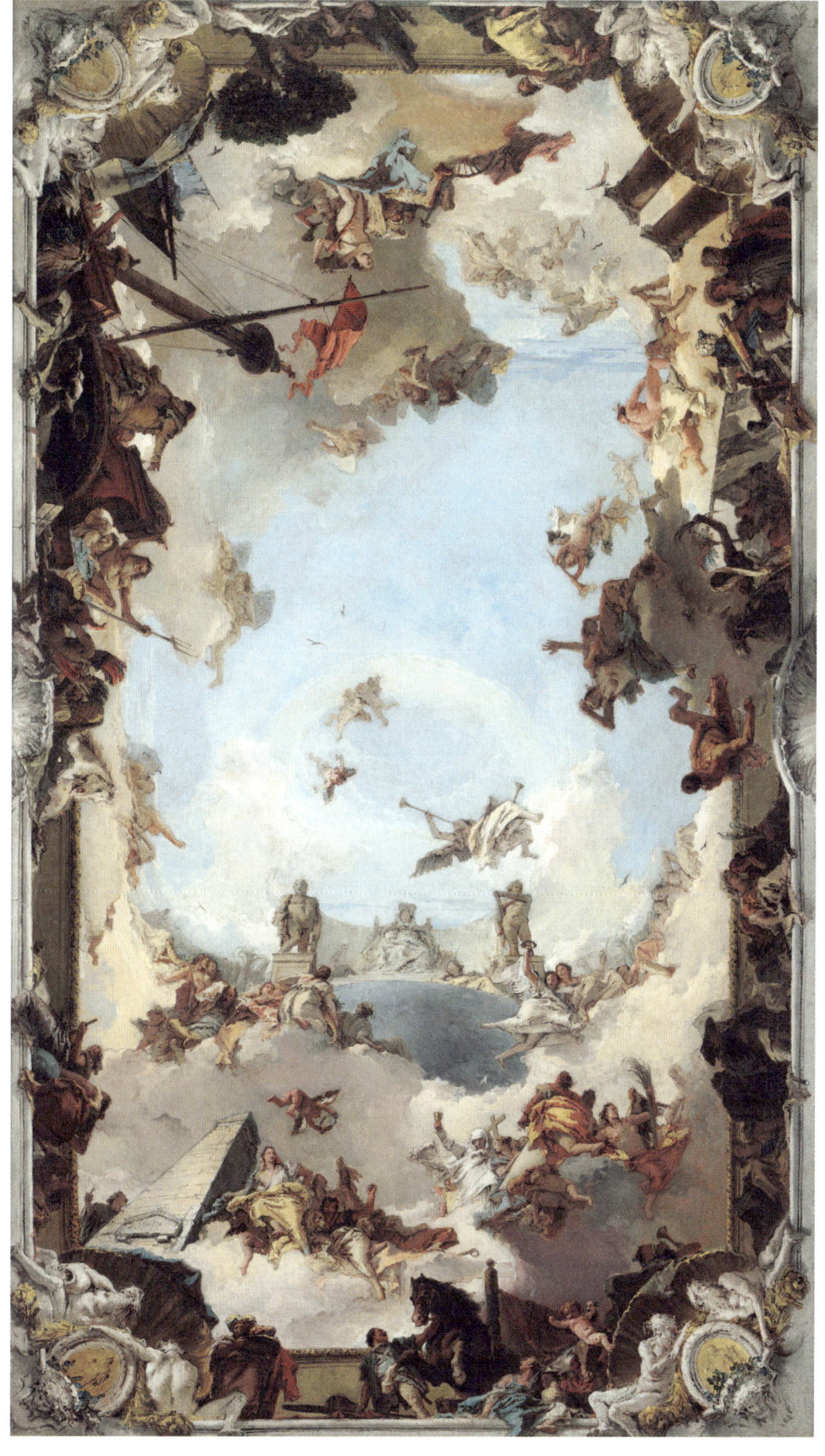

of bodies and forms that in turn produces a remarkable equality among figures of all types — angels, heroes, gods, and kings all alike. As Calasso remarked, in this world of light, "the ecclesiastics and the aristocratic families, the courts and the dynasties all move away. They become so many pretexts. So what is left, then? The pure exhibition of the world, with all its apparatus of ceremonies and fatuousness"[11] — and, one might add, without the contradictions that Goya found impossible to ignore in such compositions.

Consider again the enormous Treppenhaus ceiling, said to be the largest ceiling fresco in all of Europe. The exoticism associated with Asia, Africa, and America is scarcely diminished by the more prosaic imagery that Europe is accorded. Moreover, the painted light circulates freely throughout the entire work, in part because the natural light of the remarkable Treppenhaus allowed for it. Tiepolo's fresco for the throne room in Madrid, *The Glory of Spain*, was by contrast substantially less compelling in its use of light, in part because the natural light in the space was far less supple. As Svetlana Alpers and Michael Baxandall remarked, Tiepolo "could work with mobile, structured light of many types, even when it came to quite intractable forms. What Tiepolo could not work with was inert light. In the huge Throne Room in Madrid, for example, the ambient lighting for *The Glory of Spain* is a morose and single-track affair from deep-set windows low down on one side only," and "one of the things that defeated the attempt to rejuvenate subject matter from his earlier years was clearly the limp site lighting."[12]

It is altogether possible, even likely, that Goya had seen Tiepolo's throne room ceiling before he painted the San Antonio frescoes. Goya had served as painter to the king (*pintor del rey*) since 1786, where he was employed along with Ramón Bayeu to make the cartoons for the Royal Tapestry Works. As of 1789, Goya was court painter. (He was named first court painter the very year after the San Antonio frescoes were completed.) If Goya had indeed seen the ceiling in the throne room, as seems likely to have been the case, then it is entirely possible that the disparity between what Tiepolo wanted to achieve with effects of light in *The Glory of Spain* and what he was actually able to accomplish may have helped Goya consolidate whatever doubts he might already have had about proceeding with a fresco according to the conventions that Tiepolo epitomized. Without the play of light to lend a semblance of naturalness to such implausible compositions as *The Glory of Spain*, Tiepolo's conventions could seem improbable or absurd. A critical intelligence such as Goya's would have easily been led to question them. Manet later referred to them as "boring."[13]

To return to Goya's frescoes: the painted railing that girds the scene of the central dome of San Antonio is but one of several elements that pose problems for determining fundamental things about the image, including the perspective from which it asks to be understood. What form of aesthetic intelligence does it require of the beholder? To concentrate on the different groups of figures within the image, notwithstanding their fascinating and powerful social typology, may obscure some of the larger enigmas of the work, including those of perspective and composition. These are the means through which Goya came to confront the question of what it meant — of what it meant for painting as an art — to represent a miracle within the context of the contemporary secular world. The principles of visual perspective, which are inner-worldly, stand at odds with the very idea of a miracle, which requires formidable powers of imagination, not to say belief, to support the idea of an efficacious spiritual force acting in the human world. This was a question that Goya was to address in numerous other works, including the night visions of the *Caprichos*, his images of truth and time, in various scenes of witches, and in drawings for enigmatic architectural projects and monuments. In those works, he raises the question of whether a secular perspective of any kind can finally account for everything that a critical intelligence needs to engage with in art. In the San Antonio frescoes, the question is whether the presentation of a miracle to a group of "ordinary" *madrileños* can also make itself intelligible to the beholder of the painting, who stands in a position — both literally and figuratively — that lies outside the work and that seems to be irreconcilable with it. I note that the paradox of the beholder's position in this work is fundamentally different from the one that Michael Fried describes as significantly "modern" in relation to Courbet's monumentally large breakthrough works, such as the *Burial at Ornans*.[14] There, the composition virtually impels the beholder into its space, creating a powerful sense of visual incorporation, not least because the scale is larger than life, while at the same time the painting includes a figure who mirrors the posture of the external beholder.

With two significant exceptions — the frescoes in the dome of the Basilica del Pilar in Zaragoza (1772 and 1780) and *Burial of Christ* (1771–72) (Figure 1.8) — Goya's religious paintings prior to the San Antonio frescoes did not raise such questions. Many of those works are conceived within a framework of belief that is at once religious and aesthetic; their adherence to artistic convention is consistent with what might be thought of as Goya's precritical stance. Wonder could be integrated unproblematically into these works in part because they confront the spectator with few questions and make relatively few visual demands. Indeed, the representation of wonder within them seems to *relieve* the beholder of most intellectual or affective challenges by so easily accommodating the beholder's gaze. So, too, the principles of perspective and the conventions of composition support the sacred context that these early religious works presuppose. Among the works in question are the paintings for the Charterhouse of the Aula Dei just outside Zaragoza, the small *Burial of Christ* (also painted in the Zaragoza years, now in the Museo Lázaro Galdiano in Madrid), the portraits of the four Doctors of the Church (St. Ambrose, St. Augustine, St. Gregory, and St. Jerome) done just before the frescoes in San Antonio, and the work commissioned by the Count of Floridablanca for a side altar in the church of San Francisco el Grande in Madrid showing San Bernardino of Siena preaching before Alfonso of Aragón (Figure 1.9). These works are sustained by an aesthetic of belief that works through the conventions

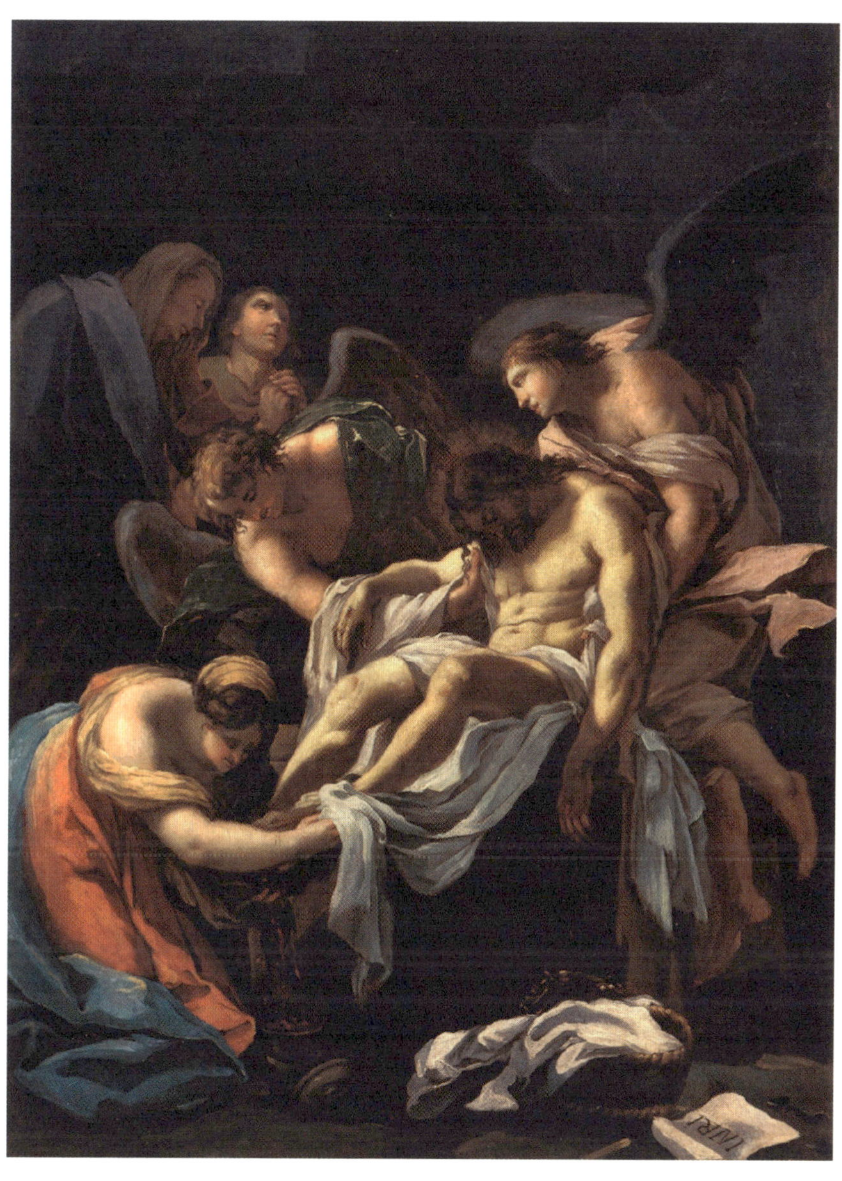

Figure 1.8.
Burial of Christ, ca. 1771–72. Oil mural transferred to canvas, 115 × 112 cm.
Lázaro Galdiano Museum, Madrid.

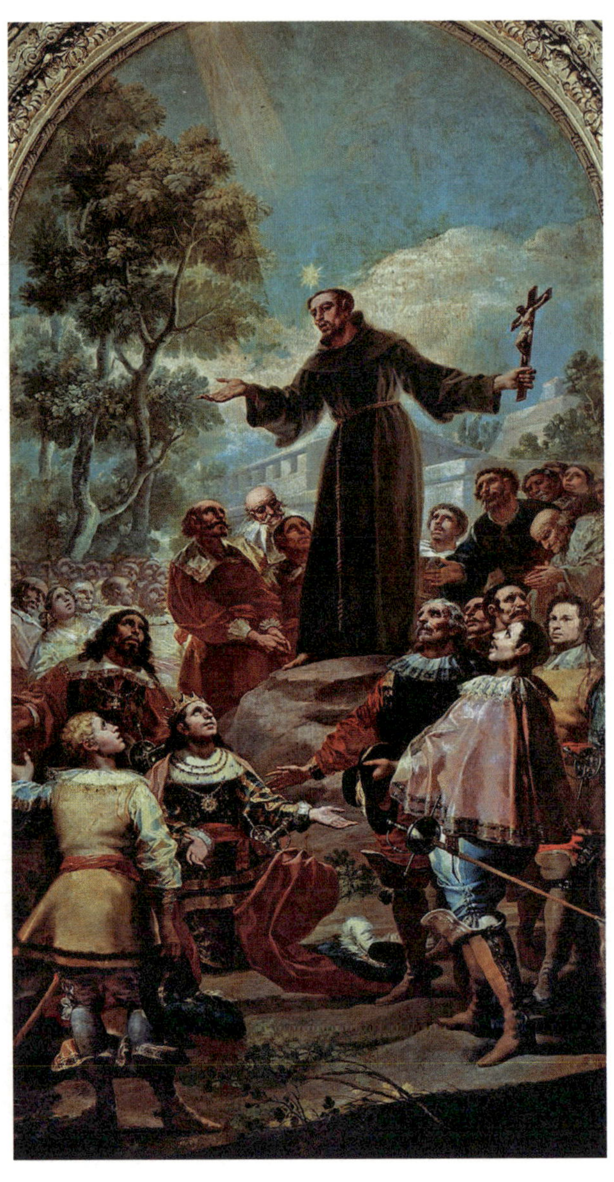

Figure 1.9.
The Sermon of Saint Bernardino of Siena, 1781–83. Oil on canvas, 480 × 300 cm.
Royal Basilica of San Francisco el Grande, Madrid.

of religious painting. They rely on the use of narrative forms, on sculptural modeling, and on effects of color in order to lend a sense of depth and dimension and, especially in the case of the portraits, of "liveness," to their subjects.

Among Goya's religious works in Zaragoza were the seven large paintings he did in oil directly on plaster, rather than as frescoes, for the Charterhouse of the Carthusian Monks, the Aula Dei. Granted, the works have been severely compromised because of the deterioration of the surface of the walls; subsequent efforts at restoration amounted to the repainting of large portions of them. But the subject matter and narrative form of the paintings tell much nonetheless. These are all New Testament stories: the Annunciation to Joachim, the Birth of the Virgin, the Betrothal of the Virgin, the Visitation, the Adoration of the Magi, the Presentation in the Temple, and the Circumcision. They are all rendered according to neoclassical norms for the treatment of narrative subjects in art. Architectural elements within these paintings provide a secure visual orientation for the spectator, as they also seem to do for the figures within each of the scenes. (By contrast, it is remarkable how Goya uses the architectural element of the railing in the San Antonio fresco to circumscribe the scene *and* to render it precarious.) In one of the Aula Dei works, the *Betrothal of the Virgin* (Figure 1.10), the figures gesture in the rhetorical ways that were associated with the style of Jacques-Louis David, whose works were known in Spain. But in Goya's early religious paintings, such gestures have the effect of *ignoring* the presence of the beholder, rather than *indicating* it, not so much by denying the beholder as by unquestioningly presupposing the stance of a believing spectator.[15] In contrast to the dome of San Antonio, the images in the Aula Dei accept as unproblematic the elemental fact that they would be viewed frontally. Moreover, they achieve coherence as a group of narrative scenes, much as Goya's tapestry cartoons make best sense when understood as an ensemble in the context of the various rooms for which they were planned.[16]

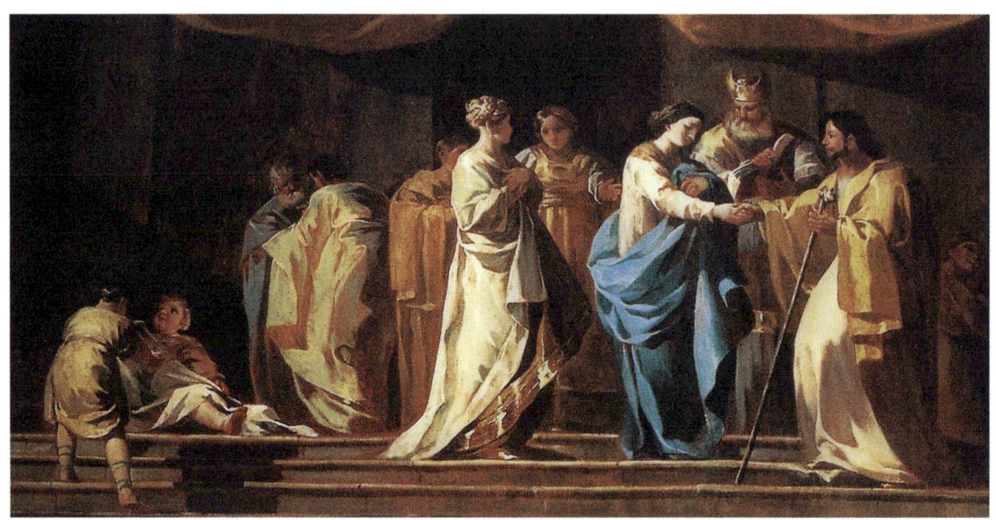

Figure 1.10.
Betrothal of the Virgin (detail), 1774. Oil on plaster.
Charterhouse of Aula Dei, Zaragoza, Spain.

As critics have noted, the sheer scale of the Aula Dei paintings also meant that there was more space on the walls for Goya to cover than might rightly be occupied by any of the central scenes they treat.[17] His recourse was to add background landscapes, folds of drapery, and incidental structures of various types (steps, pedestals, platforms, and so on) in order to make up the difference. In San Antonio, by contrast, Goya transformed the curved picture plane on which the main action was represented into a vast social "canvas" in the concave round. Above the internal spectators is a landscape and a sky that draw the eye dizzyingly toward an empty nothing-ness; the landscape anticipates passages in some of the later works in which Goya nearly abandons figuration altogether. This is a space that reads as if governed from above by a final vacancy, bereft of any forces that might carry the miracle worker or his father heavenward.

The work as a whole derives power from the sheer visual drama of the circular composition and from the steep curvature of the dome, which terminates in a vacant central cupola. Indeed, Goya seems in the San Antonio frescoes to have been responding to the power of empty space — to its ability to suggest the hollowing out of a context that had once been filled with the signs and effects of religious belief.

These features of the San Antonio frescoes are even more remarkable in contrast to the relative conventionality of some of Goya's other religious commissions, such as the two frescoes for the Basilica of the Virgen del Pilar. One, *The Adoration of the Name of God* in the small choir (*coreto*), was completed in 1772; the other, larger work, painted on the main cupola in 1780, is *Mary, Queen of Martyrs* (Figure 1.11).

It's worth a detour to consider these images. Janis Tomlinson rightly notes that Goya adopted the perspective of easel painting for *The Adoration of the Name of God by the Angels* (Figure 1.12).[18] For my purpose, this also meant adopting the illusion that the circumstance of the fresco was something other — something at once more painterly and more secular — than a church, and that its material support was not in fact a wall. This was a relatively sober work,[19] fundamentally neoclassical in its conception and firm in the power of belief that supports the figures in it. The image shows a heaven full of angels and saints, buoyed up on layers of clouds, all arranged in strongly receding perspective, ascending the vertical plane toward an apex. At the point of that apex and at the highest position in the picture plane stands the triangular icon of the name of God. Flanking angels sing the praises of the Lord and perfume the heavens with incense.

The work for *Mary, Queen of Martyrs* was a rather different affair. This was a later commission that Goya was awarded after submitting materials first to the building committee of the basilica and then to a committee of the Royal Academy. But the project ran into trouble on both religious and aesthetic fronts. Goya had by this time completed a great number of tapestry paintings for various royal residences. Not surprisingly, he complained of having to work on the cupola under

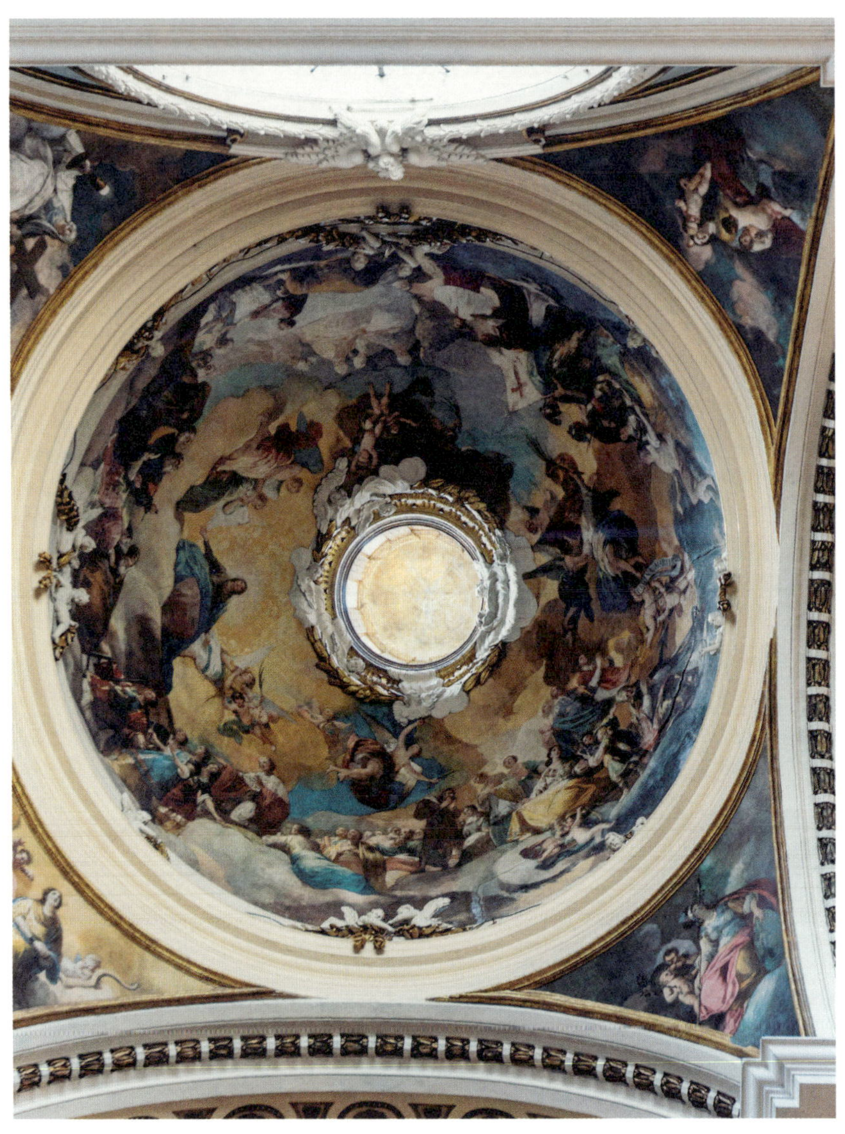

Figure 1.11.
Mary, Queen of Martyrs, 1780–81. Fresco, 212 m².
Basilica of Our Lady of the Pillar, Zaragoza, Spain.

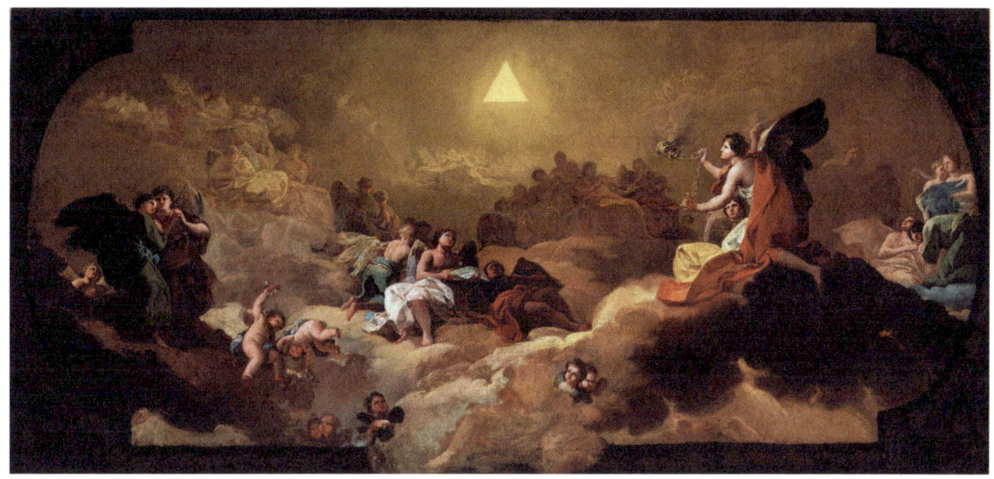

Figure 1.12.
Adoration of the Name of God by the Angels, 1772. Fresco, 700 × 1,500 cm.
Basilica of Our Lady of the Pillar, Zaragoza, Spain.

the supervision of his brother-in-law Francisco Bayeu, and alongside Francisco's brother Ramón. Goya's later sketches for four pendentives (now lost) were met with reservation when he subsequently presented these to the committee, and his work on the cupola was not found to be pleasing either. No doubt the cupola image, and the plans for the pendentives, too, showed too many traces of Goya's experience as a secular artist, but his work making the tapestry cartoons seems to have undermined the decorum that the officials would have expected to see observed in the basilica. Goya's image for the cupola, as Tomlinson notes, includes groups of "gesticulating figures swathed in colorful drapery" who seem too alive for the scene. "Even worse (in the Committee's eyes) was the fact that they almost overpower the immobile Virgin."[20]

The *Burial of Christ* painted for the palace of the Count of Sobradiel (Figure 1.8 above) is likewise conventional, with the exception of one

surprising passage. The work relies on a well-established arrangement of figures for the composition of this hallowed scene. To be
sure, the Virgin in this painting more resembles an eighteenth-century commoner than the saintly mother of Christ; to that extent,
she may be linked to some of the figures in the San Antonio fresco.
But neither she nor any of the others in the painting seems to show
any form of grief that might press itself upon the beholder or disturb
the internal order of the work. Whatever such claim the work might
make is defeated by the conventionality of its static form, which has
a deadening effect even on the figures within it. And yet among the
figures in the image, there is an angel on the right who is pictured
in motion, as if levitating. Here, it seems, Goya's effort to paint the
supernatural power of an angel seems already to have begun to draw
him to confront questions about the plausibility of the visual effects
that the supernatural might require. (In later works, such as *Flying
Witches*, he was to embrace those supernatural powers with the con-
viction of a critic who had peered into the very heart of superstition
and fathomed its seductive weirdness.)

Before turning back to the San Antonio frescoes in greater detail, it is
worth noting some further facts about Goya's earlier career. He was
admitted to the Royal Academy of Fine Arts of San Fernando in 1780
and subsequently won a commission for an altarpiece for one of the
chapels in San Francisco el Grande in Madrid, completed in 1781–83.
The work he submitted for admission to the academy in 1780 was
a *Christ Crucified* (Figure 1.13), which Robert Hughes has described
with characteristic hyperbole as Goya's "worst painting." He goes on
to describe it as a "soapy piece of *bondieuserie* . . . [conveying] a sort of
sickly, moaning piety that, if it were not for the relative liveness of the
paint and its impeccable provenance, would make you doubt it was by
Goya at all."[21] This is colorful prose, but it misses the fact that Goya
was intent on showing to the members of the academy that he could
compete on equal footing with the greatest painters of the Spanish
Golden Age — with Murillo, Zurbarán, Pacheco, Ribera, and above

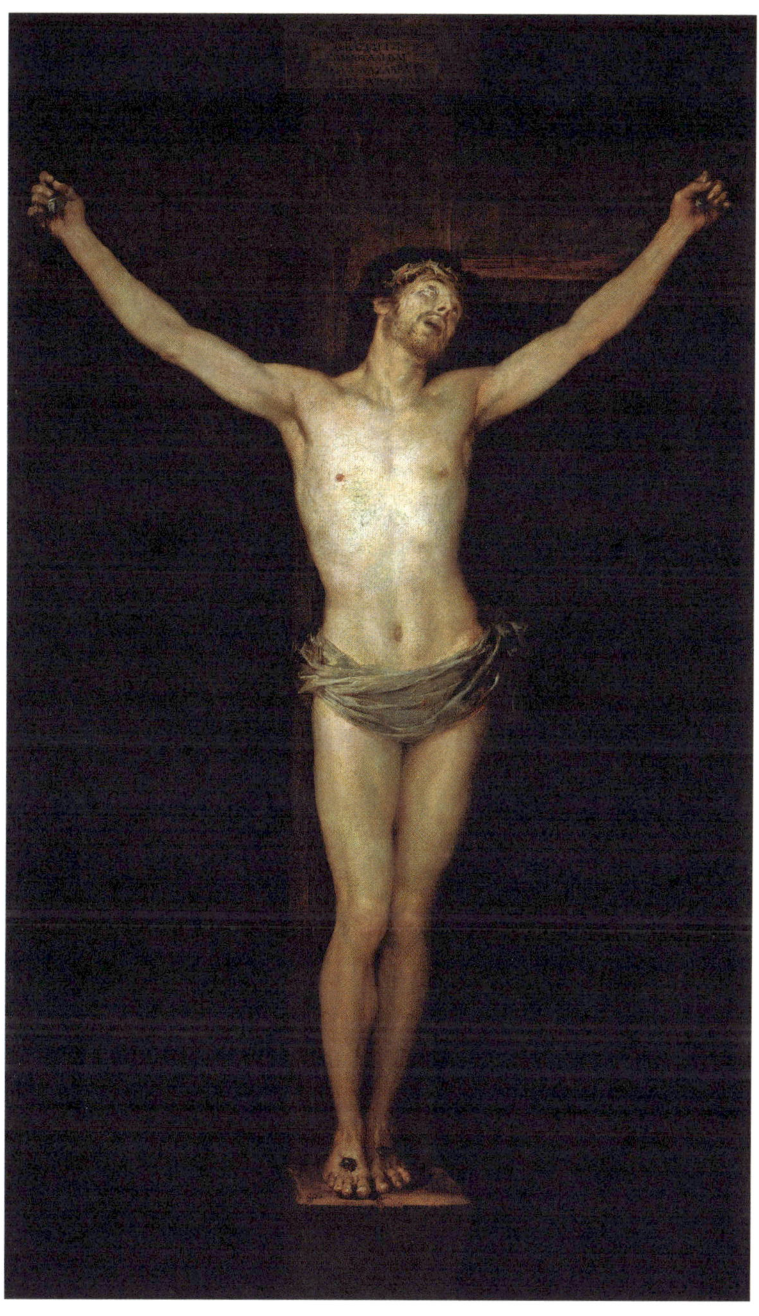

Figure 1.13.
Christ Crucified, 1780. Oil on canvas, 255×154 cm.
Museo del Prado, Madrid.

all, with Velásquez, after whom he had made numerous, studiously crafted etchings in 1778.[22] Velásquez's *Christ Crucified* was in the royal collection, and Ribera's *Crucifixion* had recently been brought to Spain from Naples by the Osunas, who were known to Goya. Goya may well have seen it in their collection at the Alameda country palace called El Capricho, realizing that they had reclaimed it for Spain.

Goya's *Christ Crucified* is important both because it shows something about his relationship to the religious art of the past — especially when the past was Spanish and was recognized as having a special importance for the development of art in official contexts — and because it reveals the role that color and sculptural form play in sustaining the illusion of an image whose subject matter is fully believed.[23] His *Christ Crucified* adheres to a sculptural ideal that is as much about Ribera or Velásquez as forceful predecessors as it is about a set of aesthetic conventions that had been masterfully adopted by an entire range of Spanish Golden Age artists. The work creates an illusion of sculptural depth that is consistent with an aesthetic desire to transcend the basic flatness that establishes one of the physical conditions for painting on canvas.[24] What Goya's *Christ Crucified* lacks is nothing that Velásquez has; rather, it is the raw intensity and material energy of the paint itself, an energy that Goya incorporated into some of his most important later works. Indeed, Goya eventually came to see the flatness of the canvas as an opportunity rather than as a constraint to be overcome; it came to be one of his most powerful ways of dealing with the power of religion in the medium of paint. The raw energy of his paint is already quite evident in a stunning Prado oil sketch for *The Taking of Christ* (1798, Figure 1.14); the final version, in the Cathedral of Toledo, transposes that raw liveness into a dramatism of light.

The side altarpiece that Goya painted for the chapel of San Francisco el Grande is altogether different in composition and purpose. The work shows the Spanish ruler of Naples, King Alfonso V of Aragón, in prayer at the feet of the Franciscan friar and later saint, Bernardino of Siena (Figure 1.9 above). In this composition, the collaborative hierarchy of church and state takes the form of a pyramidal

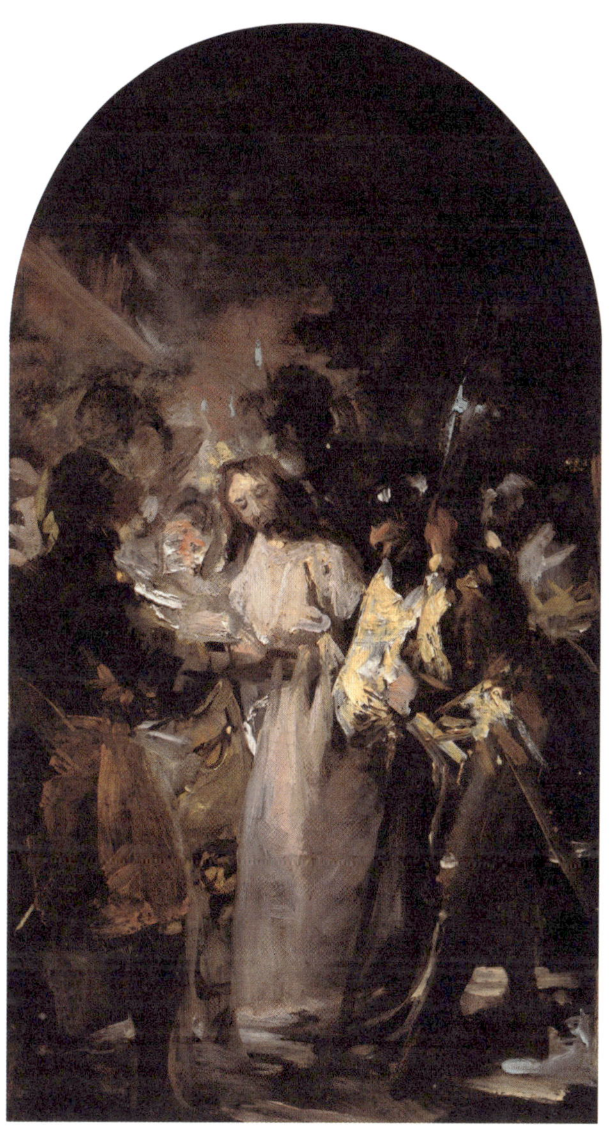

Figure 1.14.
The Taking of Christ, 1798. Oil on canvas, 40.2×23.1 cm.
Museo del Prado, Madrid.

arrangement of actors; the image is equally a statement about the piety of the Spanish ruler and the holy presence of St. Bernardino. The crucifix-wielding saint occupies the highest place in the picture, while a ray of divine grace bathes his upper body in symbolic light. (The saint's posture is one that Goya will later refer to, albeit in a much darker register, in the image of St. Francis Borgia at the deathbed of an impenitent.) The upturned gazes of the assembled spectators are reminiscent of El Greco, though the diversity of the faces suggests the direction that Goya will pursue in the San Antonio frescoes. And yet as Tomlinson has carefully observed, there is no uniform perspective holding these figures together within the visual space they occupy. This is surprising. Given the fact that the work was done as a chapel altarpiece, it was conceived with a particular kind of external spectator in mind. It was part of a visual theater that depended upon the gaze of the faithful spectators who would worship before it. It stages a mirrorlike "reenactment of what would take place in front of the painting as the officiant stands before his parishioners, mimicking the stances of saint, king, and courtiers."[25]

And yet that otherwise perfect mirroring is upset by Goya's inclusion of an image of himself on the righthand side of the scene, looking toward the faithful spectator.[26] This bit of self-consciousness may well be taken as the signature of a young artist whose career was clearly on the ascent. And while it refers to the self-consciousness of artists such as Velásquez and Rembrandt, it also suggests Goya's particular awareness of the ultimate "constructedness" of the work of art. A similar, even more prominent moment of self-incorporation is important in the portrait of the 1783 Count of Floridablanca, now in the collection of the Bank of Spain (Figure 1.15), where Goya depicts himself showing his work to the sitter, who is surrounded by the artifacts associated with his public career.

As I will discuss later, the count was responsible for a number of large-scale public-works projects, and so the painting shows the plans for the Aragón canal displayed against the table. But also lying on the floor is what appears to be a copy of volume 2 of Antonio de Palomino's

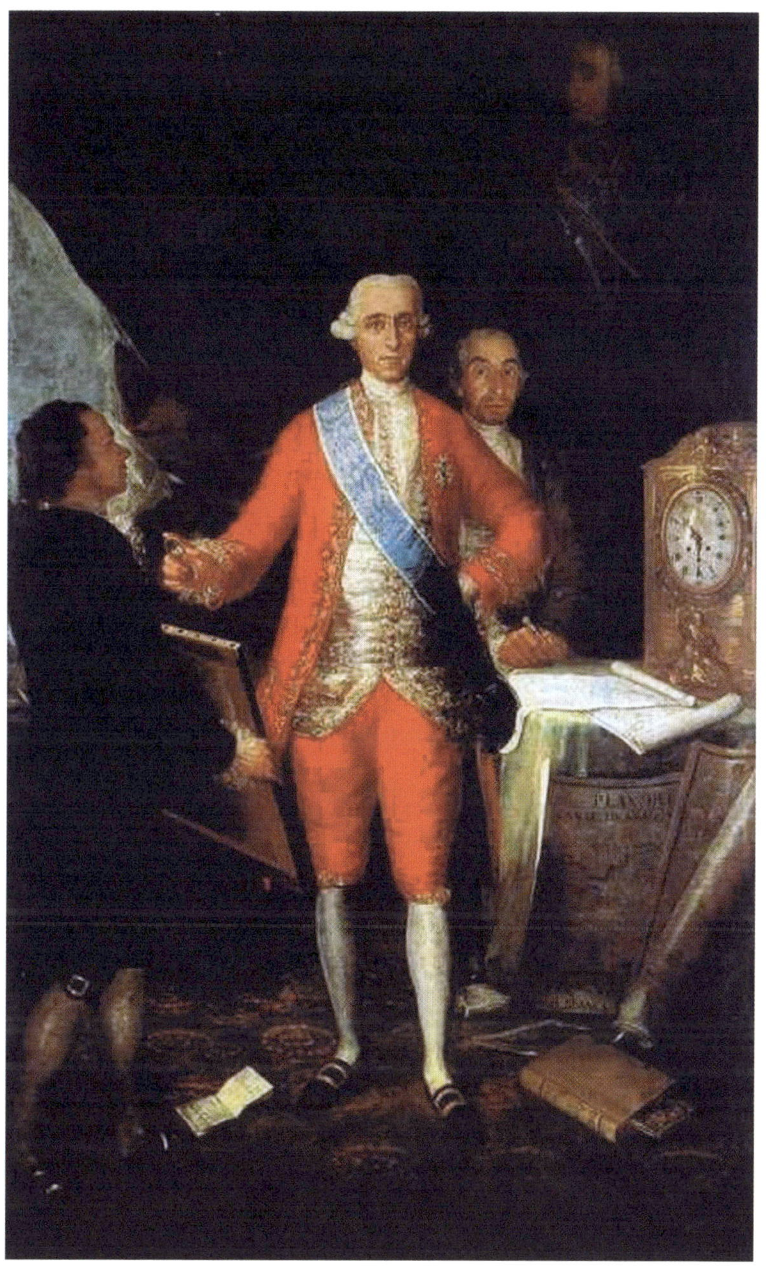

Figure 1.15.
The Count of Floridablanca, 1783. Oil on canvas, 196 × 116.5 cm.
Banco de España, Madrid.

early eighteenth-century treatise on the history and technique of art, entitled *Práctica de la pintura.* The image makes the point that painting has a place among the most highly esteemed human inventions. In the Enlightened sense, painting and engineering are both arts, and the fact that one is "liberal" hardly means that it is lesser than any of the mechanical arts. Palomino's treatise, also known as the *Museo pictórico y escala óptica,* deals extensively with visual perspective; it recognizes that painting has its basis in optics, thus in mathematics, but requires mathematics and invention in equal measures. As Goya said in his statement to the Royal Academy of Fine Arts, the source of art lies in the power of human invention, which may well take its bearings by "nature" rather than by preestablished rules; yet artifactual creation gives rise to a visual world that can be shown as unmade for the very same reason that it is itself made. This becomes quite apparent in Goya's aquatints and later paintings.

The fresco in San Antonio marks a radical departure both from the model that Tiepolo had provided and from Goya's earlier religious works. It is an earthbound work in spite of the fact that it concerns a miracle scene. Moreover, its position overhead and on a concave surface led Goya to confront a series of questions about the conditions under which any image must be constructed so as to be viewed as "natural." Given the fact that Goya's rendition of the miracle scene was earthbound rather than heavenly, it became imperative for him to fathom whether flatness, characteristic of painting on canvas or on a wall, was in fact *necessary* and whether it could be reproduced on a concave surface. The answer to that question involved the technique of anamorphosis, which Goya had practiced during his Italian years. (I will return to Goya's relationship to anamorphosis later in his career in Chapter 6.) Briefly stated, an anamorphosis is a deformed image that appears in its true shape only when viewed in some highly indirect way, typically from a hyperbolically oblique angle. It is, according to one common understanding, the distorted projection of an image on a plane or curved surface that, when viewed from a particular angle or as reflected in a curved mirror, appears regular and in normal proportion. In one common type of anamorphosis, termed "oblique," the unconventionality arises from the fact that the image must be viewed from a position that is very far from the frontal angle from which we normally expect pictures to be seen and understood. In another common form, sometimes termed "catoptric," the image must be seen reflected in a distorting mirror, typically cylindrical or conical in form, in order for it to be resolved and make sense. The images on the dome of San Antonio are in effect a resolved anamorphosis, which is to say that Goya paints them in a way that is visually intelligible on a curved surface rather than on a flat one.

The most influential treatise on painting in Goya's time referred to above, Palomino's *Museo pictórico* (the three parts of which had been reprinted in 1795–97), includes a detailed discussion of the alteration of conventional perspective demanded by curved surfaces; there is special treatment of the techniques required for painting on concave ceilings. Palomino describes the anamorphic effects of these situations as a forms of "deformation" (*deformación*).[27] Beyond Goya's familiarity with Palomino's treatise, recent scholarship has shown that Goya was interested in the effects of anamorphosis from at least as early as 1771 when he was in Italy. The recently discovered Italian sketchbook includes several experiments with anamorphic images. Among these are the preparatory drawings for a painting of *Hannibal Crossing the Alps*, which Goya eventually entered into a competition at Parma. The sketches in question read as nonsense except when viewed from a radically oblique angle, from which they clearly appear as faces (Figures 1.16 and 1.17).[28]

In the years preceding the frescoes of San Antonio, Goya also painted *Last Supper* in Cádiz (1796–97) (Figure 1.18), which, while not exactly anamorphic, is nonetheless rendered from a perspective that is oblique in the extreme. The compression characteristic of the Aula Dei works such as *The Betrothal of the Virgin* has been replaced by a heightened depth. The apostles sit on the floor with Christ, reclining in various angled positions. They are seen from a perspective that

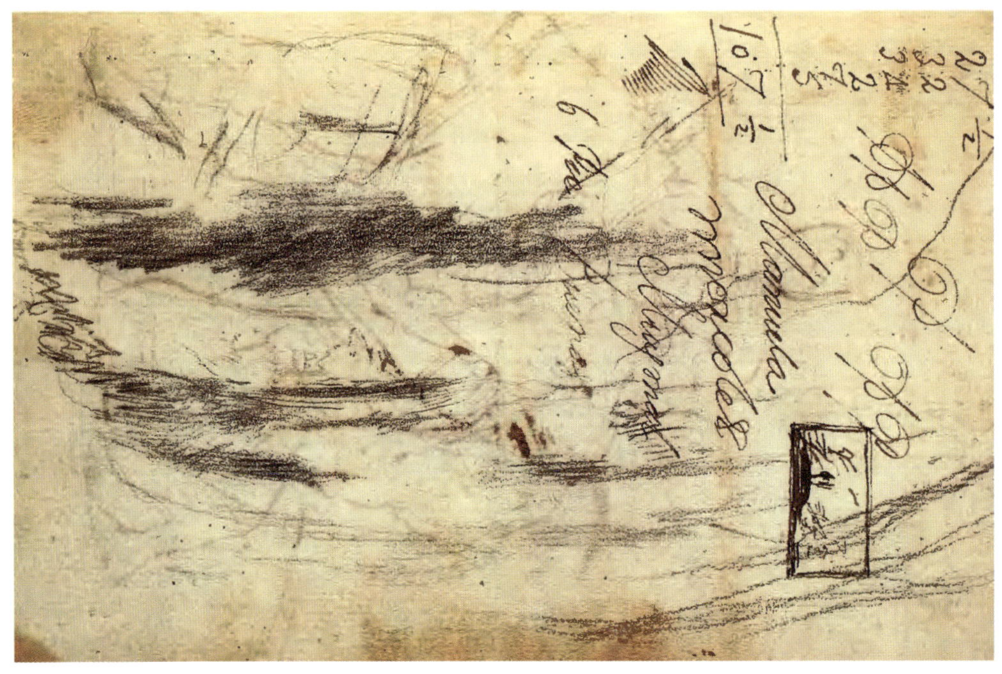

Figure 1.16.
Hannibal Crossing the Alps, ca. 1771. Red chalk on paper, 13 × 18.7 cm.
Italian Sketchbook, Museo del Prado, Madrid.

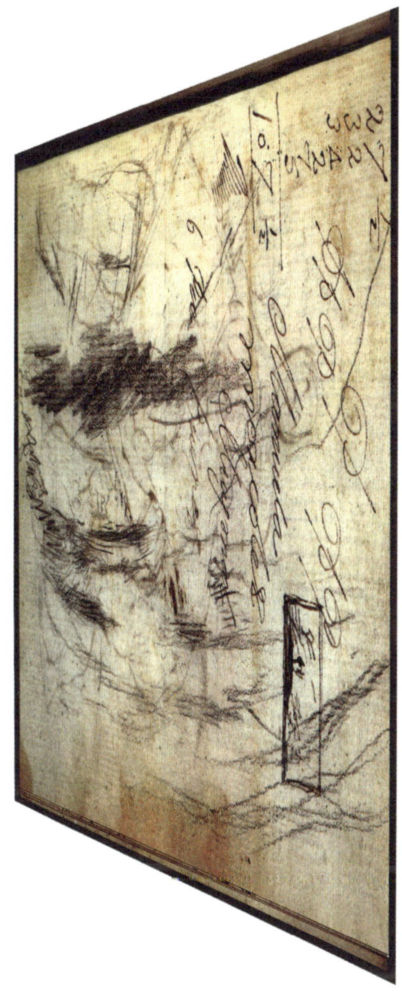

Figure 1.17.
Hannibal Crossing the Alps (anamorphic reconstruction).
Courtesy of Institut Amatller d'Art Hispànic, Barcelona.

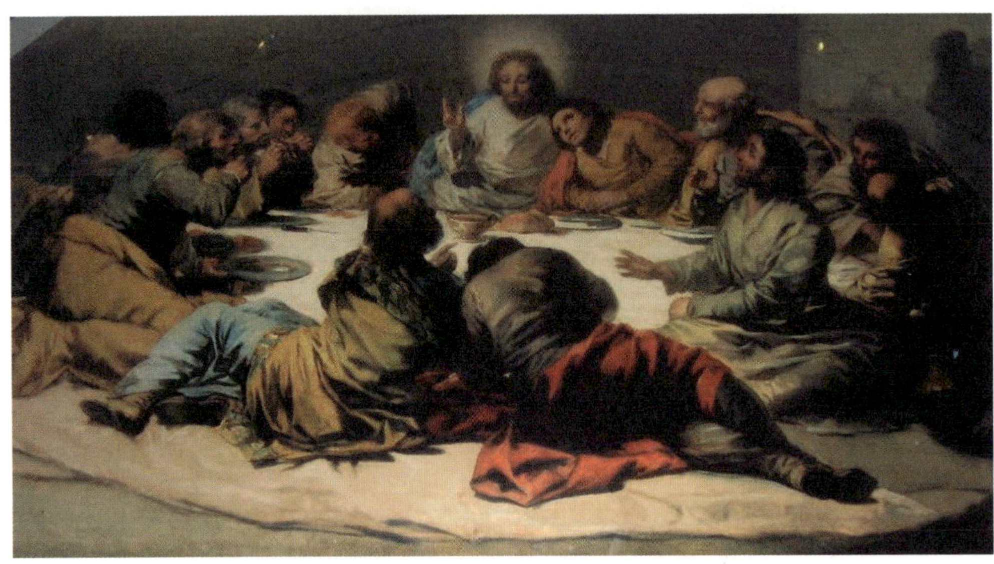

The Last Supper (detail), ca. 1796–97. Oil on canvas.
Oratorio de la Santa Cueva, Cádiz.

attempts to approach the impossible flatness of a purely horizontal view, receding deeply toward an empty background. It is probably no accident that in Goya's speech to the Academy of San Fernando, he praised Carracci, among a very few named artists, quite possibly, while in Rome, he had seen Carracci's *Dead Christ* (Figure 1.19), as well as Caravaggio's *Supper at Emmaus*, both of which press Albertian principles of perspective to the extreme. Goya said that Carracci was particularly important because he gave free rein to his students — he "revived Painting that since the time of Raphael had fallen into decline, with the liberality of his genius, he gave birth to more disciples, and better than as many practitioners as there has been, leaving each to proceed following the inclination of his spirit."[29] Whereas these images involve forceful and purposive distortions — in

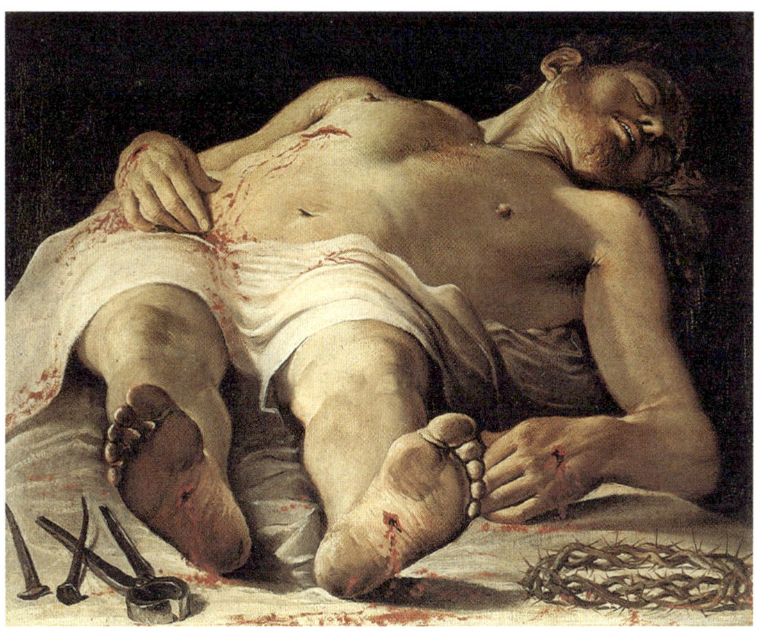

Figure 1.19.
Annibale Caracci, *Dead Christ*, 1583–85. Oil on canvas, 70.7 × 88.8 cm.
Staatsgalerie Stuttgart, Stuttgart, Germany.

the case of the Carracci so as to present the figure of the dead Christ in all the extremity of its suffering — the perspective technique that governs Goya's San Antonio fresco is, by contrast, the resolution of an anamorphic image; the work makes visual sense as a flat image in the round because it has been projected onto the distorting concave surface that is required to view it clearly. In this way, it is an example of a kind of illusionism that asks us to look beyond the surface that supports it. The implications for an understanding of the constructedness of any image are profound, especially so because the thematic content of this particular image is a miracle scene.

Some of the figures in the San Antonio frescoes call forth the idea of a contextual space, typically social; such is the case with the *majas* and the *celestina*. But others, such as the so-called "ecstatic figure," can scarcely be placed at all. Moreover, the various groups of figures seem to share little by way of relationship with one another. They form a circle not because there is any formal or thematic closure in the work, but simply because that is the form of the work's material support. In terms of composition, Goya's fresco in San Antonio de la Florida is also one of his most important efforts in the genre of ensemble painting. The work is seldom regarded in this way, in part because discussions of the genre of ensemble painting tend to concentrate either on Dutch group portraits or on the more modern ensembles that begin with Courbet's large-scale works and reach at least until *Guernica*. Goya's fresco is distinct with regard to both these traditions. When the San Antonio fresco is viewed as it must be, from below and in the round, there is no absolute focal center for its ensembles. To see it at all requires the viewer to rotate an upward gaze around all points in an unstructured circle. The symmetry that positions the "ecstatic figure" directly opposite St. Anthony introduces one element of visual orientation, but it hardly changes the fact that the image sprawls across the circle without structural articulations, save for the loosely defined groupings mentioned above.

Goya's fresco works consciously with the fact that its orientation is not horizontal in any physical sense. And yet the image reads thematically as if its underlying thematic ground does lie in the horizontality of the social and secular space in which the miracle is set. The horizontal elements of the image, all parts of its thematic presuppositions, stand in contradiction with the shape of the dome itself. In acknowledging the material support of the work and in constructing the illusion of flatness on the basis of it, Goya began to approach an issue that later modernist painting would find crucial. Modernist painting struggled, in one of its modes at least, to resist the tendency to imagine all objects of sight as located in a semblance of three-dimensional space; rather, modernism sought to accept objects in painting as conditioned by something prior and potentially antithetical to that — by the flatness of the canvas. Hence, Clement Greenberg, writing of what modernism sought to oppose, would remark that "all recognizable entities (including pictures themselves) exist in three-dimensional space, and the barest suggestion of a recognizable entity suffices to call up associations of that kind of space."[30] Goya's work in the San Antonio frescoes presages modernism, though in a somewhat different way. In it, he coupled an acknowledgment of the physical conditions of the illusionistic image with a reassessment of unquestioned alliances between religious belief and the aesthetic conventions of composition, form, and color that had for so long supported one another. This, in turn, set the stage for the development of a critical project that would address itself equally to the conventions of visual representation and to the world that such images were ostensibly about.

CHAPTER TWO

A Promise of Happiness?

What, then, are we to make of Goya's tapestry cartoons, many of which have long contributed to Goya's reputation as a "painter of light" and all of which devote themselves to secular subjects? The cartoons (large-scale painted oil sketches) are works that Goya made over a series of years relatively early in his professional career, beginning when he was first employed to produce works for the Santa Bárbara Royal Tapestry Factory in 1775 and extending over two distinct periods (1775–80, and 1786–92). Some of these paintings are so light and luminous, their subjects so full of grace and beauty, that it is difficult to understand how they could have been made by the same artist who also created the *Caprichos* (1799) and who later went on to make the Black Paintings on the walls of the house known as the Quinta del Sordo. Anyone viewing them would be remiss not to take notice of their grace and ease and in many cases of their innocence, as well. Images such as *The Parasol* show Goya as a great colorist and offer some hints of what his mature work might have been like had he been a Watteau or a Fragonard. (Fragonard was roughly his contemporary, but Goya's works bear comparison with both.)[1] Goya's tapestry cartoons were nonetheless created to reflect a distinctively Spanish social landscape; moreover, many of them include hints of violence, unsettling distortions of balance and perspective, and suggestions of the darker motives that dominate the *Caprichos* and the Black Paintings, reminding us just how misleading it can be to regard any single image of Goya's in isolation from the larger body of his work.[2]

The tapestry cartoons also raise questions about the difference between "autonomous" art and "decorative" art. In fact, none of these paintings was conceived as a work of art in its own right; none was meant to be hung or viewed for its own sake. Though we view these works now, whether in the Prado or elsewhere, in museum settings, they were in fact made for decorative purposes, and only in an indirect way, at that. Goya's tapestry cartoons were converted into far simpler paintings by the artisans at the Royal Tapestry Works of Santa Bárbara; these far less nuanced works were in turn the images from which the tapestry weavers worked. Not surprisingly, the earliest of Goya's tapestry cartoons are themselves relatively schematic, for example, *Hunt with Birdcall* (Figure 2.1) and *Dogs and Hunting Equipment*, both from 1775. He was producing works for a group of painters at Santa Bárbara who could not afford to be subtle. They had to demarcate colors clearly in order for the weavers to be able to choose when and where to use the appropriately colored threads.[3] The resultant tapestries themselves were meant to decorate the walls of the royal residences at El Escorial and El Pardo. All of them needed to conform to the requirements of particular indoor architectural spaces; they had to respond to the constraints of size and proportions dictated by their intended placement.[4] In fact, Goya's paintings for the tapestries were long considered unimportant and lay forgotten for many years. They were rediscovered only in 1870, lying in the basement of the Royal Palace in Madrid, when the majority of them were transferred to the Prado Museum. In their day, they were never intended to be seen.

These facts are worth bearing in mind because they help underscore the fact that while the cartoons were never intended to be taken as independent works of art; the tapestries for which they were made were meant to serve the pleasures of Goya's royal patrons. Goya was initially paid by the piece for the first of the cartoons, but then received a salaried post when he was named "painter to the king"

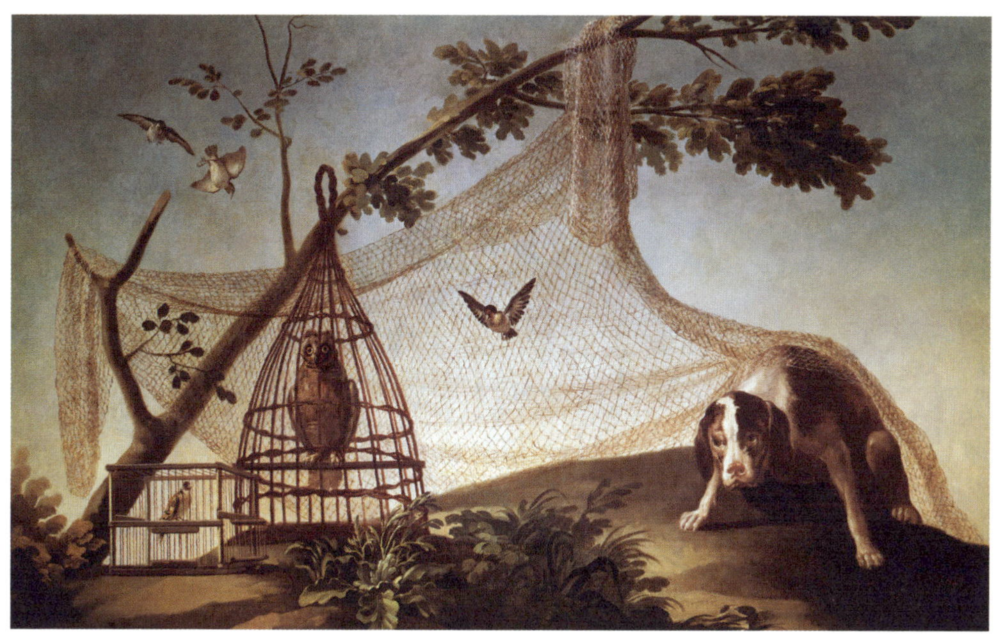

Figure 2.1.
Hunt with Birdcall, 1775. Oil on canvas, 112×179 cm.
Museo del Prado, Madrid.

(*pintor del rey*) in 1786; he was promoted to "court painter" (*pintor de cámara*) with the accession of Charles IV to the throne in 1789, and to "first court painter" in 1799, the same year in which the *Caprichos* appeared. It was also during this time that he was commissioned to paint a number of portraits of important aristocrats including the Duke and Duchess of Osuna and the Count of Altamira.

In working on the cartoons, Goya turned quite quickly away from the static, blocklike images that characterize the earliest of the series and rapidly developed a way of making works that were important and viable independently as art in spite of the decorative context out of which they emerged. Indeed, Fred Licht has gone so far as to claim that Goya was the very first painter whose cartoons were more important than the finished tapestries for which they were intended. His words are worth quoting:

> When we speak of nineteenth-century tapestries before Goya, it is almost a matter of indifference whether we mean the cartoons or the finished, woven tapestries. Boucher, Fragonard, and Audran express themselves as completely in woven tapestries which they never touched, as they do in their autograph cartoons. These artists accepted without doubt or question the essentially ornamental function of art.... With Goya's tapestry cartoons, however, the situation reverses itself quite dramatically: His cartoons are viable, perhaps even great, works of art. The finished tapestries are miserable failures. He was the first artist to face the modern problem of art versus ornament, and his conclusions were also typically modern: He rejected the ornamental.[5]

The question, however, is how Goya managed to make works of art that were viable in themselves and, moreover, to develop their critical potential in spite of their intended use. The critical work of the tapestry cartoons is situated within an artisanal context—a context that required a high level of technical competence and that counted on certain skills and procedures as inherent to the making of art.[6] But the viability of Goya's cartoons as independent works of art means that he found ways to see beyond that context even while working within it.[7] Given the patronage context within which he was working, Goya had to find ways to reckon with the expectations of his royal patrons.

Not surprisingly, the tapestry cartoons take a set of normative views about contemporary society as their baseline; indeed, one could say that they reflect a set of normative views about the nature of society as such. The critical forces at work in them emerge against the backdrop of these normative views — views about the diversity of the various character types that make up "ordinary" Spanish society, views about how the members of different social classes ought to and do behave, and views about the nature of human relationships in general. On the surface, at least, the tapestry cartoons offer sympathetic

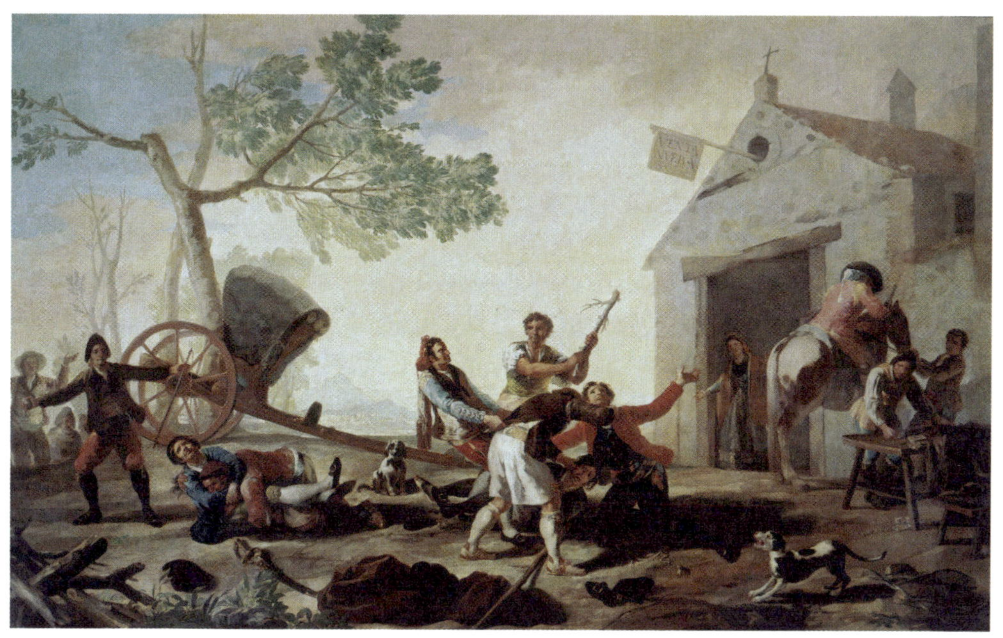

Figure 2.2.
The Fight at the New Inn, 1777. Oil on canvas, 274 × 414 cm.
Museo del Prado, Madrid.

depictions of a wide array of social types, which F. D. Klingender attributed to the court's growing realization, following the Madrid riots of 1766, that they had to take serious account of the people.[8] The "people" in this case included *majos* and *majas* (characterized as "gay spokesmen of the native tradition,") workmen and merchants, innkeepers and coachmen, children at play, and elegantly dressed *petimetres* ("dandies") who took their fashion cues from France. This is, to the casual observer, an art that displays its subjects tastefully in spite of the fact that some of the figures may be rough-hewn and ill-mannered (the characters in the *Fight at the New Inn* (Figure 2.2) stand out as a prominent example).

On the surface, though, these works convey a general sense of happiness shared by the members of a society in leisure activities, and sometimes in work and commerce as well; we see individuals inspecting the wares of a crockery merchant or of an orange seller or looking at the bric-a-brac for sale at a fair in Madrid. The codes that regulate social behavior all seem to be functioning well in these pictures. This includes the discreetly coded sexual innuendos that appear in the works designed for the antechamber to the royal bedroom at El Pardo. *The Swing* (Figure 2.3) and *The Ball Game* have been singled out in this regard.[9]

Moreover, the world of the tapestry cartoons suggests the ostensibly benign view that society exists and can be sustained independently of conflictive political forces or class differences. Goya gives us (that is, gives his royal patrons) "ordinary" people and those of higher classes happily hunting and dancing elegantly, for example, *Dance on the Banks of the Manzanares* (Figure 2.4), playing ball or flying a kite, making a picnic, returning from the grape harvest, or listening to ballads. Indeed, the behaviors depicted in them are not restricted to courtly types, but include many of the activities of "country folk." This is not surprising since the tapestries themselves were meant to provide a pleasing and varied background for the activities of the extended royal family in their residences outside of the royal palace, that is, in contexts where politics were secondary to other activities. In fact, the king insisted on "rural and ludic" scenes in his initial commission for the tapestries; the later works were specifically to include "comic and rustic themes" (*cosas jocosas y campestres*).[10]

In the world of the tapestry cartoons, the norms of taste, pleasure, and society all support one another. The underlying aesthetic frameworks from which these images emerge (but which they ultimately challenge) are largely those of the beautiful and the picturesque, reflecting the alignment of the Enlightenment aesthetic principles of (good) taste, good behavior, and easily accessible forms of pleasure.[11] Given this fact, as well, it is not surprising to find that

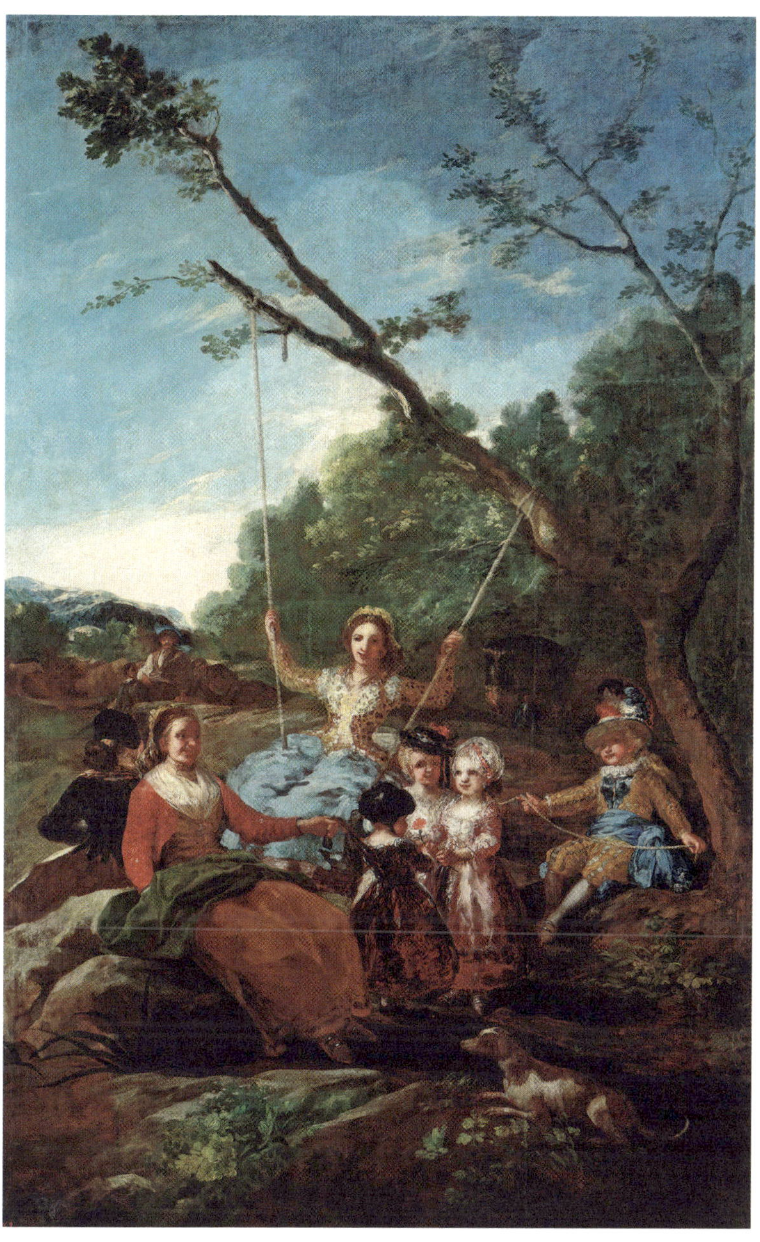

Figure 2.3.
The Swing, 1779. Oil on canvas, 260×165 cm.
Museo del Prado, Madrid.

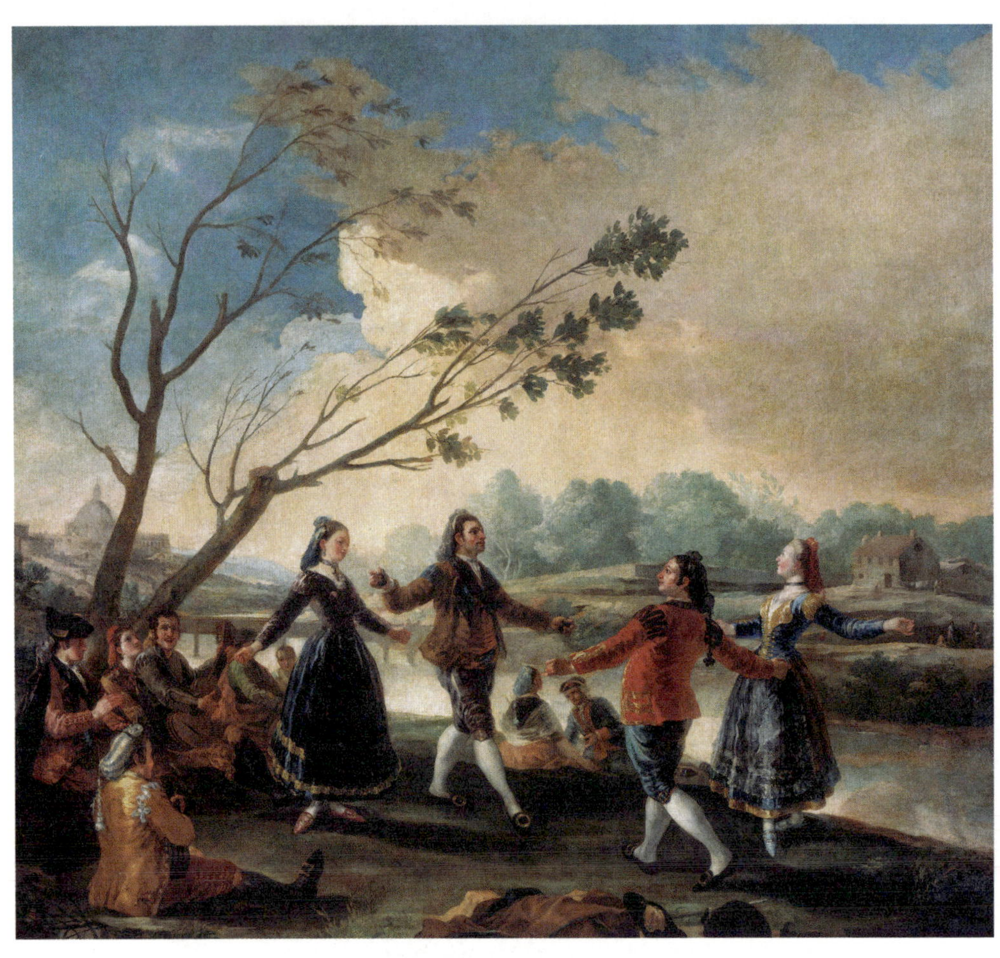

Figure 2.4.
Dance on the Banks of the Manzanares, 1777. Oil on canvas, 272×295 cm.
Museo del Prado, Madrid.

Goya's tapestry cartoons do not foreground the critical function of art, either with regard to the subjects they treat or with respect to the role they envision for art in relation to the social world. Having just been introduced to the royal court and having recently earned his first commissions and not long thereafter an official, salaried post, Goya was hardly in a position to do so in any overt way. And yet many of the tapestry cartoons do raise unsettling questions that are consistent with Goya's project of critique. Those questions alert us to a critical stance not only as regards a particular social world but as regards the nature of society and the role of art in relation to it. The result is a set of works that do more than reflect a world pictured in order to please royal tastes by providing reassuringly happy images of Spanish society. They present the grounds for a critique of normative assumptions about the alignment between decorative art and the promise of happiness with which such art was associated in those contexts. And they challenge any stance that would assume that the relations that form the social world were naturally given. Over the course of painting these works, Goya came to see that the social vision most pleasing to the court stood in tension with his own views of the social world, which were grounded in a far more liberal and critical political stance.

There are three interrelated perspectives from which the work of critique is identifiable in Goya's tapestry cartoons. The first of these perspectives is narrative. Understanding these works as narratives responds to the fact that "reading" is indeed what the cartoons require, since a great many of them present scenes that make sense only if we understand them as excerpts from larger stories. Those stories are built out of narrativized social codes, represented visually, and can be (re)constructed by attending to the actions of the characters and the details of their circumstances. To this end, the cartoons rely upon an illustrative approach to painting and are underpinned by the assumption that an image carries meaning insofar as it is part of a larger social context. That context is encoded within the image in just the ways that Roland Barthes indicated when speaking about the *studium* in a photograph. Whether in photography or in painting, the *studium* refers to embedded meanings — meanings that are available to everyone and that are presented through a shared vocabulary. They are hardly unique to Goya's work and not surprisingly find their way into the popular plays of Goya's contemporaries, including those of Leandro Fernández de Moratín.[12] The *studium* is what one expects to find; it is what can be assumed — which is also to say that it can be grasped almost without thinking or viewing carefully.[13] The tapestry cartoons are replete with these assumed meanings, and yet they often disrupt whatever background or story line one might be expecting to find in them by pointing to troubling implications or to disturbing, secondary narratives. They break the codes through which their stories are told, and they challenge the assumptions on which the dominant narrative and social codes rely. While they may evoke images of social happiness, especially in images that suggest the naturalness of social norms, they also carry the seeds from which that happiness comes undone, sometimes because the norms required for its attainment have no basis in nature or run contrary to it.

Second, as the series evolves, the tapestry cartoons begin to work more consistently *against* conventional principles of visual organization. This is especially true of the cartoons that Goya painted last, in 1791–92. They tend to isolate one of the central figures in the scene and treat the relationship between that figure and its context in ways that raise questions both about the compositional integrity of the ensemble and about the "rightness" of the social relationships they depict. This anticipates the technique that Theodor Hetzer identified in the *Caprichos*: Goya "intensifies the single, isolated motif until it becomes significant in itself. . . . This is what transforms his occasionally commonplace scenes into something gigantic, uncanny, incalculable."[14] Though the themes of many of the cartoons may be conventional, and while many of them were influenced by images drawn from both popular and iconographic traditions (for example, the cartoons depicting the four seasons), these disruptions mark the places where Goya was making important departures from those traditions. The later cartoons, though not only these, increasingly disrespect the principles of visual unity and circumscription that prevail in the earlier works. It has been recognized that the later cartoons demonstrate a freedom from the relatively conservative influence of Goya's teacher, Ramón Bayeu. But what matters most is the direction of his departure from Bayeu and from his other predecessors in making the tapestry cartoons.

Just how we are to interpret the disturbances that we find in the cartoons is nonetheless an issue that needs to be considered in recognition of the temptation to overread them in light of Goya's later, darker works. While this practice, which Ortega y Gasset labelled "mirroring effect" (*espejismo*), is one to avoid,[15] some of those connections are undeniable, and critics have been reluctant to notice the critical work of the tapestry cartoons, much less embrace it, even where they argue for the "modernity" of these paintings. For example, Valeriano Bozal has argued that the cartoons mark the emergence of a "modern visual language," especially when compared with the works of Goya's predecessors. Why? Because they are, in his words, "more lively and verisimilar, more picturesque, more convincing in everything having to do with the representation of everyday life, ordinary characters, and places."[16] But it is not the relative realism or liveliness of the tapestry cartoons that marks their importance or their modernity; rather it is the emergence from them of a critical way of seeing the social world and, specifically, a critical response to the presentation of the social world as natural and as happy by virtue of its harmonious relationship with nature.

Third, and related to both of these, are the technical and material conditions that were involved in creating the tapestries for which Goya's cartoons were intended and to which he was exposed through his ongoing involvement with the Santa Bárbara Tapestry Works. The cartoons demonstrate an engagement with the technical, artisanal processes involved in a multistage image-making practice, just as Goya's later *Caprichos* and aquatints do in their own ways. In the cartoons, the material conditions involved in the making of art were integral to the construction of an aesthetic vision grounded in the project of critique, in part because that specific image-making process was not at all a simple mirroring of the world but involved producing images of the world that required several stages of reversal. Goya's alertness to those processes, which I will explain below and in the later discussion of the *Caprichos*, enabled him to see the world "otherwise" and to recognize the ways in which the conventions of representation played a normalizing role with regard to relationships that are in fact quite skewed. Some of the distortions that find their way into the tapestry cartoons are in fact Goya's ways of representing the truth to a world organized otherwise not to see it. This fact becomes all the more prominent in the *Caprichos*.

Narrative Painting, Normative Work: The Albertian Background and Beyond

In order to understand the emergence of a critical stance within the tapestry cartoons, it is important to gauge them against the established norms for painting that had been inherited from a tradition that roots in the Italian Renaissance and were set forth in Leon Battista Alberti's fifteenth-century treatise, *De pictura (On Painting)*. (Alberti's treatise was translated into Spanish in 1784 and was cited in the most prominent Spanish work of the time, Palomino's 1795 *Museo pictórico*.) Alberti concentrates on two principal elements of painting, one revolving around questions of perspective derived from what he understood about the fundamentals of optics and the other revolving around questions of narrative. Alberti is of course known best for his theory of artificial perspective, which explained how to construct the semblance of a three-dimensional space on a flat surface, yielding an image seen as if from a single point of view that remains constant even as the viewer shifts position. The principles of perspective as he articulates them establish the position of the viewing subject as that of an "absolute" spectator, whose neutral vision is structured according to the geometrical rules by which rays of light are thought all to orient themselves around a single, "centric ray" within the visual field. But Alberti also understood that the use of perspective enables the artist to create an ensemble, a composition of figures, that serves the *historia*, the narrative function. Group composition is in fact of the highest importance for Alberti. The image of a lone figure, which Alberti characterizes as a "colossus," is far inferior to a composition that tells a story.

Behind the Albertian *historia* is a long tradition of art wherein the aim was to illustrate stories from the Bible, in large part for instructional purposes.[17] Goya's frescoes in San Antonio de la Florida are related to it, though in the unconventional ways described above. Alberti had already modernized this earlier tradition, first by addressing himself to secular contexts and second by invoking nature as the artist's fundamental reference point without appeal to any higher, spiritual authority. Specifically, he argued that the best way to compose a painting with an eye to the *historia* is to observe nature, which he described as "the wonderful maker of things."[18] The many other issues that Alberti discusses — including which kinds of compositions provide the greatest pleasure and which kinds of balances and contrasts work best in art — are subordinate to the orientation toward nature and to the interests of the *historia*.

The term "nature" nonetheless requires some elaboration, first because it does not mean just the "natural world" as represented in the form of landscapes, seascapes, pictures of the sky, and so on. Rather, it includes everything that Alberti's predecessors have referred to as "creation." It includes the human world and especially the physical world of human beings. These are the factors that made Alberti such a significant point of reference for the development of secular art, beginning in the Renaissance and continuing long afterward until the time when artists such as Goya — indeed, Goya specifically — began to question those principles of composition and move beyond them. While the notion that painting should strive to create a perfect likeness of nature was in fact ancient — Pliny the

Elder famously recounts in the *Historia naturalis* how Zeuxis made a painting of grapes so lifelike that birds tried to eat them — Alberti was the one who aligned the idea of nature as a norm with the technique of artificial perspective. This alignment extends all the way to Ernst Gombrich's landmark study *Art and Illusion*, which holds that painting, as a record of perception, is a mode of cognition and implicitly *not* a form of critique. Indeed, Alberti provides the undergirding for what Norman Bryson, in his critique of Gombrich and perceptualism, calls the "natural attitude" in painting.[19] One could say that the critical function of art — both as regards modern art in general and as regards Goya specifically — had to assert itself *against* the normative emphasis on nature and the orientation around narrative that Alberti's principles helped establish.

Goya's Innovations

When Alberti refers to nature, he means to say that the painter should not take his bearings from mythologies or fantasies, nor should he invent things on his own. The painter's teacher and guide should be the world of things as they are observed. When Goya described some of the tapestry cartoons as his own inventions ("de invención mía"),[20] he was clearly departing from Albertian principles. For example, his image of *Blind Man's Buff* (*sic*) (Figure 2.5) is reminiscent of Rubens's image of a dance among mythological figures and villagers (1630–35), which hangs in the Prado and which Goya may well have seen among the works in the royal collection, which he inventoried as part of his duties as pintor de cámara.[21]

In contrast to Rubens, however, there are no mythological figures in Goya's cartoon, but rather members of the upper classes playing a favorite game.[22] But "of his own invention" also means that Goya did not model certain images in question after ones already in existence.[23] Where, then, did he find his inspiration for those paintings? Goya himself spoke of his sources of inspiration as Velásquez, Rembrandt, and nature,[24] but the reference point in Goya's cartoons is not just the natural world (which is certainly present in them, as the

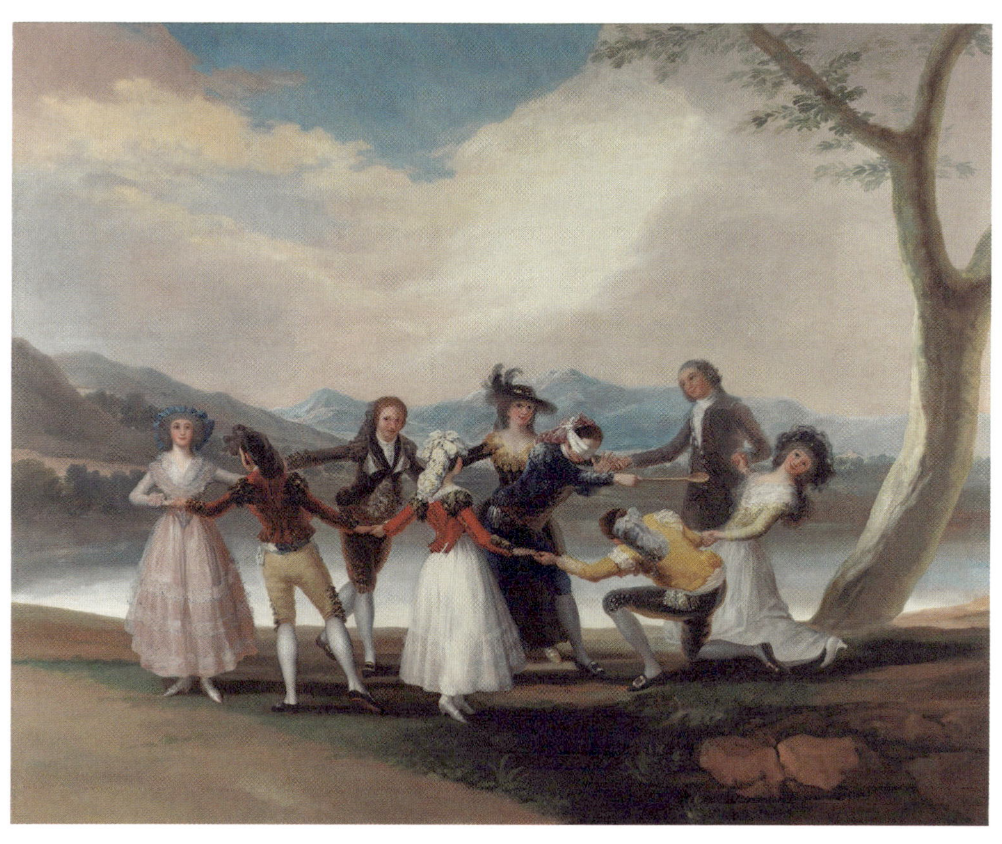

Figure 2.5.
Blind Man's Buff [sic], 1788. Oil on canvas, 269×350 cm.
Museo del Prado, Madrid.

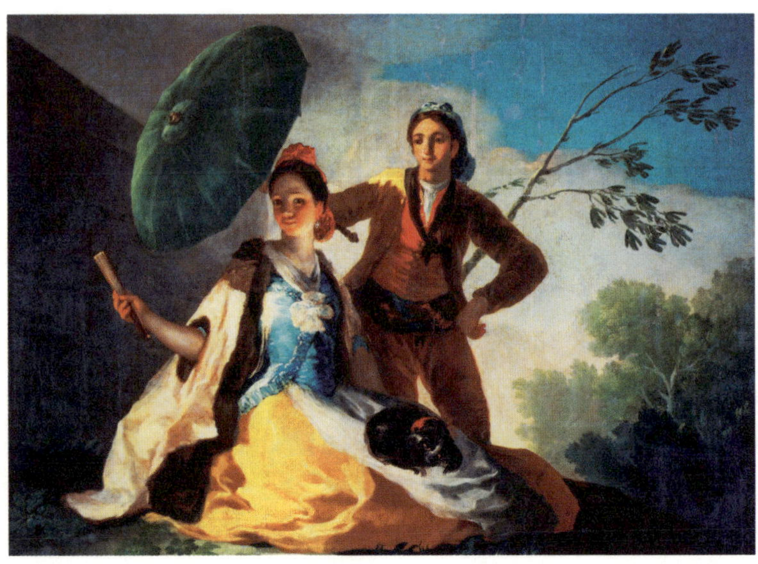

Figure 2.6.
The Parasol, 1777. Oil on canvas, 104 × 152 cm.
Museo del Prado, Madrid.

cartoons of the four seasons show), but *society* and especially those sectors of society that exist independently of the institutions that constitute *civil* society. The narrative component (the *historia*) of the tapestry cartoons revolves principally around this social world, and the sources of happiness in them are produced when social practices seem to be in concert with the natural world; for example, the ostensible subjects of *Picnic on the Banks of the Manzanares* and *The Parasol* (Figure 2.6), along with *Dance on the Banks of the Manzanares*.

This point is central to the tapestry cartoons, which fully register the expectation that art, and especially decorative art, should reflect a harmonious alignment between the natural and social worlds. This expectation is of course utopian, and it is moreover at odds with the increasingly modern understanding that social practices are *not* natural and so *require* justification. To justify social practices was hardly the ambition of the cartoons, yet to represent an alliance between nature and society would have had the unintended effect of accepting the legitimacy of social practices *without* having to justify them. Writing of the relationship between artisanal practices and the evolution of naturalism in the arts, Pamela H. Smith has argued that beginning in the Renaissance, "[n]ature increasingly came to be regarded as an authority to which to make appeal when other traditional sources of legitimate authority failed or were not available."[25] But in spite of the "naturalism" of the tapestry cartoons, Goya makes us aware of those instances where the justification of social practices on the basis of their "naturalness" seems questionable, at best. Indeed, where society and nature are at odds is just where the cartoons challenge accepted images of happiness at the social level by demonstrating where and why human beings engage in activities that contravene the order of nature or where narratives do not lead to their anticipated happy endings. If the cartoons do invoke the normative status of nature and of narrative, it is ultimately in order to question the social practices they help sustain.

Those questions take many forms. In *The Pottery Seller* (Figure 2.7), the coachmen drive off into a nondescript distance while the noble-woman looks out from her elegant carriage. The group seems to be leaving the scene rapidly or, perhaps, not to be stopping at all. The footman at the rear of the coach is reeling backward while the pottery seller seems to be negotiating with a man whose face we cannot see since his back is turned toward us. The action is fragmented, displaced across many centers of attention, in spite of the fact that the light shines centrally on the figure of the pottery seller. The promise of narrative cohesion is thwarted, and the attempt to reconstruct a single line of action is made impossible because there are multiple centers of focus. The impressively large wheels of the carriage and the body of the coach itself—ostensibly mere "props" in the same way the crockery and the dog might be thought of as props, ancillary to character and action—assume as much importance as the

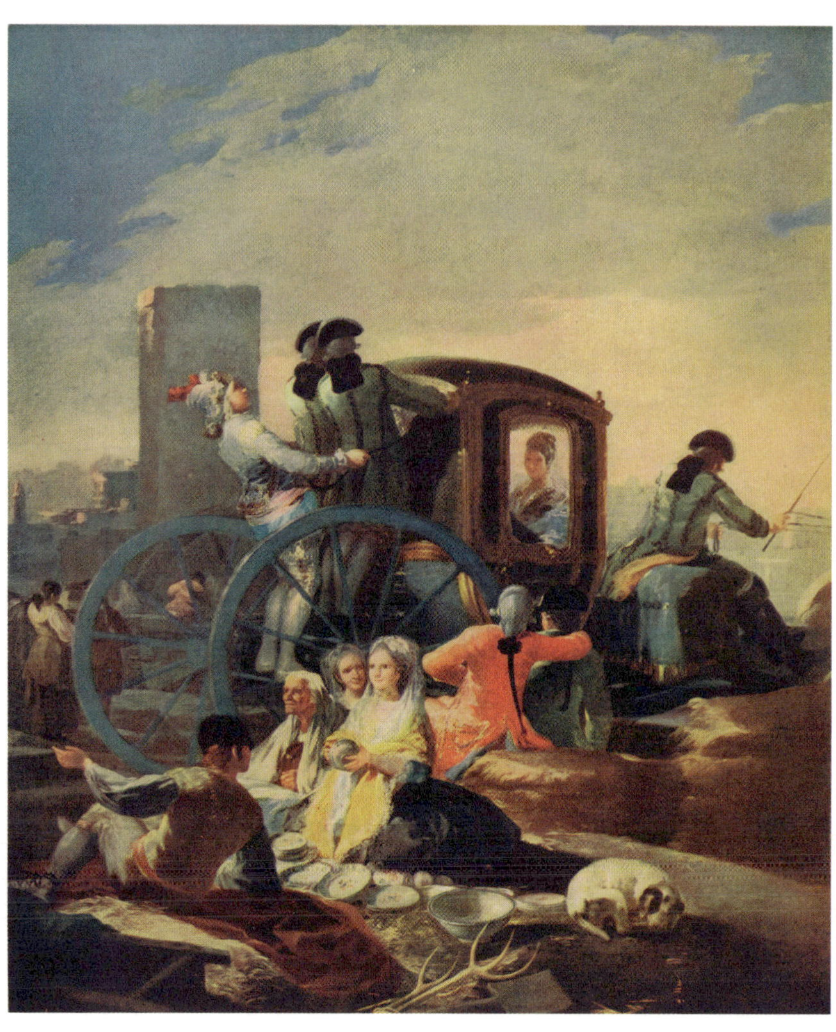

Figure 2.7.
The Pottery Seller, 1779. Oil on canvas, 259×220 cm.
Museo del Prado, Madrid.

characters in the scene. And still, all the relevant social codes remain visible. We recognize clearly that the individual in the coach is a noblewoman (the coach window provides an elegant frame for her, offering us a nearly perfect view through an Albertian "window"); we see what she observes, save the face of the young man. Likewise, we recognize the countryside coding of the pottery seller and those around her — the old hag, who may well be a *celestina* or procuress, and the young man, who may be talking amorously to the seller. We wonder what wares are actually on offer here, an issue raised more provocatively still by the figure of the orange seller in *Picnic on the Banks of the Manzanares*.[26] And through all this a dog lies sleeping, as if nothing unusual at all were going on.

The ostensible narrative of the image concerns one thing, the pottery seller. But the image conveys a different sense, which has to do with what the noblewoman sees in the relationship between the seller and the young man facing her. And there is more to observe that is outside her field of view. Specifically, there are the horses driving the coach, which are not visible in the image at all, and the footman who is thrown back by its motion. Indeed, Goya's depiction of the motion of the coach comes from a set of forces of which we see only the effects. In sum, there is something more at work here than the two narratives that the image represents, and something more than the two competing centers of attention, the one involving the crockery seller and the noblewoman-observer. There are multiple narratives at work here, and at least two desires and two potential and incomplete centers of attention, one revolving around the crockery seller and the noblewoman-observer and the other best attributed to an off-scene force (the horses) that disturb what we see.

The issues lying just below the surface in *The Pottery Seller* disturb the expected narrative, not least because the diffusion of focus creates an image with competing points of attention, some of which lie outside the frame of the image itself and point to narratives that diverge from what we expect, that is, a study in contrasting segments of society. The issues in *The Fight at the New Inn* (Figure 2.2 above) are upsetting in a more explicit fashion, both due to the nature of the action itself and the way Goya pictures it. The cartoon depicts a fight that has broken out in front of a dilapidated inn, which ironically advertises itself as "new."[27] The scene is situated on the outskirts of Madrid in an area now known as "Ventas" and known then as "Ventas del Espíritu Santo."[28] It was a place where muleteers, coachmen, ruffians, and gamblers used to gather; the inn as we see it in the image is located at the intersection of two roads. The narrative action seems to originate in a game of cards, depicted off to the right, which has gotten out of control.[29] The center of the image is dominated by the remains of a brawl. A man lies on the ground and is about to be beaten, while another combatant is being subdued off to the left. This fragmented scene hangs together visually, if at all, by virtue of an empty cart placed diagonally across the central field of view. We can surmise that it may have been drawn by the horse standing off to the far right. But perhaps most notable of all are the reactions of the internal observers of the scene, who express astonishment, confusion, and dismay at what has happened: the innkeeper has rushed to the door to investigate the commotion, and four individuals approach the scene from the left, one in particular whose outstretched arms remind us of the looks of astonishment among the observers of the miracle of St. Anthony in Goya's fresco and of the anonymous victim of the shootings in *The Third of May, 1808.* The point is not just that a pastime activity has turned violent but that the violence fragments the narrative, as reflected in the organization of the composition itself.

But is the card game really at issue? There is at least one alternative to the expected story about a card game gone wrong. What may have happened is that the habitués of the inn were lying in wait to ambush the driver of the carriage. His arrival may have interrupted their card game. The driver may have realized what was about to happen, engaged the locals, and ended up in a brawl with them. If this is so, then the violence in this image is radical, not accidental or occasional. It has prompted one official Prado commentator to the following dark conclusion: "Drawing out the worst in himself, man is turned into a savage, worse even than the beasts, as indicated by the two dogs in the composition, who observe the scene without getting involved, the one lying calmly, the other barking nervously."[30] To conclude this of many of Goya's other works, even of this period — for example, *Highwaymen Attacking a Coach* (*Asalto de la diligencia*, 1786–87) or the later *Attack on a Coach* (1793) — would hardly be surprising. To posit it within the tapestry cartoons is shocking. It suggests that Goya did not believe, as Rousseau thought, that a *return* to a state of innocent nature is impossible for human beings and that their only option is to make the best of civil society. Rather, it suggests that there is part of nature, a violent part, that remains within human beings, no matter how "civilized" they may appear.[31]

The Wedding (Figure 2.8) works in quite a different way. The image proposes an easily read social critique and a strong compositional organization through which another, more subtle critical narrative emerges. The iconographical tradition suggests that *The Wedding* is a representation of the course of life and that this couple are at a central juncture at the bridge of life, between youth and old age. That tradition also alerts us to the signs of the groom's pride and ambition.[32] But this image also tells the story of an arranged marriage, a marriage between a beautiful woman and a very wealthy man who is obviously quite ugly. Though the image breaks the rules of perspective (perhaps intentionally so, in spite of its strong architectural elements),[33] the arc of the massive stone bridge creates an emphatically secular arch over and around the central characters. Well to the right of the center, the father of the bride looks on with resignation. In spite of the fact that his daughter will be wealthy, she seems scarcely to be interested in the groom. The promise of a life of luxury seems to be enough for her.[34] But the priest, dressed in black, shows a cynical smile,[35] and a boy off to the far left who greets the wedding party with outstretched arms — again reminiscent of the gestures of amazement in the frescoes in San Antonio de la Florida — leads us to

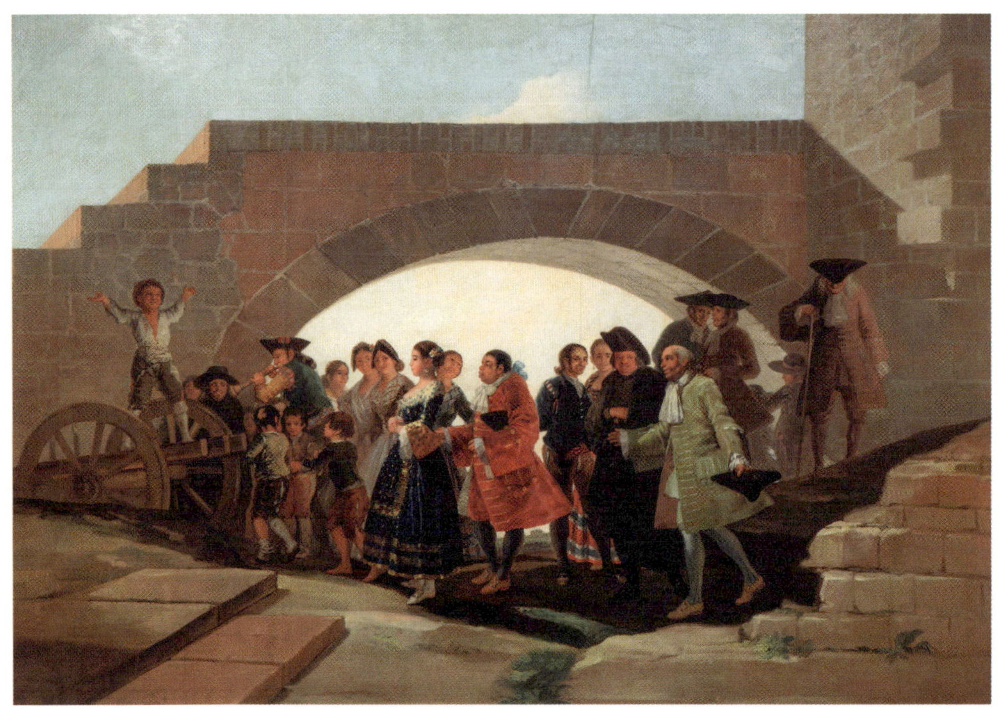

Figure 2.8.
The Wedding, 1791–92. Oil on canvas, 269×396 cm.
Museo del Prado, Madrid.

ask what is in fact so surprising: that a wedding is happening, or that *this* wedding is happening?

However, knowing that arranged marriages were not uncommon,[36] there might be something else that is provoking this astonishment, some other narrative that both the conventional interpretations mask. Indeed, the expected social critique masks a narrative about colonialism and race, which neither the iconographical tradition nor the story of an arranged marriage has prepared us for. The groom in this image is unmistakably dark skinned, in addition to being fat, ugly, and rich. His features are simian, almost grotesquely so. Hers are properly "Spanish," her complexion olive toned and her hair and eyebrows dark. Her demeanor is poised, while he is over-eager. We can only speculate where his wealth might have come from, and given his looks, it is altogether possible that he is a *criollo* who has come to Spain with a fortune made in the colonies. The differences between them, which this marriage will try hopelessly to bridge, are more those of race than of beauty or wealth. Manuela B. Mena Marqués aptly cites the Spanish eighteenth-century representations of the different castes (*pinturas de casta*) in relation to this image, among them Luis de Mena's *Castas o escenas de mestizaje* (ca. 1750) and José de Ibarra's *De mestizo y española, castizo* (ca. 1750), and images relating specifically to interracial marriage (for example, prints by Juan de la Cruz Cano y Olmedilla: *De negro y española nace mulato* and *De mulato y española nace morisco*).[37] But there is more to say. We note from the bride's olive complexion that she must also have elements of other than "pure" *castiza* blood in her, as nearly all Spaniards did. The upshot is this: that this other narrative, a narrative about race, is not simply an exposure of racial differences or prejudices but an indication of the fact that nearly everyone is blind to it — all except perhaps the boy whose astonishment alerts our own gaze.

The Wedding is one of many cartoons that raise questions about what is natural and what is not and whether the social order can in fact ground itself in appeal to the natural order of things. These are

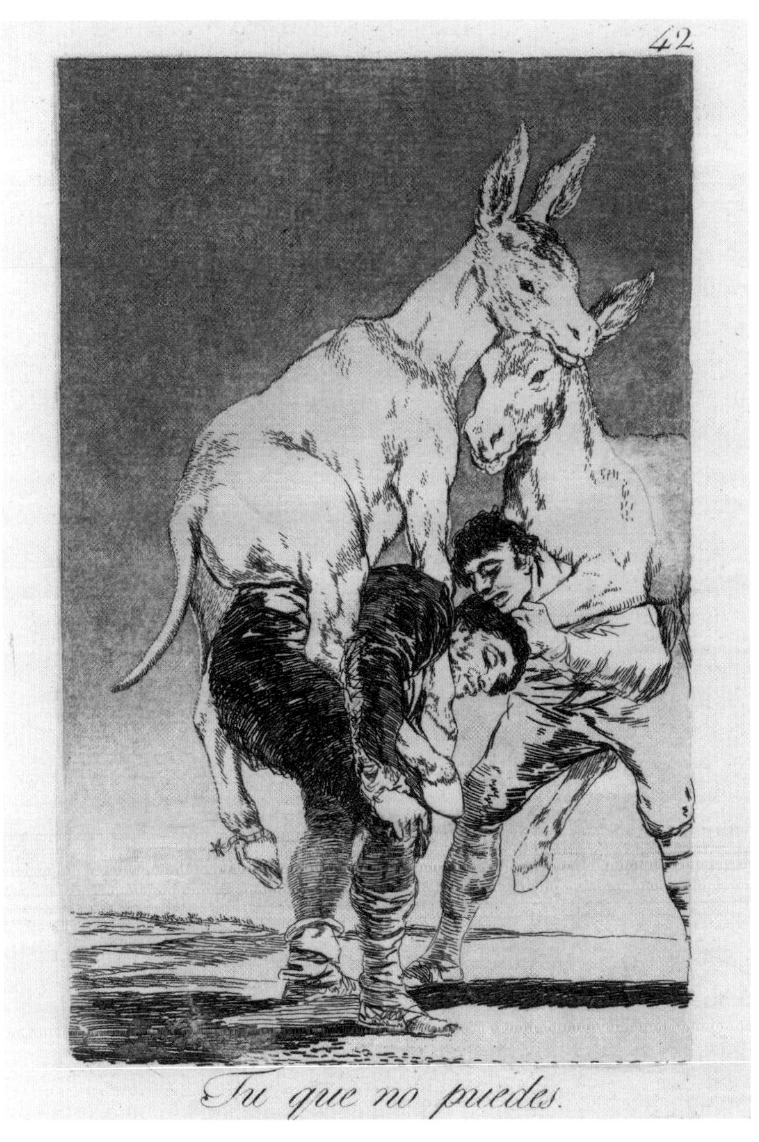

Figure 2.9.
"*Tú que no puedes*" ("You who are not able"), *Caprichos*, no. 42, 1797–98, published 1799. Etching and burnished aquatint, 21.8 × 15.2 cm.

cartoons in which the relationship between human beings and the world is out of balance, whether because it is shown to be out of proportion or scale or because it is the characters in question that are engaged in activities that violate the workings of nature. (These are the factors that become full blown in an image such as no. 42 of the *Caprichos*, *"Tú que no puedes"* ["You who are not able"], Figure 2.9), in which two men are carrying beasts of burden rather than the other way around.)

The Stiltwalkers (Figure 2.10) shows human beings doing something they were never designed for. (Tomlinson shrewdly relates this directly to *The Wedding*, in which "Goya's protagonists aspire to become what nature never intended them to be.")[38] This stunt is an expression of daring that contravenes what human beings ought to do and that reappears in some of Goya's bullfight images that I will discuss later on; it goes against where they ought to stand in relation to the earth and to others around them. It is the *embodiment* of a distortion of perspective, in this case, in the service of love and courtship. The men on stilts are approaching a second-story window that can barely be seen in the upper righthand corner of the image. The extreme and literal unnaturalness of social conventions is unmistakable; more subtle is the fact that neither the men nor the woman in the window are in a position to notice it, much less get beyond it.

Anticipating the **Caprichos** *and the* **Black Paintings**

It bears noting that a number of the cartoons anticipate the critical project that comes into full view in the *Caprichos* (1799). Jean Starobinski said in his chapter on Goya in *1789: The Emblems of Reason*: "Goya's tapestry cartoons … are already 'caprices.' … From the outset Goya shows people sunk in melancholy, scenes of violence, accidents, murders."[39] As I will discuss in the chapter to follow, the work of the *Caprichos* is largely one of "unmasking," that is, showing society how it is, rather than how it perceives itself to be, and demonstrating that it fails to see itself as it is. That project requires the artist first to identify and to expose the distortions — principally

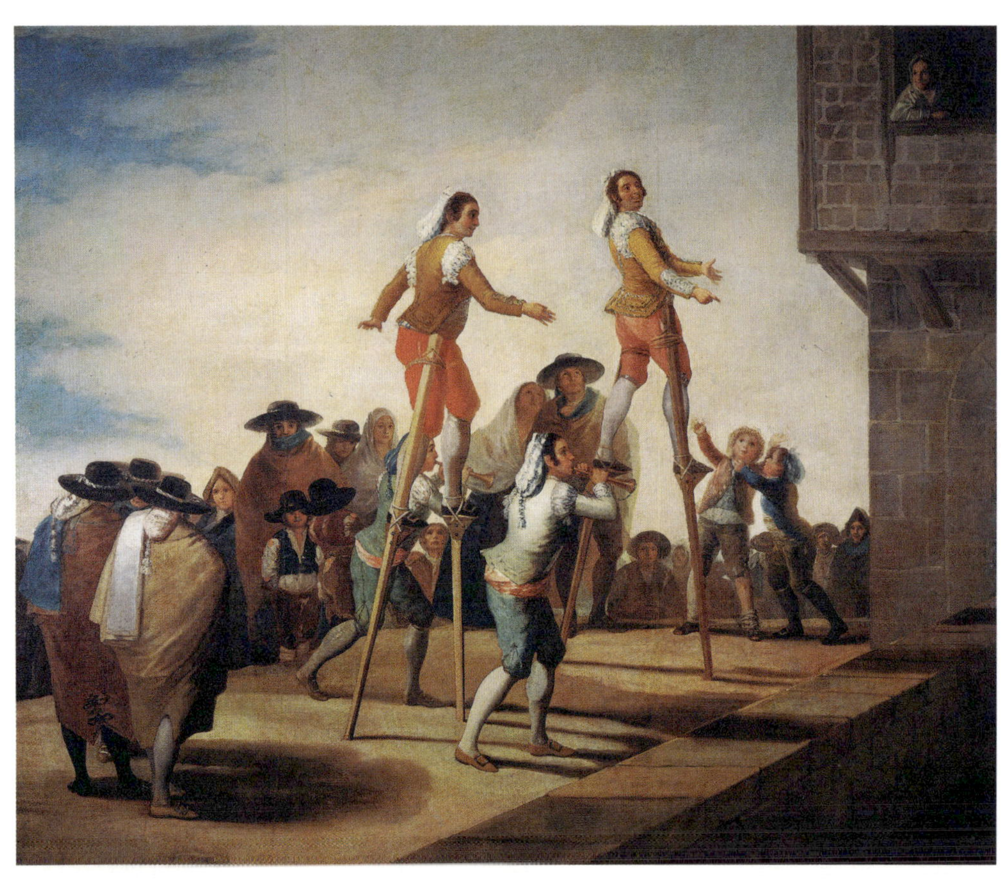

Figure 2.10.
The Stiltwalkers, 1791–92. Oil on canvas, 268×320 cm.
Museo del Prado, Madrid.

those of self-perception — that impede a clear vision of things as they are. But the tapestry cartoons work differently, even as they anticipate the *Caprichos*. The issue they raise is the relationship between the forms of behavior that mark social relations as happy and stable and underlying impulses, including impulses of violence, that break through social conventions and raise doubts about the very possibility of "society" as such. In anticipating the *Caprichos*, many of the cartoons expose the troubling fact that conventions never wholly "socialize" human nature, never wholly eliminate the antisocial motives of aggression. So it is not surprising to find anticipations of the Black Paintings in the cartoons, as well.[40] *Blind Man's Buff* (Figure 2.5 above) anticipates the *Duel with Cudgels* in the Quinta del Sordo (Figure 2.11). The cartoon would have us understand that the bonds of love help lend structure to society and that love is blind. But the further message is that love is a dangerous and violent force, operating capriciously. The blunt wooden spoon promises none of the bittersweet pain of Cupid's arrow, which blends pleasure with the pain of its sting. Indeed, we are not too far away from the naked violence of the *Duel with Cudgels*, where there is no social varnish at all. At this level, human behavior and animal behavior are disturbingly similar. Indeed, one of the cartoons, *Two Cats Fighting* (Figure 2.12), dispenses with human behavior altogether and depicts naked animal aggression and its companion, naked terror.[41]

Surprisingly or not, issues of "unnaturalness" are especially prominent in the cartoons of children. Critical discourse around Goya's images of children in the cartoons has concentrated on their genealogy in paintings of the young Christ and John the Baptist and in images drawn from mythology.[42] But Christological and mythological precedents can distract from what these images also show: that Rousseau notwithstanding, neither the condition of childhood nor the original state of (human) nature is one of innocence. Indeed, nature itself has to be tamed in order for human beings to interact with it. The many images of hunting in the cartoons reflect this fact, as does *Boy Riding a Ram* (Figure 2.13).

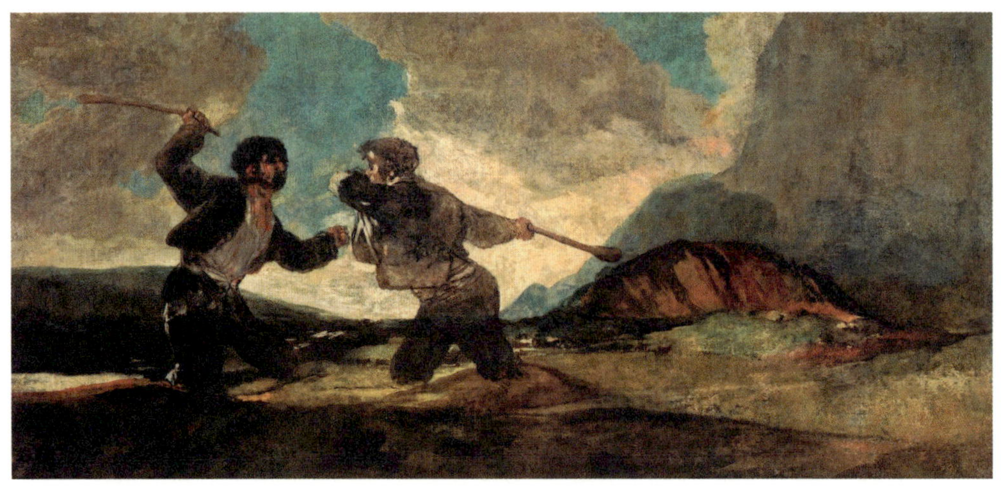

Figure 2.11.
Duel with Cudgels, ca. 1820–23. Oil mural transferred to canvas, 125×261 cm.
Museo del Prado, Madrid.

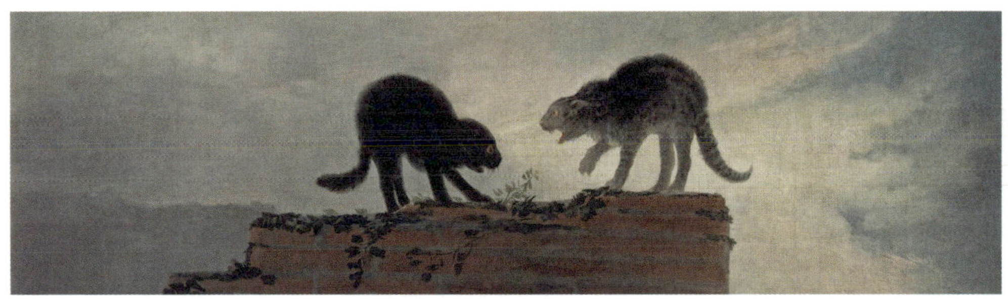

Figure 2.12.
Two Cats Fighting, 1786. Oil on canvas, 56.5×196.5 cm.
Museo del Prado, Madrid.

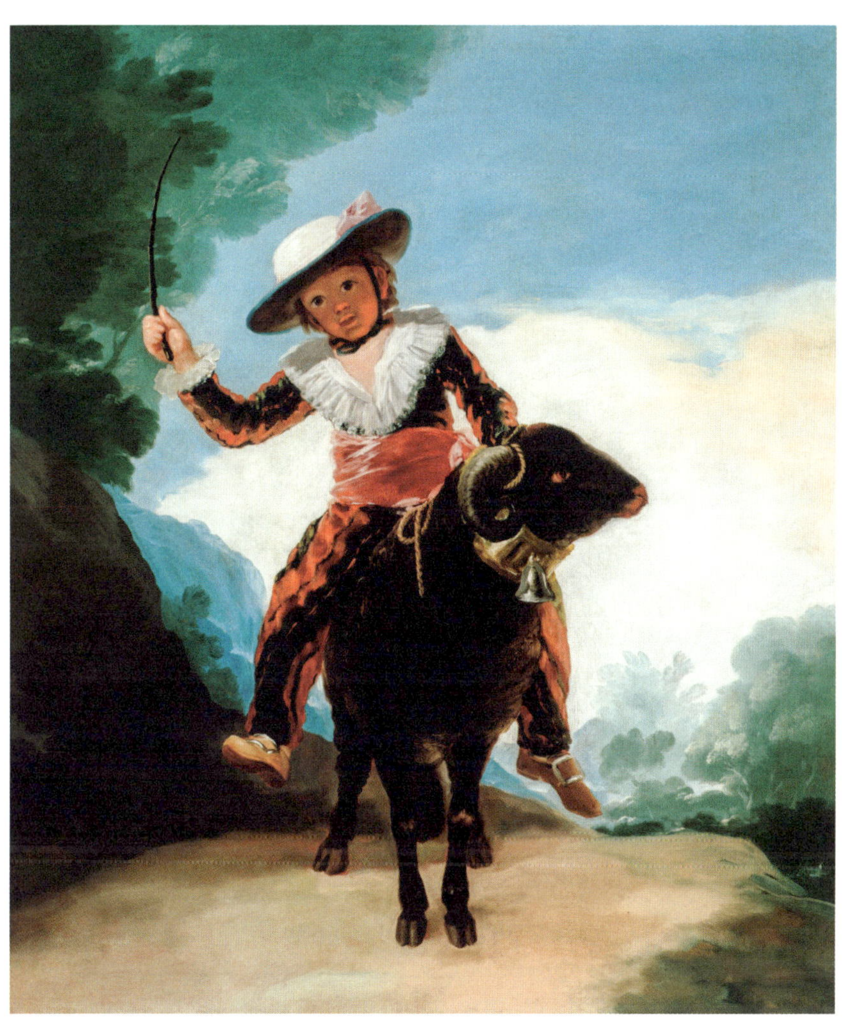

Figure 2.13.
Boy Riding a Ram, 1786–87. Oil on canvas, 127.2 × 112.1 cm.
The Art Institute of Chicago.

The image of two boys playing and holding two muzzled mastiffs is remarkable for the sheer mass of the outsized dogs, in relation to which the two boys appear as little giants.[43] From what we can read of the inscription on one of the collars, the dogs are in the royal service ("DEL SoR"). The dogs appear large enough to be the size of small horses, but Goya also distorts that magnified view so that the boys are enlarged rather than dwarfed by the massive dogs (Figure 2.14).

The images of boys picking fruit (1778) and of boys climbing a tree (1791–92) suggest that even the most innocent of activities involve imbalances of power, the domination of certain individuals by others. Especially in *Boys Picking Fruit,* the perspective is distorted so that the boy in the tree appears unnaturally large and imposing with respect to the others. Perhaps the most emphatic of all these is *The Game of Horse and Rider* (Figure 2.15), where the boy who is riding on the shoulders of the other is painted in light and displays a special joy, while the one who is carrying him, painted in shadow, labors under his weight. (The distortions of size in this image presage one of the most memorable of Goya's prints from the *Disparates, The Simpleton* [Figure 2.16].) The scene is mirrored in reverse in the background off to the left, where Goya reminds us that this game was also a balancing act, pitting play against the forces of nature, as in the much earlier work, *The See-Saw* (1780).[44]

Finally, I would note that whether due to the distorted proportions with which they are painted or the activities in which they engage, the children in the tapestry cartoons seem to be protoadults rather than children in the customary, natural sense. For instance, children riding in a carriage are dressed as if they were miniature grown-ups, and when boys are dressed up in costumes, they play at being soldiers. Some of this may be attributable to the fact that "childhood" as we know it was a later invention of the social imagination and related practices. For boys to dress up as soldiers might seem to be an innocent game. But given all the firearms in Goya's works — only a few of which are put to socialized activities in the form of sport (hunting) — how can we not read these boys as future soldiers, rather than as the "toy

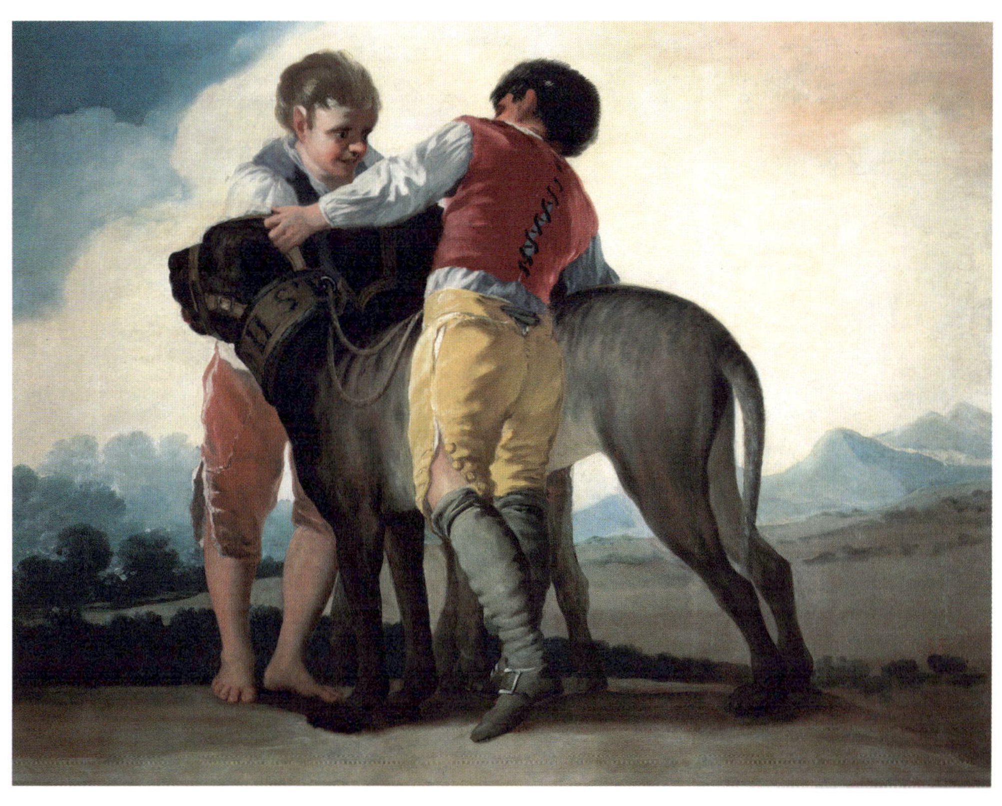

Figure 2.14.
Boys with Mastiffs, 1786–87. Oil on canvas, 112×145 cm.
Museo del Prado, Madrid.

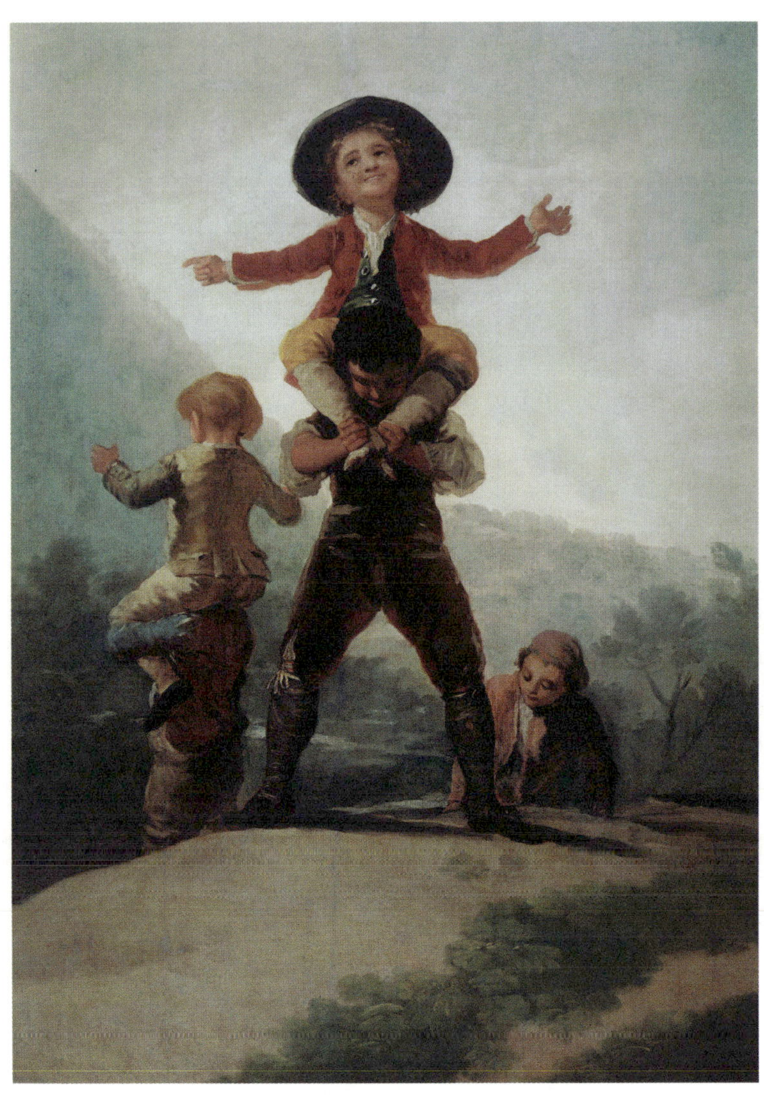

Figure 2.15.
The Game of Horse and Rider, 1791–92. Oil on canvas, 137 × 104 cm.
Museo del Prado, Madrid.

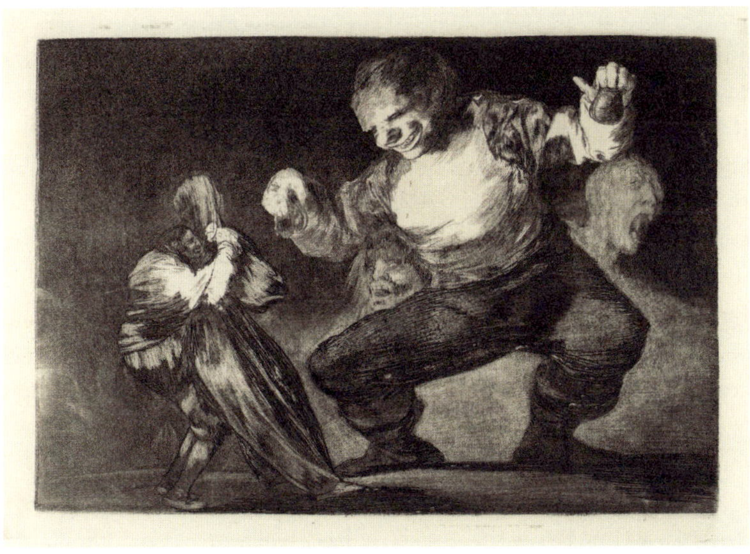

Figure 2.16.
"Bobalicón" ("The Simpleton"), *Los Disparates,* no. 4, 1815–19, published 1864.
Etching, burnished aquatint, drypoint, and burin, 24.1×35.4 cm. Museo del Prado, Madrid.

soldiers" they pretend to be? Goya may well have an insight into their future that they themselves could not.

Reversals and Inversions

I conclude this chapter with a brief set of remarks about the tapestry cartoons meant to support the suggestion that Goya was engaged throughout in his career in reflections about the material construction of images. These remarks follow on the discussion of how Goya deconstructs and reconstructs images in conjunction with the frescoes in San Antonio de la Florida. We will see more of this in relation to the making of the etchings and aquatints.

The technique of tapestry making that was used in the Santa Bárbara Tapestry Works exposed Goya to a process in which a final

87

image, the tapestry, was arrived at through a series of reversals. In addition to the process mentioned above in which an oil painting model or cartoon was transformed into a more schematic image so that the separation of colors required by the weaving process could be accommodated, tapestry weaving required the weaver to sit *behind* the loom, facing the sketch, which was in turn oriented toward the loom.[45] The image was thus viewed from the front but woven from behind. Moreover, the "high-warp" method of weaving used at Santa Bárbara reverses the left-right orientation of the cartoon, since the weaver is copying the front of the cartoon from the back of the tapestry. Because left and right were reversed, the painter, in turn, needed to create the cartoon in the direction opposite from the one intended for the completed tapestry.[46]

Goya understood this requirement and certainly saw this process many times over the course of his involvement with the Santa Bárbara tapestry works. This no doubt encouraged him to see the world "otherwise." And it may well have helped prepare him for the work he would do in etching and aquatint, where the copper plates had to be engraved with the *reverse image* in orientation (left/right) and where the process involved *removing* material where the printed marks would appear. This aspect of the etching process, I suggest in Chapter 4, was directly aligned with a crucial feature of the work of critique as Goya carried it out in the *Caprichos*. Seeing "otherwise" was in fact key in his development of his critical art. It required seeing things as opposite to or as inversions of the way in which they ordinarily appear, and with that, realizing that seeing things this way could provide access to the truth that might not otherwise be evident. Goya learned the process of seeing things "otherwise" early on in his career, and in the case of his paintings for decorative tapestries, in a genre where it would hardly be expected.

CHAPTER THREE

Goya, Modernity,

Aesthetic Critique

Among the stories often told about the evolution of modern art, there is one that would seem to accommodate Goya quite well. This is a story that locates the chief accomplishment of modern art in the achievement of abstraction, in securing freedom from the obligation to make images that resemble or represent the "world," and thus in establishing art's independence from all other worldly spheres of activity. Key to this story is an account of the way in which art abandons any subject other than itself and represents nothing — nothing outside itself. It is a story about art breaking free, becoming independent, establishing its full autonomy. Without wishing to dispute the merits of this story in general, there is nonetheless another account to be considered and another understanding of art's relationship to all the things that might seem to stand outside it. Goya has an especially significant place in it. This alternative account countenances a more complex relationship between art and the worldly domains around it, placing art in an engaged position of critical reflection on those domains. It is also an account that attends to art's reflection on the social and material bases on which it is made. On this account, it is important that art retain some discernible relationship to the things from which it distinguishes itself, and one of the conditions for that to happen is for art to remain connected to the project of figuration, that is, the creation of images that bear some connection to the things we recognize in the world. How to resemble the world while engaged in a critical relationship with it is an important question, some of the answers to which will emerge over the course of what follows. My overarching argument is that this is, in fact, the path that Goya followed, and that close consideration of his relationship to one of the key figures in the development of modern European art — Manet — will, by force of contrast, reinforce this claim and help illuminate how Goya undertakes a discernibly modern project in art that is centrally involved in the project of critique. It will show how Goya's project remains fully engaged with the issue of art's ability to speak to the worldly contexts around it.

To this end, I proceed with a painting by Manet that has particularly close ties to Goya, even though it is a painting that no longer exists in anything close to its original form. The image in question is Manet's *Dead Toreador* (Figure 3.1). It is in fact a fragment of an earlier work, entitled *Incident in a Bullfight*, that Manet showed in Paris at the Salon exhibition of 1864 (Figure 3.2). The original composition went through several iterations before being finished and is available to us now only as a reconstruction on the basis of curatorial evidence (Figure 3.3). Manet's original *Incident* was an odd composition, seemingly built out of separate elements: the figure of the dead toreador in the foreground, the *toreros* clinging in the background to the perimeter fence of a rather schematically depicted arena, and in between them, something that appears to be a blotch or stain suggesting the partial outline of a bull. Its compositional structure can be traced to some of Goya's bullfight paintings, as will become clear in due course.

When *Incident in a Bullfight* was shown in 1864, the reaction to it by critics was fiercely disapproving, even to the point of sarcasm. Some dismissed it as "primitive." One commentator objected to "the rigid bullfighters spaced out mechanically around the arena like fence posts." Another complained about the "shapeless mass in the middle of the arena that is at the same time a bull, a rhinoceros, and a Paris sewer rat." Others compared the blotch of a bull to "a

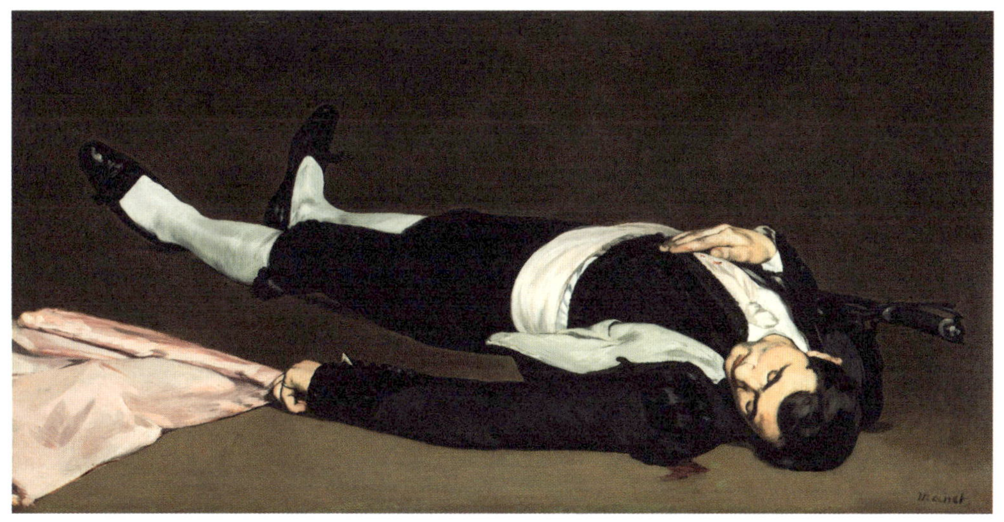

Figure 3.1.
Édouard Manet, *The Dead Toreador*, ca. 1864. Oil on canvas, 75.9 × 153.3 cm.
National Gallery of Art, Washington, D.C.

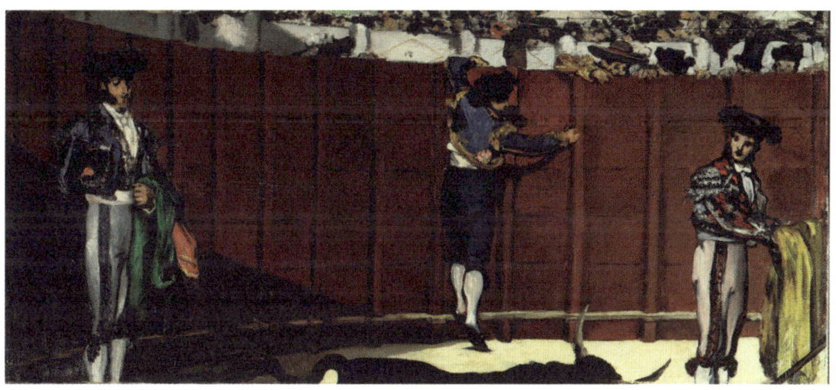

Figure 3.2.
Édouard Manet, *Incident in a Bullfight,* ca. 1864. Oil on canvas, 47.9 × 108.9 cm.
The Frick Collection, New York.

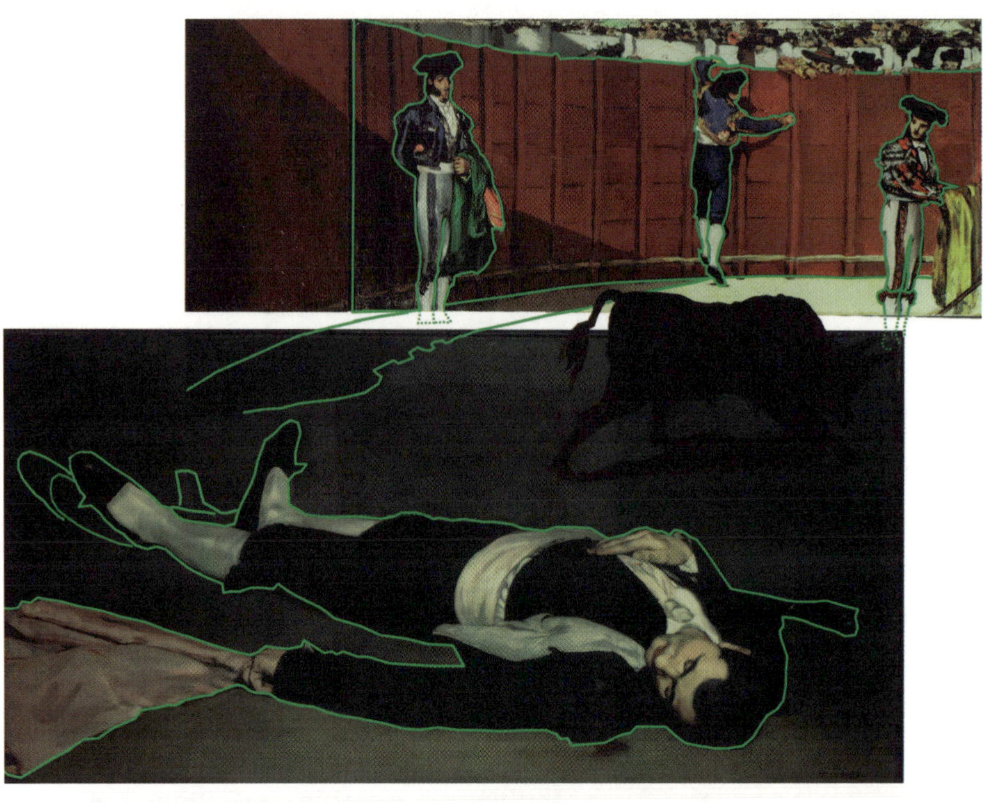

Figure 3.3.
Reconstruction. From Susan Grace Galassi, *Manet's 'The Dead Toreador' and 'The Bullfight':
Fragments of a Lost Salon Painting Reunited* (New York: Frick Collection, 1999), p. 13.

bit of spilled ink or to shoe polish." Critics scorned Manet's wide-angle perspective and condemned his choice of color for the sand.[1] In response to these attacks, and many more like them, including cartoon caricatures in the Paris newspapers, Manet made a radically bold and destructive move: he literally cut the figure of the dead toreador out of the painting, attacking the canvas with the equivalent of a pocket knife, thereby destroying the original composition, but leaving the dead bullfighter isolated and intact. The gesture was as dramatic an example of modernist iconoclasm as one could imagine, certainly for the 1860s, when such an act still seemed extreme. It was indeed iconoclasm in the root sense — the destruction of the image — though here in the more nuanced sense of the destruction of the composition in a way that ended up yielding one lone image. In part as his way of responding to the compositional conventions demanded by his critics and the art-historical past, Manet reacted by turning — productively, in the end — against his own work. And by so doing, he generated a far more disconnected, fragmentary, and powerful image than what he had originally constructed in *Incident in a Bullfight*. (See Figure 3.1 above.)

The *Dead Toreador* does not present any of the compositional difficulties that the critics saw in *Incident in a Bullfight* because it eschews composition altogether. But it presents a host of new challenges that are in turn characteristic of aesthetic modernism in one of its dominant modes. The figure of the dead toreador is entirely bereft of context. The figure is situated on the ground, lying in a way that asks us to apprehend everything that might be inactive, artificial, and inert about a subject (the bullfight) that is conventionally associated with dramatic actions, with pageantry and drama and display — a subject that was linked in the popular imagination to a form of tragic spectacle that was long regarded as uniquely Spanish. (It was in fact largely due to the French perception of Spain as an exotic land that bullfighting came to be seen this way.) Indeed, the image stands in stark contrast to some of Manet's other bullfight compositions, which conform far more closely, even if problematically, to

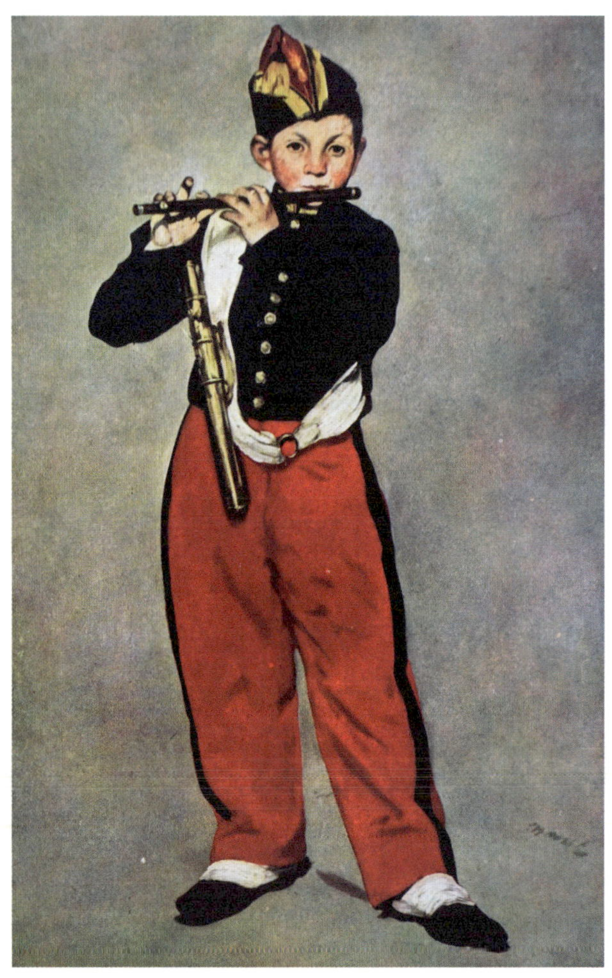

Figure 3.4.
Édouard Manet, *The Fifer*, 1866. Oil on canvas, 160×97 cm.
Musée d'Orsay, Paris.

prevailing conceptions of what such a spectacle ought to be. (I will turn to them below.)

What we see in the *Dead Toreador* is an image that negates or rejects the contextual supports that the other figures in a composition might provide. In that regard, it is related to some of Manet's portraits of lone individuals, for example *The Street Singer, Stéphane Mallarmé*, or *The Fifer* (Figure 3.4). But even more than any of those portraits, it is a powerful example of how an artist's confidence in the power of the image to be what it is, in and of itself, depends upon a refusal of the aesthetic principles and presuppositions of perspective, of proportion, and of a central narrative or drama. For this reason, Manet's painting is an especially useful point of reference for outlining some of the dominant views about modernity in art and for connecting those to Goya's critical project. In part through the various refusals just mentioned, the *Dead Toreador* offers a moment in the construction of visual modernity through a process of *aesthetic* self-critique, a process in which the true subject of art ultimately comes into view as being nothing other than what it itself presents, and not anything in the world. The story of Manet's *Dead Toreador* is clearly about de-composition, but there is something further at work in it, because in looking *at* the strangely isolated figure of the toreador, we are also confronted with a disruption of the conventions and preconditions of our looking — that is, the conditions of perspective, of spatial orientation, and of composition that were designed to sustain our engagement in a world made to appear as if it were created *for us.*

Aesthetic Critique

This view about modernity in art, which associates aesthetic modernity with the process of self-reflective aesthetic critique, was most famously espoused by the influential critic Clement Greenberg, whose writings on art reflected the view that art moves onward by directing its critical gaze reflectively and inwardly toward its own procedures and presuppositions; that important art is art that grapples with the material conditions out of which it is shaped and with the very substances and supports out of which it is made; and that in the process art finds its "true subject" to lie nowhere other than in itself. It is a line of thinking that leads to a valorization of modernist abstraction, and especially of abstract expressionism, as the apogee of the autonomy won by art's self-reflexiveness. It is a path that would seem to secure art's independence from the domains of society, politics, religion, and so on, not least in the interest of securing its *equality* with all of them. The work of aesthetic self-reflection is regarded as the motive force behind the decomposition and disfiguration of the image in modernism. It provides one rationale for the pulling, the stretching, and the blurring of figures that led to abstraction and to the point where we seem no longer to be looking *through* a transparent medium or at an arrangement of figures, but rather are looking *at* the medium by which the figures seem to have been reabsorbed.

The *Dead Toreador* is an instance of painting in which some central subject (in this case, the bullfight) is occluded, and it presages instances in which the figural subject is nearly eliminated and where there is nothing discernible, or almost nothing, there. This occlusion is implicit in the construction of the salon version of Manet's *Incident in a Bullfight*, about which all the critical objections — the complaints about his use of color, about the stiff remoteness of the *toreros* in the background, and about the blotchy bull in the middle — might never have occurred had there been a well-constructed, central action of the kind that would have been appropriate for the painting of tragic events, for history paintings, or indeed even for narrative-based genre paintings of the kind we see in Goya's tapestry cartoons. Instead, Manet was drawn to create a work (the original *Incident in a Bullfight*) in which the action, the actors, and the scene itself were fundamentally disjointed, hence a work that offered not one of the conventional means by which a central event could readily be reconstructed. Moreover, from what is left, we don't know whether in the end to regard the *Dead Toreador* as the fragment of a tragedy or not,

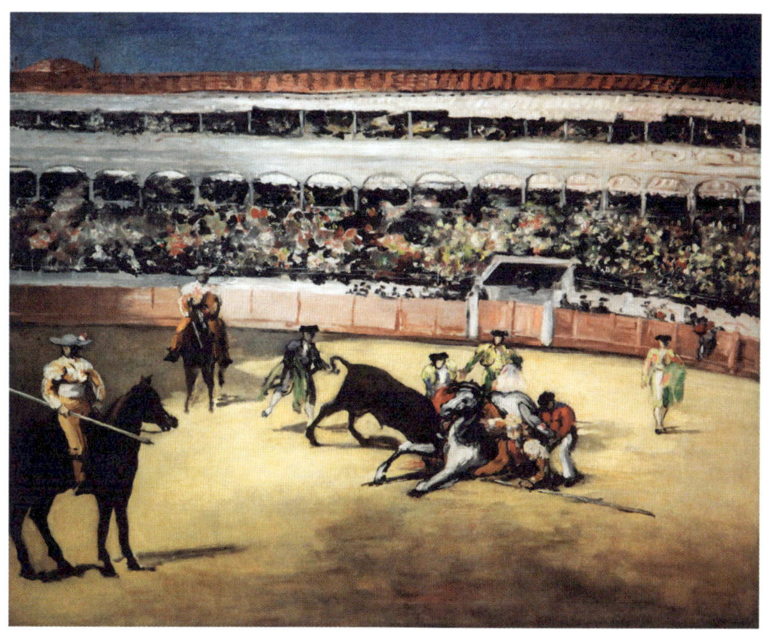

Figure 3.5.
Édouard Manet, *Bullfight*, 1865–66. Oil on canvas, 90×111 cm.
Musée d'Orsay, Paris.

because the subject matter of the painting is left out; what might have been the principal action is never given to us directly to see. This occlusion is likewise true of some of Manet's other bullfight scenes in which the climactic moment of the protracted spectacle, the kill, is surrounded by so many blurred figures that it becomes nearly impossible to observe. We are unable to see what really *is* going on within the confined space of the bullring, which after all was designed for the witnessing of a spectacle (Figure 3.5).

These examples and this account feed directly into the conventional story about modernism as a movement away from figuralism and toward abstraction, with Manet as one of its heroes. The story is neither uncontroversial nor unproblematic. Certainly with respect to the tradition of figural compositions in the nineteenth century, one needs to reckon with other, sometimes more complex forms of negation than this version of aesthetic modernity would suggest. And one ultimately needs to answer questions about whether and how art can itself survive the force of a critique that would seem to isolate it so drastically from all other forms of social and historical practice to the point that it refuses to see itself as a semblance of the world at all. This is where the example of Goya plays a crucial role. Indeed, my reason for thinking about Goya in this context is based on the premise that his work offers a viable alternative to just such concerns. With respect to the status of the figural subject as an "excerpt from" or synecdoche of the world — a likeness of it — for instance, Goya's work would seem to suggest that the work of art is at once like the world and fundamentally unlike it, the *double* of the world and also its *antithesis*. It gives us the world seen *otherwise*. It is, to invoke Adorno's language in *Aesthetic Theory*, the "determinate negation of the existing world order."[2] How does this happen and evolve, this likeness that is an unlikeness and vice versa? And what, after all, is "the world" in a context like this?

Wholly germane to this last point is Manet's unusual still-life painting of an almost formless asparagus (Figure 3.6), painted in 1880, in which the vegetable seems to melt into a viscous nothingness, or rather, into the paint out of which it is formed. It might seem difficult to say *why* the image of the asparagus is so much about paint, but it is. Perhaps it is because there was nowhere else for the intensity of an image like the *Dead Toreador* to go other than to a further reflection on the very medium out of which it was formed. There are potential models for this kind of dis-figuration in Goya, as for example the *bodegón* ("still life") composed of ribs, loin, and head of mutton (Figure 3.7), where the meat is already on its way to becoming (but does not become entirely) a formless mass of paint.

Both images, of asparagus and meat, are examples of still-life painting, but both are vastly different from the disciplined

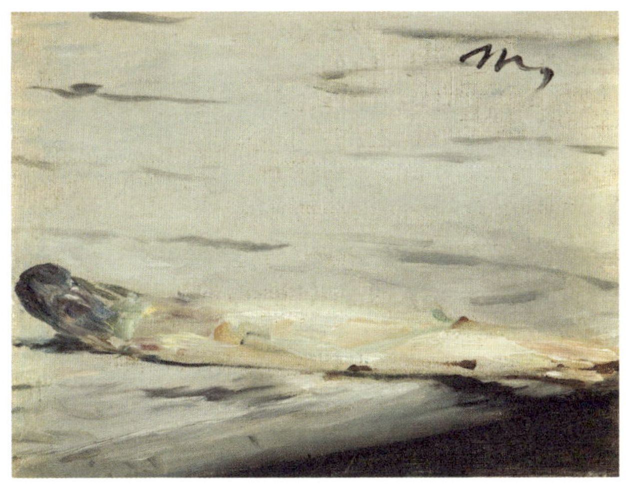

Figure 3.6.
Édouard Manet, *Asparagus*, 1880. Oil on canvas, 16.9×21.9 cm.
Musée d'Orsay, Paris.

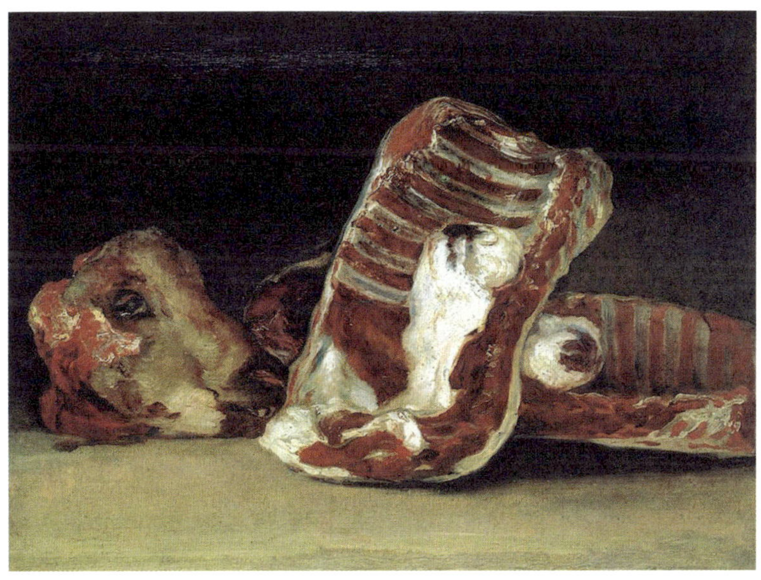

Figure 3.7.
Still Life of a Lamb's Head and Flanks, 1806–12. Oil on canvas, 45×62 cm.
Musée du Louvre, Paris.

realism — the consummate illusionism — of the preceding European still-life tradition. The question is whether we can fully explain the processes of de-composition and dis-figuration as being driven solely by the force of aesthetic reflection and exploration, that is, by the discovery of new frontiers through the rejection of the conventions of the past. In Goya's case, at least, the answer seems no, or not entirely. There are a set of known historical circumstances surrounding the image to be taken into account. These include the fact that it was almost certainly painted while Goya was living in exile in Bordeaux during Madrid's *año de hambre* ("year of the famine") from 1811 to 1812. The image is no doubt a response in paint to the destructiveness of the famine, a visual record of the decomposition of the very things, then so scarce but most necessary for life. In short, there is an active relationship between the "external" circumstances surrounding this image and the otherwise "aesthetic" work also evident in it, that directs attention both toward the very medium out of which the image is made and toward the historical circumstances surrounding it.

The Subject of Painting

More fully considered, the issue involves something more than the question of whether an image does or does not *resemble* the world. Consider Goya's *Semisunken Dog* (Figure 3.8), which involves both the literalness of a figure that lies in plain sight, even if only partially so, and an expanse of paint that borders on a kind of sheer nothingness. The little dog — its head only — seems to be all but powerless as it peers up and gazes toward a formless mass of color that might be sand, a hill, or a vast nothing of anything but color. The figural subject of the painting is overwhelmed, its body eclipsed, drawn nearly to the null point, and all but displaced in terms of visual weight by the indeterminate color mass that might well have served as its ground or background. There are X-ray studies that suggest that the large color field in the painting may have begun as a landscape; perhaps we can read the final work as an erased or abstract landscape or as a kind of

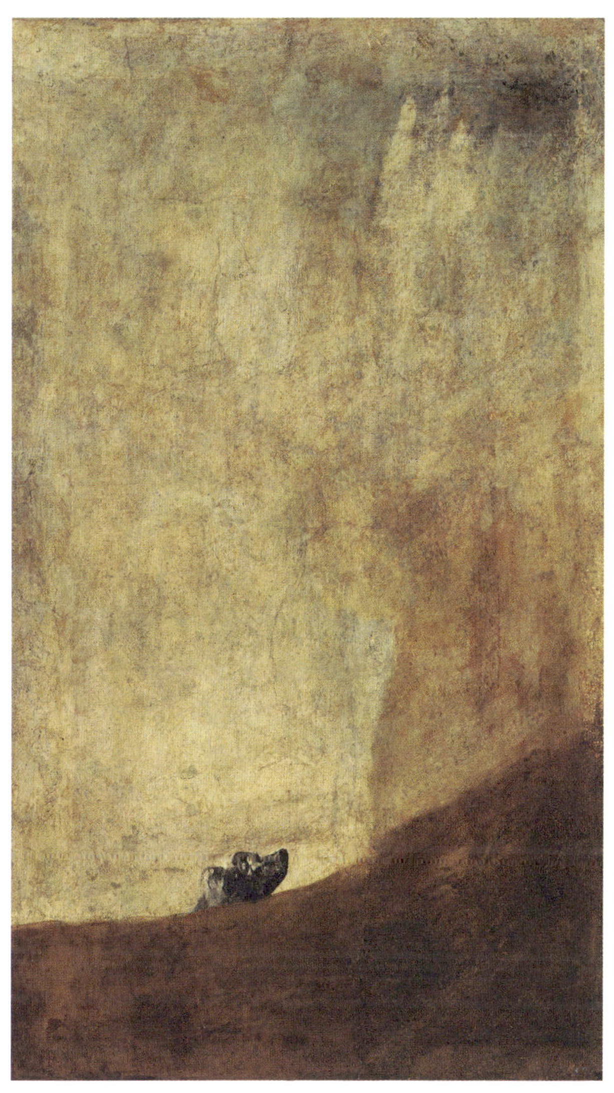

Figure 3.8.
Semisunken Dog, ca. 1820–23. Oil mural transferred to canvas,
131×79 cm. Museo del Prado, Madrid.

negative ground against which the image of this apparently helpless dog is set. And yet even while we are given an image, Goya's painting is in the end no more just about a dog or a landscape than Manet's lone wilting asparagus is just about food or Goya's *bodegón* about meat.

How do we explain these works that *are* and *are not* about their figural subjects? It might be said that these works involve the simultaneous assertion and denial of what they show. On the side of whatever works *against* the image, there is a force of negation that seems to be rooted in something other than a modernist exploration of painting's presuppositions, or in a struggle against the traditions of the past, or in an exploration of the means and media out of which images are made. Indeed, if one considers Goya's painting of the dog even briefly against the iconographic tradition to which it is related, we can see the extent to which he is painting what is and is not there. The dog in Goya's painting might seem to echo the tradition rooted in works such as Dürer's *Melancholia I* and his *Saint Jerome*. But there is scarcely any visual resemblance or citation of Dürer. What Goya somehow renders in the juxtaposition of the diminished dog and the overwhelming ground is neither an icon of melancholy nor a more realistic dog, but the anxiety of viewing an image that is so bereft of context, just as this dog is masterless.

I will turn below to say more about the simultaneous assertion and denial of the literal subject in Goya and what it means in relation to the issue of negation, but first I want to examine how this process—the work of aesthetic self-reflection in the service of an engaged critique—plays out in two of Goya's best-known historical paintings, the uprising of *The Second of May, 1808* (Figure 3.9) and the executions in *The Third of May, 1808* (Figure 3.10), presents a crucial moment in Spanish history as utterly chaotic and disorienting.

The sprawling and uncontained action of *The Second of May, 1808*, while arrayed against a roughly diagonal background, has no clear focal point, in part because of the genuine historical turmoil of this moment. The work was the result of Goya's effort, six years after the fact and under a restored government, to reckon with the official

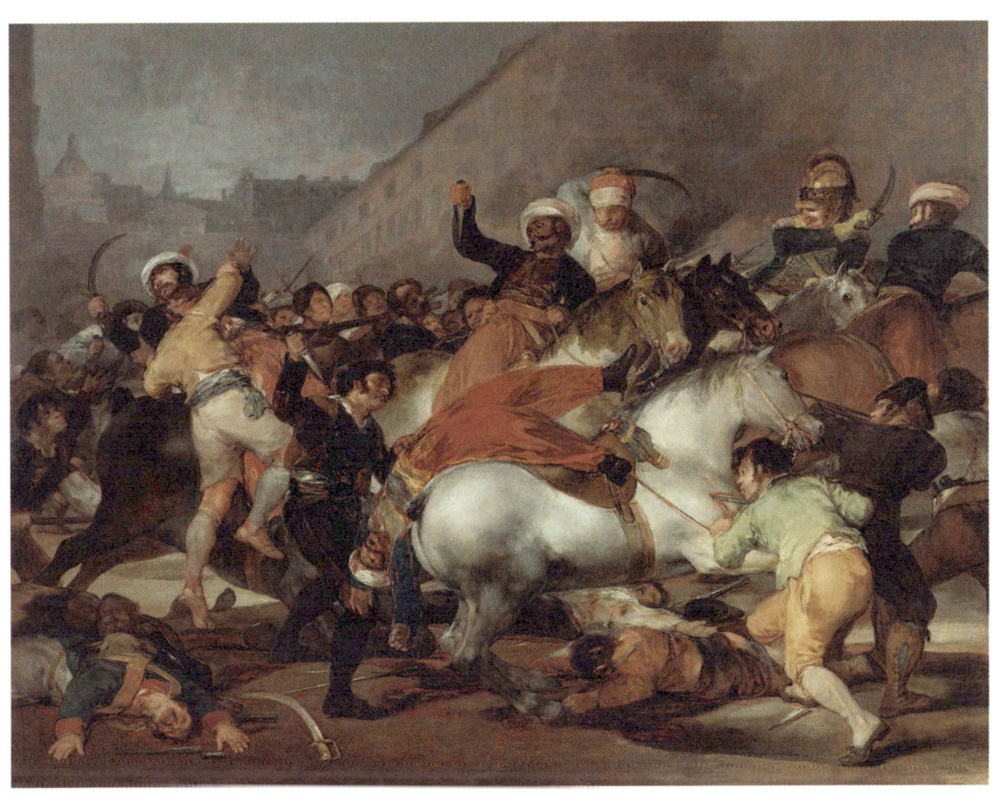

Figure 3.9.
The Second of May, 1808, 1814. Oil on canvas, 266×345 cm.
Museo del Prado, Madrid.

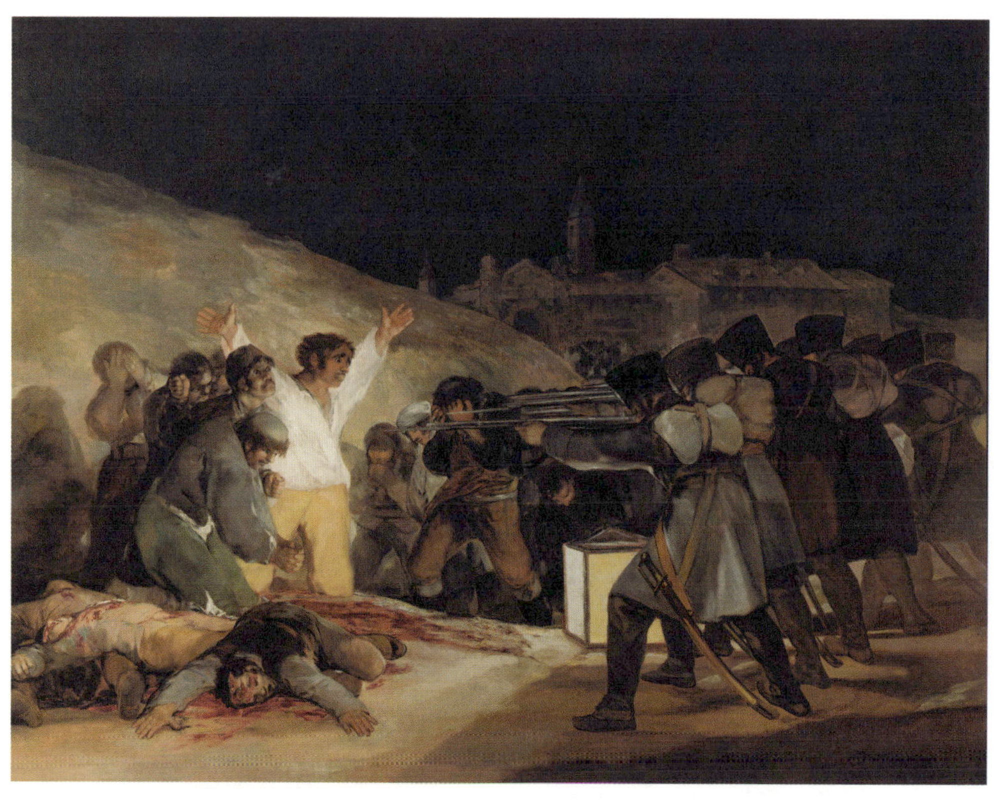

Figure 3.10.
The Third of May, 1808, 1814. Oil on canvas, 266×345 cm.
Museo del Prado, Madrid.

task of memorializing events he had himself also lived through. Goya had personally experienced the French occupation of Spain that began in 1808 when Napoleon used the pretext of reinforcing his army in Portugal as a way to seize the Spanish throne, leaving his brother Joseph in power. (Goya was for a time sympathetic to the ideas brought in from France, though not at the time the painting was made.) Attempts to remove members of the Spanish royal family from Madrid in early May of 1808 provoked a widespread rebellion in the city. We may rightly conclude that the innocent, uprising *madrileños* are portrayed in the painting as victims of the elite Mamelukes of the French Imperial Guard, who charged and subdued the rebellious citizens under order from Napoleon's brother-in-law and a marshal of the French Empire, Joachim Murat. But the rebels are also depicted as vicious counterassailants in their own right. Indeed, the chaotic violence and moral ambiguity of the scene conjures something of the Reign of Terror in France, except that this was not France in the eighteenth century, but Spain in the early nineteenth century, and that the occupying forces were the agents of the imperial power of one of Europe's most "enlightened" countries. In fact, Spain had long feared that the French Revolution might spread. The prime minister, Manuel Godoy, issued a decree in 1793 forbidding anyone "to insert any paper or book containing news, favorable or adverse, of matters concerning the Kingdom of France."[3] The sprawling and strewn figures in the painting, victims and assailants alike, are subject to a process of deindividuation that pushes the conventions of figuration and the genre of history painting to their limits (Figure 3.11).

The Second of May is about a subject too terrible to be depicted with clarity. It is about a moment in history as collective chaos, one in which the distinction between those on the "right side" of history and those on the "wrong side" was remarkably unclear. Moreover, one could also say that according to this canvas, there is no individual subject-agent *of* history, because the individual has been *destroyed by* history; indeed, there may not even be a collective agent in the

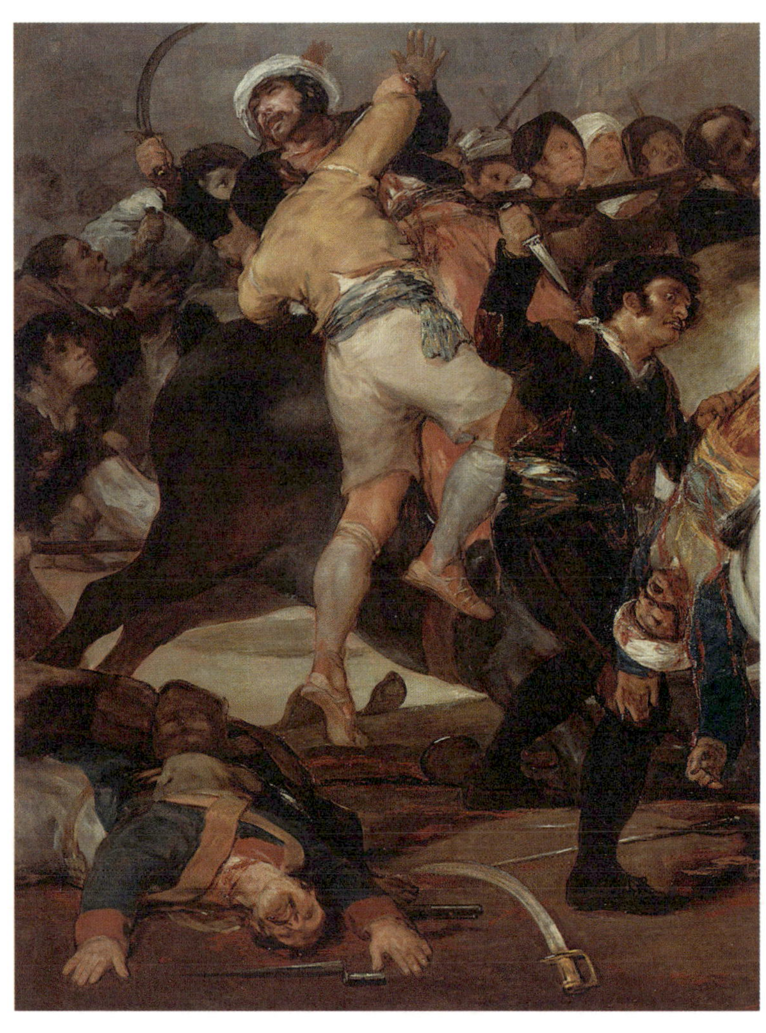

Figure 3.11.
The Second of May, 1808 (detail), 1814. Oil on canvas.
Museo del Prado, Madrid.

conventional sense, either, but only desperate groups who transmit the powerful forces of which history is ultimately composed.

As is well known, *The Second of May* was followed by an equally famous painting, maybe even a more famous painting, if one is to judge by its influence: *The Third of May, 1808*. Manet took this work as his model for the *Execution of Emperor Maximilian* (Figure 3.12), as did Picasso for the *Massacre in Korea* (Figure 3.13). Here, it is also clear that the story of modernity and critique in Goya cannot simply be aligned with the view that understands art as propelled by the force of internal self-reflection, much less than with the notion that the work of critique in artworks leads to the triumphant independence of the aesthetic sphere from all other worldly domains. Indeed, *The Third of May* seems rather to be the negation of negation, ultimately positive in its figural and compositional assertions; moreover, it moves in a direction that would seem to rescue and reassert the primacy of the individual subject. It's often said that the painting shows the terror of an individual positioned in contrast to the anonymous regiment of executioners. This is no doubt true, but in contrast to the massive chaos of *The Second of May*, here we see a powerful assertion of figuration directed toward the project of reasserting the dignity of the individual, if only by means of outrage at the violence done to this one *madrileño*. This particular image brings the clarity of a painter's insight as witness to the truth — not merely his vision of the world — to bear upon the unjust punishment of one particular rebellious soul who was caught up in the turmoil of history. Yet in visual terms, the image could not be more different from the one Goya painted of the events of the previous day.

The contrasts between Goya's *Third of May* and Manet's *Execution of Maximilian* are illuminating. Manet's image has been closely aligned with the view of art that regards the negation of the figural subject as one of the achievements of modernism. The Manet painting has indeed elicited much commentary in this regard, including by André Malraux and Georges Bataille. It has also been read in an essay, "Modernism, Manet, and the 'Maximilian': Executing Negation," by

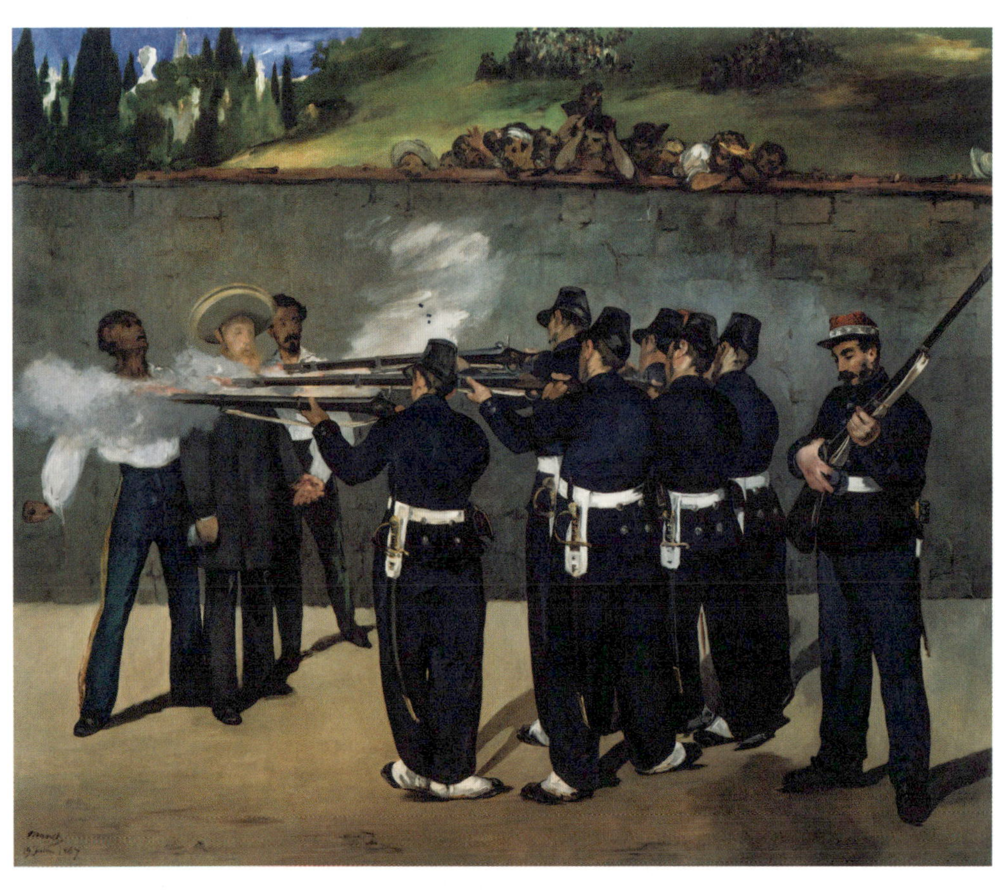

Figure 3.12.
Édouard Manet, *Execution of Emperor Maximilian*, 1868–69. Oil on canvas, 252 × 305 cm.
Kunsthalle Mannheim, Mannheim, Germany.

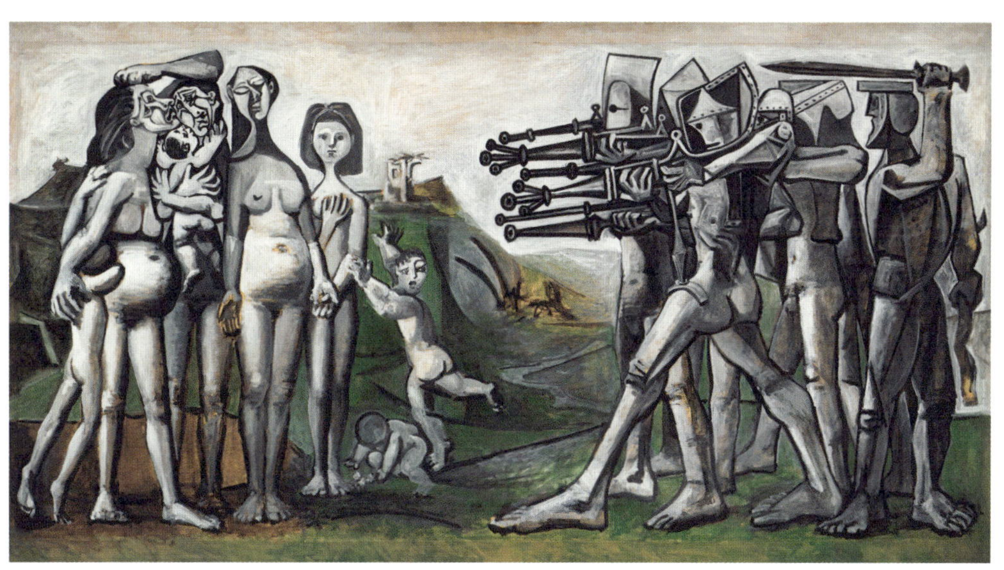

Figure 3.13.
Pablo Picasso, *Massacre in Korea*, 1951. Oil on plywood, 110×210 cm.
Musée Picasso, Paris.

Neil Larsen, as part of a book entitled *Modernism and Hegemony*. One of Larsen's aims, with which it is hard to disagree, was to insert history back in to an art-historical enterprise that had come to focus on aesthetic critique as the privileged route of access to the truth by reminding us that the aesthetic history we find championed around Manet's *Execution* cannot possibly be reconciled with the political history at stake in the events it depicts. The history of aesthetic modernism wants to tell a triumphant story in which the negation of the subject is the means through which painting is able to reveal the truth in general — the truth of what, for lack of a better term, might simply be called "Being." But in relation to the Manet painting, this seems to elide the fact that the execution of Maximilian was a moment in the very difficult assertion of Mexican independence against European (Spanish) control.

In the course of historicizing the Manet *Execution*, however, Larsen endorses some of the most traditional views about Goya's reference work. He regards Goya's *Third of May*, in contrast to Manet's *Maximilian*, as conventional, heroic, Christological, and finally, Spanish. The latter term is meant to be damning: "In Goya, as in the iconographies of a Crucifixion, a visual priority is accorded to the place of the victim.... Goya represents a violent death that takes on a meaning only within the narrative enclosure that begins and ends in the life of its collective and eponymous hero (the defenders of a traditional Spain against a Napoleonic Modernity)."[4] These remarks may be nothing more than the casual reassertion of inherited views. What I *do* want to suggest is that *The Third of May* is importantly about something else and that what Goya does in it contributes to a very different understanding of the role of art in relation to the project of critique within the panorama of modernity. The victim's outstretched arms in *The Third of May* do indeed suggest a crucifixion, but this is a secular and modern sacrifice, one that art can depict but scarcely redeem (Figure 3.14).

As a secular enterprise, art is not in the business of redemption. Moreover, the scene is illuminated by a lantern that glows with the terrible force of Enlightenment. And this is perhaps the most important point. The lantern plays two roles. It is the source of the light by which the truth of these shootings can be seen and so implicitly supports the artist in his role as witness to the truth. But it is also the light that allows the French regiment to see their target. Indeed, it seems that well before Horkheimer and Adorno, Goya understood something about the dialectic of enlightenment, that is, about the ways in which the historical Enlightenment was all too prone to reinforce the barbarism from which it hoped to get free. As one of Goya's French contemporaries, Louis-Sébastien Mercier, saw, it was in fact an excess of rationalism that brought revolutionary destruction to Europe: "Every day the sciences open up some new avenue. In the midst of these new,

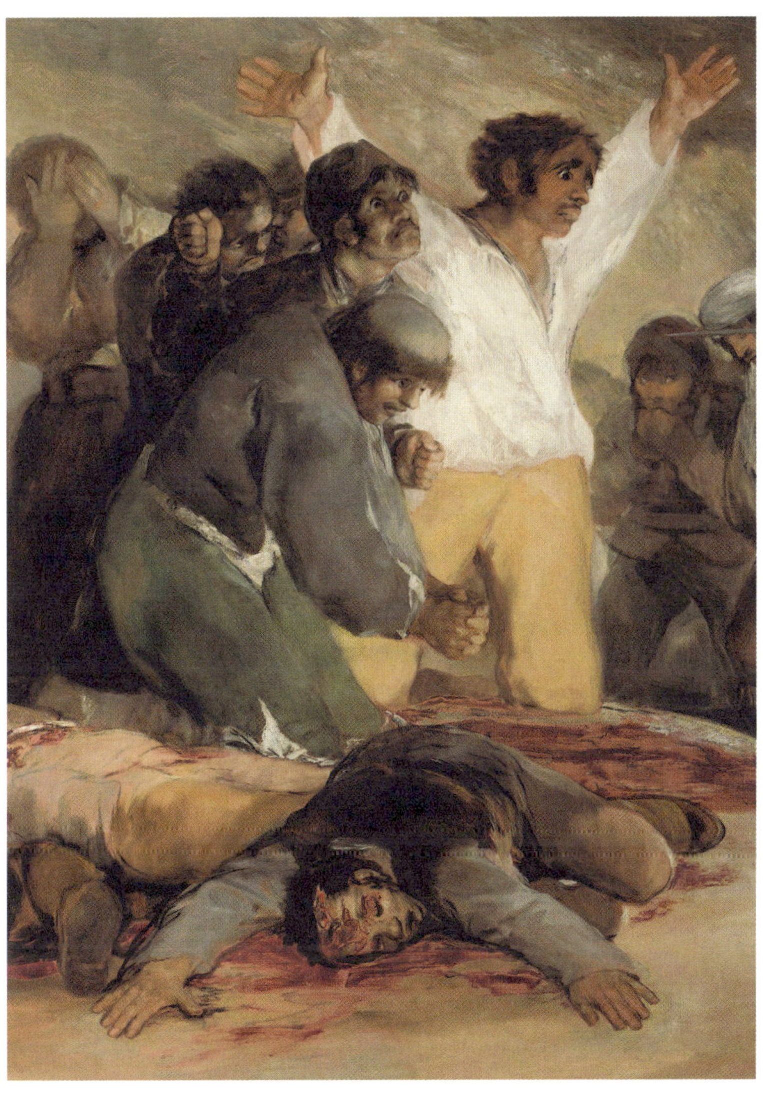

Figure 3.14.
The Third of May, 1808 (detail), 1814. Oil on canvas.
Museo del Prado, Madrid.

aspiring arts, will we end up with the ferocity of the same barbarous ages that our reason was to defeat?"[5] Goya was drawn to a similar understanding by pursuing the internal logic of art, with which he was deeply involved, but also by his experience of the contradictory, nearly impossible set of conditions and options he saw presented within late eighteenth-century and early nineteenth-century Spain. Within that historical panorama, it was never possible for him entirely or finally to embrace the values of the Enlightenment for which he did no doubt have hope, but it was even less possible for him to imagine a return to the stubborn superstitions of the Spanish past.

In sum, the historical basis for the work of critique in Goya's work incorporates the relentless exploration of these two impossible alternatives, an exploration that proceeds from within each of them, that succeeds in identifying the ways in which the one is often nested within the other, and that ultimately discovers the need to resist a premature rush to judgment about the need for Enlightenment in response to the Spanish past. The critique of the Spanish past is not enough. Because, if Enlightenment is positioned as overcoming of the darkness of that past, the truth is that it is liable to negate itself. Enlightenment, we might say on the basis of the *Third of May*, stands in need of further critique, a process that could best be called an enlightenment about Enlightenment. (This involves recognizing that — to use Hegel's salient metaphors — what is a "perfume" can also be an "infection.")[6] As a consequence, the very notion of "the Enlightenment" becomes something dynamic, not just a simple abstraction.[7] Indeed, Goya allows the object of critique itself to reveal the things that work internally against it and does not provide an exemption for art itself.

Consider the aesthetic investment that he makes in his portraits of intellectuals, many of whom are painted in the most disciplined and decorous way imaginable (Figure 3.15). These three-quarter-length portraits display a remarkable respect for the dignity of the subject. They are permeated by an acknowledgment of the values held by the sitter, whose posture in turn conveys an implicit respect

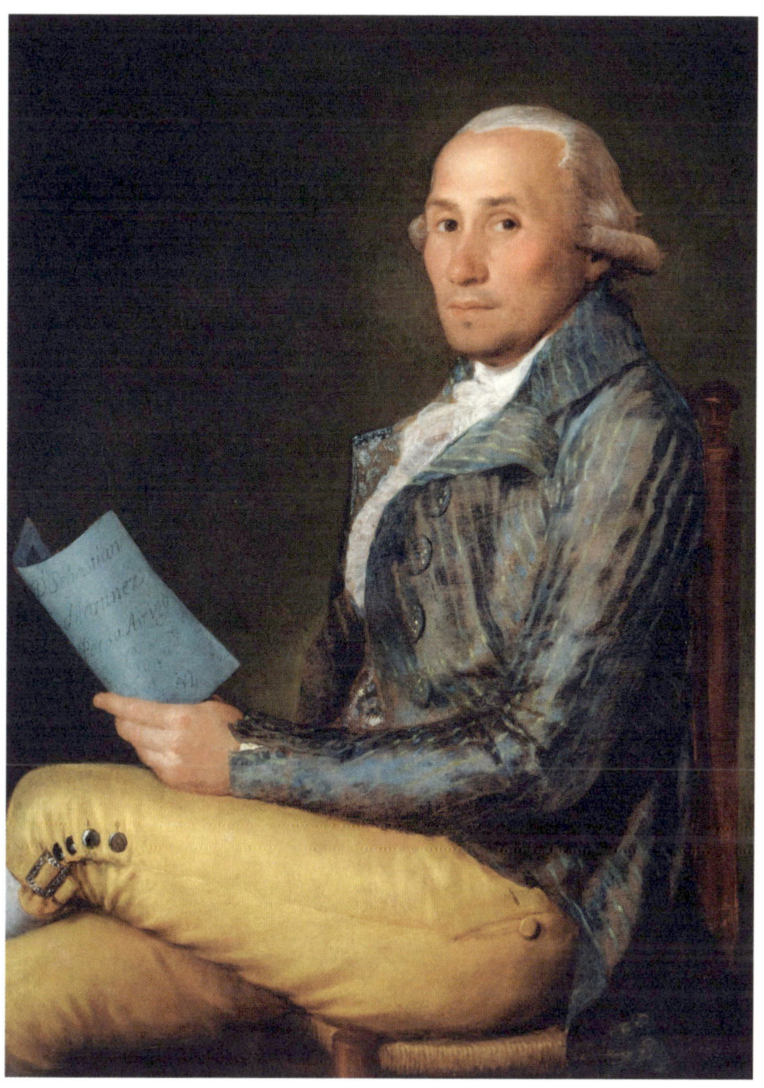

Figure 3.15.
Sebastián Martínez y Pérez, 1792. Oil on canvas, 93×67 cm.
Metropolitan Museum of Art, New York.

for the artist. The manner of dress, the hair, the attention to sartorial detail in the images all convey a degree of personal dignity and social decorum. They are also emblematic of Goya's affinity for Enlightenment ideals, which is to say that his critical relationship to those ideals emerges from within. Indeed, the more troubling elements of these images are ones they themselves disclose. Consider the raised eyebrows in the portrait of Don Sebastián Martínez, or even more so, the boredom and melancholy that appear to haunt the figure of Gaspar Melchor de Jovellanos at his desk (Figure 3.16).

Indeed, neither the Enlightenment investment in learning as championed by the circle of *ilustrados* with which Goya was associated nor the aristocratic commitment to good breeding turns out to have enough energy to sustain itself in these paintings. We recognize that one counterpart of intelligence is boredom and that another is skepticism. As for "good breeding," we see the results all too clearly in his 1814–15 portrait of Fernando VII (Figure 8.2, below). The elaborate robes cannot quite compensate for the unpleasantness of the face. Indeed, while some of Goya's portraits of aristocrats are as proper as the costumes his sitters wear (for example, the Duke and Duchess of Osuna, 1788), there are others where we are given a frank look at the artifice and emptiness behind the made-up scenes. The group portrait of the family of the Infante Don Luis de Borbón (1783–84) is a case in point. The Infante is not himself the central subject of the painting, even though he was one of Goya's most significant patrons at the beginning of his career; his wife, María Teresa de Villabriga, is. The action depicted is nearly a boudoir scene, though quite a modest one, showing María Teresa getting her hair done. The happy Infante is pictured in profile, playing cards. Goya positions himself off to the lower left, observing the group, attempting to paint the scene from an all but impossible angle. The result is a composition that leads us to wonder what its central subject truly is — whether it is this behind-the-scenes moment itself or Goya's self-conscious witnessing of it. But there is something stranger still about the painting, and that is the vastness of light that washes over the central portion of the

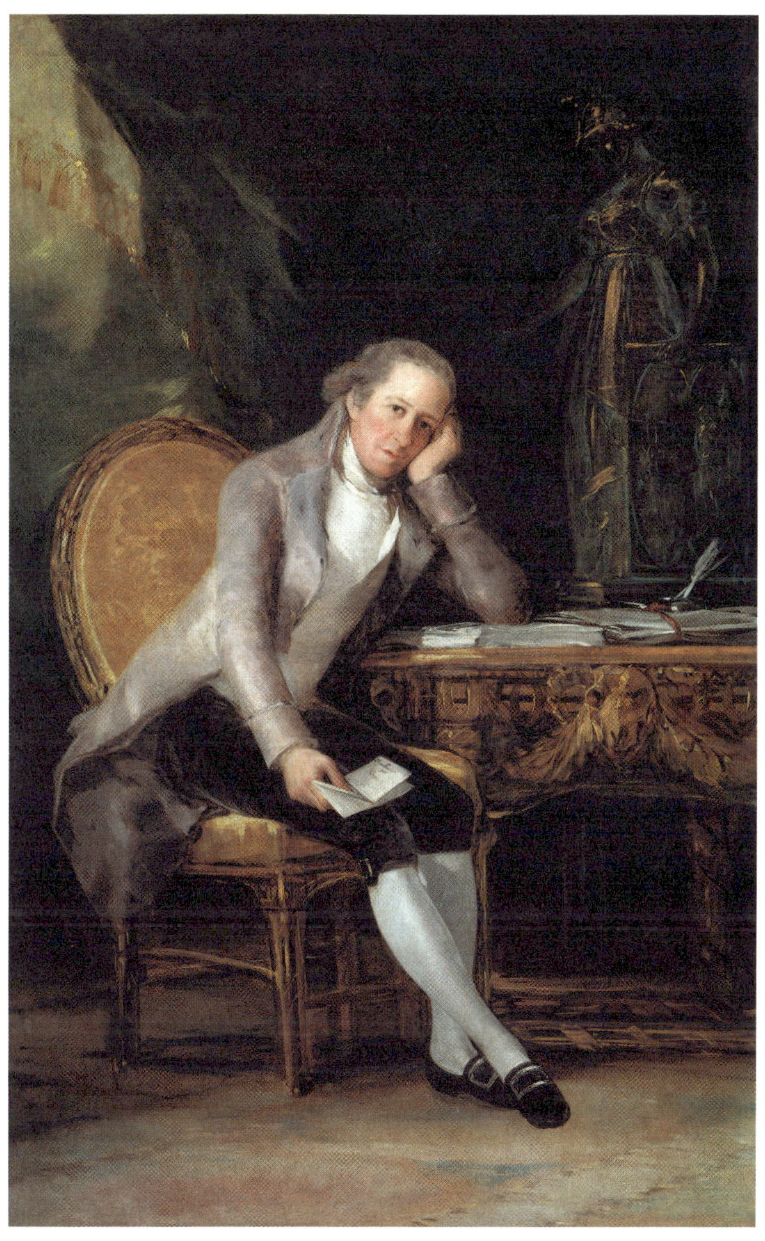

Figure 3.16.
Gaspar Melchor de Jovellanos at his Desk, 1798. Oil on canvas, 205×133 cm.
Museo del Prado, Madrid.

scene, improbably emanating from a lone candle. While not quite the ghoulish light that haunts Goya's nighttime images of witches and bogeymen, it tinges the painting with a combination of artificiality and eeriness that harkens to images such as *The Witches' Sabbath* in the Quinta del Sordo. It is one example of the ways in which Goya's images often position themselves on the ambiguous edge of light and dark and play with the ways in which the one can so easily be transformed into its opposite other. That process could, of course, lead to an endless spiral in which no object is left unscathed and in which the artist is eventually left with no ground on which to stand. Goya's approach is sufficiently thorough and deep to raise such concerns. He comes close to a kind of negation that seems to court absolute nothingness and self-destruction, but his art survives the prospect of nihilism precisely because in his hands, the project of critique remains aware of its own vulnerability.

The ambiguous edge of light and dark, of play and violence, that can be detected in some of the tapestry cartoons is even more prominent in many of his images of bullfighting, including the two that most likely inspired Manet's original composition—one very early, "Dragging the Bull Away" (*El arrastre*, 1793), and another very late, *Bullfight, Suerte de Varas* (1824, Figure 3.17). The compositions are strikingly similar to the one Manet tore apart. In *Suerte de varas*, the actors confronting the bull are massed in a swarm of paint, while a dead horse lies inert on the sand in the background, wholly disconnected from the center of the action, which Goya paints in a way that makes it impossible to discern many of the individual figures from the paint out of which they are made. There is a prominent, circular wall separating the stands from the ring, a dead bull being hauled off by a group of mules, and what appears to be a dead horse lying on the sand as well (though admittedly no dead bullfighter). Some *toreros* and others converse in two groups in the space toward the outer edge of the ring. But perhaps the most shocking thing about the painting is something that Manet captured in *Incident in a Bullfight* of 1864:

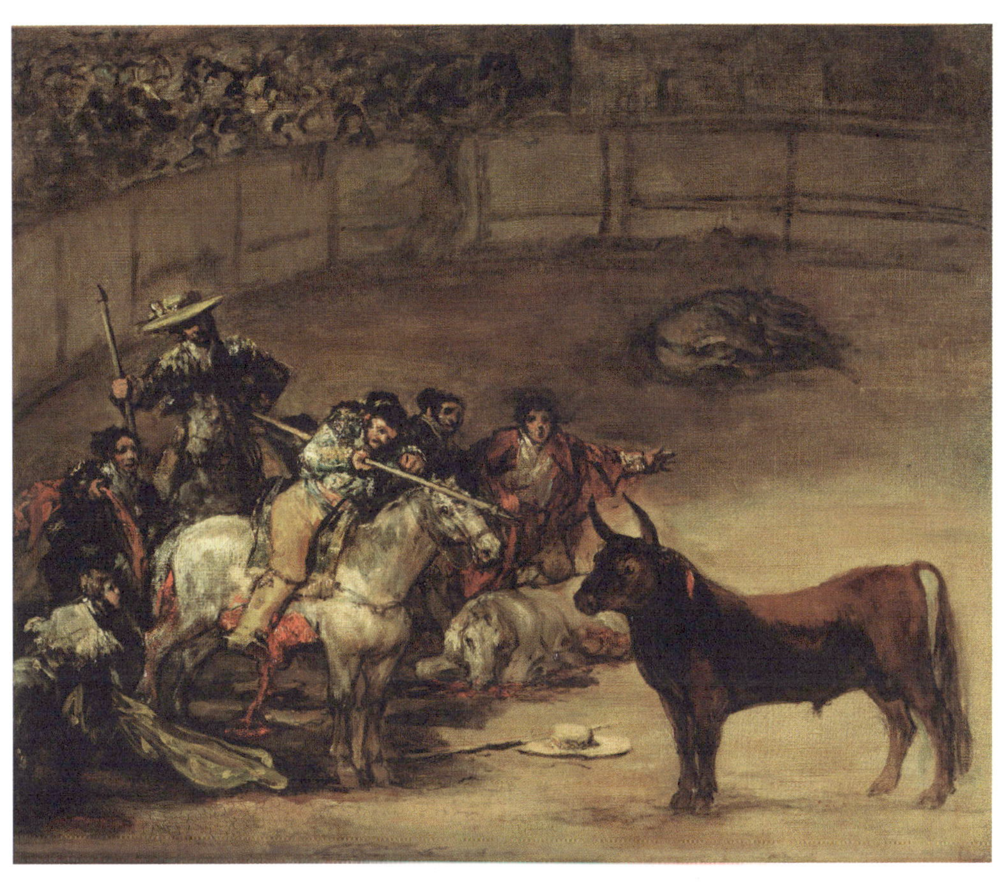

Figure 3.17.
Bullfight, Suerte de Varas, 1824. Oil on canvas, 49.8×70.8 cm.
J. Paul Getty Museum, Los Angeles.

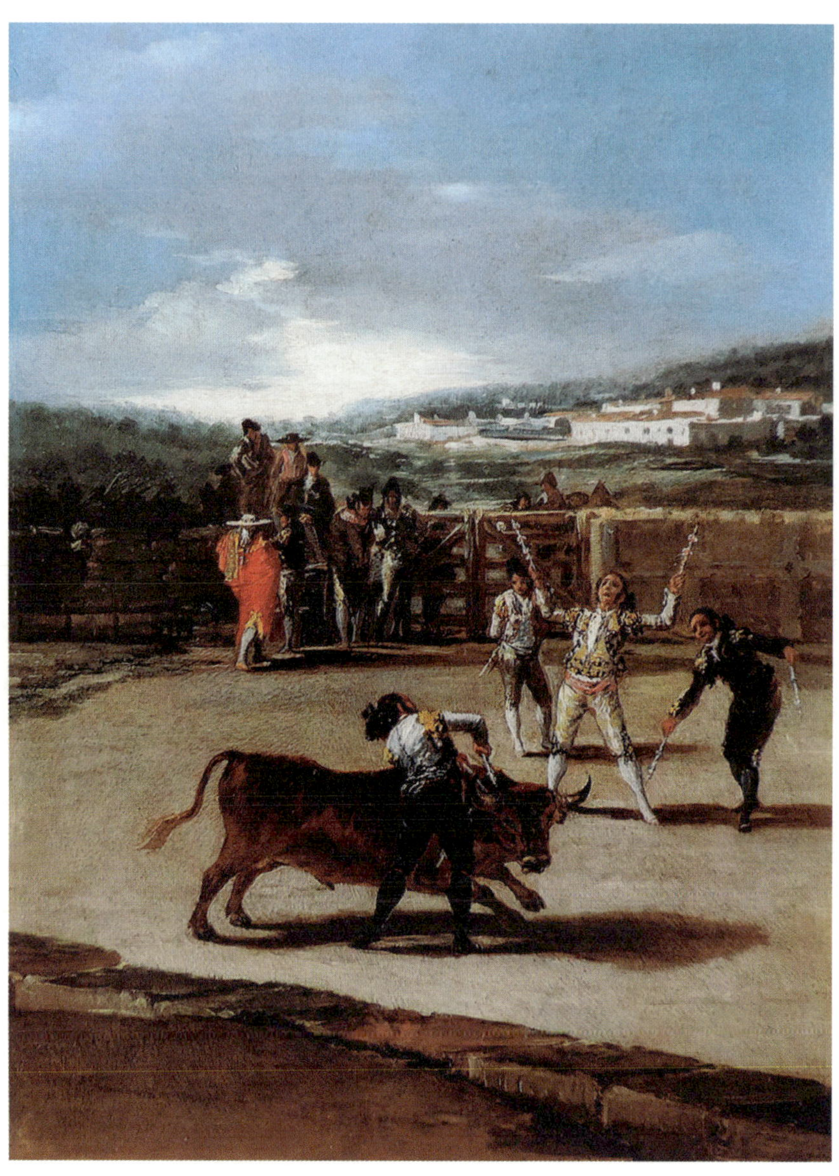

Figure 3.18.
Banderillas in the Countryside, 1793. Oil on tin, 43.1×32 cm.
Colección Masaveu, Oviedo, Spain.

the sharp contrast between the celebratory excitement of the fans, brilliantly attired in multicolored costumes, and the deathly flat and dull monochrome figure of the bull. Needless to say that bullfighting was both popular entertainment and spectacle, but Goya will not let the viewer forget that it was one that ends in death. That is its fore-ordained end point, one that neither diminishes the brilliance of the spectacle nor is reduced by it. Each of the elements in this contradictory pair of lively spectacle and dull death asserts itself unchecked, such that the painting always insists that we remember to regard each one from the other's vantage point. Indeed, the contradictions internal to the bullfight are transferred to the composition itself, which refuses to synthesize them into a unified story. In fact, there is no story. The painting is meant to capture a moment after the action has concluded.

The subject matter (bullfighting) and the way Goya dealt with it across his career are in many ways exemplary. Bullfighting was of course quintessentially Spanish and something for which Goya felt a personal, lifelong affinity. He engages with it from relatively early on (for example, *Banderillas in the Countryside*, 1793 [Figure 3.18]) to very late (the *Tauromaquia* series of 1816 and the large-scale *Bulls of Bordeaux*, 1824–25). Three elements are consistently at work across these images: first, an awareness that there is but a sliver of difference that separates the play of sport from violence; second, an awareness of the precarious relationship between spectator and action; and third, an appreciation of the difficulty involved in showing and in witnessing the truth. These render the images both more interesting and more troubling than had they been done simply as occasional pieces or just as illustrations of the sport and spectacle. While the *Tauromaquia* series no doubt began as illustrations for the 1801 edition of Nicolás Fernández de Moratín's *Carta histórica sobre el origen y progresos de las fiestas de toros en España* (first published in 1777), the series is intent on showing the sometimes absurd violence that is integral to the sport. It has been described as a "parenthetical element" in Goya's work, situated as it is in between the *Disasters of War* and the *Disparates*.[8] But it is intimately connected to both, as well as to the earlier tapestry cartoons. There is hardly anything parenthetical about it.

Of the *Tauromaquia* plates that bear titles drawn from Moratín's text, several are designed to track the history of the sport in Spain, from plate no. 1, showing the Spaniards of ancient times hunting bulls on horseback, to an image picturing the Cid spearing a bull (no. 11), to a plate showing the introduction of *banderillas* ("harpoons") by the Moors (no. 7), to plates illustrating the derring-do of well-known mid-eighteenth-century bullfighters including Martincho (Figure 3.19), Juanito Apiñani (Figure 3.20), and others.

But this is hardly a documentary series — no more than the *Caprichos* is meant to document daily life in Madrid.[9] Janis Tomlinson rightly recognized Goya's intentions as more complicated than what her more literally minded predecessors, Juliet Wilson Bareau and Enrique Lafuente Ferrari, had believed. In her view, reading the series as a history of the bullfight in Spain is contradicted by a fact as basic as the published order of the plates, which shows "little concern for chronology."[10] Tomlinson cited the possible influence on Goya of antibullfighting propaganda, including treatises such as the *Oración apologética en defensa del estado floreciente de España, dicha en la plaza de toros*, which took bullfighting to be symbolic of the most barbarous and retrograde elements of Spanish society in the reign of Charles IV, and yet she also recognized that the series defies interpretation as satire. It seems better to say, as Tomlinson does, that *Tauromaquia* may reflect Goya's own ambivalence as both aficionado of the sport and enlightened critic of it.

But the deeper issue revolves around the question of what the bullfighting images are in fact *about* and what that can tell us about Goya's position with respect to the story of modern art. On the one hand, the bullfighting images are clearly about something other than the emergence of "art itself" (its materials, techniques, and compositional powers) as a domain independent of everything else. The role of all of those aesthetic elements is interwoven with the ostensible subject of the works, bullfighting. And yet these works are hardly just

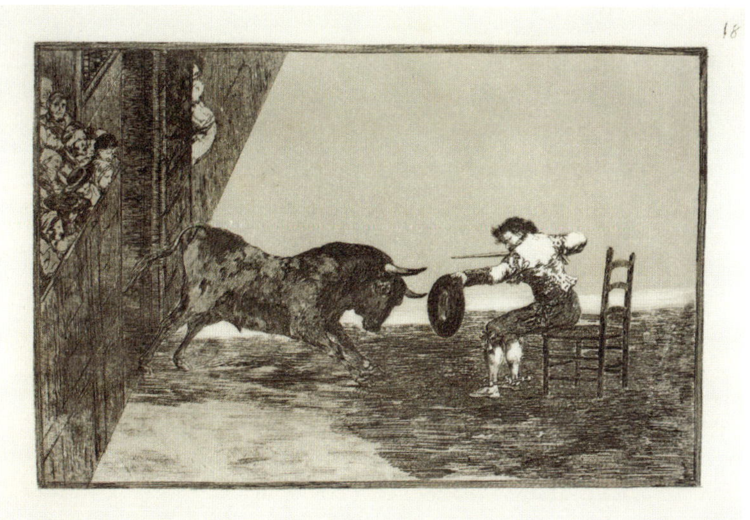

Figure 3.19.
The Daring of Martincho in the Ring at Zaragoza, *Tauromaquia*, no. 18, 1816.
Etching, burnished aquatint, and drypoint, 30.2×42.2 cm.

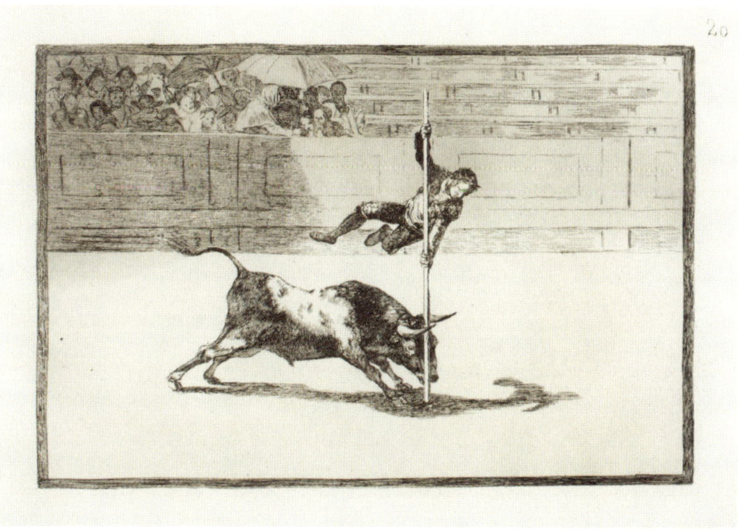

Figure 3.20.
The Agility and Audacity of Juanito Apiñani in the Ring at Madrid, *Tauromaquia*,
no. 20, 1816. Etching and aquatint, 30.5×42.2 cm.

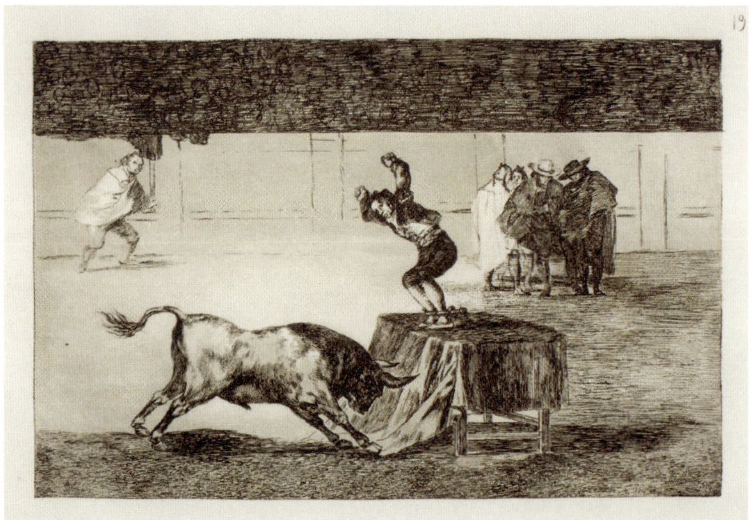

Figure 3.21.
Another Madness of His in the Same Ring, *Tauromaquia*, no. 19, 1816.
Etching, burnished aquatint, drypoint, and burin, 30.3×43.6 cm.

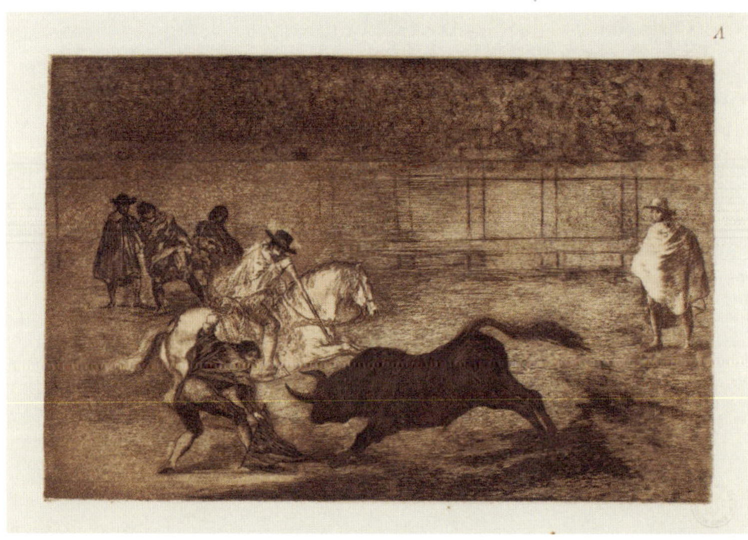

Figure 3.22.
Unpublished print "A," *Tauromaquia,* 1814–15. Etching, aquatint, burnisher, burin,
drypoint, and brown ink, 35.2×45.5 cm. Museo del Prado, Madrid.

about bullfighting. On the contrary, they involve issues that radiate from the topics they show in ways that make evident the power of art to engage with matters rooted in basic human drives, with the relationship between individual and collective action, with questions of religion and superstition, with history (for example, the Spanish past and its popular and ethnic traditions), and with questions about the relationship between spectators and actors.

Some of this is achieved by a focus on the extremes of the sport, as in the acrobatic image showing Apiñani balancing on a pole as he swings across and in front of the bull (no. 20, Figure 3.20, above) or Martincho standing on a covered table, ankles bound together, poised to leap over a charging bull (no. 19, Figure 3.21).

As with all virtuoso performances, these clearly involve some element of risk, but that risk is ever so real in a sport where the actor risks his life, hoping, of course, that the bull will be the one to die. Are these examples of strength and dexterity, or of utter foolishness? Plate no. 38, *The Death of Pepe Hilo* (who was a well-known *torero* and author of a book on the art of bullfighting, the *Tauromaquia o arte de torear*) makes the question unavoidable. But the series is suffused with death even where no creature dies. Consider no. 34, in which the figure of the bull is entirely black and flat, yet charged full of energy that suggests nothing if not what Freud would later call the "death drive" (Figure 3.??).

Moreover, all this death is surrounded by suggestions of fear and superstition. In the first of the *Tauromaquia* plates to show the role of Moors in the development of the sport (no. 4), there is a dervish-like figure in the background, positioned on his knees and with his arms outstretched, as if in the posture of someone either invoking or exorcising spirits. Indeed, the movement of capes and headgear, the creation of large, shadowy spaces, and in particular, the Moorish fig-ures in some of the images establish clear affinities with the *Caprichos* and *Disparates*.

The images that make up the *Bulls of Bordeaux*, for their part, are intimately connected with issues raised by Black Paintings and with the *Second of May*. Just as the Black Paintings are in effect transpositions of some of Goya's earlier images into the key of darkness, these lithographs display an irresistible attraction to the violence inherent in sport and play. The compositions of *"El famouso American, Mariano Ceballos"* ("The famous American, Mariano Ceballos," no. 14) and *"Dibersión de España"* ("Spanish entertainment," no. 16, Figure 3.23) are dominated by swirling, snakelike lines of figures controlling the foreground, while the background is composed of anonymous figures lining the interior of the ring and by indistinguishable masses of spectators in the stands.

Modern Duel (no. 12) links to a subject familiar both from the tapestry cartoons and the Black Paintings, while *Andalusian Dance* (no. 11) is hardly just a happy scene; grimacing faces and grotesque cries stand out from the heaping mass of people surrounding the dancer. Indeed, the bullfighting images are exemplary because so many of them contain within the bounds of a single image the sharp contrasts that mark Goya's work overall. Their strategies are significantly more emphatic than those at work in the tapestry cartoons, which similarly, but more subtly, include elements that undermine their own cheerfulness and similarly suggest that violence may be ineradicable and integral to any form of human activity and indeed to happiness itself. The final image of the series (no. 18, simply entitled *Bullfight*) presents a slaughter of horses and bulls reminiscent of the chaos of *The Second of May*. It includes the barest glimpse of the curve of the barrier and the spectators in the stands behind. The image is as much about the forces of chaos itself as it is about bullfighting.

As noted earlier, it may be expedient to think that the contrasts and reversals in Goya's work can be explained as a function of external factors — his biography, his illnesses and deafness, his love affairs, his shifting political stance, his corresponding financial situation, and so forth. While these factors are undeniably informative and important, the contrasts and contradictions at issue do not respond to entirely circumstantial causes; they are present throughout Goya's work. Moreover, their importance is relative to an art

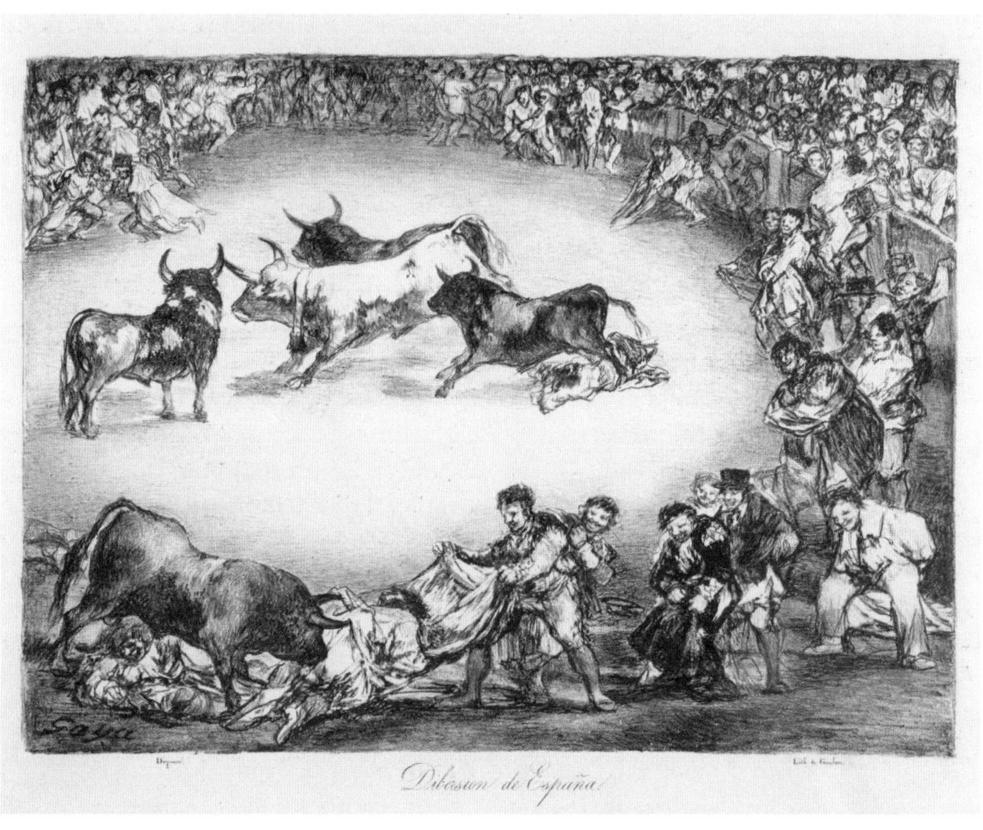

Figure 3.23.
"*Dibersión de España*" ("Spanish entertainment"), *The Bulls of Bordeaux,* 1825.
Lithograph, 42.2×53 cm.

deeply involved in reflecting upon its role in relation to everything that stands outside it, whether it be events happening on the world-historical stage or those presenting themselves as forms of popular entertainment happening in a bullfighting arena. They are at the same time part of an aesthetic project involved in reflecting upon the conventions that condition and enable it and in pressing the limits of its ability to refuse those altogether. As distinct from the kind of negation discussed by Malraux and Bataille in relation to Manet, one that is in effect a cancellation, Goya was relentlessly searching to discover the limits of negation itself. In doing so, he was able to discern the importance of whatever the process of negation allowed to be discovered. Understanding the limits of negation was central to securing the ability of art to show the truth about the worldly domains with which it engages while acknowledging the fact that everything, including art itself, inevitably stands, however unwittingly, within some place of ideology or untruth.

This view has implications for the particular kind of seeing that involves witnessing and that would seem to be part of the figural literalism that some have claimed is Goya's anticipation of photojournalism. Among the *Disasters of War* are some truly horrific images, about which there will be much more to say in Chapter 6. In them, we see maimed and dismembered bodies, the most brutal aggressions, a treatment of the human that comes out of human nature, but one that borders on the inhuman (Figure 3.24, *Disasters of War*, plate 3). Some of these images echo the strategies of *The Second of May* and *The Third of May* (Figure 3.25, *Disasters of War*, plate 15). However, one of the *Disasters* seems especially to speak with a sharp literalism and to ask us to accept the etching as a direct and unselfconscious critique of the atrocities of war. The caption reads *"Yo lo vi"* ("I saw it," plate no. 44 of the *Disasters of War*, Figure 3.26).

But here is a perfect example of a case where we need to look beyond the literal words or image to find what Horkheimer and Adorno described in *Dialectic of Enlightenment* as "the admission of

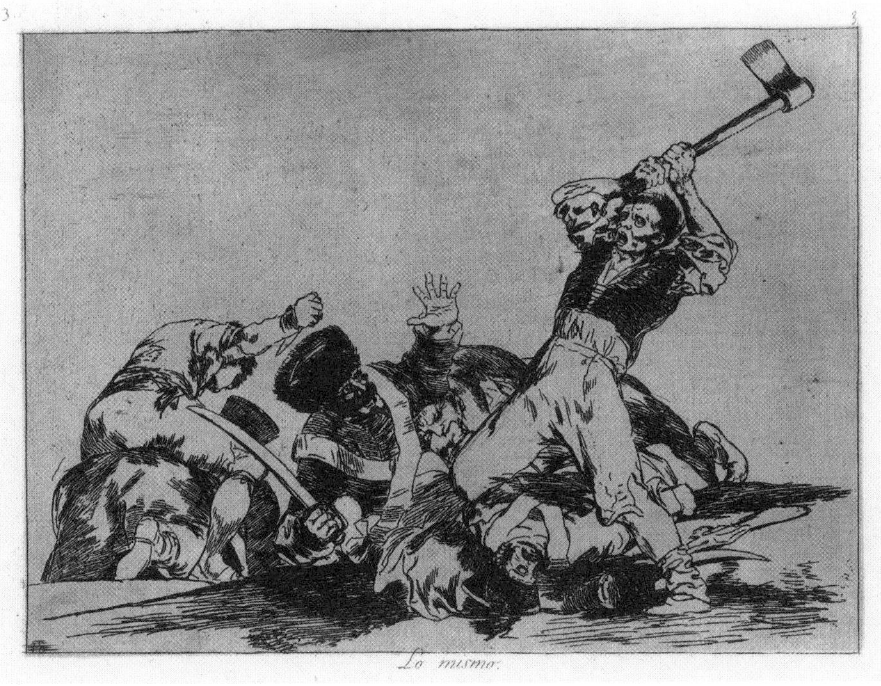

Figure 3.24.
"*Lo mismo*" ("The same"), *Disasters of War,* no. 3, ca. 1810–15, published 1863.
Etching, aquatint, burin, drypoint, and burnisher, 16.2 × 22.3 cm.

falseness that cancels [the image's] power and hands it over to truth."[11] For we do not really know whether these words give voice to what the crowd has seen and attempts to name — the invisible thing from which it flees — or whether the words articulate what the artist claims to have witnessed. In that case, the further question might well be: How could anyone have witnessed this and survived? And yet it seems that none of the other alternatives one might propose — for instance, that the artist or the crowd saw *nothing*, that there was *nothing to be seen*, or that whatever was imagined as seen was in effect hallucinated — can

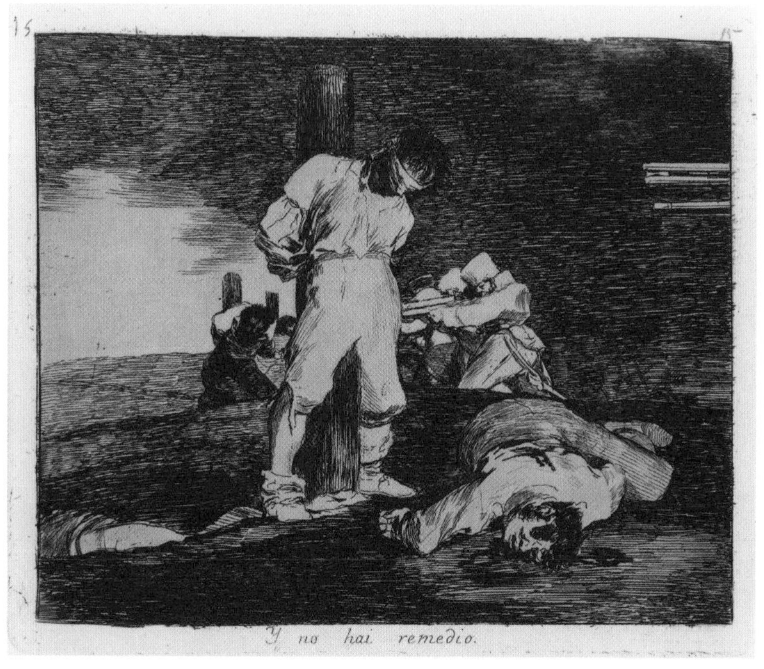

Figure 3.25.
"*Y no hai remedio*" ("And there is no help"), *Disasters of War,* no. 15, ca. 1810–15, published 1863. Etching, aquatint, drypoint, burin, and burnisher, 13.9 × 16.4 cm.

possibly stand. This implies a particular kind of witnessing, one that depends upon a special relationship between art and the worldly affairs it is meant to address. Goya wants to establish a position for art that both asserts and denies claims for the priority of the literal figure, the claims of the artist as witness of the truth, and indeed art's engagement with the world-destroying powers of violence. As the *Caprichos* in particular suggest, it is important not to read the work of art in this regard as criticism but as a form of self-conscious critique. I will return to the *Caprichos* in this regard in Chapter 4.

It is essential to speak about the project of "art," and not just "the

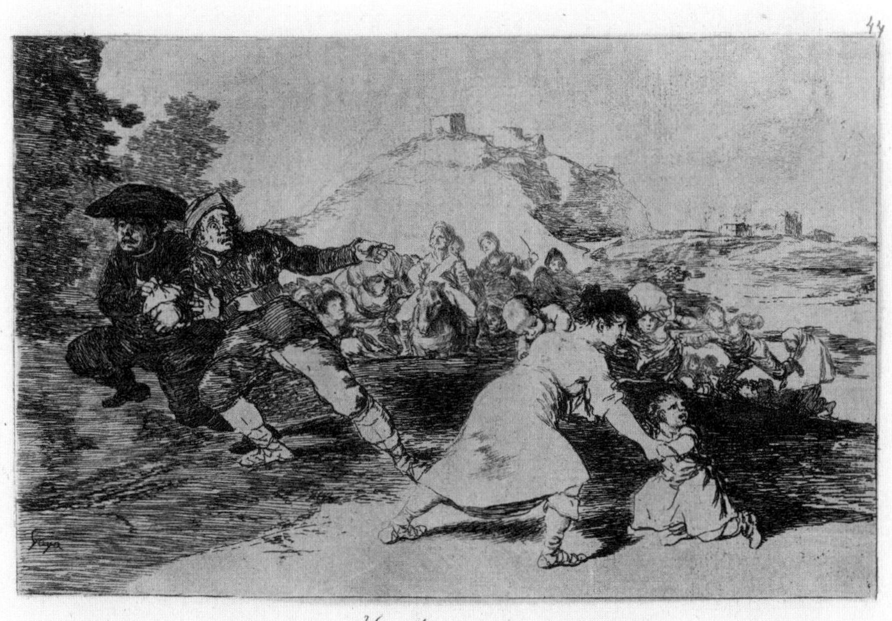

Figure 3.26.
"*Yo lo vi*" ("I saw it"), *Disasters of War*, no. 44, ca. 1810–12, published 1863.
Etching, aquatint, drypoint, and burin, 16.1×23.9 cm.

artist," in relation to critique, not because there can be one without the other, but because Goya seems very much to want to question the subject position of the figure with whom we would most closely associate this whole enterprise, that is, the artist. Consider two examples from among Goya's many self-portraits. The first is clearly in visual dialogue with Velásquez's *Las Meninas* and works to an extent just as *Las Meninas* does—through an oblique presentation of everything in its frame and their visual inferences, as well, including the artist himself (Figure 3.27). But there is something quite distinct about Goya's painting that lies in the fact that while he, the painter, is the

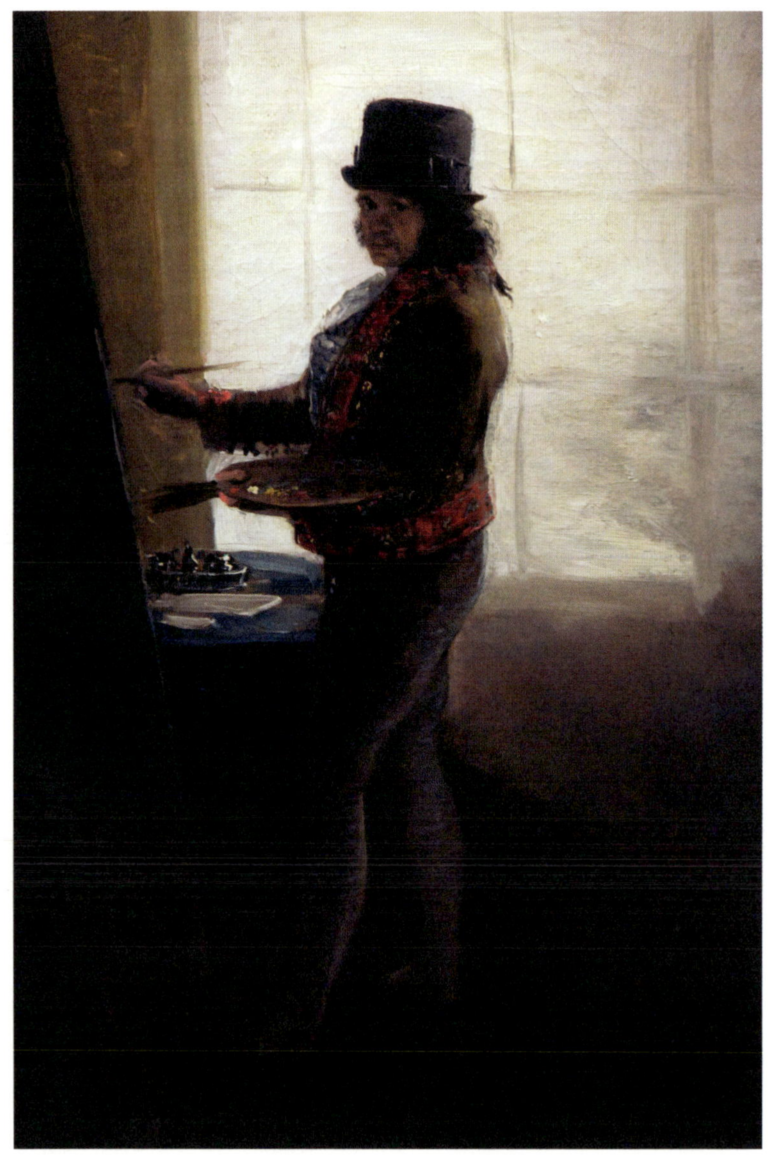

Figure 3.27.
Self-Portrait at an Easel, 1790–95. Oil on canvas, 42 × 28 cm.
Real Academia de Bellas Artes de San Fernando, Madrid.

ostensible subject of the work, he does not picture himself in the mirror in which he must see himself, but leaves it to the viewer to infer the mirror in which he views his own image-model. In the background of Goya's self-portrait is a window whose barely visible, gridlike pattern suggests another sort of canvas on stretcher, but again with no image; better said, it serves as a frame through which the precondition for any image, the light, is transmitted. In between the blank canvas back and the light source, as painter of nothing visible, looking at something we cannot see, is Goya, the artist. This is a portrait of the artist both as involved in and standing independent of his own subject self; it is indeed a picture that raises questions about the position of the artist vis-à-vis an enterprise whose subject might be anything, but that cannot be nothing, and that in this case is the stance of the artist vis-à-vis painting.

There is perhaps no better way to pursue this deft positioning than with reference to one of the most important sets of Goya's etchings, the *Caprichos*, which is introduced by the second of the self-portraits in question (Figure 3.28). Plate no. 43 of the *Caprichos* (Figure 3.29) is very well known. It presents an ambiguity that aptly captures the contradictions surrounding the question of rational enlightenment. It is equally the sleep of reason and the dream of reason that may produce monsters. The sleep of reason yields a world of bogeymen and specters (for example, plate no. 64, *Buen viaje*), while the dream of reason produces a view of happiness that is either incapable of self-reflection or unable to notice what reflection might teach about the root of destructive forces. Is it important to remember that one of the preparatory drawings for this image, made in 1797, contained the words "*Ydioma universal*" ("Universal language") inscribed on the pedestal.[12] The caption below the image reads: "*The author dreaming. His only intention is to banish prejudicial vulgarities and bear firm witness, with this work of fancy, to the truth.*" According to the preparatory drawing, then, the sleep of reason is a precondition for the truth to be revealed.

The contradictions of this particular plate of the *Caprichos* are a

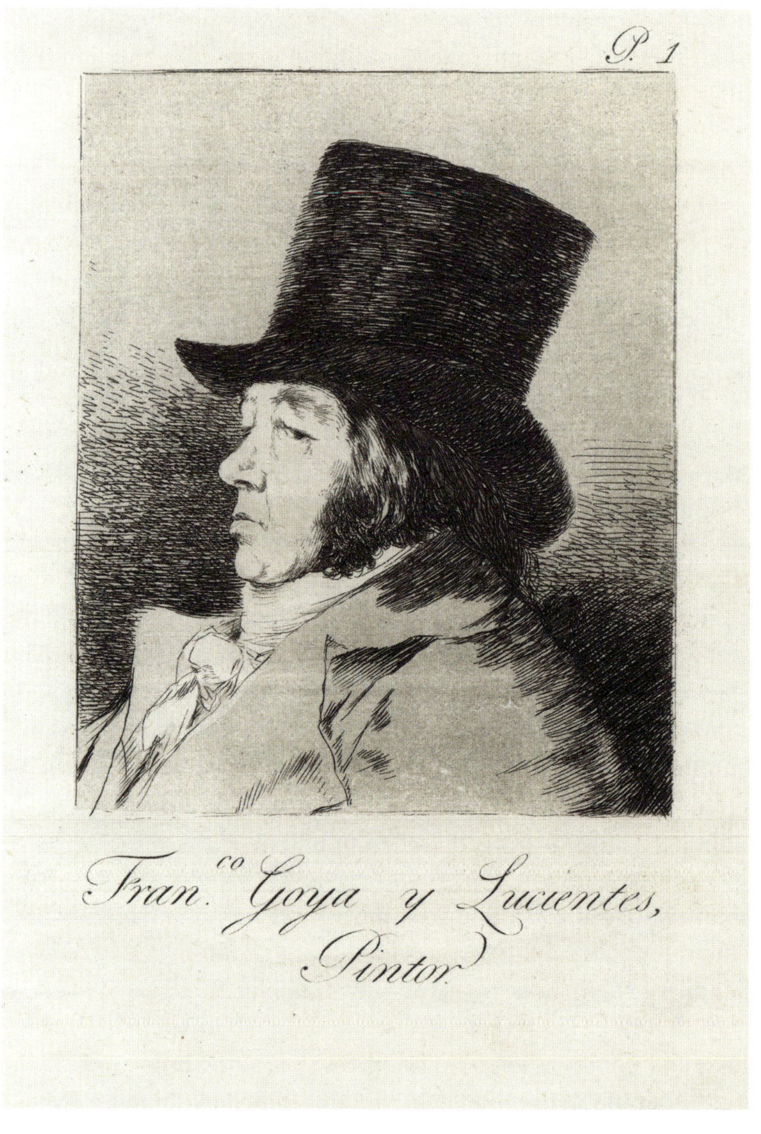

Figure 3.28.
"*Francisco Goya y Lucientes, Pintor*" (Francisco Goya y Lucientes, Painter), *Caprichos*,
frontispiece, 1797–98, published 1799. Etching, aquatint, drypoint, and burin,
22×15.3 cm.

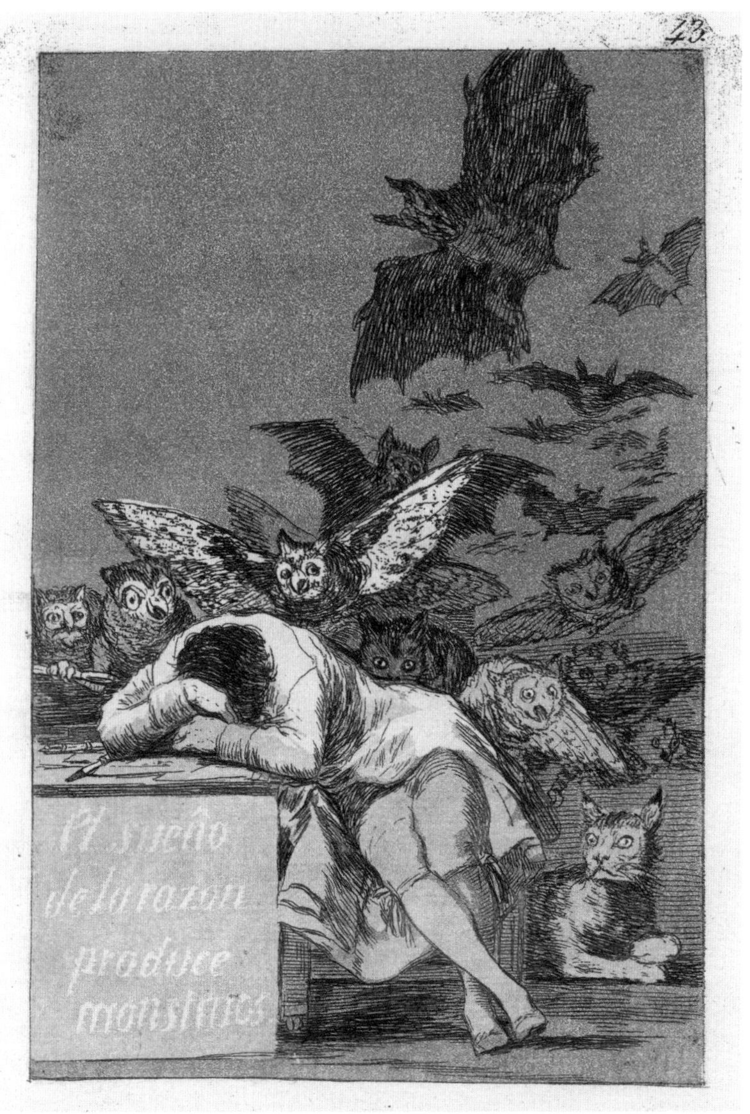

Figure 3.29.

"*El sueño de la razón produce monstruos*" ("The sleep of reason produces monsters"),
Caprichos, no. 43, 1797–98, published 1799. Etching and aquatint, 21.8×15.2 cm.

good example of the ways in which an image cancels what it shows or says by affirming what it cancels. But what else is there other than sleep or dream? A first line of response would suggest that there is criticism, which requires a kind of alertness that is able to capture the self-incriminating contradictions of the world and reflect them back to itself. And this is in fact what Goya does throughout much of the series by portraying forms of ignorance and superstition that believe in themselves regardless of how implausible or ridiculous they might be. The *Caprichos* contain ample evidence of this, as we will see further in the chapter to follow. But this is mostly a matter of criticism and not critique, and to take the *Caprichos* simply as criticism would place them in the same category as Hogarth's satires or the work of other artists who turned to printmaking because its reproducibility allowed for social criticism to be circulated on a relatively wide scale. The question for the series of the *Caprichos* as a whole has rather to do with the stance of anyone who would undertake such a thorough and relentless critical practice in a fully self-conscious way. Who can do this? Who can do this and survive?

A typical answer to this question would of course be the philosopher — that the philosopher is somehow able to construct a platform that can survive its own critical thrust. But we know, from the frontispiece to the *Caprichos*, again, that for Goya, this is not the philosopher, or at any rate not the philosopher who simply takes a stance for Enlightened reason. The reason is that such a stance is insufficiently self-conscious. It fails to recognize what Hegel so brilliantly captured in his critique of the Enlightenment, that is, its failure to understand that "since what is object for me is that in which I recognize myself, I am for myself at the same time in that object in the form of *another* self-consciousness."[13] For Goya, it is the artist who stands in the best position to recognize this truth, which when applied to the work of self-representation would imply a conscious self-distancing.

This is indeed just how Goya imagines himself in the frontispiece of the *Caprichos*. Consider the opening self-portrait (Figure 3.28, above) again. He identifies himself as a "painter," though ironically the *Caprichos* are not paintings. He gazes with a critical and ironic eye, not directly. His top hat suggests a certain worldliness and, most of all, an affinity with the very same social world on which he is about to cast his relentlessly critical gaze. (Manet's *Philosopher* and *Absinthe Drinker* may well have drawn their inspiration here, though both figures are far more aloof.) This figure is not only an artist but a man of the world, which is also to say that he is also *of* the very same world from which he would distance himself. He knows and acknowledges this. More specifically, he is a figure who looks awry, or askance, with a sideways glance that attempts to deflect its own critical force so as to survive it. He is an image of the cynic, where cynicism describes whatever may be required to survive the project of a critique in a way that can allow it to go on.

CHAPTER FOUR

The Limits of Representation

What did etching bring Goya? An end to illusion and seduction.
— Malraux, *Saturn: An Essay on Goya*

There is a conventional place for painting in canonical theories of the modern individual — the philosophical subject as opposed to the figural subject of painting — where "modern" refers to the period that stretches roughly from the European Renaissance, through the Enlightenment, and up until what came to be called modernism and its aftermath, "postmodernism." As described in the previous chapter, the mode of visual representation dominant in painting since the Renaissance played a crucial role in establishing the paradigm of the subject as an "absolute spectator" from which modernism sought to break free. But from the Renaissance until modernism, visual representation was integral to the development of the modern subject's understanding of itself as having access to the truth of the world. In a landmark philosophical essay, "The Age of the World View," Heidegger characterized that process as one that resulted in the transformation of the world into a picture. Heidegger argued that every age is oriented by some particular metaphysics and that the metaphysical orientation of modernity was epitomized by a self-conscious subject whose relationship to the world was grounded in the paradigm of representation. This means that the modern subject relates to the world as one relates to a picture; the equivalent would be putting a frame around an image rendered from a constant point of view that establishes the basis for what subjects consider real and true or not. But what kind of picture and what kind of frame matter deeply to these claims. The position of the modern subject evolved together with a set of conventions of visual representation that allowed for the creation of the semblance of three-dimensional space through the use of "artificial perspective" (sometimes called "painter's perspective"),[1] described above. This established the sense that the world bounded within it is fully and transparently available, able to accommodate the full range and depth of human experience, and grounded in a position that does not change according to the stance of any particular spectator. It creates a world that is endowed with what Michael Kubovy called the "robustness" of perspective. In his words, "the visual system [of artificial perspective] does not assume that the center of projection coincides with the viewer's vantage point. For if it did, every time the viewer moved, the perceived scene would have to change."[2] Because artificial perspective establishes a stability that transcends the circumstances specific to any particular individual, it creates the semblance of a validity that one might well call "metaphysical."[3] It was, at any rate, central to what Heidegger regarded as the metaphysics of modernity. For related reasons, the invention of artificial perspective has often been associated with the concept of an ideal "point of view," thought of as the hypothetical position of the Albertian sort from which one can gain access to a distanced and true view of a given scene. As we will see below, this is the very ideal that Goya's first major foray into the world of prints made for publication — the *Caprichos* — shows to be especially fraught.

There are, to be sure, *theoretical* limitations to this view about representation, many of which have been pointed out since Heidegger's essay. One is that this view is itself bounded by metaphysics. It regards the modern subject as if it were the instantiation of a set of philosophical views. Placing metaphysics before everything else, it says nothing about how the modern subject came into being socially, politically, historically, or in relation to any other set of practices. Nor does it establish anything other than a philosophical perspective for the critique of subjectivity. While it certainly supports the fact that the development of "artificial perspective," as a paradigmatic example of representation, holds a place of great importance in the culture of modernity, it offers no clues about the role of art vis-à-vis other domains of practice. Least of all does it leave open the possibility that art might articulate a critical stance with respect to a culture grounded in the alignment between perspectival representation and truth.

This is where Peter Sloterdijk's more recent critique of subjectivity can be useful since it brings questions of theory and practice together at the outset and in ways that turn out to be especially helpful in understanding what Goya was up to in the *Caprichos*. He argues that to be a subject involves "taking up a position from which an actor can make the transition from theory to practice."[4] Not surprisingly for a thinker whose major works include a *Critique of Cynical Reason*, he goes on to explain that making this transition depends on the release of inhibitions to action, that is, finding the right "disinhibitions" that allow the subject to act: "This transition usually takes place once an actor has found the motive that liberates them from hesitation and disinhibits them for action."[5] In premodern times, the most powerful force of disinhibition was compulsion through external command.[6] In modernity, however, the source of this compulsion was turned inward: individuals within the culture of modernity "will seek to find methods to place the commanding authority inside the hearer of the commands themselves, so that they seem only to be obeying their interior voice."[7] The modern understanding of individual moral autonomy, best articulated by Kant, is wholly consistent with this view since autonomy in the Kantian sense turns on the ability to create obligations for oneself, to give oneself the law (*auto nomos*). Indeed, it is central to the Enlightenment project as Kant envisioned it, where Enlightenment involves rejecting tutelage in order to be able to think for oneself.

Goya clearly came to recognize the broad limitations of the model of visual representation, especially as he developed a sense of what art was called upon to do in relation to the realm of practice in the world. This recognition is especially evident in the *Caprichos*, which unlike Goya's earlier works were not commissioned by any individual or institutional patron but were undertaken by him wholly on his own.[8] For various reasons, the *Caprichos* violate many of the conventions of representation. (The same holds true, and perhaps more emphatically so, for the *Disparates* and the *Disasters of War*.) The woman sitting in the background in *"Ni así la distingue"* (Figure 4.1) for instance, is too small in relation to the figures in the foreground, even though she controls the action. The dead body in *"A caza de dientes"* (Figure 4.2) seems to be hanging from nowhere (though likely from the limb of a tree that has been cut out of the frame).[9] The background in *"Bien tirada está"*—and so many other images in the series—is a wash of gray-tone ink that does nothing to help situate the figures in space. Many of the images (for example, *"Se repulen," "Si amanece, nos vamos,"* *"Duendecitos"* [Figure 4.3], and numerous others) offer intentionally grotesque distortions of the human form, distortions that *require* a transgression of the norms of artificial perspective. They do so in order to suggest that something other than conventional painter's perspective is required if certain truths are to be shown. Additionally, there are the captions, which add a discursive component to each visual image. They add a *speaking* to the *showing*, and these discursive additions in turn function rhetorically to reveal the limitations of the conventions of visual representation. The captions are both enigmatic and essential; they are parerga that illuminate the socially grounded contradictions that the conventions of representation tend to suppress, and they emphasize things that the visual conventions of artificial perspective might well find improper or disturbing.

I will return to these issues over the course of this chapter. But it is directly important, in relation to them, to ask about Goya's relationship to the shifting locus of "disinhibition" in his time. Goya was confronted by a world where many external sources of command

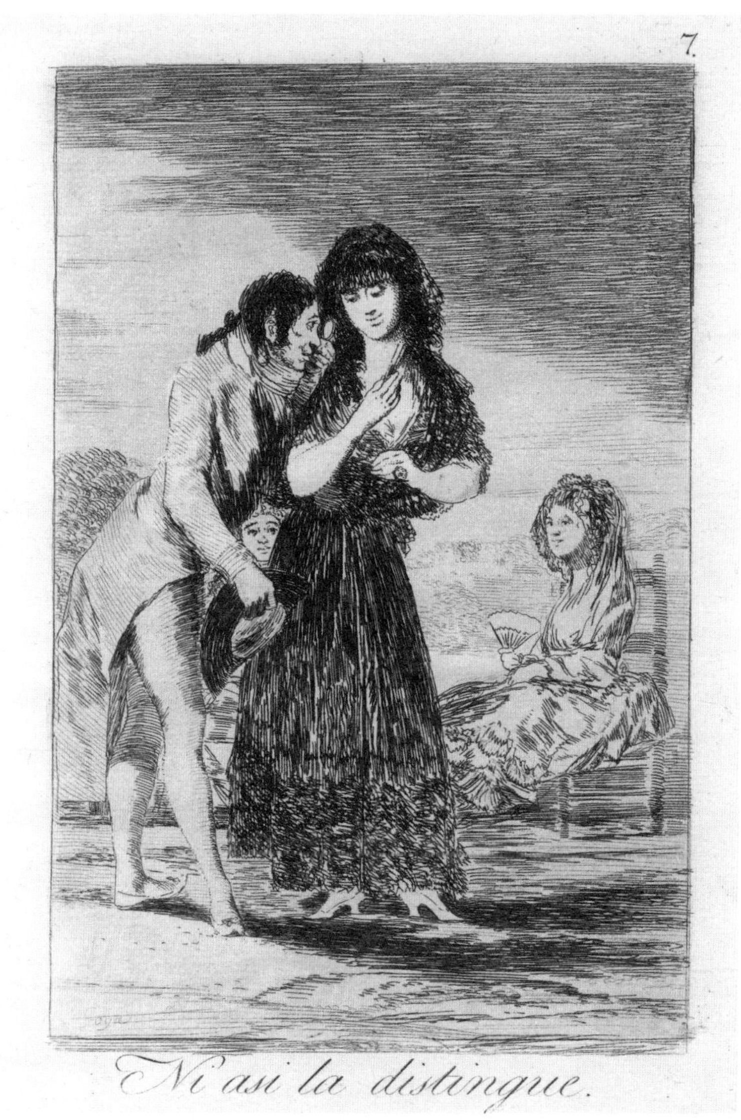

Figure 4.1.

"*Ni así la distingue*" ("Even thus he cannot make her out"), *Caprichos*, no. 7, 1797–98, published 1799. Aquatint and drypoint, 20×15 cm.

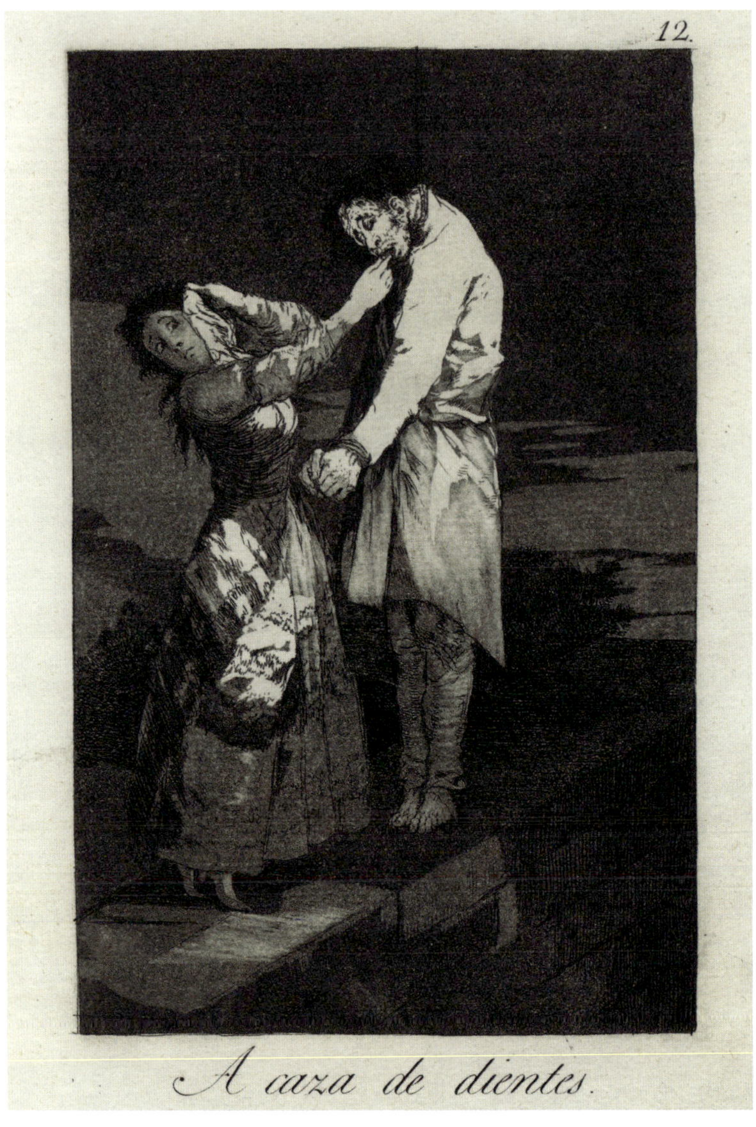

Figure 4.2.
"*A caza de dientes*" ("Out hunting for teeth"), *Caprichos*, no. 12, 1797–98,
published 1799. Etching, burnished aquatint, and burin, 21.9×15.3 cm.

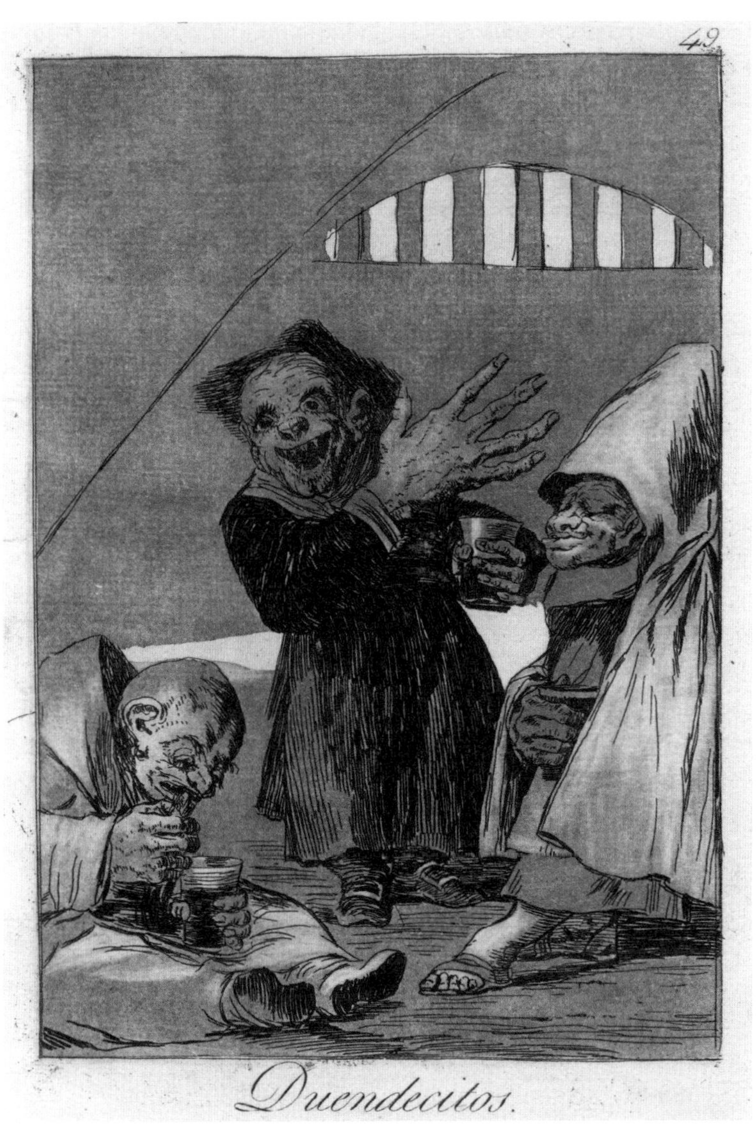

Figure 4.3.

"*Duendecitos*" ("Hobgoblins"), *Caprichos*, no. 49, 1797–98, published 1799.
Etching and burnished aquatint, 21.7×15.2 cm.

continued to play a substantial role in shaping action and belief and correspondingly in which subjects had not fully taken responsibility for themselves, that is, had not fully recognized their autonomy. What stands in the way of that recognition often involves a blindness to the source of those commands — to the power of religious institutions, of inherited superstitions and traditional beliefs, of normative social relationships, and of unquestioned assumptions that perpetuate collective ignorance as they pass from generation to generation. But rather than speculate about the possibilities offered by new and different sources of disinhibition or envision some kind of radical freedom or sovereign moral autonomy as an alternative ideal, Goya concentrates on the mechanisms by which the various external commands that played such a large role in motivating human subjects to action were concealed or outright denied. While he no doubt understood that the work of unmasking might be a necessary step for the creation of new ways of imagining the world, his goals were hardly utopian in any naïve sense, and certainly not in the *Caprichos*. This is no doubt a function of Goya's understanding of the particularly difficult position of art, in between theory and practice: that even while recognizing that what needs to be shown and while able to reach beyond conventions, art is blocked in the effort to intervene directly in the world.

This difficulty is worth dwelling on. To be sure, in exposing the beliefs that make human beings less autonomous and free than they might be, Goya's *Caprichos* and related works clearly do something other than "theorize" — that is, construct universal, ideal standpoints from which things *ought* to be viewed or that show how they *ought* to be. The responsibility they assume, as a form of practice, is to show what the conventions of representation help hold in place while also acknowledging the constraints that bear upon any form of practice that restricts itself to the work of showing, whether as a representation of the world through the techniques of perspective or otherwise. The conventions of artificial perspective were well suited for producing the semblance of a "true likeness" of nature and were remarkably able to accommodate the demands for empirical truth.[10] But they were rather unequipped to deal with instances in which appearances were designed either to conceal things that are real or to mask intentions that are true. The greater challenge comes in the face of a world that seems to be constructed around the *principle* of concealment, such that there is no point from which to recognize these things.

In order to deal with such circumstances, Goya had to work on two fronts. One involved an effort at social criticism, with which the *Caprichos* are conventionally associated, that is, pointing out the flaws and deceptions at work in the world around him. Another involved a project of critique, that is, a reflection on the limitations of the conventions of representation, including the difficulty involved in isolating a position within the social world from which to see the truths that society endeavors to hide. Finding that position would in principle be a prerequisite for any form of action, yet the passage from the work of showing (and in the case of the *Caprichos*, also of saying, given the captions) to the work of doing marks what would seem to be an inherent limitation of the work of art. Whether and how Goya presses up against this limit is a question that is as relevant for the *Caprichos* as it is for the *Disasters of War*.

By the time he published the *Caprichos* in 1799, Goya was working at a level where he seemed capable of doing nearly anything as an artist. His capacities were extraordinary, and his prestige was great. He had gained ascending appointments at the royal court and had been named director of the Royal San Fernando Academy of Fine Arts in 1795. His works had ranged widely. In addition to the extensive tapestry cartoons, there were the religious paintings, culminating in the frescoes in San Antonio de la Florida discussed in Chapter 1, a number of commissioned portraits for aristocratic families and individuals — including six portraits commissioned for the Bank of San Carlos (forerunner of the Bank of Spain) — as well as numerous sketches and drawings, along with some etchings, most significantly the ones made after Velásquez's paintings. Throughout his work preceding the *Caprichos*, Goya came to recognize that the practice of representing anything in perspective called for adherence to a set of visual conventions that were hardly absolute and yet that had come to acquire the status of norms, backed by the sense that they were able to convey the truth of nature, its "true likeness." At the same time, it became increasingly evident that the work of representation and the conventions of perspective would not be enough to confront the realities of the social world — that there were things needing to be acknowledged that were outside the scope of what could be represented and indeed that the conventions of representation served to conceal. As hinted above, one response to this realization was the introduction of discursive supplements to the images of the *Caprichos*, the *Disparates*, and the *Disasters of War*. Specifically with respect to the *Caprichos*, the viewer might expect that the words accompanying the images would render their visual enigmas more intelligible, but the captions are sly and evasive and often point obliquely to contradictions within the social world that the figures represented in the images can't themselves see. Each caption has an unmistakable rhetorical force and is positioned as a counterforce to the acts of concealment and self-deception that the images show. But even as they are made plain, those contradictions are hardly resolved by the act of adding a discursive supplement to a visual representation.[11]

Goya's involvement with the conventions of representation and the use of perspective is bound up with his engagement of the history of Spanish art. Velásquez was no doubt a principal influence on Goya when it comes to his deep understanding of what it meant to represent anything using the techniques of artificial perspective. Goya's portrait of the royal family (1800–1801) makes an obvious allusion to *Las Meninas*, as does his self-portrait at the easel (1790–95). The number of etchings that Goya made after Velásquez's works is remarkable, including copies of *Los borrachos* (*The Drunkards*), made in 1778, and *Las Meninas* (Figure 4.4), done some time between 1778 and 1785, as well as a large number of solitary figures.[12]

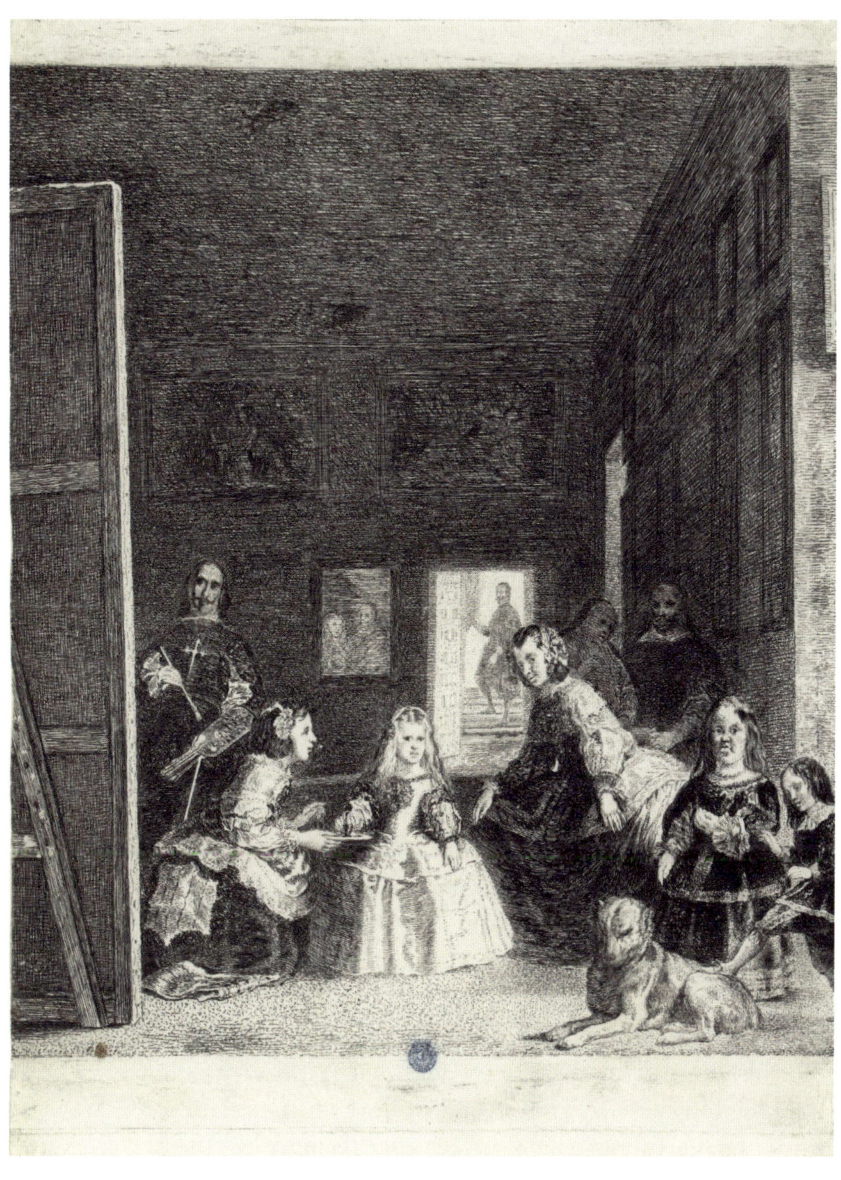

Figure 4.4.
Las Meninas, after Velásquez, ca. 1778–85.
Etching, aquatint, drypoint, burin, and roulette, 40.5×32.5 cm.

The full list of these etchings gives some sense of the depth of his involvement with Velásquez: *Philip III; Margaret of Austria; Philip IV; Isabel of Bourbon; A Prince of Spain; Pernia, Called Barberousse; The Buffoon Don Juan of Austria; Ochoa, Porter of the Palace; Aesop; Menippus; The Drinkers; Las Meninas; Don Baltasar Carlos; Don Gaspar de Guzmán, Count of Olivares; The Dwarf Sebastian of Morra; The Dwarf El Primo.* It has long been said and is no doubt true that Goya copied Velásquez as part of a relatively new national project to place examples of great works of Spanish art in wider circulation, as had become the custom in other European countries.[13] Goya adopted Velásquez as an instructional model, not only because Velásquez was an artist whose example was worthy of honorific treatment, but also because Goya sought to promote the national legacy and establish his own place within the history of Spanish art. While it would be hard to encapsulate what Goya absorbed from Velásquez in a few simple terms, one thing is clear: that beyond what Goya learned from his more immediate Italian and Spanish teachers, Velásquez drew him to concentrate on the basic elements of representation and to do so with a remarkable intensity. On initial viewing, it would seem that the etchings after Velásquez simply subtract the dimensionality and depth that color contributes to Velásquez's paintings in favor of austere contrasts and flattened tones. Yet Goya attempted to reintroduce a sense of depth into his etchings, even while working within a framework that admits only gradations of black, gray, and white.[14] This effort adds an intensity not present in the original paintings, a concentration that Goya heightens by focusing his attention both on the subject of representation — that is, the figures in the image and their arrangement in space — and on the means by which a painted image is recreated in a wholly different artistic medium and by different techniques. Goya's etchings concentrate demonstrably on the relationship between the marks made on a surface (in this instance, the plate, covered with a wax medium) and the resultant printed image. The resulting intensity of his engagement with Velásquez is exemplified, among other ways, in the manner in which Goya worked — perhaps even overworked — his version of *Las Meninas*. Critics have often deemed this one of the less successful works in this group of etchings, and indeed, Goya was himself quite unhappy with it, reportedly destroying the plate after it was finished.[15] But it is nonetheless highly revealing of the focused attention that he intensely devoted to Velásquez.

Goya's intensity also illuminates differences between his work and Velásquez's. Velásquez found ways of making his subjects worldly and engaging, even if they were mythological figures such as Mars and Venus; moreover, he drew upon various techniques of representation through colored paint on canvas in making the work of artificial perspective seem as natural as possible — the play of light and reflections, mirrors, framing devices, and the use of color, as well. These were the ingredients for the seemingly magical creation of the semblance of a world. Indeed, of all the artists preceding Goya, Velasquez's work could be seen as the culmination of conventions that began in the Renaissance and had become normative. His use of color in the service of perspective in fact epitomizes advice given as early as Giorgio Vasari's writings on technique in the long preface to his *Lives of the Artists* (1550). When painting in perspective, Vasari advised the use of color as a way to ensure that the convergence of "supporting" lines would disappear. Here is Vasari's account of what ought to happen as the painter progresses from the small sketch, through a large-scale cartoon, to the final painting: Painters

> draw the perspectives in the same schemes that have been adopted on a small scale in the first drawing, enlarging them in proportion. If in these there should be perspective views, or buildings, that are enlarged with the net, which is a lattice of small squares that are made large on the cartoon, when reproducing everything correctly, for of course when the artist has drawn out the perspectives in the small designs, taking them from the plan and setting up the elevations with the right contours, and making the lines diminish and recede by means of the intersection and the vanishing point, he must reproduce them in proportion on the cartoon.... Perspectives are beautiful in so far as they appear correct when looked at, and diminish as they retire form the

> eye. . . . The painter must take care too, to make them diminish in proportion
> by means of delicate gradations of colour that presuppose in the artist correct
> discretion and good judgment.[16]

This is exactly what Velásquez does in works such as *The Surrender at Breda*. But at the same time, Velásquez's paintings often leave space for the subtle acknowledgment that art can in the end make only a semblance of a world.

For his part, Goya sought to distill the fundamental components of Velásquez's images, sans color, both in order to capture their essential ingredients and also to confront the fact that any act of representation is in fact an illusion produced on what is essentially a worked surface. What is sometimes said about Goya's etchings, and not always inaccurately — that they reach toward the depth that coloration would otherwise provide — needs to be modified in relation to this particular group: that they subtract color in order to make manifest in more starkly visible ways the means by which color conspires to yield the semblance of depth that helps create the illusion of a world. Doing so introduces an opacity into images whose painted models inevitably seem more transparent and natural; yet that opacity is part of what it takes to disclose the means whereby the seeming transparency of the art of representation was brought about. Ultimately, it leads to a critique of the assumptions around transparency that the practice of representation carries with it, namely, that art gives us a "true likeness" of the world. In the case of many of the *Caprichos*, we are made quite aware that what we see as the background is itself the material ground of the image because it contains visible traces of the physical surface from which the image emerges.

This is a subtle revelation, because the *Caprichos* are both etching and aquatint. The process of making an aquatint involves soaking a resin-coated surface (a copper plate) in an acid bath; this produces a soft, continuous wash over the plate that in turn allows for a continuous gradation of dark and light tones, which could not be achieved by even the most talented use of crosshatching. The surface of the plate is thus a material ground that becomes a visual background in the image. That background preserves its material origins, but it is often a blankness. It does little, if anything, to provide visual context for the image, and certainly not context of the kind that might illuminate or resolve the contradictions within the image. If anything, the background functions rather more like a blank screen onto which the image in question is projected, as if Goya were reproducing the effects created by the ancient technique of the *lanterna magica* (magic lantern).[17] (Goya's involvement with techniques of projection will become further apparent in Chapter 7.) I will turn shortly to how these effects work in the two different sections of the *Caprichos*, but the immediate inference to be drawn from the set as a whole has to do with the fact that Goya recognizes both that the work of art is constructed and that it does not assume that an external world simply presents itself to us, such that the task of the artist can be one of re-presentation. What we think of as "the world" is itself constructed and often in ways that are designed to conceal rather than reveal the true nature of things. Time and again, the *Caprichos* and related works are engaged in a process of denaturalizing conventions in order to show just this.

Coming to terms with the nature of representation and with the conventions of perspective and reckoning with their material basis in a worked surface certainly helped establish Goya's understanding of the difficult place of art between theory and practice. But this difficulty notwithstanding, it was understanding the underlying assumptions that attach to the use of painterly perspective that allowed Goya to place art in the service of a critical project that extended well beyond the aesthetic realm. Foremost among those assumptions was the Enlightenment notion that the world is a "black box," or a series of such boxes, into which we can peer and that we can ultimately illuminate by various means, some philosophical and others practical or aesthetic.[18] To wit, the work of representation in art is premised on the belief that the world is fundamentally illuminable, even if there may be some isolated places of darkness within it. It is consistent with the work of Enlightenment that involves a movement from opacity to clarity, from the darkness of ignorance and superstition to the light of rationality, bounded by an understanding of the contours and limits of what we can and cannot know. In the preface to the first edition of the *Critique of Pure Reason* (1781), for instance, Kant outlined the need for this boundary-setting work in very explicit terms: "Human reason, in one sphere of its cognition, is called upon to consider questions, which it cannot decline, as they are presented by its own nature, but which it cannot answer, as they transcend every faculty of the mind."[19] What is required is a project of critique, or in Kant's words:

> the establishment of a tribunal to undertake the most laborious of all tasks — that of self-examination, and to establish a tribunal, which may secure it in its well-grounded claims, while it pronounces against all baseless assumptions and pretensions, not in an arbitrary manner, but according to its own eternal and unchangeable laws. This tribunal is nothing less than the critical investigation of pure reason.[20]

In establishing this "tribunal," reason gains in power specifically, by "choosing the various objects of thought, it is able to define the limits of its own faculties, and even to give a complete enumeration of the possible modes of proposing problems to itself, and thus to sketch out the entire system of metaphysics."[21] Placing boundaries around what can and cannot be known, Kant establishes the conditions of possibility whereby the light of reason can enter the "black box" of the world and turn it into a well-lit space, a box fully illuminated by the light of reason.

The notion of the illuminated black box is relevant to Goya's relationship to the project of critique for two reasons, one of which has to do with his understanding of the principles whereby that notional box is formed and another of which has to do with what he finds when he peers inside. What Goya learned about the nature of representation and its limits speaks to the first of these; it is a subject to which I will return in later pages of this chapter. But I want to point out here the fundamental tension within an Enlightenment premise that illuminates the interior of the black box allowing us to control its unruly contents. That tension aids the subject to pass from theory to practice in ways that will promote individual and collective happiness. Goya's recognition of that tension, which is already visible in the tapestry cartoons and emphatic in the *Caprichos* and the Black Paintings, is based on two premises. The first is that there is no necessary alignment between the principles of happiness and the work of art, especially the work's adherence to the principles of representation by which we are able to see the world as if from a "God's eye" perspective; the second is that inside the black box is a set of unruly forces that scarcely know themselves to exist. What Goya illuminates when he peers into the black box is the darkness of human nature itself. To be sure, not everything that is dark in Goya has traceable roots; as the Black Paintings suggest, that darkness is most vexing when it is not reducible to any particular cause at all. Yet that darkness can sometimes be linked to identifiable causes, many of them social and many of which are concealed by the very things that impede the ability of the subject to act as an autonomous individual: blind adherence to the clergy, belief in the power of superstition, and faithfulness to a series of self-serving motives including fear, greed, vanity, jealousy, and pride. All of these motives are supported by a lack of self-awareness that enables a blindness about their role in the subject's movement to action.

To see the darkness of human nature as both social (and potentially corrigible) and essential (and therefore incorrigible) is vastly different from what an Enlightenment thinker such as Kant believed. For Kant, everything in nature can serve some good: "Even poisons are serviceable; they destroy the evil effects of other poisons generated in our system, and must always find a place in every complete pharmacopoeia."[22] Kant does of course admit the possibility of radical evil and he provides a long discussion of it in the first part of *Religion within the Limits of Reason Alone*. But even to inquire why human beings might actually choose evil if there is in fact a moral law is a question that *presupposes* the existence of a moral law. Kant's statement assumes that human agents can and must act consciously and likewise that the world is transparently available, available to be known by us and available to us as a sphere in which action for the good is always possible.

Understanding the world as available to be known by us is fully consistent with the general assumptions at work in the paradigm of representation, in which the visual work of art draws on the techniques of perspective to create the semblance of a window through which we gaze upon the world. That has been fundamental to painting since Alberti's treatise. (Alberti: "On the surface I am going to paint, I draw a rectangle of whatever size I want, which I regard as *an open window* through which the subject to be painted is to be seen.")[23] The represented world is in principle an illuminated world, a "white box" of intelligibility in which action (the *historia*, in Alberti's terms) takes place. Goya was not unfamiliar with such ideas and saw them exemplified in some very concrete projects undertaken by powerful men for the benefit of the greater good. Consider his 1783 portrait of the Count of Floridablanca (see Figure 1.15, above), who was a prominent political figure known for his involvement with large-scale engineering projects, especially hydraulic works, canals, and dams. On the table in the portrait are maps, and on the floor is a plan for building the Aragón canal alongside the Ebro ("Plano del Canal de Aragón / Al Excmo. Señor Floridablanca, año 1783"). The clock that figures prominently in the painting underlines the fact that these are worldly works, works that must be completed with precision and on time. I will return to this example in the final chapter for what it has to say about Goya's commitment to the ideal of the public good.

But in the *Caprichos*, both elements of this paradigm are subjected to intense pressure. The work of representation is subjected to a critique because its purely conventional status had become naturalized, while the passage to action is limited both by a sense of pervasive social deception and by an awareness of what art can and cannot do. It has long been established that the eighty plates of the *Caprichos* can be divided into two sections, with a self-portrait frontispiece (no. 1) that frames the entire series. Plates 2 through 42 are set in the conscious, waking world, while plates 44 through 80 are set within the world of sleep and nightmarish dreams. The famous "*El sueño de la razón pro-duce monstruos*" ("The sleep of reason produces monsters") (no. 43; see Figure 3.29, above) is the hinge between the two. (This is the only plate of the series that does not carry a caption outside the frame; the phrase "El sueño de la razón produce monstruos" appears in white on the side pedestal of the desk.) The image and its genealogy have been the subject of countless commentaries, most of which regard it as a statement of what can happen when the vigilance of reason wanes. The image is likely a response to the frontispiece of the second volume of Rousseau's *Philosophie* made by Charles Monnet, published in 1767. It may also owe a debt to Quevedo's satirical *Sueños*, written over the years between 1605 and 1622. But behind the figure asleep at his desk in Goya's image are bats and owls and a lynx with piercing eyes. The owl is a frightening figure but also one long associated with wisdom, and famously with the wisdom that arrives at the hour of darkness, since owls can see in the dark. The lynx had long been thought of as having supernatural powers of sight. The suggestion is not just that the sleep of reason releases demons but that some demons may have powers of insight that are not available to ordinary vision. While hovering in the background, these figures suggest a dialectical inversion of the belief that things can be seen most clearly when they are brought out into the daylight, when the "black box" is fully exposed to the power of light. Indeed, Goya saw that in the daily conduct of business, participants in the social world would tend all too easily to misrepresent or mask the motives behind their actions. Intentionally or not, these are subjects who introduce all kinds of opacities into the world of light. To expose that fact is the work of the plates that make up the first half of the *Caprichos*—to illuminate what is best seen in the dark is the work of the second series of plates.

To proceed with some examples from the first half, no. 6 (Figure 4.5) shows a world in which deception is so pervasive that nobody rec-ognizes even himself ("*Nadie se conoce*" ["Nobody knows himself"]). Here, the caption speaks a truth beyond what the image on its own can show. It points from outside the image space to the very things

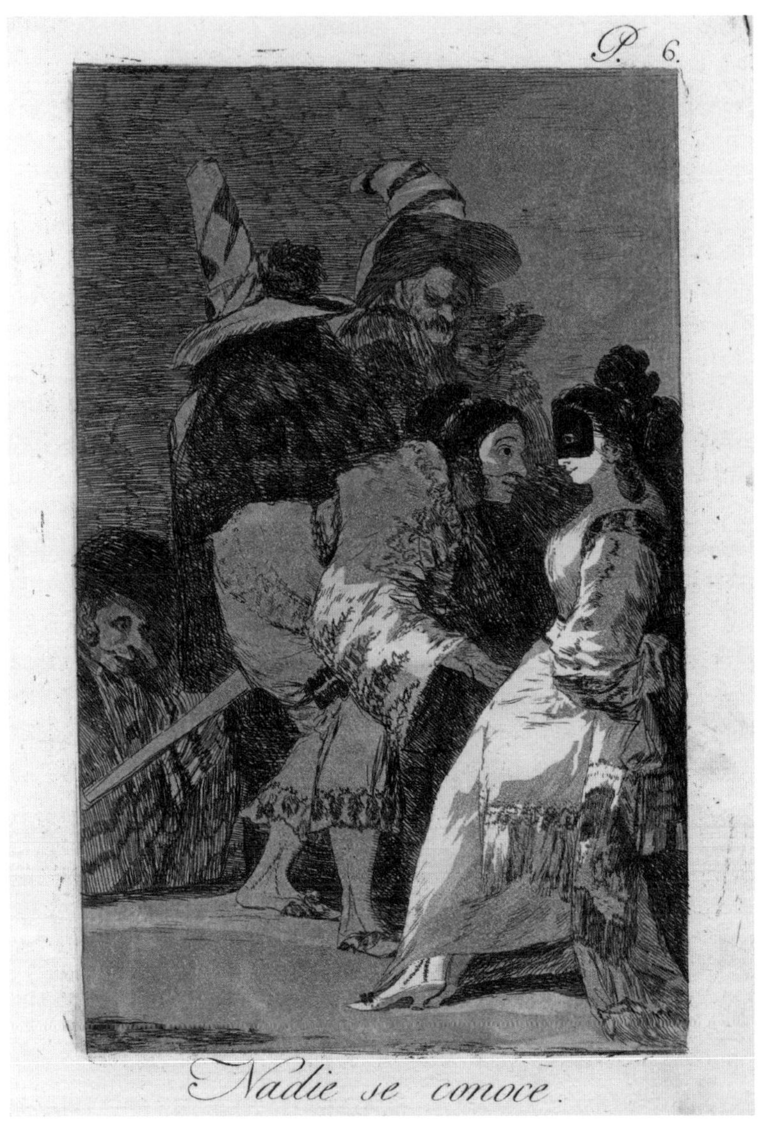

Figure 4.5.
"*Nadie se conoce*" ("Nobody knows himself"), *Caprichos*, no. 6, 1797–98,
published 1799. Etching and burnished aquatint, 21.9×15.3 cm.

that the figures in it cannot see. Carnival costumes and masks are not in this instance meant for the benign purposes of "pretend," for entertainment or for the temporary loosening of norms or the breaking of taboos.[24] Goya had come to know and to understand that image repertoire well from Tiepolo's Venetian carnival images, which incorporate many figures masked in black,[25] but his are different and portray raging desires that lurk in the darkness, scarcely visible. Indeed, what Goya attempts to do in so many of the images of the first half of the *Caprichos* is to show the very things that are apt to go unrecognized or that are actively suppressed in the everyday social world. These include the forces that motivate individual to sometimes perverse actions, but they also include the mechanisms by which those motives go unacknowledged. Self-deception plays an especially important role in the process. In no. 7, holding a monocle to his eye, a suitor looks at a young lady, while a figure who may well be her mother is depicted in the background, sitting calmly in a chair. The caption reads "*Ni así la distingue*" ("Not even thus will he make her out"), suggesting that neither better eyesight nor a closer view will help the suitor penetrate the young woman's ruses (Figure 4.1, above).[26] At issue is not physical sight, rather it is the need for insight into her motives, which a monocle cannot possibly give him. The point is that he is not sufficiently aware of what he needs in order to see, that is, to understand her.

In other images, the meaning of the caption turns on a deft play of words, adding the force of wit to Goya's biting social criticism. "*Ya tienen asiento*" ("They already have a seat [bottom]") (no. 26, Figure 4.6) puns on the double sense of "*asiento*," which means both "seat" and "understanding."[27] These girls with their seats on their heads have no hope for intellectual understanding ("*asiento*"), because their intelligence is already situated in their seats — which we can take as meaning their rear ends. Wit had a long-established role in artworks that combined text and image, principally prints. The tradition of the *emblema*, epitomized in the works of Alciati, is exemplary in this regard. But the *emblema* tends to be enigmatic; its aim is to speak a compressed truth, and each one would characteristically revolve

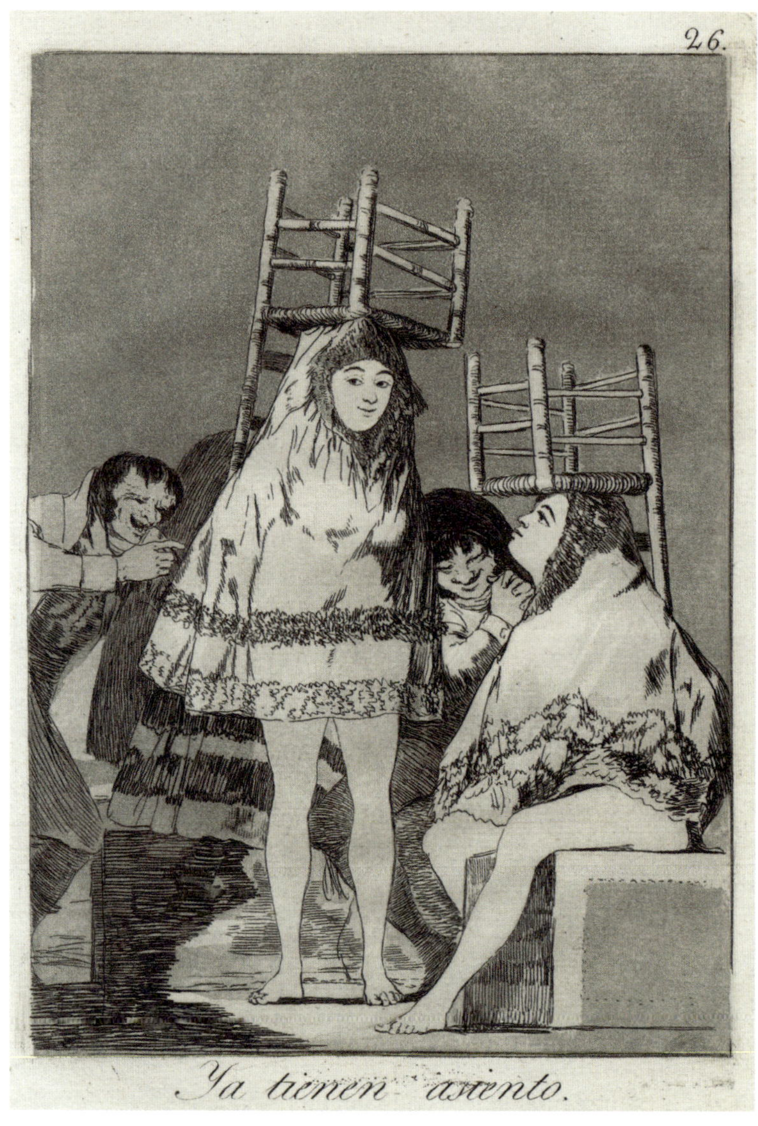

Figure 4.6.
"*Ya tienen asiento*" ("They already have a seat"), *Caprichos*, no. 26, 1797–98, published 1799. Etching and burnished aquatint, 21.7 × 15.2 cm.

around the mutual reinforcement by text and image of some central symbol. This is very different from what we see in Goya, where the verbal explanation redoubles the double entendre that we see represented in an image that is otherwise unintelligible.

Plate no. 14 (Figure 4.7) resonates with the tapestry cartoon depicting the wedding of a bride to a wealthy groom who is horribly ugly. The *Capricho* shows the young woman scarcely able to countenance her fiancé, while the groom-to-be sports a voracious grin, and onlookers in turn gawk and shield their eyes. The caption is crucial and provides a good measure of how different the *Caprichos* are from even the most critical of the tapestry cartoons. It reads: "¡*Que sacrificio!*" ("What a sacrifice!"). The meaning does not seem mysterious, but it raises a question whose answer is far from clear: "For whom? — whose sacrifice?" On a first pass, we are likely to assume that the sacrifice is hers and that she has bargained away her beauty and her future for his money, but the sacrifice is his, as well, since although he may not realize it, there is little chance that any happiness will come from this match.[28] (Cf. plate 5, "*Tal para qual*" ["Two of a kind"], and plate 27, "*¿Quien más rendido?*" ["Who is more overcome?" — Figure 4.8]. In the latter, the suitor pretends to be "overcome" emotionally, while the lady ignores the fact that she will be "overcome" physically.)

Part of what matters about ¡*Que sacrificio!* is that the caption says something beyond what is represented. It shows the representation to be insufficient to the task of exposing the double deception (indeed, the double self-deceptions) at the heart of the image. As noted above, we might in principle expect captions to clarify the meaning of puzzling images. But the rhetorical force and enigmatic quality of so many of the captions of the *Caprichos*, like this one, undermine any such expectation. ¡*Que sacrificio!* gestures rhetorically toward what might well be known or shown about this pair, but that is inevitably avoided in proper social discourse, spoken, if at all, in hushed asides. As soon as the conventional pathos and sentimentality that appear at the surface level of this caption crack, we are exposed to a potentially bottomless

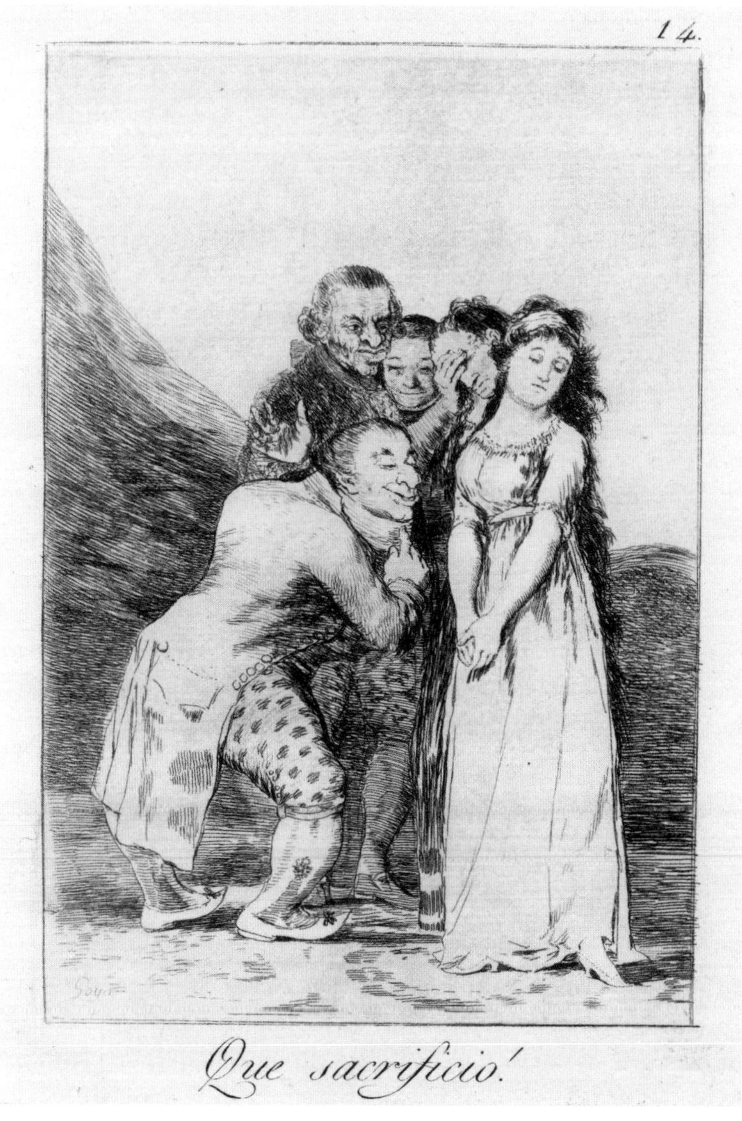

Figure 4.7.
"*¡Que sacrificio!*" ("What a sacrifice!"), *Caprichos*, no. 14, 1797–98, published 1799.
Etching, burnished aquatint and drypoint, 20.3 × 15.2 cm.

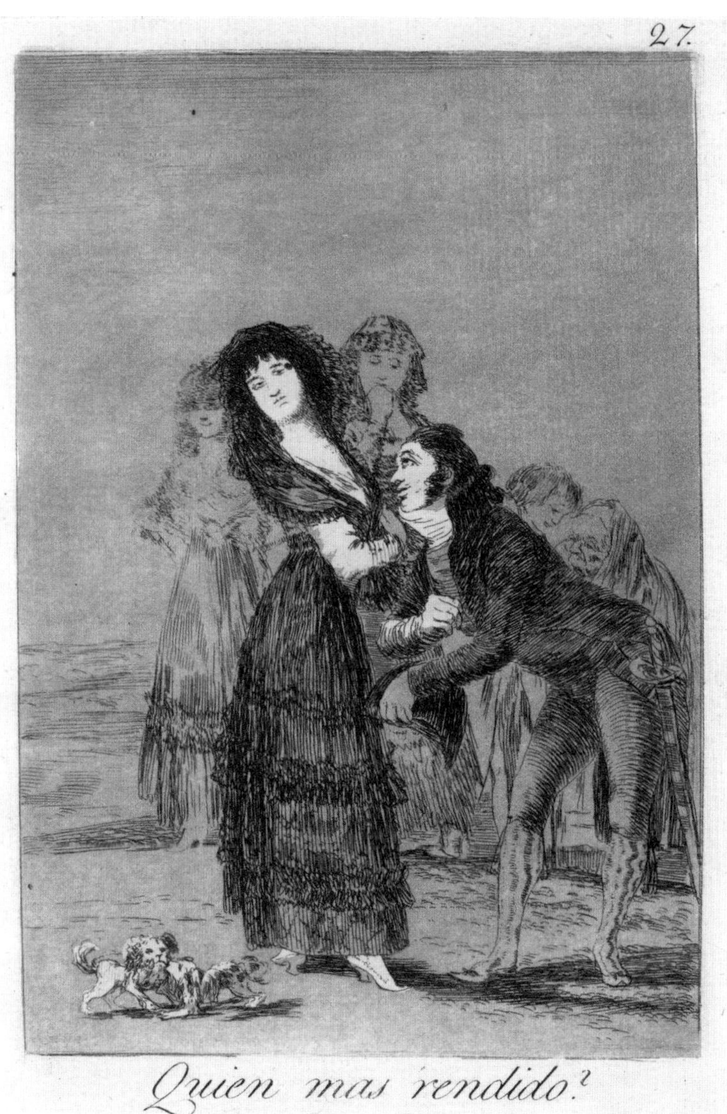

Figure 4.8.

"*¿Quien más rendido?*" ("Who is more overcome?"), *Caprichos*, no. 27, 1797–98, published 1799. Etching, aquatint, and drypoint, 19.8×15.1 cm.

critique of the social world and in particular of those social relations that are driven by love and desire among women and men.

The "bottomless" nature of that critique is significant. Many of the *Caprichos* are images that refuse to offer any internal position from which to represent the truth of things in a coherent and consistent fashion, especially in the social world. Indeed, Goya rarely, if ever, locates any position within the social world that would be free from deception or immune to critique, and indeed, many of the *Caprichos* insist on the fact that society reinforces its own behaviors so as to shut out the possibility that its weaknesses might be recognized and changed. Among the primary mechanisms for this reinforcement — this "disinhibition" — are the institutions that serve to transmit values across generations. These are, to be sure, among the very same vehicles that Goya identifies as contributing to the blindness and self-deception that keep people chained to their weaknesses and indebted to the very forces that might allow their autonomy to emerge — the institutions of education, medicine, and the church, along with the social institutions of courtship and marriage. Not surprisingly, they are also among the very institutions that Goya's Enlightenment peers sought to reform. To take just one example, Jovellanos and his colleagues drafted a *Plan de educación* in 1798 at the request of the king.[29] The treatise opens by lamenting the sad state of education in contemporary Spain. What Goya sees, however, is a society so deeply inbred in its ways that there is virtually no opening for educational reform, certainly not through traditional methods. This social obstinacy and imperviousness to change thread their way through a variety of the *Caprichos*, each one of which brings some particular version of that recalcitrance into focus.

Consider plate no. 25 (Figure 4.9), "*Si quebró el cantaro*" ("For he broke the jug"). The young boy in the image is being beaten by a woman (presumably his mother), brandishing a shoe as her weapon of choice. The jug, broken into shards, is pictured in the foreground, while in the background, the freshly cleaned laundry hangs out to dry. The image is dominated by the brutish ugliness of the woman's

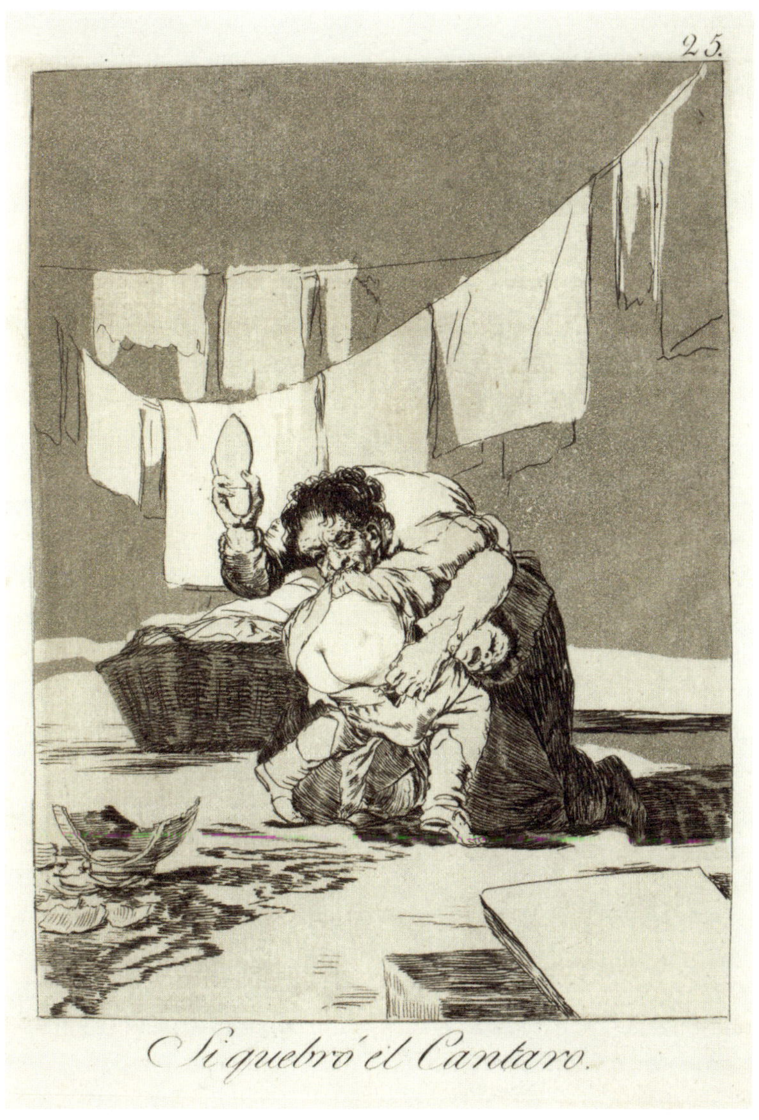

Figure 4.9.
"*Si quebró el cantaro*" ("For he broke the jug"), *Caprichos*, no. 25, 1797–98, published 1799. Etching, aquatint, and drypoint, 20.9 × 15.2 cm.

face, by the boy's exposed bottom, and by his pathetic grimace. She will wash the laundry over and over again, and each time it gets soiled, it will be cleaned. But if she beats this boy each time he makes a mistake, his face and his bottom will not continue to look so innocent. His distress, and moreover, her repeated actions, ensure that his face will eventually look like hers. (Cf. no. 15, in which the young woman taking advice is bound to look like the old hag giving it if she decides to follow it, and no. 46 [Figure 4.10] in which the practice of "correction" results in physiognomic distortions.) In fact, the image is not just a critique of the mother's cruelty, but a critique of the process by which figures like her come about. To change the course of things would require an intervention of some sort, perhaps a reform in childrearing.

That is urgently needed but seemingly impossible in a society where nobody seems to grow up. See, for example, no. 4 (Figure 4.11), *"El de la rollona"* ("Nanny's boy"). The failure to achieve the maturity of character that would form the basis for true moral autonomy is a feature of the pervasive inbreeding that we see across so many of the *Caprichos*. In no. 37 (Figure 4.12), an ass decked out in pretentious garb gives instruction in reading to a younger ass. The caption reads "*¿Si sabrá más el discípulo?*" ("Perhaps the pupil will know more?").

On one level we understand the critique of pretense and recognize that the symbols of learning are no indication of knowledge, and even less of wisdom. An ass is an ass, no matter what. And if education is handed down from ass to ass, as this *Capricho* seems to suggest, what real chance is there that things will change? In plate 40 (Figure 4.13), a donkey doctor attends to a dying patient, and the caption asks "*¿De qué mal morirá?*" ("From what sickness will he die?"). On one level, the calamity roots in the ignorance of physicians. But the deeper tragedy is that there is nobody to tell the patient that he is being treated by an ass (and the ass is of course too ignorant to know it himself — that is part of what defines him as an ass). It would be an understatement to say that the two shadowy figures in the background of this image make no efforts at disclosure. They are for all

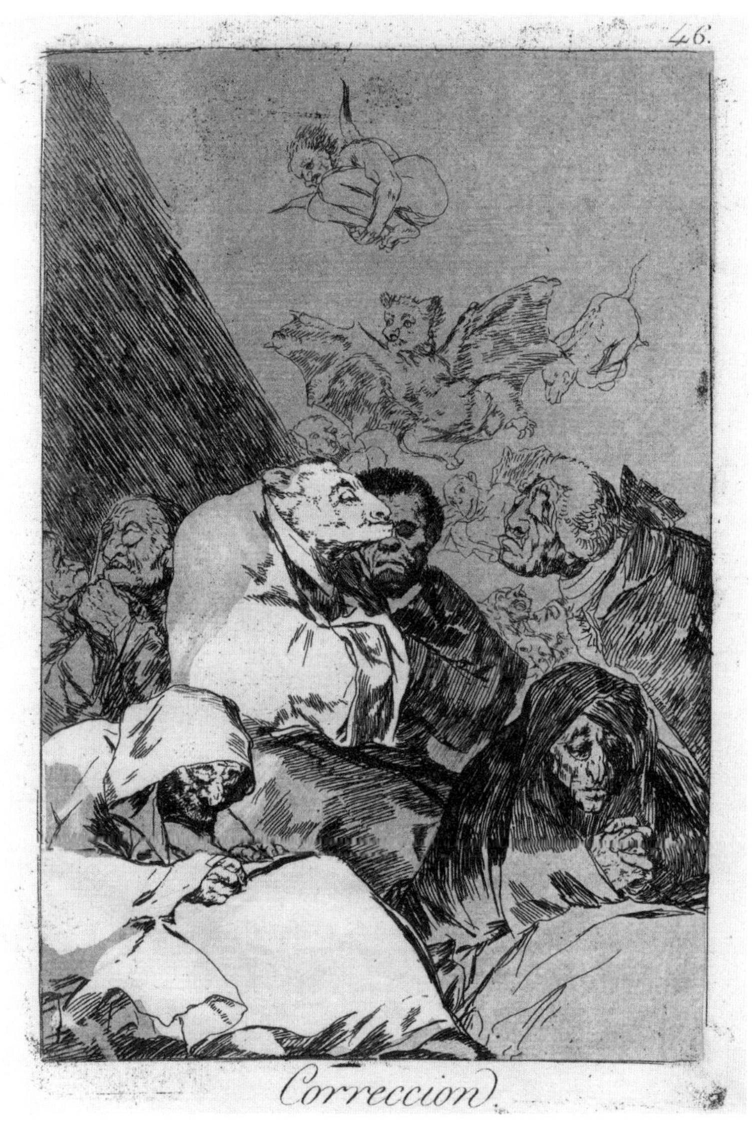

Figure 4.10.
"*Corrección*" ("Correction"), *Caprichos*, no. 46, 1797–98,
published 1799. Etching and burnished aquatint, 21.7 × 15 cm.

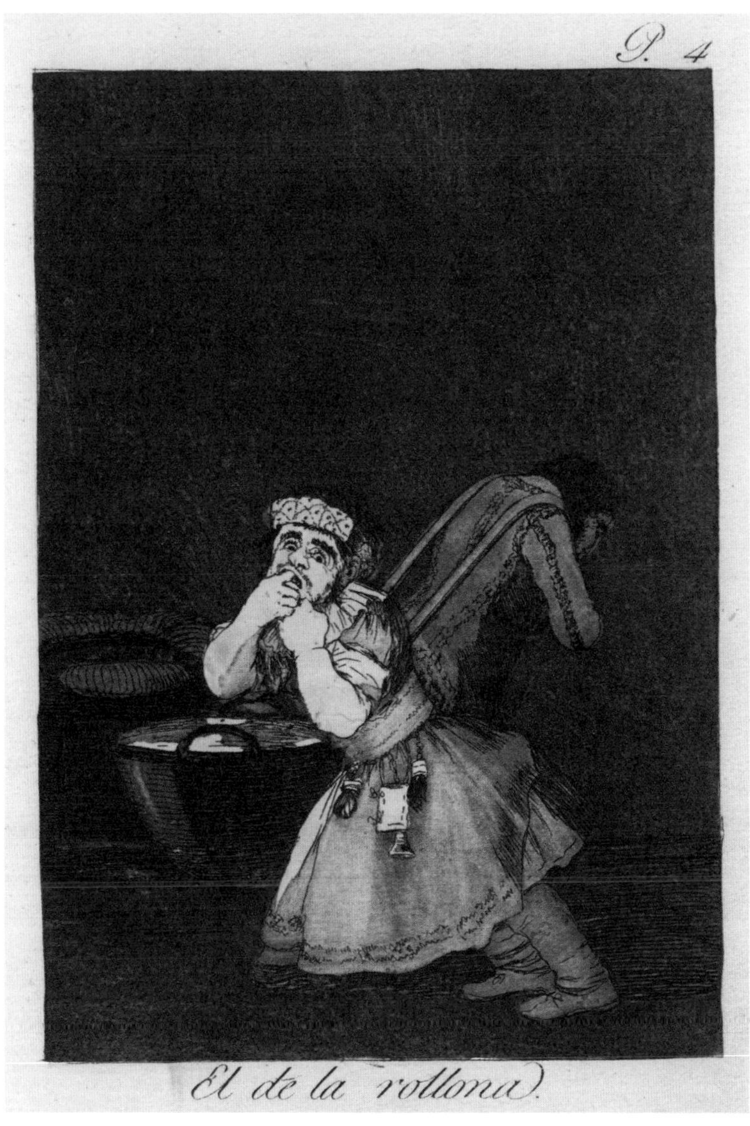

Figure 4.11.

"*El de la rollona*" ("Nanny's boy"), *Caprichos*, no. 4, 1797–98, published 1799. Etching and burnished aquatint, 20.9 × 15.7 cm.

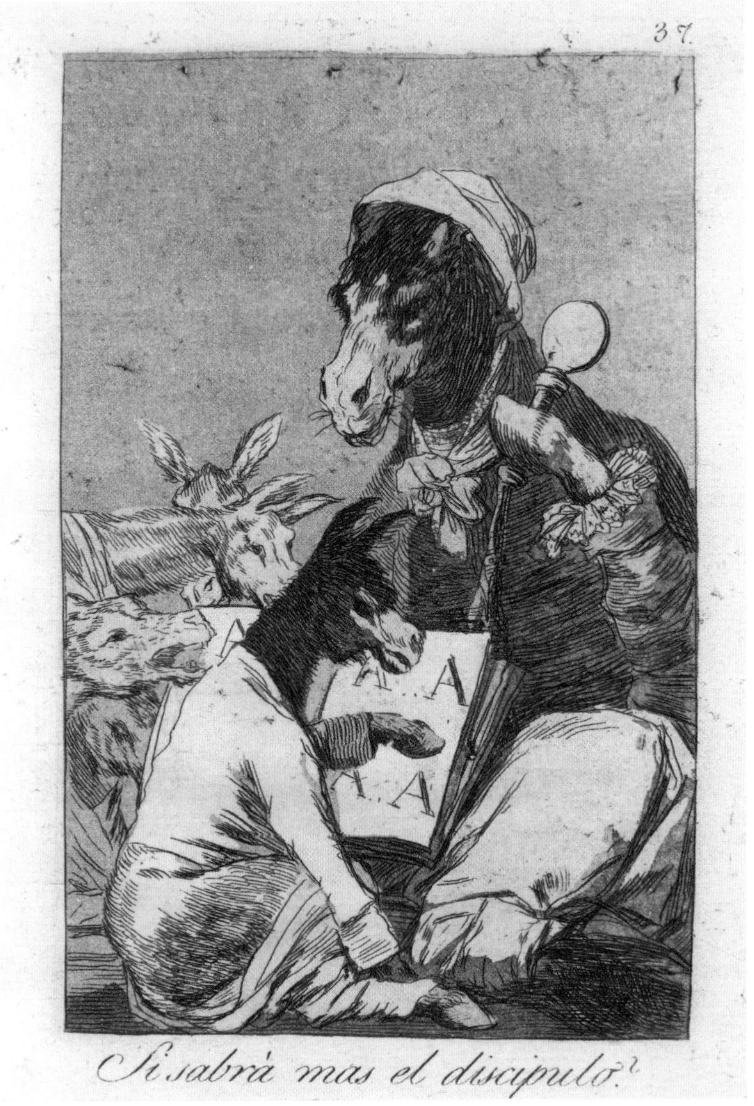

Figure 4.12.

"*¿Si sabrá más el discípulo?*" ("Perhaps the pupil will know more?), *Caprichos*, no. 37, 1797–98, published 1799. Etching, burnished aquatint, and burin, 21.8 × 15.3 cm.

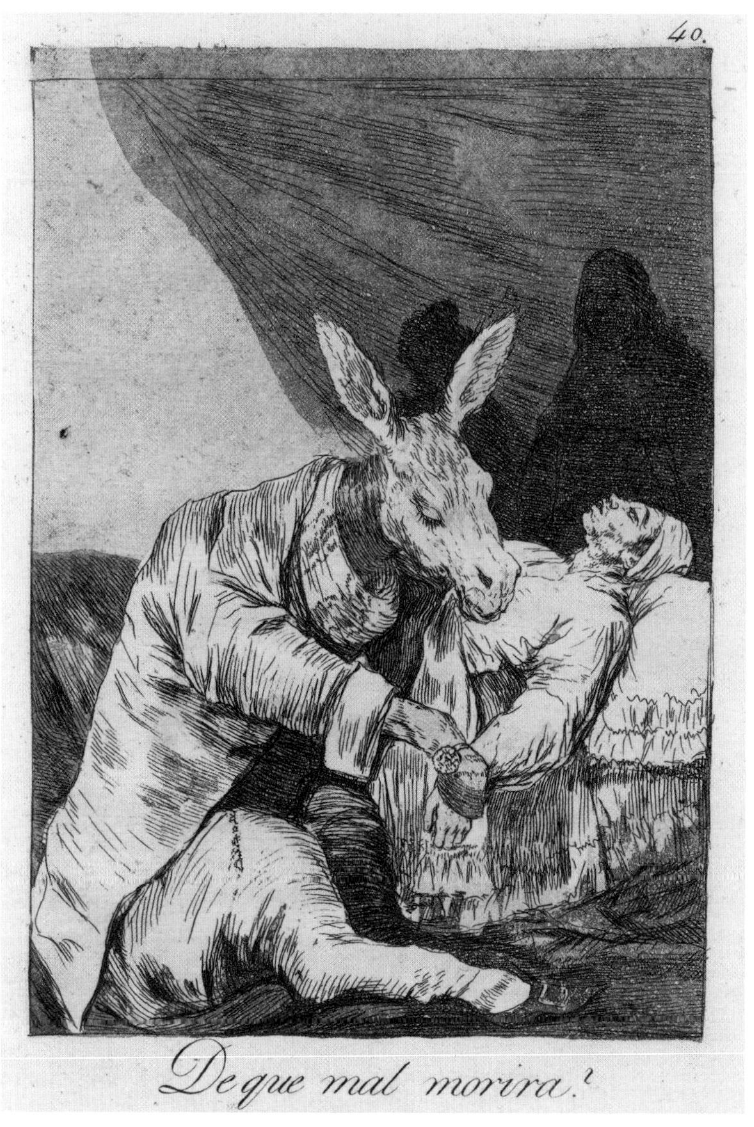

Figure 4.13.
"*¿De qué mal morirá?*" ("From what sickness will he die?"), *Caprichos*, no. 40, 1797–98, published 1799. Etching, burnished aquatint, drypoint, and burin, 21.6 × 15.2 cm.

intents and purposes complicit in the tragic farce. So, too, with the image of a monkey who plays music to the utter delight of a donkey (no. 38, "*Bravísimo*"), while a few onlookers in the background laugh mockingly at their mutually invisible stupidity. Finally, there is plate 39, "*Asta su abuelo*" (Figure 4.14) which can be translated either as "As far back as his grandfather" or "Even his grandfather."

In either case, the point is clear: the donkey in the picture, who according to the manuscript commentaries is studying a book of genealogical records, finds nothing but images that look just like himself as far back as he can see or at least as far back as his grandfather. (The first English description of the plate identified the image as the "Genealogy of a nobleman.")[30] The meaning most often attributed to this *Capricho* is indisputable: that the preoccupation with lineage and with the tracing of one's ancestors is the business of fools.

But there is an additional point to be made about it, consistent with all the other images just discussed, namely, that fools make fools, that is, that social forms reproduce themselves; that when they become inbred, they leave little opportunity to gain any perspective on the fact that this reproduction of deception is an enabling of the social structure itself. This is what makes us unwitting fools (asses). As no. 41 suggests in showing the portrait of an ass painted by a monkey (Figure 4.15), the only thing that this society seems to hope for — and it is a cynical hope in the negative sense of that term — is a beautification of something that is fundamentally debased. Indeed, it is only from the oblique position of the caption that Goya is able to insert a wedge into the social reproduction of self-deception. And while the *Caprichos* struggle with the fact that they cannot themselves change these things, they do acknowledge the fact that saying (in the captions) is no greater a guarantee of change than the work of showing (in the images themselves).

One might have reason to think that the work of the *Caprichos* could have concluded with the completion of the first set of plates. They go to great lengths to expose the mutually reinforcing self-deceptions

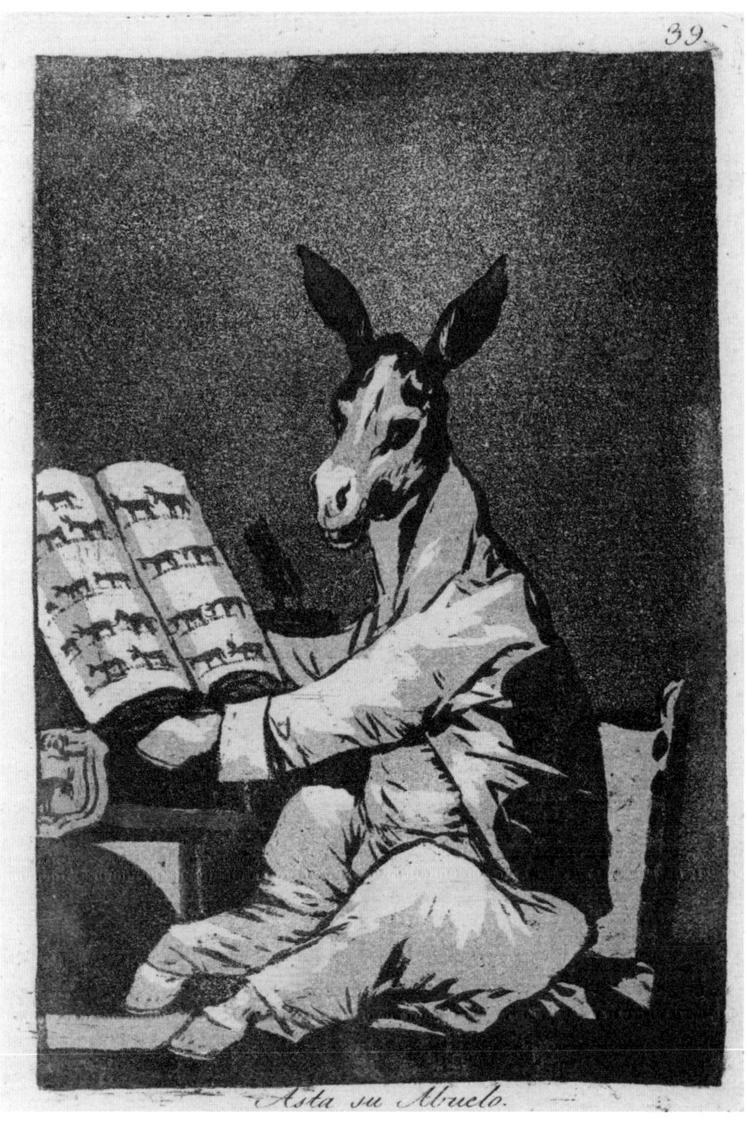

Figure 4.14.
"*Asta su abuelo*" ("As far back as his grandfather"), *Caprichos*, no. 39, 1797–98, published 1799, aquatint, 21.7 × 15.2 cm.

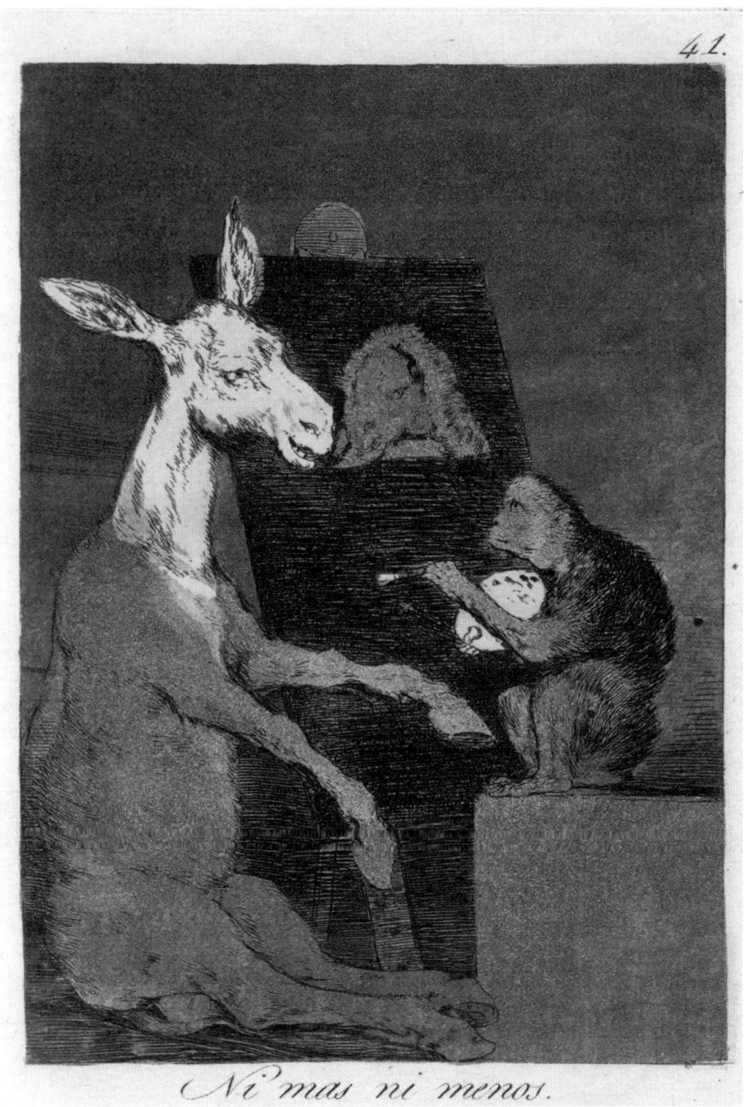

Figure 4.15.
"*Ni más ni menos*" ("Neither more nor less"), *Caprichos*, no. 41, 1797–98, published 1799. Etching, burnished aquatint, drypoint, and burin, 20×15.2 cm.

that pervade the social world. Additionally, they challenge the principles of representation that aligned the establishment of a fixed visual perspective with the illumination of the truth. They expose the limits of visual representation to the possibility that some clarifying, discursive statement might resolve the contradictions and enigmas that are made visible. Yet they also demonstrate the limitations of art — even in this hybrid form — to pass from a trenchant and multifaceted critique of the social world to an active response to it. I will turn in a discussion of the *Disasters of War* to some even more striking examples of Goya's struggle with this last issue, but for now, the question is why, given everything he was able to capture in the first set of plates in the *Caprichos*, Goya was inclined to create the set of images that make up the second half of the series.

The answer I would propose is twofold. First, understanding that representation involves light and that institutions and behaviors in the social world around him were designed perpetuate obscurity, Goya could see that there were things to be explored in the relationship between truth and representation that could best be accomplished under the cover of darkness. Second, the context of darkness, and specifically of sleep, affords the opportunity to delve into motives that could all too easily be suppressed while awake and also affords the opportunity to explore how art might respond to the possibility that it could have access to motive forces (passions, desires, and so on) that manifest themselves only when the vigilance of the conscious mind is suspended.[31]

Not trivially at stake is the question about what kind of sleep we are to assume. Is this the metaphorical sleep of reason, in which the mind is ostensibly awake and yet responding to all kinds of irrational influences in spite of the fact that they *present* themselves as rational (or at least as acceptable)? Or is it the condition of physical sleep, in which the censorship of our conscious mind is lowered, which in turn allows our nightmarish fears to be released? If those nightmares are merely individual, there might be no great concern; they could be regarded as idiosyncratic or as part of some personal pathology.

Similarly, an individual lapse in reason could be remedied by the proper conduct of reason. Whichever is the case, physical sleep or the dormancy of conscious reason, Goya's suggestion is that the power of illumination by daylight has a limited reach. The questions I would raise in considering examples from the second series of the *Caprichos* plates are accordingly these: What can an artist make visible in the darkness, if there were the power for it to be shown? What can be seen *only* in the darkness? And what might that in turn tell us about the things we see — or think we see — during waking hours?

Indeed, much of what Goya depicts in the second half of the *Caprichos* depends on an inversion of the Enlightenment trope according to which we see things best by the light of the day, that is, by shining the light of reason into the black box of human nature and social relations. There are some things, these images suggest, that are made visible to us best in the darkness, just as the images projected by a magic lantern can best be seen when the room is dark. (Consider the inversion of light and shadow in the night sky in no. 51 [Figure 4.16], "*Se repulen*" ["They preen themselves"].) This inversion of the Enlightenment trope is entirely consistent with the insights at play in the first half of the *Caprichos*, but in the second half are more nakedly exposed. Consider the extremity of "*Y aún no se van*" ("And still they don't go," no. 59, Figure 4.17), which shows individuals attached to their vices even as they approach the grave. We see teachers and pupils bound in educational formalities that ensure that nothing will be learned (no. 47, "*Obsequio al maestro*" ["A gift for the master"]); we witness the roots of solemnity (no. 63) and of devotion (no. 70) in the same kinds of superstitions that go into the making of witchcraft (Figures 4.18 and 4.19). The grotesque figures in no. 70 suggest that the line between devotion and superstition is virtually nonexistent and that both require the stupidity worthy of an ass. (The devout figure on the right in no. 63 — "*Miren que grabes [sic]*" ["Look how devout they are"] — underscores a similar point.) Likewise, we see individuals who are bound to one another because they are chained to their desires (plate no. 75, "*¿No hay quién*

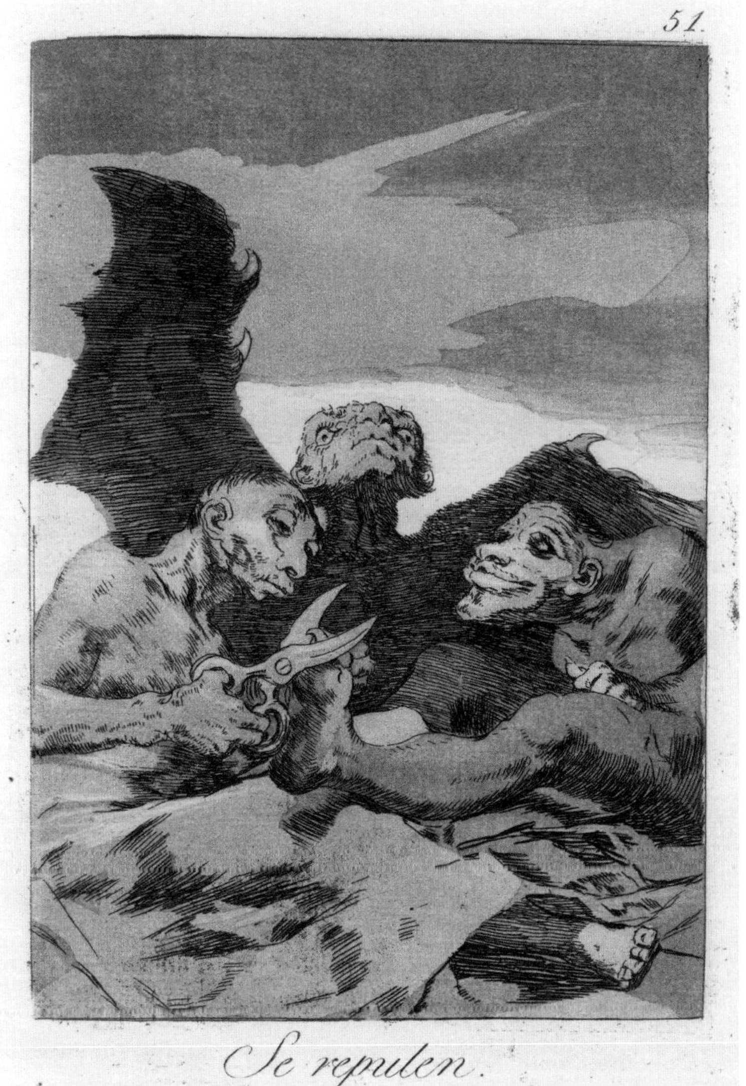

Figure 4.16.
"*Se repulen*" ("They preen themselves"), *Caprichos*, no. 51, 1797–98, published 1799. Etching, burnished aquatint, and burin, 214×14 cm.

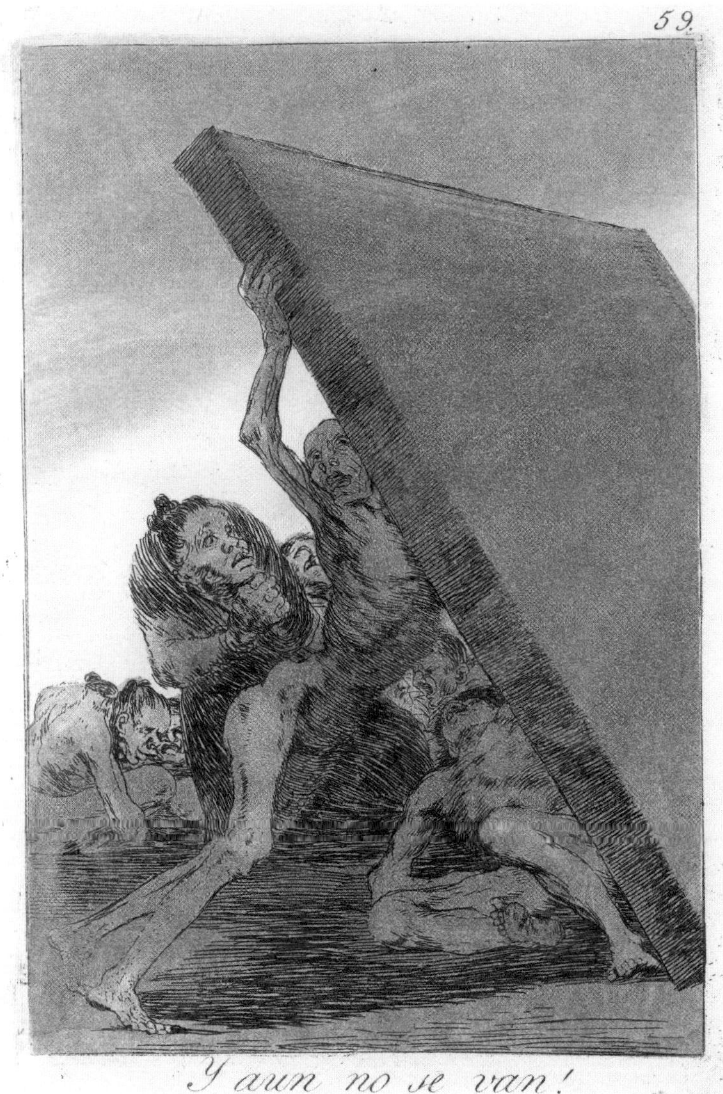

Figure 4.17.
"*Y aún no se van*" ("And still they don't go"), *Caprichos*, no. 59, 1797–98,
published 1799. Etching, burnished aquatint and burin, 21.9×15.2 cm.

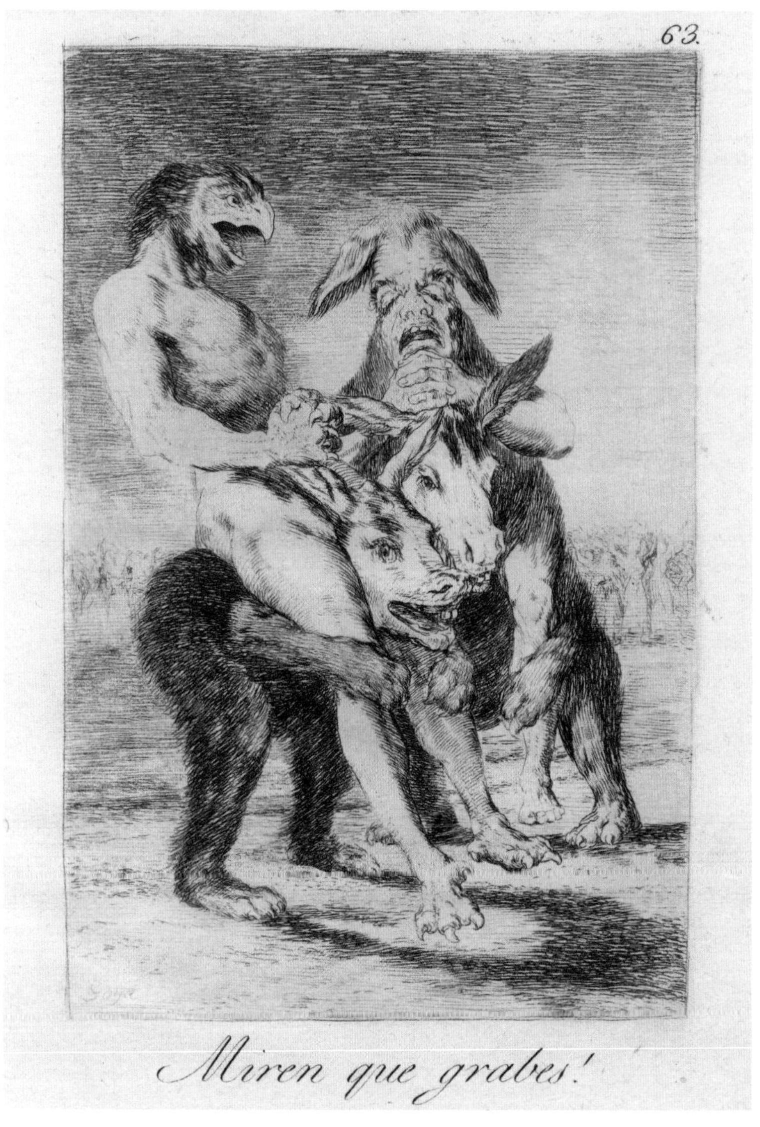

Figure 4.18.
"¡Miren qué grabes!" ("Look how solemn they are!"), *Caprichos*, no. 63, 1797–98,
published 1799. Etching, aquatint, and drypoint, 21.5 × 16.3 cm.

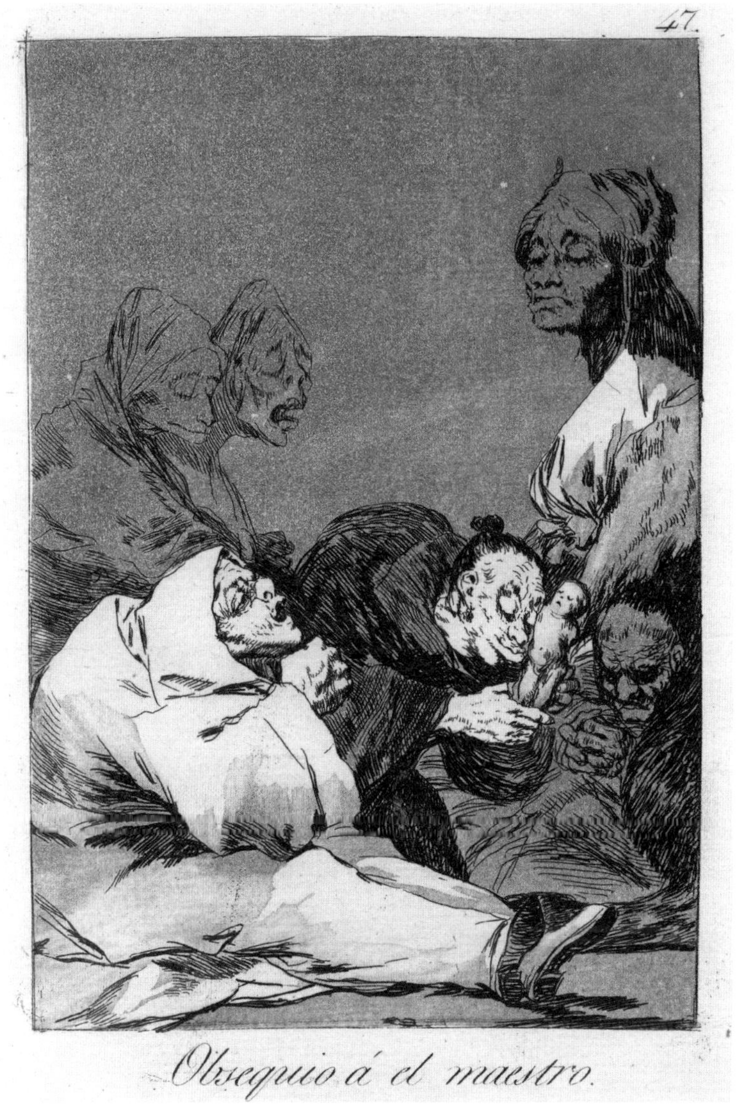

Figure 4.19.
"*Obsequio á el maestro*" ("A gift for the master"), *Caprichos*, no. 47, 1797–98, published 1799. Etching and burnished aquatint, 20.8×15.3 cm.

nos desate?" ("Is there no one who can untie us?"). No. 75 (Figure 4.20) is the counterpart of no. 62 (Figure 4.21), in which a lecherous old couple is entangled in a grotesque act of lovemaking, barely escaping the clutches of a monstrous figure who would draw them into the abyss.

The world of the second half of the *Caprichos* is a world turned upside down and in which individuals are locked into their reversions. (Cf. no. 77 , *"Unos a otros"* ["One to another"]). In this is upside-down world, the individuals are locked into perverse inversions (as in the case of the fake bull and the picadors in no. 77). In no. 42 (Figure 2.9, above) the world of men and beasts is upside down because all are beasts of one sort or another. In this particular plate, the background provides no point of orientation; shadows fall on the ground from an unlocatable source of light. Or consider the arrogance of the soldier in no. 76 (Figure 4.22): he orders the war wounded around and attacks them, just as he did the enemy.

The nocturnal sequence comes to an end with the final plate (no. 80), *"Ya es hora"* ("It is time now," Figure 4.23). The image shows what appears to be a group of monks awakening sfrom a deep sleep, their mouths agape with giant yawns. The commentary in the Biblioteca Nacional manuscript is revealing and speaks directly to the contrast between what can be seen by night and what is concealed by day: "As soon as it dawns they flee, each one his own way, Witches, Spirits, visions and fantasms. It's a good thing these people only let themselves be seen at night and in the dark! Nobody has been able to figure out where they hide during the day."[32] The present-day online curatorial commentary by the Prado ascribes the caption to the figures in the image and apparently believes them to be screaming.[33] But this clearly seems wrong and entirely misses the fundamental irony of the image, namely, the irony that concerns the fundamental motif of "awakening." Waking up, returning to consciousness, bringing things into the light of day where we would expect them to be made visible are all tropes that are turned on their head, since we know that awakening will return us back to the world of the first part of

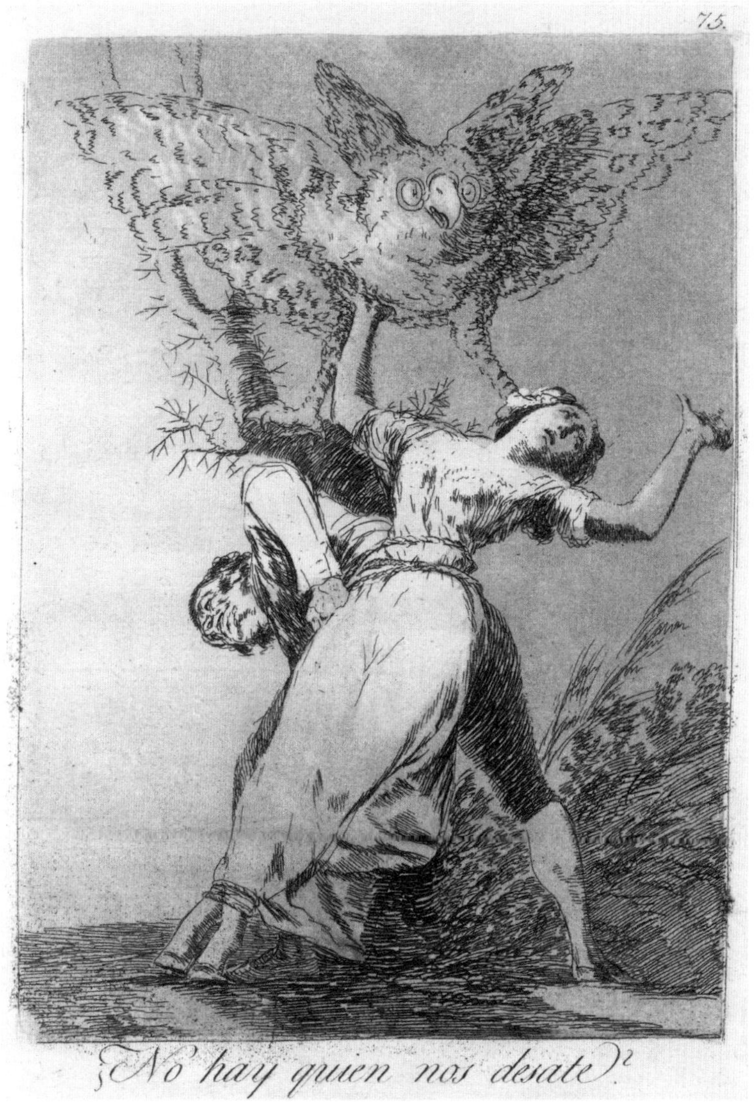

Figure 4.20.
"*¿No hay quién nos desate?*" ("Is there no one who can untie us?"), *Caprichos*, no. 75, 1797–98, published 1799. Etching, and burnished aquatint, 21.8×15.2 cm.

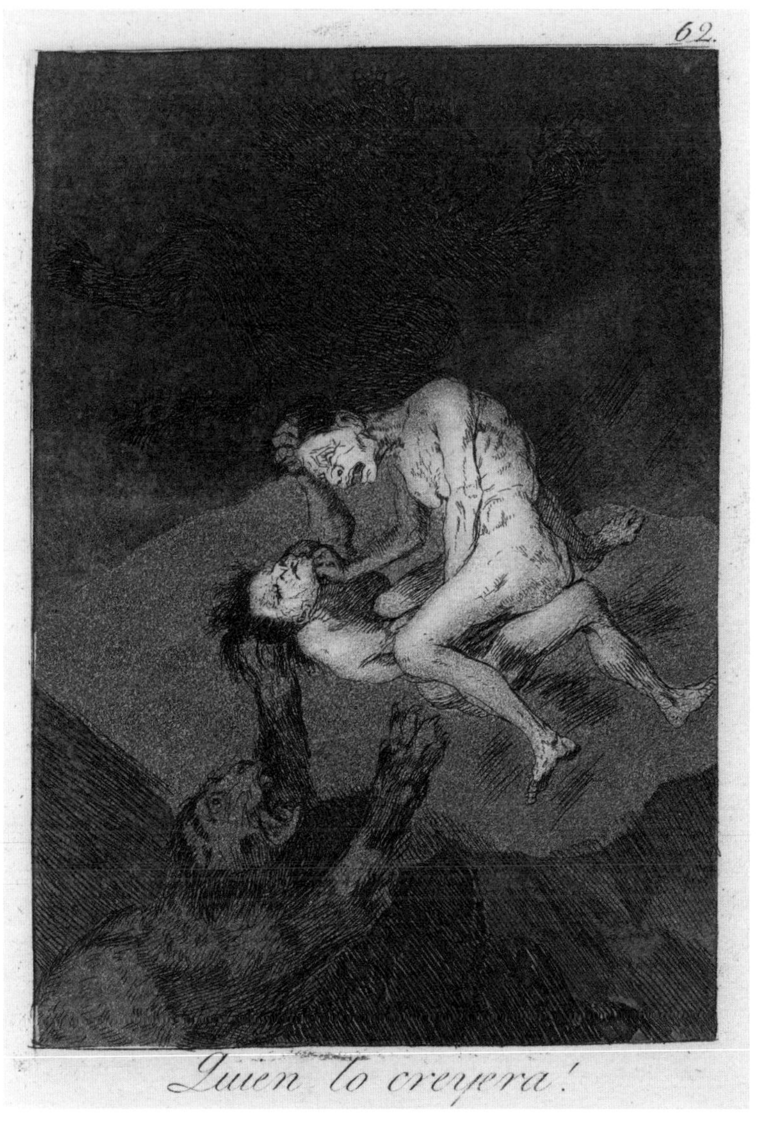

Figure 4.21.
"*¿Quién lo creyera?*" ("Who could believe it?"), *Caprichos*, no. 62, 1797–98, published 1799. Etching burnished aquatint, and burin, 20.3×15.1 cm.

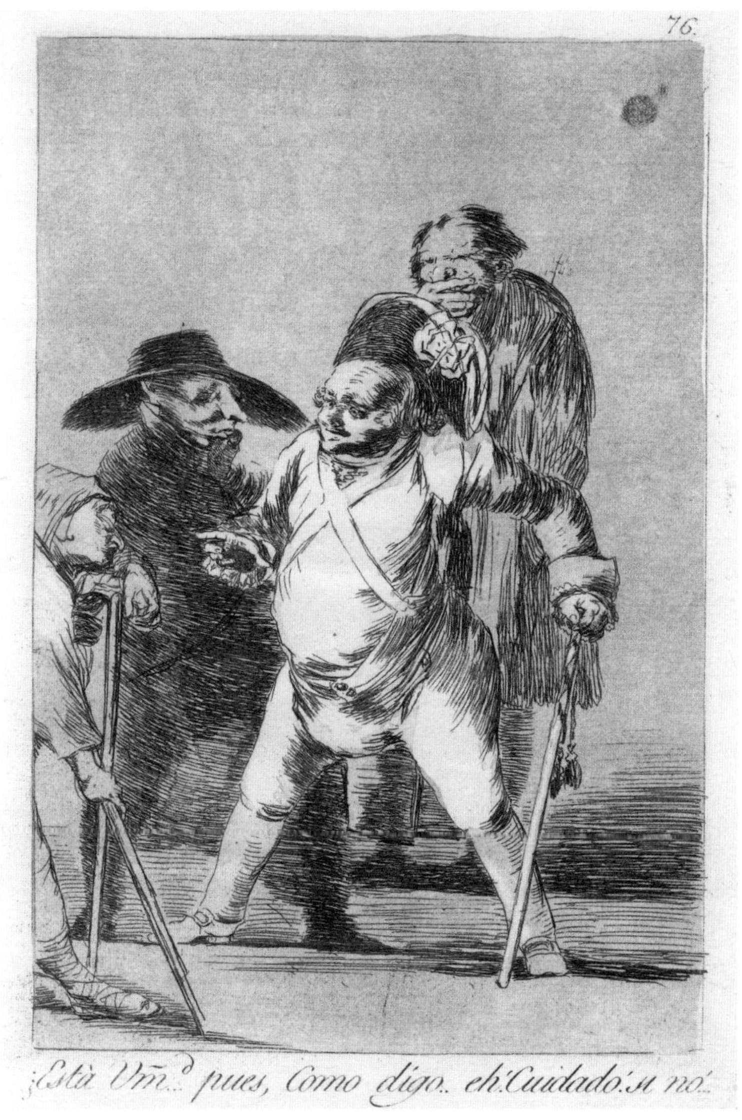

Figure 4.22.
"¿Está Vmd…pues, Como digo…eh! Cuidado! si no…" ("You understand?…Well, as I say…
eh! Look out! Otherwise…"), *Caprichos*, no. 76, 1797–98, published 1799.
Etching, burnished aquatint, and drypoint, 21.7 × 15.2 cm.

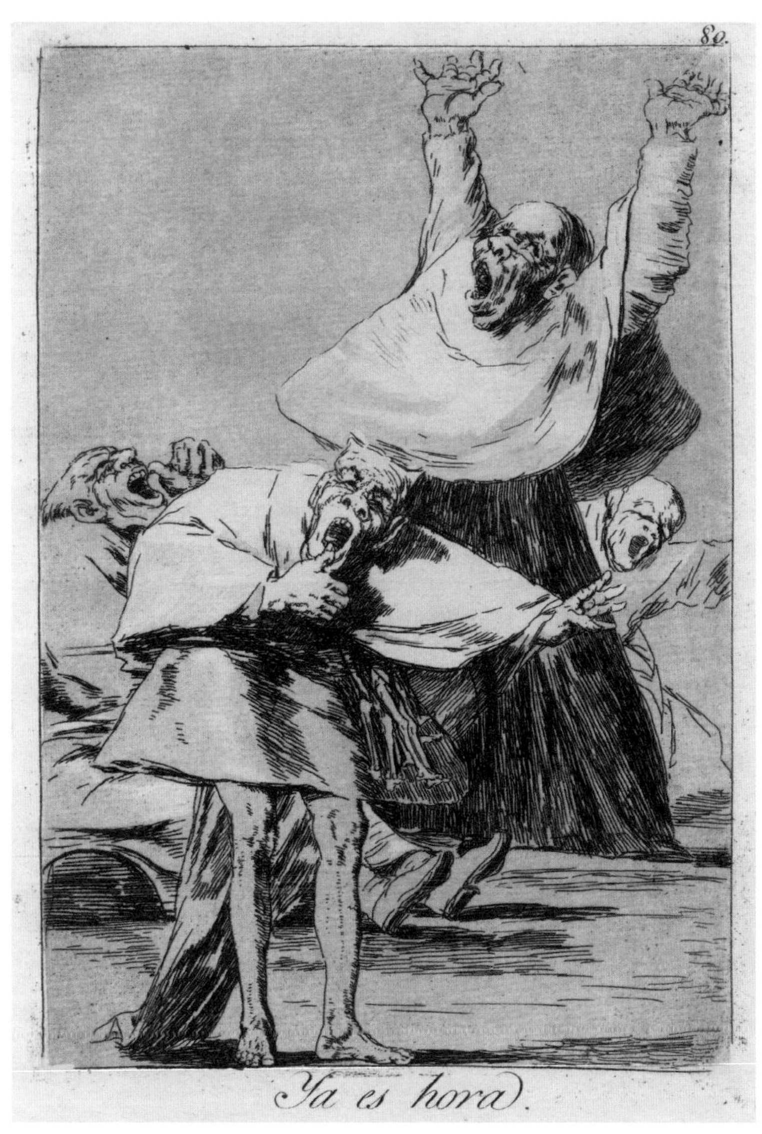

Figure 4.23.
"*Ya es hora*" ("It is time now"), *Caprichos,* no. 80, 1797–98, published 1799.
Etching, burnished aquatint, drypoint, and burin, 21.7×15.2 cm.

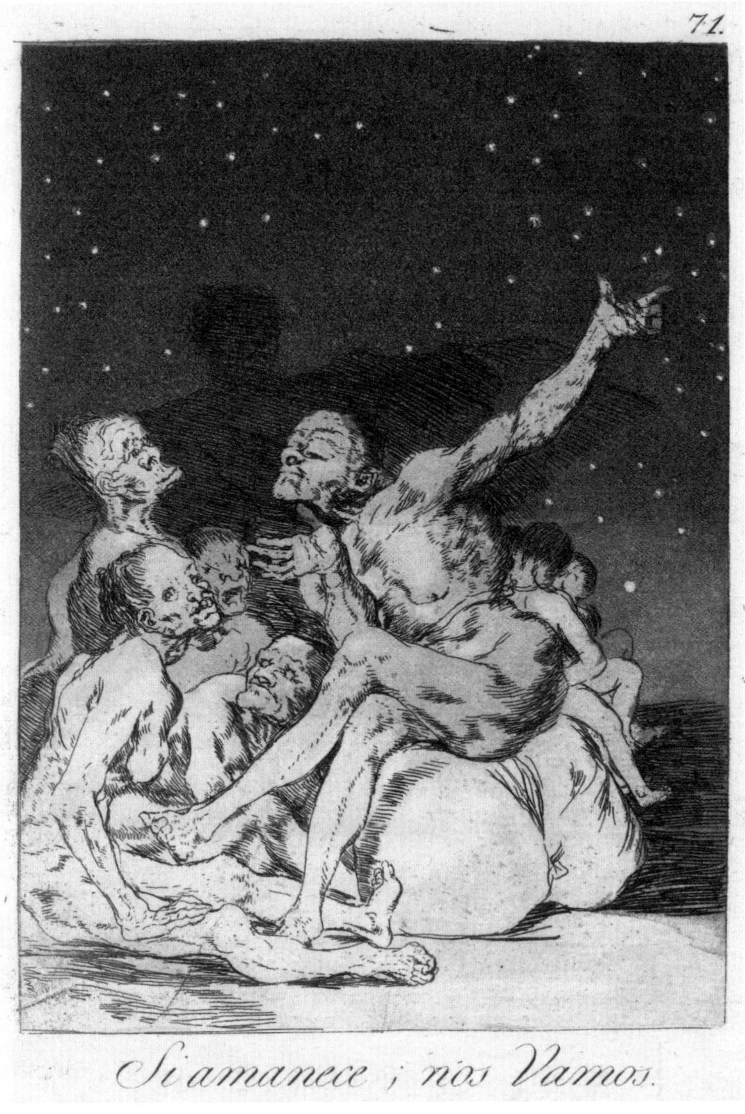

Figure 4.24.
"*Si amanece, nos vamos*" ("When day breaks, we will be off"), *Caprichos*, no. 71, 1797–98, published 1799. Etching, burnished aquatint, and burin, 20.2 × 15.2 cm.

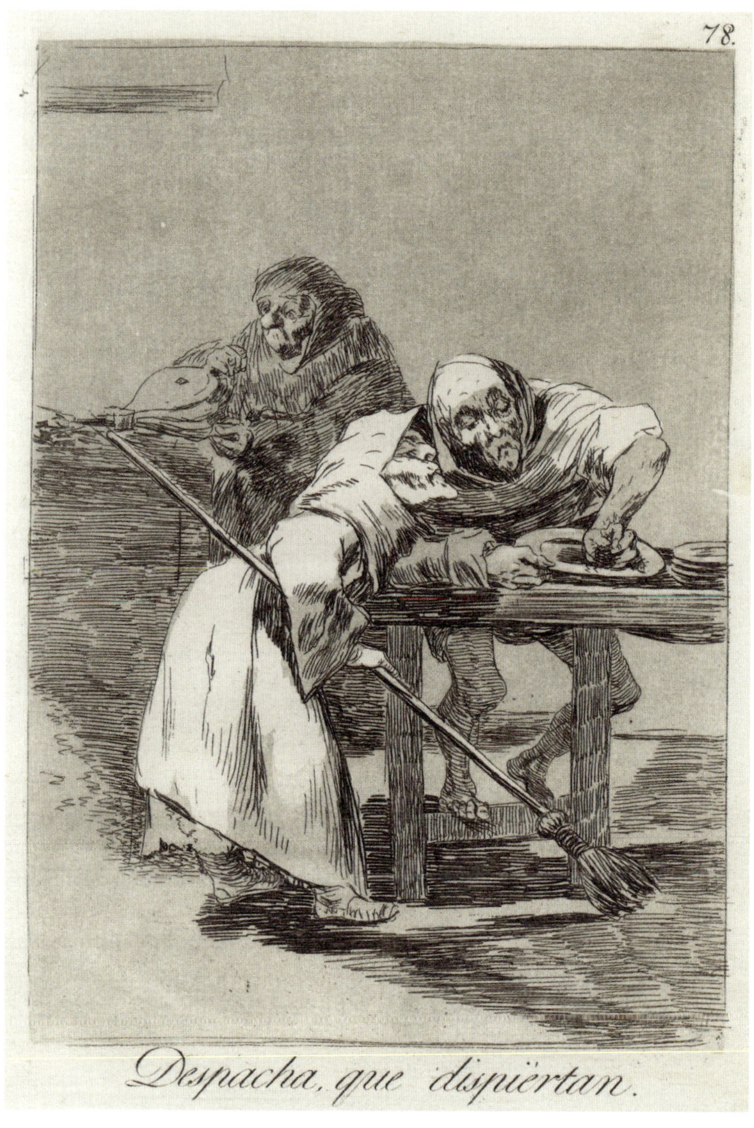

Figure 4.25.
"*Despacha, que dispiertan* [sic]" ("Hurry up, they are waking"), *Caprichos*, no. 78, 1797–98, published 1799. Etching and burnished aquatint, 21.8×15.2 cm.

the *Caprichos*. A number of the later images in the second half of the *Caprichos* lead up to this final plate. The great shadow in the background of no. 71 ("*Si amanece, nos vamos*" ["When day breaks, we will be off"], Figure 4.24) points ironically to the threat that daylight poses to the horrible creatures whose activities thrive at night.

In no. 78, "*Despacha, que dispiertan* [sic]" ("Hurry up, they are waking," Figure 4.25), night provides concealment for whatever these sorry figures might be doing as they finish cleaning the kitchen (the Ayala manuscript commentary suggests they are on a binge). Other figures make sure to steal a drink before the dawn (no. 79, "*Nadie nos ha visto*" ["Nobody has seen us"]).

Once we have seen all this and more, no. 80 (Figure 4.23) signals a return to the day, that is, to a world in which everyone seems to work hard to avoid recognizing what is true and in which nobody is able to see the contradictions in which they are enmeshed, except perhaps the artist with a critical gaze. In both parts of the *Caprichos*, the captions help signal those contradictions. But the further irony is that the captions can do this only from the outside and that even from the outside, they have no ability to change the things to which they point. But perhaps that was enough. The *Caprichos* were clearly a disruptive form of seeing and were withdrawn from sale in the same year they appeared in print after only twenty-seven copies had been sold.

CHAPTER FIVE

Conflicts of the Faculties:

Goya and Kant

The drama of the Enlightenment has often been conceived as a struggle between the secular illuminations of reason and the archaic forces of darkness, superstition, and deceit, whose resurgence threatens to undermine the rational world. On the one side stands a vision of human beings as guided by rational ideals, as obedient to the claims of reason, and as respectful of the inward, rational call of duty and of the moral law; in contrast stands the vision of a figure such as Goya, attesting to the persistence of all that is archaic, demonic, and repressed in enlightened cultural life. It may of course seem that in doing so, Goya roundly contradicts or simply refuses the project of Enlightenment, rejecting out of hand the Enlightenment's faith in reason and its attempts to justify morality through it. In Arthur Danto's review of the influential catalogue and accompanying essays *Goya and the Spirit of Enlightenment*, for instance, the *Caprichos* are described as the complete antithesis of the Enlightenment's moral world. They show us "whores and fools, bawds and ninnies, thieves and asses, all engaged in mutual exploitation, with menacing birds and animals as witnesses.... There is not even a God to save us. The best we can do is acknowledge the black truth."[1] Similarly, it is plausible to regard paintings such as *The Third of May, 1808* and the etchings in the *Disasters of War* as Goya's attempt to reckon with the corrosive effects of the Enlightenment on social and political life.[2] While it may be tempting to see Goya's work on balance as the result of a rejection of the Enlightenment views that he sometimes embraced, this has long been recognized as insufficient by the contributors to *Goya and the Spirit of Enlightenment*. Still more apt is the view of Tzvetan Todorov who clearly positions Goya as more enlightened than the Enlightenment itself: "His thought has its point of departure in the spirit of Enlightenment that he finds around himself; but, quite quickly, he finds its limits and discovers its blind spots. Educated in the spirit of Enlightenment, he learned how to discover the things the Enlightenment leaves in the dark. The nocturnal forces [that] direct human behavior no less than the will or reason does."[3]

What is less often recognized are the complexities and contradictions of the Enlightenment. In mapping Goya's relationship to the Enlightenment, we need an understanding of Enlightenment that takes its internal tensions fully into account. Indeed, we do well to recognize that the Enlightenment was a field of never fully resolved internal contradictions that some figures did indeed *attempt* to resolve rather than as the site of a simple opposition between, for example, an ethics based in reason and abandonment to no ethics at all or between the privileged rational faculties of thought and will (as exemplified by philosophy above all) and those more worldly domains, such as law, medicine, engineering, agriculture, and the arts. To regard the Enlightenment culture as a field of sometimes irreconcilable principles, regardless of the adherence to reason as a way to believe otherwise, may in turn help in dealing with the interpretive difficulties posed by an artist (for example, Goya) who respects the Enlightenment's implicit ideals in certain genres (for example, portraiture) while thoroughly challenging its world in so many others (for example, the *Disasters of War* and the Black Paintings of the Quinta del Sordo). Rather than resolve the apparent contradictions within Goya's work by reference to personal and biographical factors that tend to lead us away from the images themselves, we can see each of the various frameworks through which Goya's work demands interpretation as independent and irreducible; the demands the images make of the viewer, whether entirely sustainable or not, are not meant to be synthesized under some single grand scheme. This displaces the overly schematic contrast between Goya the painter of "light" and Goya the painter of "darkness" in favor of a view in which the dominating trope of the Enlightenment (that is, light) is itself exposed as resting on grounds that it cannot fully illuminate and indeed as proposing projects for which its own principles cannot always find uniform foundational supports.

Consider the conceptual instability inherent in the very notion of a rational critique. As is evident in the grammatical genitive in Kant's title, *Kritik* der *reinen Vernunft, Critique* of *Pure Reason*), it is difficult to discern what is the subject and what the object of rational critique.[4] If reason is the *object*, then who or what maintains the vigilance that would be required in order to keep reason vigilant and pure? And if reason is itself the *subject*, then who — whose desires, imperatives, or rules — can motivate and propel this critique forward? In Goya, a similar instability is exemplified in, among other ways, the absence of a single position from which to read the caption that accompanies the central image of the *Caprichos*, discussed above, "*El sueño de la razón produce monstruos*" ("The sleep of reason produces monsters," see Figure 3.29, above). When taken in conjunction with the self-portrait frontispiece of that collection, the ambiguity of this image-caption pair suggests the tendency of Enlightenment rationality to reverse and cancel itself, that is, for it to negate itself by the very deployment of critical reason.[5] While signaling the consequences of a failure to maintain the vigilance and self-regulation that the successful exercise of reason would demand, the image also reminds us that the activities of reason may themselves produce monsters.[6]

Initially, it might seem that the autonomous proceedings of reason in Kant's first *Critique* are simply an effort to continue and perfect the project begun with the Cartesian aim to keep merely contingent, external factors (including historical and empirical ones) from impinging on the work of pure thought. But in this case, it remains unclear how pure reason could be differentiated into the separate functions or faculties that describe the modes of knowledge necessary for it to operate in the world, including the functions necessary for ethics. This might explain why a thinker such as Kant was so hard-pressed to affirm pure reason's relevance to the realm of practice, as he does both in the *Critique of Pure Reason* and in his lectures on ethics. While the notion of "*pure practical* reason" is not entirely oxymoronic, it does rest on the thinnest reed of thought. Similarly, if Kant's goal were simply to analyze empirical knowledge under the scrutiny of pure reason, he would not have felt obliged to pursue each *Critique* through a dialectic in which reason proposes to address its own internal crises and to correct its own misguidance through a series of self-regulating clarifications. This attempt at self-correction is no doubt an essential element of Kant's project of critique, but it also ensures that reason travels within its own orbit, scarcely touching the external world.

Kant was wedded to the idea of reason's autonomy, and so unlike Goya, he presupposed the irrelevance of the preexisting contexts of belief — contexts that reason saw itself as having successfully overcome:

> I appeal to the most obstinate dogmatist, whether the proof of the continued existence of our soul after death, derived from the simplicity of substance; or of the freedom of the will in opposition to a general mechanism of nature, drawn from the subtle and objective practical necessity; or of the existence of God, deduced from the concept of an *ens realissimum* — the contingency of the changeable, and the necessity of a prime mover — has ever been able to pass beyond the limits of the schools, to penetrate the public mind, or to exercise the slightest influence on its convictions.[7]

This was Kant's point of departure for his interpretation of human freedom and the basis for a critique of religion in which a series of potential illusions resulting from illegitimate, "morally transcendent" ideas are seen to result in fanaticism, superstitions, false illuminations, and thaumaturgy — "sheer aberrations of a reason going beyond its proper limits and that too for a purpose fancied to be moral (pleasing to God)."[8] Kant's critique of religion in this passage from *Religion within the Limits of Reason Alone* is fully consistent with the goals and methods established in the first *Critique*, where he wrote that "criticism alone can sever the root of *materialism, fatalism, atheism, free-thinking, fanaticism,* and *superstition*, which can be injurious universally; as well as of *idealism* and *skepticism*, which are dangerous chiefly to the Schools, and hardly allow of being handed on to the public."[9] The position that Kant explicitly takes in *Religion within the Limits of Reason Alone* is that the reliance on the power of grace is an aberration of thought that cannot be reconciled with the workings of reason, "for the employment of this idea would presuppose a rule concerning the good which (for a particular end) we ourselves must *do* in order to accomplish something, whereas to await a work of grace means exactly the opposite."[10] Kant resolves the dilemma — inherited from thinkers such as Pascal, according to whom belief is valid insofar as it is absurd (because nothing rational can be said about faith) — by making the possibility of faith dependent on the limits of knowledge ("I have therefore found it necessary to deny *knowledge*, in order to make room for *faith*").[11]

As discussed in Chapter 1, it is customary to regard the process of secularization as a function of the loss of spiritual confidence or as the preservation and transposition of practices whose original function and purpose lie in the past into the contemporary world.[12] Indeed, in writing of Goya, Fred Licht thought that all of modern religious art could be described in these terms but seemed only to see the downsides: "Of all the many paintings of religious subject matter that were painted during the nineteenth and twentieth centuries," he says, "not one can lay claim to being an *opus sacra*. Even the finest — Delacroix's *Lamentation* or Puvis de Chavannes' *Legend of St. Genevieve* — *moving* though they be as works of art or as personal expressions of faith, never had the force to function in the manner of altarpieces — to function, that is, as cynosures of communal worship."[13] And yet Goya shows that while the process of secularization may originate in a need to overcome the irrationality inherent within the presecular world, the result is highly *un*stable and *in*complete.

Consider once again the frescoes in San Antonio de la Florida in Madrid. On one level, their purpose was to place the miracle of Saint Anthony within an ordinary, secular context, set in its turn within a local church. This is no doubt true, but the fact is not just that certain elements in the fresco, such as the painted balcony, roundly contradict the spiritual character of the space customary for the lofty interior domes of churches or that the heavenly figures appear to be subject to the physical effects of gravity. Rather, it is that this spiritual scene of the miracle is rendered contingent on a precarious perspectival aesthetic. Because the image as a whole invokes a demand for coherence that it cannot meet and is rendered on a surface that would distort the figures necessary to its own composition, Goya must purposefully alter the conventions of artificial perspective applicable to paintings made on flat, planar surfaces in order to show something we can find aesthetically believable and "true." In the process, Goya draws on the conventions of earlier, rococo painting in order to reveal the degree to which the procedures of representation that had become dominant in the Enlightenment world are not so much a response to a secularization process occurring autonomously within the broad field of "reason," but are also failed attempts to limit the tendency of religious beliefs to exceed the contexts they establish for themselves, notwithstanding the dilemmas that the apparent "solution" produces.

The San Antonio frescoes have often been seen as alien to established painterly conventions. For Licht, their distortions suggest "the first forebodings of a mind that had given up a traditional faith without converting to a new and equally 'illusory' system of apprehending the purposes of our world."[14] If this is indeed so, it is only a foreshadowing of a fact so emphatically revealed in some of Goya's other works — that the Enlightenment proved unable to eradicate or to subsume the ethic of salvation presupposed by religious art. Indeed, Goya characteristically takes the salvational moment as the occasion of an encounter with a set of forces that neither religion nor reason had the power to uproot.

Consider his painting from 1788, *St. Francis Borgia at the Deathbed of an Impenitent* (Figure 5.1) in this regard. Goya's preliminary sketch shows the dying man patiently waiting for the saint to administer the last rites (Figure 5.2). While angels are poised to welcome the soul of the departed on the extreme right, on the left, a devil sneaks away, foiled by the saint's miraculous intervention. While the sketch may be read as a "presecular" allegory of enlightenment, the final version of the painting and Goya's earlier oil sketch represent a radical break both with the models on which they may have been based — especially Sebastiano Ricci's *Saint Anthony of Padua Healing a Young Man* and *San Gaetano Comforting a Moribund Sinner*.[15] In Goya's version, the dying man has convulsed into stiffness. His body lies across the bed, and the saint seems to recoil from him. (Why a saint would fear death is mysterious indeed.) His left hand is thrown up in a gesture that speaks both sanctity and repulsion, while his right hand remains scarcely able to control the miraculous, efficacious sign of salvation, the crucifix. Moreover, the crucifix spurts crimson blood, as if to insist on the material origins of religious beliefs that had, through the process of secularization, been transposed into purely figural terms. And instead of the saving power of angels, Goya has placed monsters over the dying man, as if to shock the viewer into remembering the drama of transgression and evil that had become diminished by the claims of moral reason in the Enlightenment world.[16]

In Goya, the impossibility of complete secularization derives from the ineradicability of evil, which returns, like the Freudian repressed, to remind us of the ways in which all that is earlier in culture continues to hold us bound. Those forces pervade the Black Paintings and the *Disasters of War*, the *Disparates*, as well as many other works. The images of incarceration, including the small, but exceptionally powerful *Yard with Lunatics* (Figure 5.3), offer countless instances in which something older, more archaic, pierces through the veil of civilization with which the Enlightenment had allied itself.

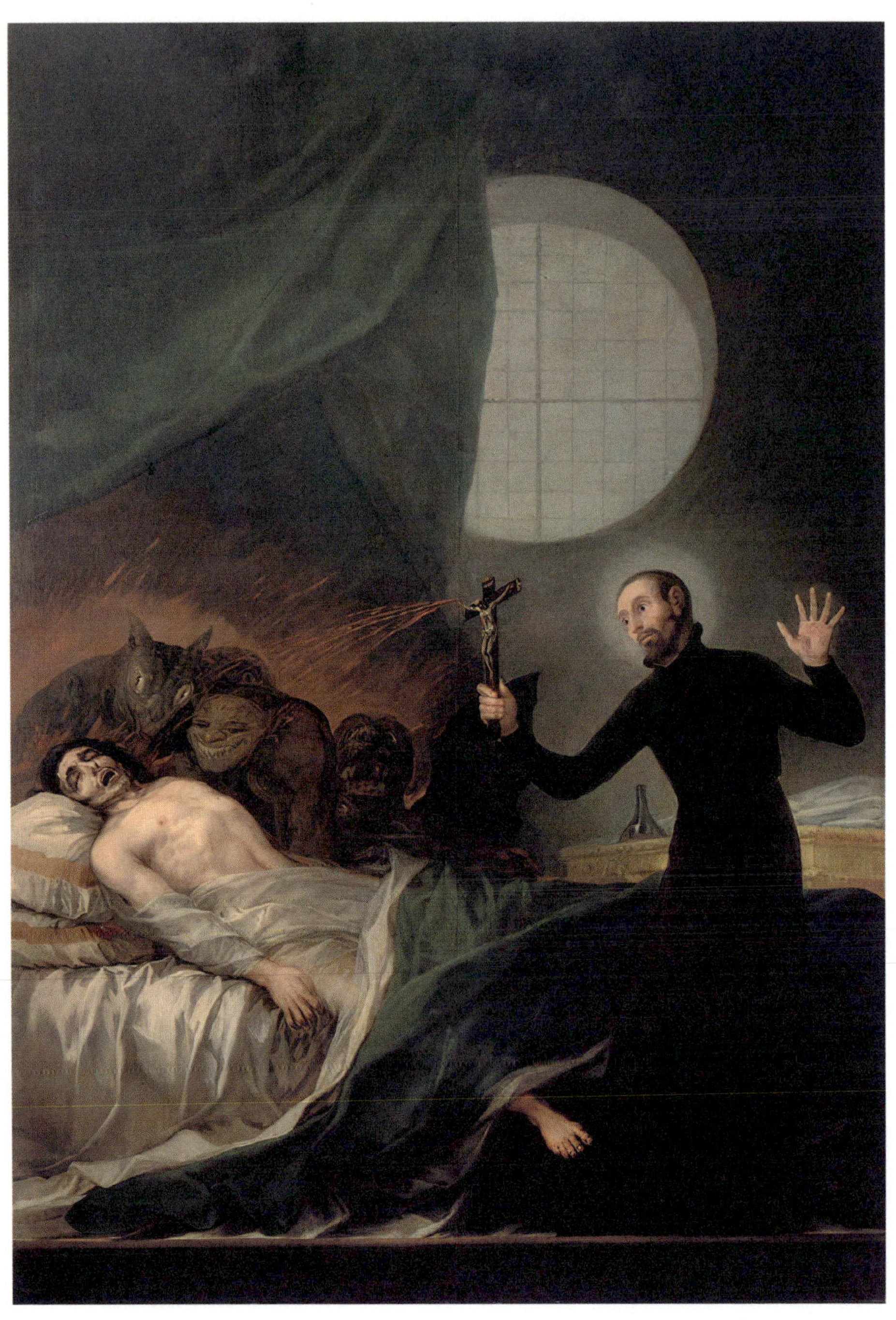

St. Francis Borgia at the Deathbed of an Impenitent, 1788. Oil on canvas, 350×300 cm.
Valencia Cathedral, Valencia, Spain.

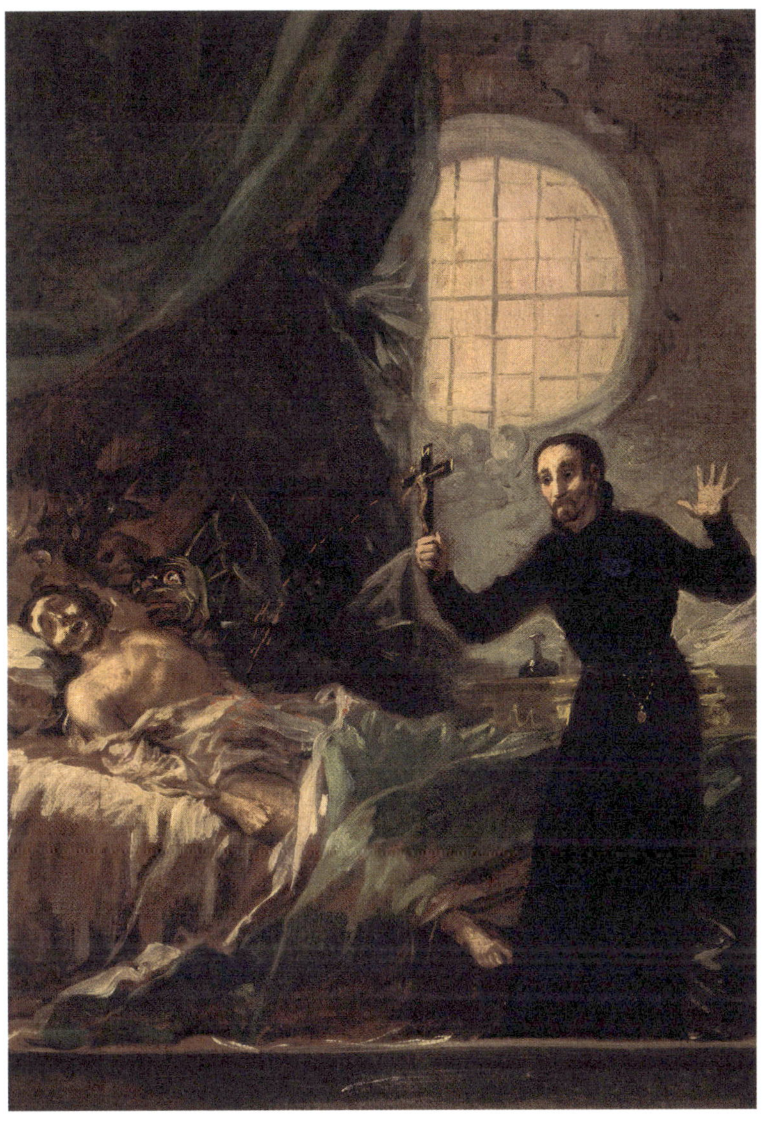

Figure 5.2.
Sketch for *St. Francis Borgia at the Deathbed of an Impenitent*, ca. 1788.
Oil on canvas, 38×29.3 cm. Private collection.

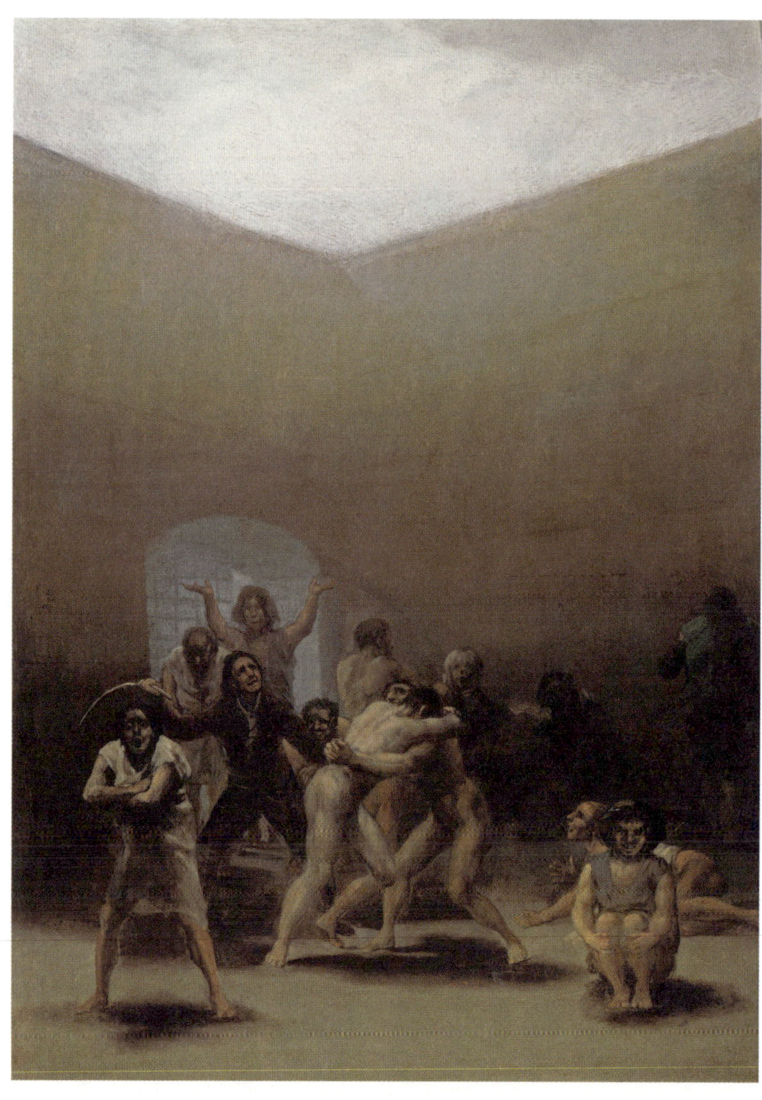

Figure 5.3.
Yard with Lunatics, ca. 1794. Oil on tinplate, 32.7 × 43.8 cm.
Meadows Museum, Dallas, Texas.

Seen from Kant's point of view, however, there was a significant difference between the idea of radical, preexistent evil and the evil that springs from the free will of human beings. The latter allows human goodness to emerge as part of the Enlightenment's self-validating story of progress: scripture

> finds a place for evil at the creation of the world, yet not in man, but in a *spirit* of an originally loftier destiny. This is the *first* beginning of all evil represented as inconceivable by us (for whence came evil to that spirit?); but man is represented as having fallen into evil only *through seduction*, and hence as being *not basically* corrupt (even as regards his original predisposition to good) but rather as still capable of an improvement, in contrast to a seducing *spirit*, that is, a being for whom temptation of the flesh cannot be accounted as an alleviation of guilt. For man, therefore, who despite a corrupted heart yet possesses a good will, there remains hope of a return to the good from which he has strayed.[17]

Indeed, it could be said that according to this view, a precondition for the achievement of the Enlightenment is a dramatic reduction, if not the elimination, of the archaic drama of transgression and salvation that Goya refuses to ignore. But as Goya's Inquisition images suggest, when transgression becomes socially normalized, religion ceases to act as the source of authoritative laws — including laws that help hold society together — and becomes transformed instead into the means by which superstitions are forcibly imposed and function as forms of state power. (See, for example, Figure 5.4, *"Aquellos polbos"* ["Those specks of dust"].)

Moreover, insofar as the secularization process demonstrates one of the principal ways in which modern institutions may attempt to appropriate and normalize the authority of religious beliefs, the ethical constraints that those subjects would accept cannot be understood without an account of the social and historical perspectives that Goya refuses to exclude — and on which he casts a sharply critical eye. Thus, his response to the Enlightenment is inextricably bound up with a critique of the illusory (because falsely self-regulating)

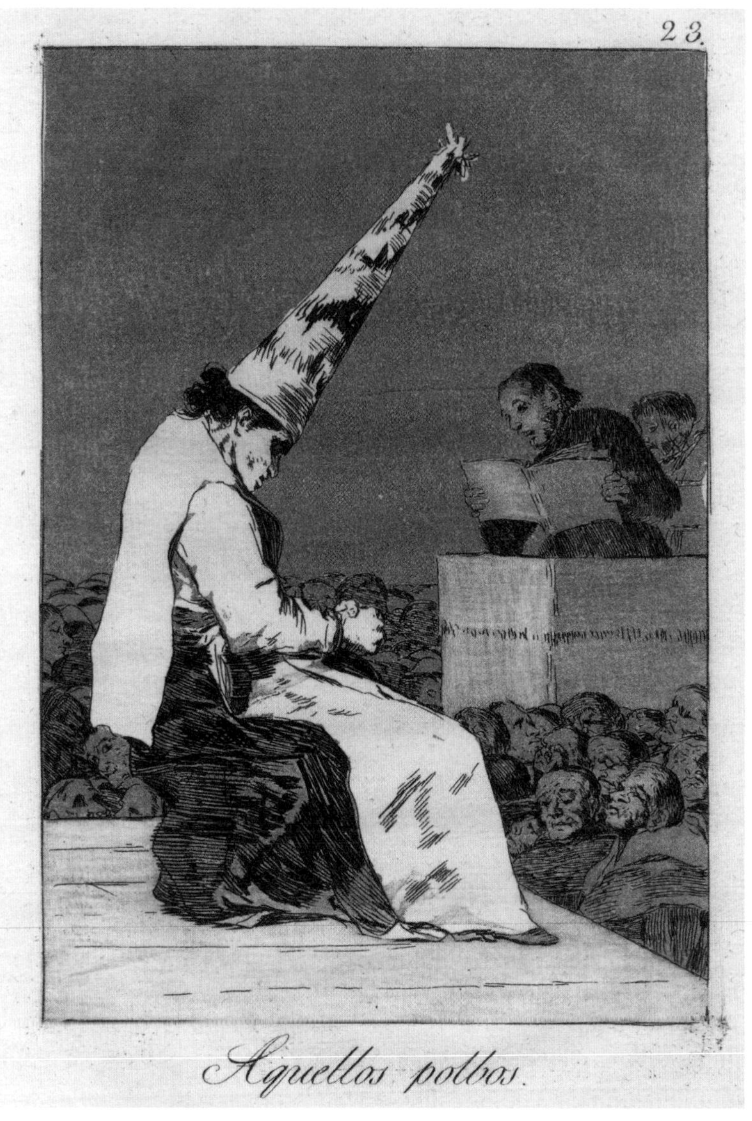

Figure 5.4.
Sketch for *"Aquellos polbos"* ("Those specks of dust"), *Caprichos*, no. 23, ca. 1797.
Red wash and red chalk on silk paper, 20×14.6 cm. Museo del Prado, Madrid.

perspectives of the modern social world. Within this world, the members of civil society (for example, the bourgeoisie) had come to regard themselves as the privileged "subjects" of history in a way that required the repudiation of the very processes through which their existence, as a social class, was brought about. Put in other terms, bourgeois society offered a way in which the contradictions inherent in modern enlightened culture could provisionally be settled[18]; but for Goya, the characteristic Enlightenment distinctions between rationality and superstition, as between the claims of reason and the impulses of desire, could not so easily be quieted. Whereas bourgeois society offered a restructuring of those tensions in the interest of creating a more habitable world — as the tapestry cartoons on the surface reflect — Goya suggests that this settlement presupposes a vision of the Enlightenment as the self-validating completion of history, which no social class could have the authority to claim. I will return to the question of history below.

To be sure, Enlightenment thinkers hardly saw all the claims of reason as uncontested. Moreover, they clearly understood that different forms of reason could, in practical matters, assert very different kinds of authority, including claims for the superiority of any one of them over all the others. Kant was especially determined to assert the priority of philosophy among the faculties of the university — specifically, its priority over the faculties of religion, law, and medicine. That is the explicit subject of the essays, *The Conflict of the Faculties*, collected and published just a year before Goya's *Caprichos*. The problems, as Kant states it, were that "the biblical theologian . . . draws his teachings not from reason but from the *Bible*; the professor of law gets his, not from natural law, but from the *law of the land*; and the professor of medicine does not draw his *method of therapy as practiced on the public* from the physiology of the human body but from *medical regulations*."[19] Each one ought to recognize its contingent nature and not attempt to mix its authority with that drawn "truly" from reason — which is to say, not attempt to claim for itself the grounds that philosophy alone can rightly assert. This has the effect of placing philosophy in a position of greater authority than any of the other faculties, which is to say that it is fundamental. This was Kant's way of resolving the conflict among the faculties. Perhaps most importantly, philosophy takes the place that theology once held as "queen of the sciences." In contrast to the faculty of theology specifically, Kant's argument was that the philosophical faculty has and must sustain freedom of expression, that is, that it must be able to have its rational arguments answered by rational arguments rather than by the equivalent of intellectual force. As regards ethics, it means finding the basis for obligations through the resources of *pure practical* reason and not from the laws of any particular land. And as regards history, it means adopting the stance of a neutral spectator who can discern the alignment between the emergence of critical reason and the arc of progress.

I will consider these issues in relation to Goya in what follows, but first it should be said that it would be mistaken to believe that the principles of Enlightenment and the adherence to reason always show up discursively, in the form of reasoned arguments. There is a visually grounded way of viewing the world that reflects the Enlightenment perspective that Kant inherited from Descartes and that Goya inherited from the pictorial tradition of the Renaissance, leading up to Velásquez (especially in relation to works such as *The Surrender at Breda*, *Las Meninas*, and the Rokeby *Venus*). As discussed in the previous chapter, this is the perspective of representation, which relies centrally on the power of framing, both visually and conceptually. Kant's first *Critique*, as further developed in the second, presented the practice of world representation as subtended by the constructive powers of the self-regulating subject. Goya recognizes those powers by acknowledging the prior pictorial tradition in the way he learned to construct images but shows in addition that the demands (of truth, authenticity, self-legislation, freedom, and autonomy) internal to that culture could not be met by the practice of representation deemed essential to its constitution. Hence, he also challenges the visual conventions that he learned. His interest is indeed in invention, rather than representation, understanding that the kind of invention he famously refers to when writing of the *Caprichos* requires a critique of the conventions that preceded him. Representation ignores the presecular history of the (modern) world and dismisses the persistence of any of the archaic forces mentioned above. It is for Kant a form of world construction that is dependent on the belief that there are no intelligible essences, no "auratic" presences, no preordained qualities, and certainly none that do not flow from reason itself; more emphatically stated, reason *produces* the forms of the world, which supersede those of nature. Representation is construction: "reason has insight only into that which it produces after a plan of its own, and that it must not allow itself to be kept, as it were, in nature's leading-strings."[20]

The supersession of intelligible essences by humanly constructed forms is of practical importance insofar as it allows for the contextualization of actions within the world and for the openness of contexts to the possibility of reconfiguration from within. It secures the possibility of human freedom and in turn underpins some central Enlightenment tenets about ethics. (I will return to this question in greater detail below.) And yet the theory of representation fails to account for the process by which the subject's formative powers themselves came into existence. Indeed, the Kantian account of reason conceals the problem of its own origins by masking the genealogical processes through which the framework of representation evolved; additionally, it is hard-pressed to deal with instances in which it proves insufficient. As in Derrida's analysis in the essay "Parergon" of the image of the *Colossus* attributed to Goya,[21] it is not only that the representational frame is unable to accomplish the work of regulation it is intended to carry out and so undergoes a process of internal reversal and collapse. The category of the sublime can help provide an account of such situations, and in Kant's version, though hardly in Goya's, the sublime ultimately provides reassuring support for the exercise of rational powers. The additional problem with representation is that it fails to question

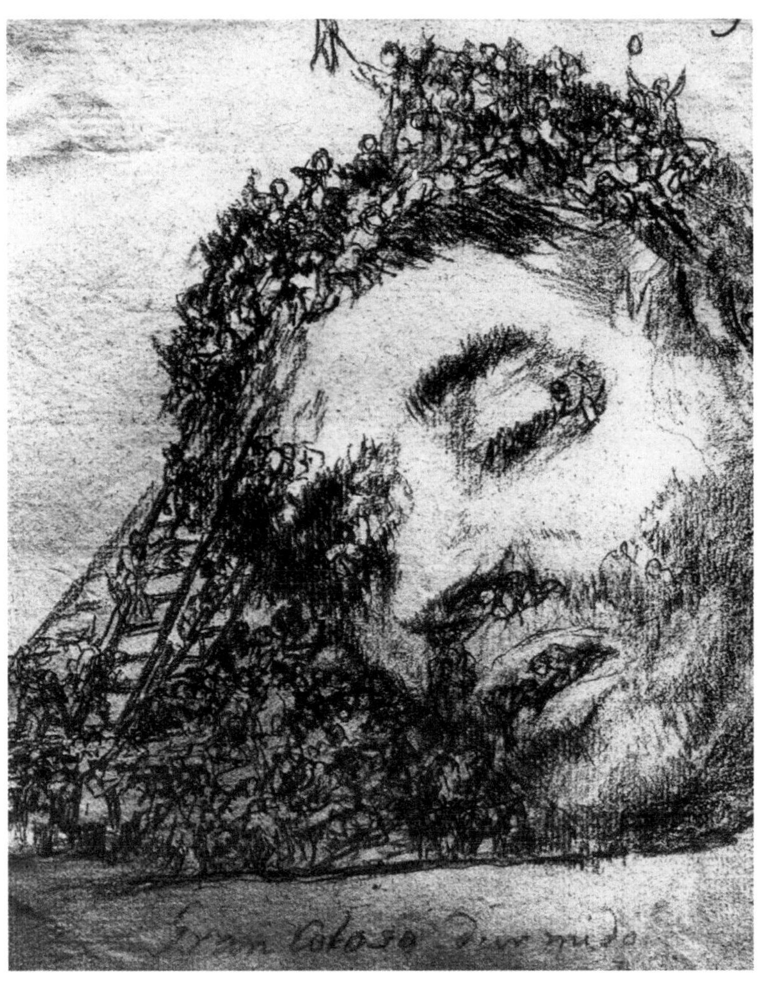

Figure 5.5.
"Gran coloso dormido" ("Large sleeping giant"), ca. 1824–28. Lithographic pencil,
19.2 × 15.4 cm, Album G3. The State Hermitage Museum, St. Petersburg.

the understanding that it does in fact have the power to create or origi-nate a world. It is not inherently self-conscious, even though a figure such as Velásquez certainly made it so). As happens with Kant's resolu-tion of the "conflict of the faculties," the overarching thrust of world representation is to construe the spheres of history, society, desire, and belief as contingent on and implicitly as inferior to itself. Whereas for Kant, the power of the subject to frame or constitute a world within which action is possible and where history bends to the arc of moral progress follows from the power of reason (more about which in rela-tion to history below), Goya's work would seem to suggest that no frame can adequately contain the world that the imagination attempts to present. The *Colossus* that Derrida discussed may only be attributed to Goya, but the authenticity of the "*Gran coloso dormido*" (Figure 5.5) from the so-called "First Bordeaux Album" (1824–28) is not in doubt and shows us a figure born of the imagination and its burgeoning fears that exceeds the framing power of reason and that, indeed, cannot inhabit any presentable form. The particular force of the image, not unrelated to many of the *Disasters of War*, derives from the contradic-tory effort to show what cannot be represented.

The example of the colossus is but one in which Goya shows that the drama of the Enlightenment amounts to something more complex than an allegorized narrative in which the stubborn forces of dark-ness are vanquished by the power of reason's light. Thus, despite the fact that critics have for many years interpreted Goya's oil sketch for the work known conventionally as *Truth Rescued by Time, Witnessed by History* (Figure 5.6) as conveying a positive ethical and historical force wholly consistent with the progressive Enlightenment narrative, I would suggest that Goya's fundamental resistance to allegorization in this and most other works helps reveal the limitations of the Enlight-enment, including in its interpretation of history and in its ethical ambitions.

I will return to this particular painting for what it says about history below,[22] but first it bears noting how Goya's works can be construed as having an *ethical* force, one quite different from that

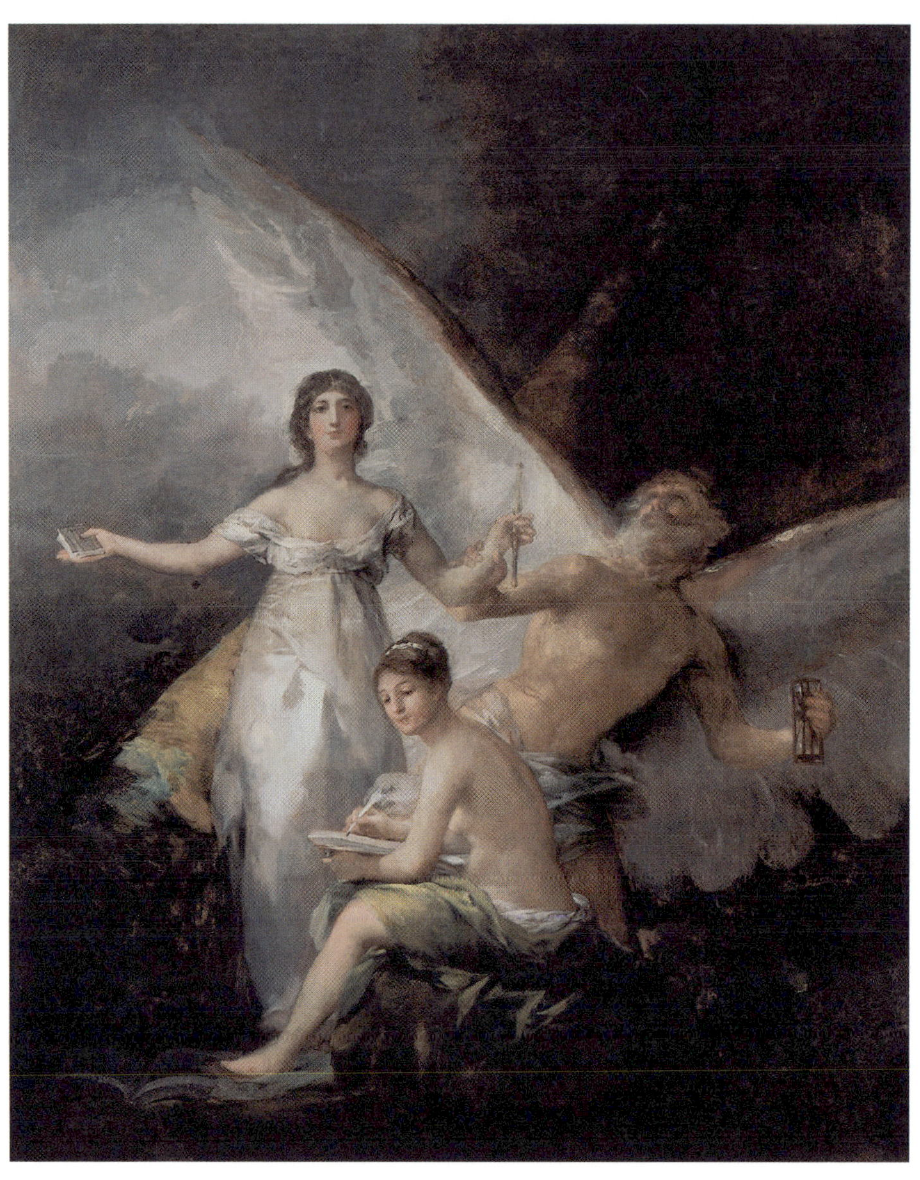

Figure 5.6.
Truth Rescued by Time, Witnessed by History, ca. 1812. Oil on canvas, 294 × 244 cm.
Nationalmuseum, Stockholm.

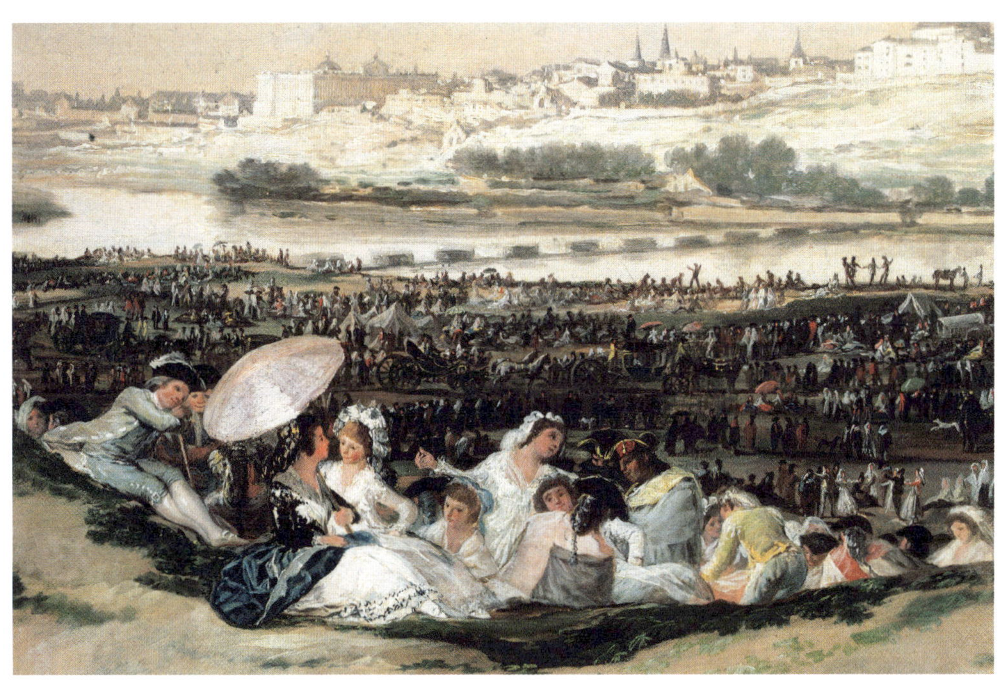

Figure 5.7.
Meadow of San Isidro (detail), 1788. Oil on canvas.
Museo del Prado, Madrid.

imagined by Kant. While Goya devotes his attention to exemplary individuals — especially in the portraits that we will discuss in Chapter 8, he also locates an ethics in the way a given work is structured. That ethics relates to the obligations to which the viewer must respond in order for the image to be apprehended as making sense. The force of that structural obligation often tugs and pulls against the ostensible "subject matter" of the work. To take one example, consider the *Meadow of San Isidro* (Figure 5.7). The work might be regarded as simply descriptive. As was not inappropriate for a tapestry image, it is about just what it shows, that is, a large-scale outdoor feast-day celebration on the banks of the Manzanares. Not surprisingly, perhaps, Goya identified it in these terms in a letter to his childhood friend, Martín Zapater.[23] The image shows a wholly secular celebration of a religious feast in which the religious element has been all but lost. The picture is further descriptive in social terms, in that the figures in the foreground are dressed in costumes clearly inspired by French tastes. But this depiction of the event and others of folk festivals clearly involved a simplification, an idealization of figures, reflecting a faith in the dignity, indeed, of the implicit nobility of humble people of the kind invoked by Rousseau. In that regard, the image goes beyond description and expresses a normative force, showing how one ought to celebrate and dress, taking the occasion of the celebration of the patron saint of Madrid as an opportunity to make the point. The painting models good dress and the good behavior that ought to accompany it, and quite emphatically so, given that this is a crowd scene, a gathering of the masses.[24] It is also a celebration of the city of Madrid of which San Isidro was the patron, here shown as a gleaming city on a hill in the far distance of the work. And knowing that the work was intended as the basis for a tapestry designed to hang in the bedroom of the *infantas* at the Pardo Palace, we can easily attribute that normative force to the implicit desire of the Spanish royal family to see themselves as benevolent and Enlightened rulers, that is, as inspired by French taste and as supporting the newly ascendant middle class.[25]

But the scene is almost too big to take in as a whole. In order to grasp it, the viewer is obliged to accept a convention that has nothing to do with the descriptive content or normative implications of the work. This is one of radical foreshortening, by which the scene is painted in the equivalent of an extreme wide-angle view. This view does not distort in the way a camera lens would typically distort at such a wide angle, but it does require that the tremendous difference between the detailed figures in the foreground and the relatively anonymous ones is exaggerated over what is in reality, that is, on canvas a very small amount of space. We can meet the obligation to apprehend the scene as a whole, but in order to do so, we must accept a tension between what description and norms ask and what visual representation requires. In other words, Goya's use of the rational convention of artificial perspective does not pretend that it can supersede the realities of secular social life. The formal resolution of the view of the meadow of San Isidro leaves contradictions intact without itself being subverted by them or without counting on an inversion of the happy world of the *pradera*, even though Goya was quite capable of doing just that, and in fact did so in the much later *Pilgrimage to San Isidro* (Figure 5.8), painted on the walls of the Quinta del Sordo — a snakelike image of huddled figures, a grotesque guitarist, shapes cloaked in black, and a landscape of sinister forms.

In the earlier image, the sense of an obligation imposed by the attempt at framing remains intact; in the latter one, the reality seems to overwhelm any sense of rational obligation. The image itself and the figures in it are driven by sheer force. But as I hope in addition to suggest, it is precisely this contrast between the acceptance, acknowledgment, or *willing* of a demand, in the case of the *Meadow of San Isidro* — a demand that remains attested at the level of representation regardless of the fact that it may remain unmet — and the inability to locate or fully frame an appropriate response to it in the *Pilgrimage* that may help us move beyond the interpretive challenges posed by some of Goya's works to a better understanding of the ways in which he challenges assumptions that underpin Enlightenment conceptions of ethics and morality.

To be sure, there is an important distinction to be made between morality and ethics. In broad terms, the former concerns good and evil; the latter concerns right and wrong. Is it possible to discern an ethics where moral claims cannot be established? There is much in modern, liberal, enlightened culture that would seem to believe so. (Consider the example of those who describe themselves as "ethically Christian," that is, whose life practices reflect a distinction between right and wrong but who do not accept religious grounds for

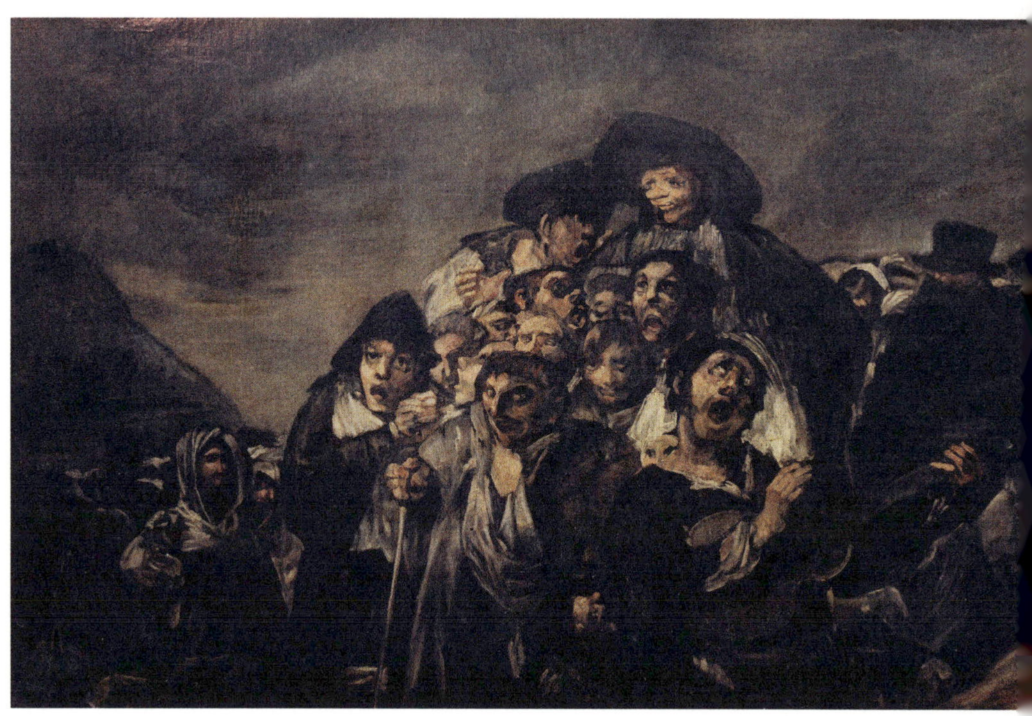

Figure 5.8.
The Pilgrimage to San Isidro, 1820–23. Mixed media mural transferred to canvas,
138.5×436 cm. Museo del Prado, Madrid.

determining good and evil.) In Goya, however, the attempt to establish an ethics by affording the viewer a stance *external* to the work, not derived from moral principles at all — as Kant might have imagined for the "ideal spectator" of history — results in an even more troubling dilemma than one might ordinarily expect, even from images of violent revolution, destruction, and war. In this regard, consider *The Third of May, 1808* and some of the *Disasters of War* (for example, no. 26, "*No se puede mirar*" ["One cannot look at this"], Figure 5.9). Through a technique that uncannily anticipates the ways in which mechanically reproduced images are cropped or cut in the photographic and

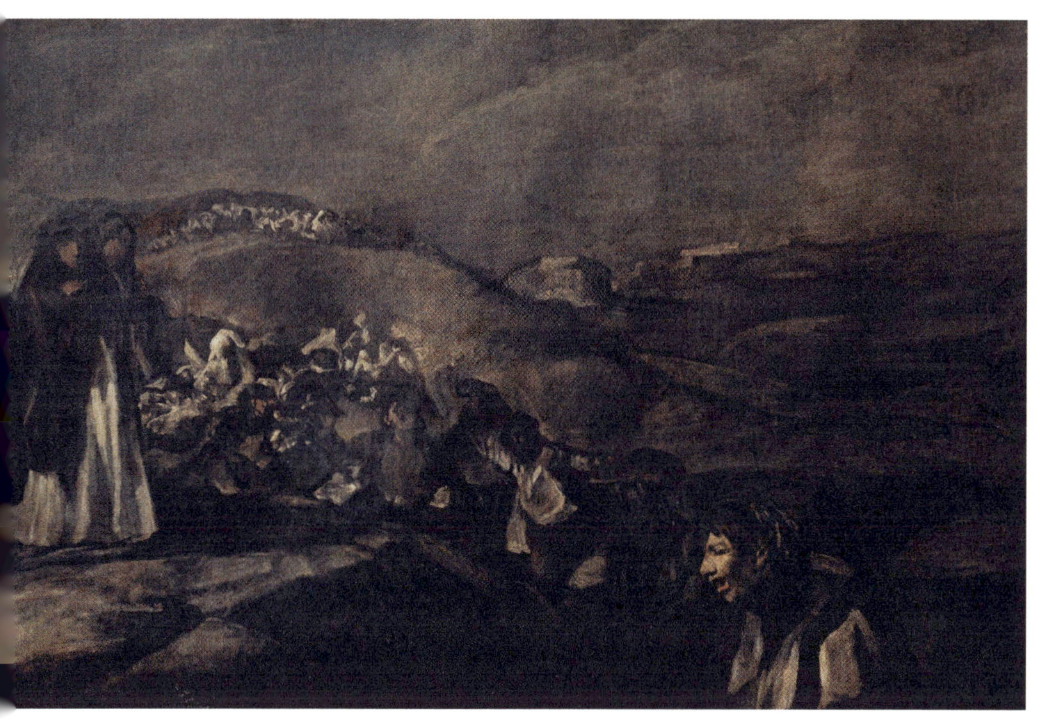

cinematic fields, the effect of the frame in such works is to implicate art itself in the very violence it helps disclose. Because the perspective of the unseen perpetrators of the violence is as compelling as the perspective of the viewer external to the image the viewer is implicated in the violence of these images in a remarkably unsettling way. Thus, rather than read Goya's efforts in *The Third of May, 1808* and the *Disasters of War* solely in *moral* terms — as claiming secure access to a universal perspective on good and evil that would allow him to criticize the atrocities of history from the "outside," it is more promising to consider the ethical challenges they pose and especially to consider

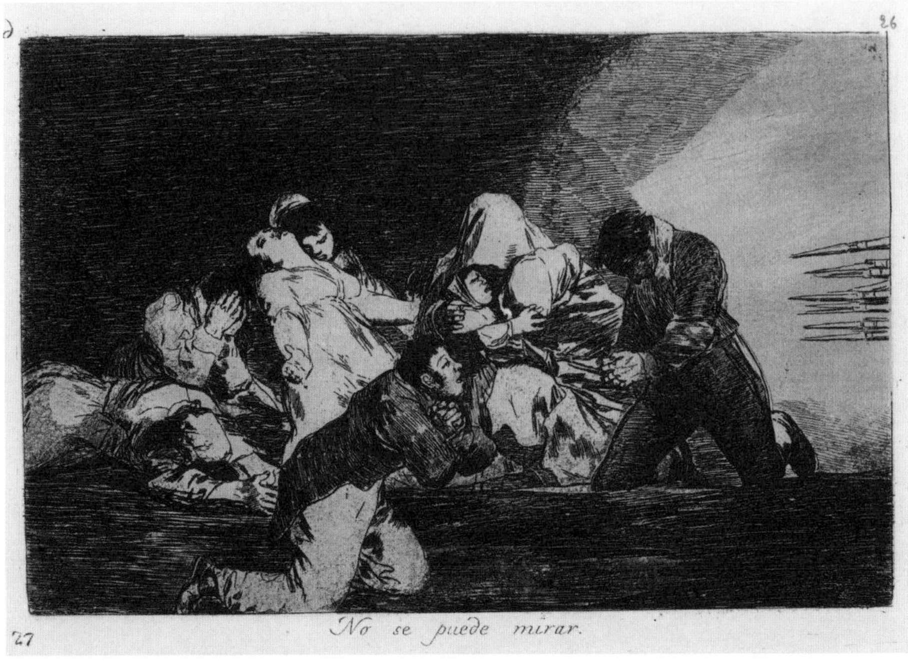

Figure 5.9.

"*No se puede mirar*" ("One cannot look at this"), *Disasters of War*, no. 26, ca. 1810–12, published 1863. Etching, burnished lavis, drypoint, and burin, 14.5×21.0 cm.

those challenges as epitomized in the vexed relationship between the external spectator and the implicit violence that the exercise of any autonomous framing power seems to create.

The contrast with Kant could not be clearer. According to principles explicitly stated in Kant's second *Critique*, the *Critique of Practical Reason*, the obligations we construe as ethical are rational and personal. They are the manifestations of a law that in turn reflects the rationality, freedom, and autonomy of the subject-self. In Kant, the ethical domain is closely aligned with that of a particular view of rational autonomy and is first and foremost a reflection of the subject's capacity for self-legislation or self-rule. This is consistent with the principle of (self-)regulation that operates quite broadly — a principle that allows the work of knowledge to be determined as legitimate, that warrants judgments to be determined as valid, and that allows individuals and their history to be conceived as having a purpose.

To be sure, there must be an element of obligation if a demand is to be felt as ethical in any strong sense of the term, and that obligation must itself be articulated in relation to some authority, origin, or source. In Kant, that source is a "law" that we (rational human beings) give to ourselves. Somewhat more broadly conceived, however, the ethical field can be seen as a function of a systematic framing power that, prior to the work of practical reason, regulates and controls the division among the various fields and faculties within which specific obligations arise. Indeed, the limits and interrelationship of these fields are articulated in the three Kantian critiques and in Kant's essays on history, which, taken together, have sometimes been referred to as constituting a "fourth *Critique*."[26] Quite apart from Kant's interest in locating the grounds for a moral law based on universalizable judgments and manifested in maxims, there is a concealed or unwritten but nonetheless recognizable ethic — a governing frame, a principle of internal regulation and control — at work within each of the separate spheres addressed by Kant: pure reason, practical reason, aesthetic judgment, and history. These spheres reflect the various modes of authority under which actions may be construed as having meaningful purposes or ends.[27] Thus, one may locate an implicit ethic within the sphere of cognition addressed by the first *Critique*; its tacit rules govern the separation of "things" from "things in themselves," of what we can and cannot legitimately claim to know, and this, in turn, drives Kant to isolate and reduce the various illusions or self-conflicts of reason in what he describes as "antinomies" and "paralogisms." Likewise, an ethic of autonomy and self-regulation governs the framework of practical reason described in the second *Critique*, which is concerned explicitly with the nature of self-legislation and with the universal moral law. An ethic of desire, feeling, and intersubjective communication is emergent from the *Critique of Judgment*, whose overarching principle may be stated in terms of a rule that forbids basing aesthetic "judgment" on "interested pleasure." The principles at work in all these critiques are transposed into the key of historical thinking in the essay "What Is Enlightenment?" where Kant argues for "man's release from his self-incurred tutelage." "Tutelage," Kant explains, consists in "man's inability to make use of his understanding without direction from another. Self-incurred is this tutelage when its cause lies not in lack of reason but in lack of resolution and courage to use it without direction from another."[28]

Thus, in spite of the obvious differences between cognition, morality, judgment, and history, there is an overarching principle that underpins the effort to maintain consistency across these various domains. This was not merely a theoretical notion. Indeed, one expectation prevalent more broadly in the culture of the Enlightenment was that the competing claims of each of these fields might somehow be acknowledged, if not fully resolved, in the formation of a neutral public space, that is, in civil society. This presents the rational face of the Enlightenment in its political or "liberal" guise. But what is constitutively true of the liberal order is true of the Kantian critiques as well: that each sphere can sustain a respectful relation with the others only insofar as it can recognize that no frame is able to give substantive shape to the general obligation that these various demands for acknowledgment create. Except from the position of an empty and abstract subject, who could be bound by no particular set of rules generated within these frames, it might be impossible to reconcile the various requirements they impose—to meet the demands of reason and history, for example, or to reconcile transcendental value and social rules, or to respond at once to the demands of knowledge and feeling. As a result of these conflicts (which can be taken to indicate the nature of Enlightenment culture as an internally fragmented, detotalized, or perspectival whole), one is forced to confront the potentially sublime pathos of actions that inherently exceed *any* framework within which their ends and authority may be contained.[29] Such actions could well appear as presenting monstrous threats to just about everything in the rational world.

Kant addresses these possibilities only in his discussion of the aesthetics of the sublime, which, as is well known, presents a threat to the sensory and cognitive capacities of human beings but which ultimately has a happy, affirmative end. Goya, by contrast, continues to make reference to the archaic contexts from which the Enlightenment's ethical authority believed to have made a categorical break. I take Goya's recognition of the persistence of archaism in the *Caprichos* not just as a revelation from an implicitly enlightened stance of the failure of the (modern) Enlightenment fully to penetrate (archaic) Spain — though it is certainly that — but also as an indication of the Enlightenment's failure to subsume completely the authority of sacred institutions. This presents a challenge to the Enlightenment's image of its own authority through a reminder of the fact that reason has origins at all.

That reason also has a history was an idea that was left mostly to Kant's philosophical successors (most importantly, Hegel) to address. But while it clearly has a history, reason does not exactly have an origin, at least as far as Enlightenment thinkers were concerned.[30] For Kant, the assumption was that the emergence of and successful collective guidance of humankind by reason would define the shape history as one of progress — as progress for the human race. The question was how we could know the shape of history as a whole when we are ourselves located *within* history. How could we take even the most promising signs of progress as conclusive evidence that the arc of history as a whole would bend toward moral progress for humanity?

It was a question that was addressed explicitly in conjunction with the French Revolution in the essay "An Old Question Raised Again: Is the Human Race Constantly Progressing?" Kant's answer may seem surprising, not so much because of his conclusion but because of his method, which could best be described as aesthetic and specifically as rooted in the fundamental visual metaphors of perspective and spectators. His focus is not on the events of the French Revolution but on the responses of the spectators — the witnesses to history. The spectators are the ones who are able to see that the events are indicative of true progress, but only because they are ideal spectators. On the one hand, they are disinterested with respect to the outcome of the revolution, while on the other hand, they are profoundly moved by its events. "This revolution," Kant writes, "finds in the hearts of all spectators (who are not engaged in this game themselves) a wishful participation that borders on enthusiasm, the very expression of which is fraught with danger."[31] For Kant, the French Revolution provided the example of a historical event that could be taken to prove the moral progress of humanity insofar as the sympathies or feelings it provoked in the spectators could be subsumed under the species of judgment available only to an ideal spectator. Specifically, the moral significance of history is visible from "the mode of thinking of the spectators which reveals itself publicly in this game of great revolutions, and manifests such a universal yet disinterested sympathy for the players on one side against those on the other."[32]

Goya's engagement of the relationship between reason and history yields very different results. Two particular works, each related to the other, help bring this to light. One is the *Allegory of the City of Madrid* (Figure 5.10). A second is the image customarily labeled *Truth Rescued by Time, Witnessed by History* (Figure 5.6). But in *Truth, Rescued by Time*, the figure of "truth" has also been taken as a stand-in for the constitution drawn up in Cadiz on March 19, 1812. However it is no less a symbol of Enlightenment itself. On that reading, the Enlightenment presents itself as a historical field in which truth is saved from the threats of time for modern culture and progress by the power of history, scientifically conceived.[33] And yet this interpretation fails to ask why history can rescue time from something — the passing of time — of which it is also composed. If the sense is that history somehow records and preserves truth for posterity — that is, history is understood as the record of events rather than as the events

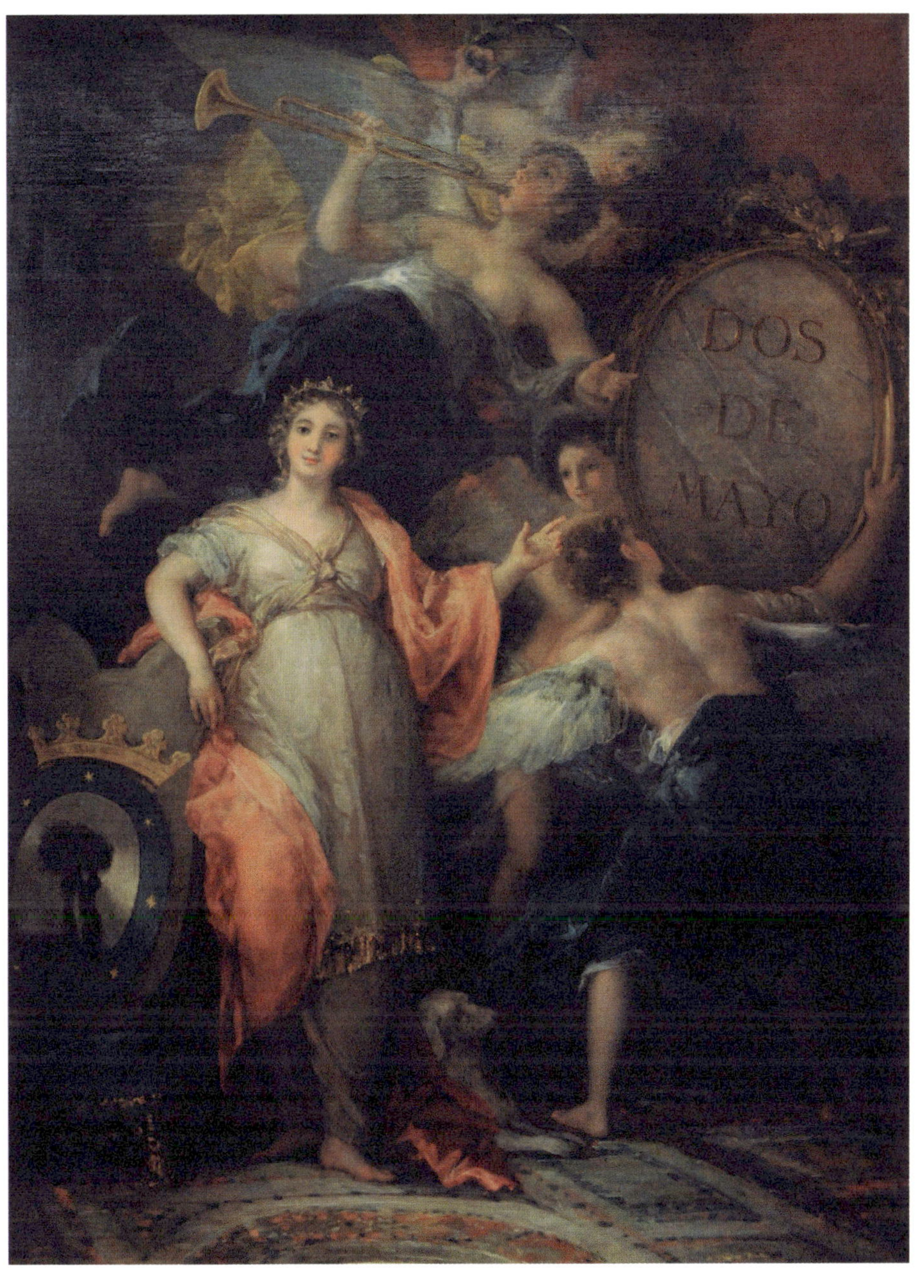

Figure 5.10.
Allegory of the City of Madrid, 1810. Oil on canvas, 260 × 195 cm.
Museo de Historia de Madrid, Madrid.

themselves — then we have to reckon with the fact that truth is also *subject to* history's potentially disorienting effects. It is worth remembering that in Spanish, *historia* means *both* the events of the past *and* the written account of the past. How, moreover, is a future created if time threatens truth and if history can tell us only about the past? This makes the nearly miraculous appearance of Truth even more puzzling. (Note that in the painting, History looks over her shoulder, toward the past.) Indeed, it seems on closer inspection that this painting tells not of time's saving power, but of the vulnerability of truth to temporality: having become conscious of its own susceptibility to the effects of time, truth cannot be apprehended directly; it is fleeting, and must be approached through the frameworks that history provides. The sense of the painting is that truth is being carried off by time and is rescued by history — from which it also follows that there is no truth directly available to us, no *permanent* truth, except what history can tell. And there is no telling what overall shape history might have.

In fact, Goya's own experience showed that there could be no secure reliance on Enlightenment ideals to provide a sure path toward moral progress. The *Allegory of the City of Madrid* is especially illustrative in this regard. In his post as first court painter, Goya initially pledged his allegiance to the French king, Joseph Bonaparte. His sympathy for Enlightenment ideas initially translated into sympathy for the usurping monarch. But the outrages committed during the conflict, against which the *madrileños* rebelled in the uprisings of the Second of May, showed how easily the forces of reason and the progressive ideals attached to them could be overwhelmed by irrational violence. Tadeo Bravo de Rivero, an alderman of Madrid and a personal friend of Goya, commissioned him to make a portrait of King Joseph I, which he did. The original image shows a woman holding the city's coat of arms in the foreground. Behind her, a group of winged spirits are holding up a medallion that originally displayed the image of the king. But in 1815, Joseph Bonaparte's image was substituted for that of Ferdinand VII, which was subsequently replaced in 1820 with the word "Constitución." (The history of the painting is more complicated still: Ferdinand's portrait was restored in 1823, but in 1872, the image of Ferdinand was substituted by the words "Dos de Mayo," which is how the work stands today.)[34]

The small oil sketch held in the Museum of Fine Arts, Boston, anticipating the *Allegory of the City of Madrid* and *Truth Rescued by Time*, confirms the interpretation proposed above. All the iconographic elements in *Truth Rescued by Time, Witnessed by History* (Figure 5.11) confirm the uncontroversial identity of the figures: truth is naked (unlike the case of the *Allegory of the City of Madrid*); the winged figure of time is shown holding an hourglass, while history, looking over her shoulder toward the past, is writing in a book presumably for the future.[35] But a very different drama plays out in the space above these figures: there is a broad shaft of light intervening from the left, while owls and bats populate the dark realm to the right, toward which time is drawing truth. Indeed, the composition is very close to images of abduction that Goya made elsewhere, including in the *Caprichos* (for example, no. 72, *"No te escaparás"* ["You will not escape"], Figure 5.12). These are hardly images of the kind of secular salvation that is sometimes associated with history. If we think in the essentially contemporaneous terms that Kant proposed, there are no spectators in these works; moreover, they hardly suggest anything close to a synthetic perspective from which to grasp the nature of a truth that is subject to time. Can a notion of progress, moral or otherwise, be gleaned from these works? Can the arc of history be read as leading toward the good? It seems doubtful. At the very least, one is forced to admit that there is no position from which to tell for sure.

It may of course be tempting to think that the authority of ethical obligations might simply be induced in the spectator-subject aesthetically or created as a function of the need to fill the space of some preexisting social, cultural, historical, or psychological need. Certainly in Kant, the vacuum created by the absence of any rational *obligation* to believe is filled by a disciplinary imperative to obey

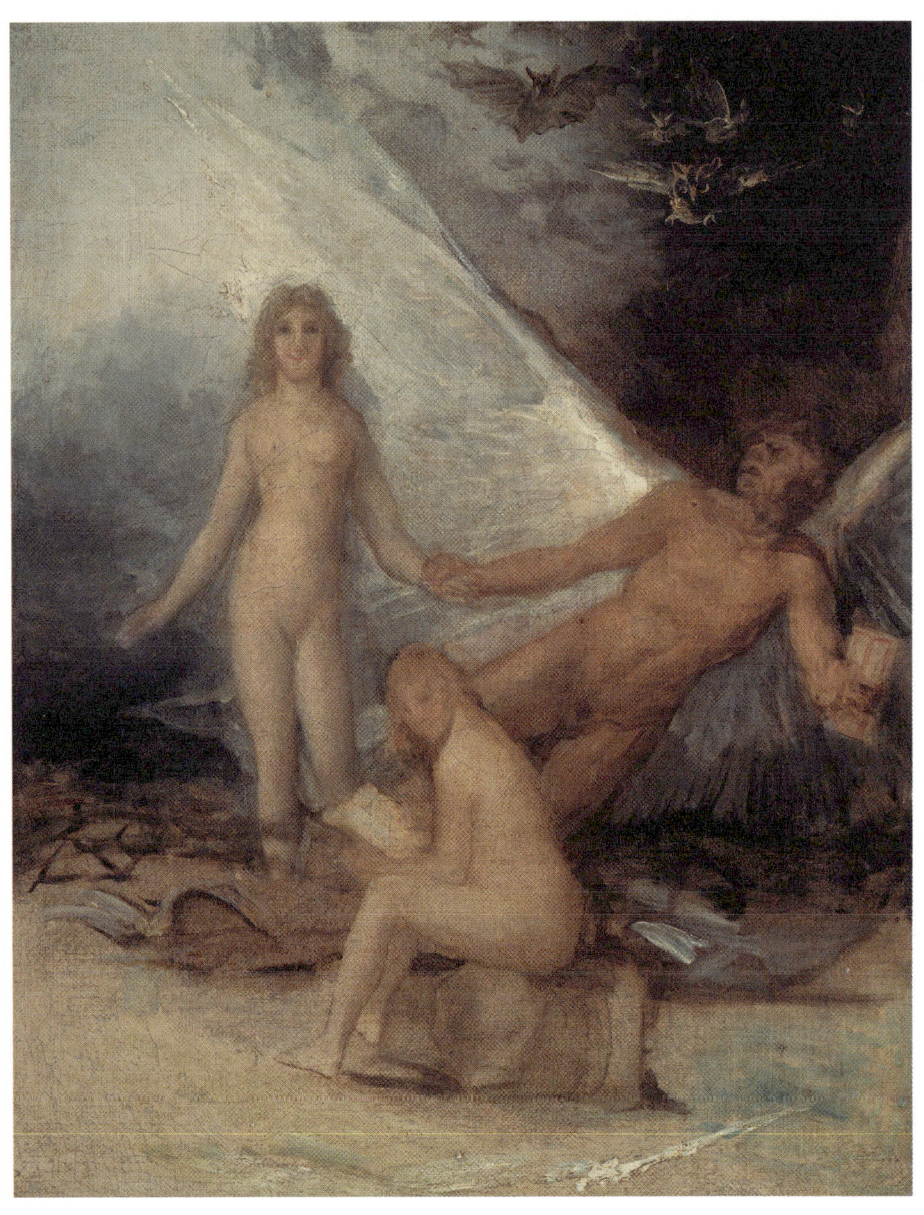

Figure 5.11.
Preliminary sketch for *Truth Rescued by Time, Witnessed by History* (fig. 5.6 above),
1800. Oil on canvas, 42×32 cm. Museum of Fine Arts, Boston.

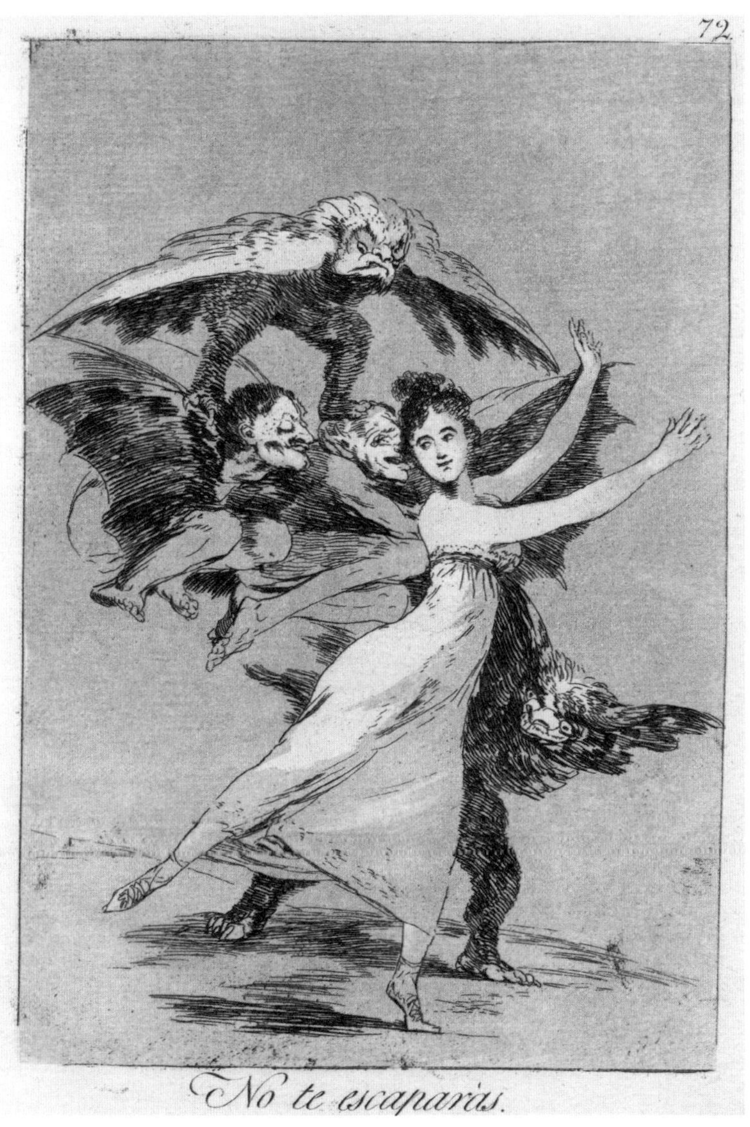

Figure 5.12.
"*No te escaparás*" ("You will not escape"), *Caprichos*, no. 72, 1797–98, published 1799.
Etching and burnished aquatint, 21.7 × 15.2 cm.

the ethical imperatives dictated by reason. As suggested above, this insures that the domain of ethics can be isolated as a function of the secular, autonomous, freely willing subject. "The good will is not good because of what it effects or accomplishes or because of its adequacy to achieve some proposed end," writes Kant, "it is good only because of its willing, i.e., it is good of itself."[36] But it was precisely because Kant's call for autonomy, which relied on a concept of the rational will as sovereign, as answerable only to itself, required man to *"make himself* into whatever he is or is to become" that the Kantian critique of religion could be seen as but a veiled form of self-domination rather than as truly liberating human beings from indebtedness to the archaic traditions of the past. But so conceived, the Enlightenment project of critique conceals the fact that the rational subject marks an incomplete break with the traditions of religious belief, which provided an authoritative ground for ethical actions in the presecular world. Goya helps us see something different, that is, that the powers of reason are genealogically descended from forces of desire, self-deception, and false belief; hence, they continue to stand in need of precisely those controls that reason itself proves unable fully to provide. In the process, Goya dramatically restages the drama of Enlightenment envisioned by Kant, according to which the principal accomplishment of reason resides in the successful critique — and overcoming — of superstition, dogmatism, and the uncritical acceptance of inherited beliefs. Understood as a corrective to the Enlightenment's understanding of itself, Goya's work is grounded in a more complex appreciation of the fact that the rational institutions of the enlightened world are not in fact autonomous, but represent the ongoing responses to the demand that the archaic sources of authority somehow be brought under control. The history of the present is laden with the freight of the past, which in turn means that ethical obligations cannot effectively be built upon the foundations of the free, rational will.

This reality runs contrary to the hopes that were increasingly accepted by the intellectuals and artists in Spain who had strong affinities for the ideals that fueled the French Revolution. These include Sebastián Martínez (himself an amateur painter), Leandro Fernández de Moratín, Evaristo Pérez de Castro, and of course, Jovellanos.[37] Their outlook was consistent with the aspirations of the growing social class that had hopes for a better life and time for leisure activities, much as we have seen in the tapestry cartoons. The ethical principles of the bourgeois social world are best exemplified in the preoccupation with locating stable frameworks for collective will formation and intersubjective agreements based on the primacy of fellow feeling or sympathy, which Kant inherited from Rousseau and which Goya takes as his focus in those cartoons. They also come into play in his masterful portraits of intellectuals of which Jovellanos is certainly the most prominent.

However, in Goya, the construction of the social world and its ethical demands is open to two countervailing threats. On the authority of images that dominate the *Caprichos*, it could be said that the establishment of the autonomous rational subject induces a for-getfulness of the link between subjectivity qua self-consciousness and subjection as a form of self-reinforcing social domination. As a result of this forgetfulness, the subject tends to conceal the pro-cesses through which it becomes *subject to* the barbarism of its own self-assertion over against the natural world. (Recall no. 25 of the *Caprichos* cited in the previous chapter, "*Si quebró el cantaro*" ["For he broke the pitcher"], Figure 4.9, above). The second threat is repre-sented in the resurgence of those archaic forms of superstition that enlightened reason, in the course of overcoming superstition, took as its principal accomplishment to have expunged. Accordingly, many of Goya's "dark" paintings represent analogues of bourgeois social life, seen neither from the perspective of a higher reason nor from the cynic's oblique vantage point but rather from the perspective of a still partially or sometimes thoroughly demonized world. As images such as *The Pilgrimage to San Isidro* (as compared with the earlier *Meadow of San Isidro*) and *The Witches' Sabbath*, Figure 5.13) allow us to see, the process of Enlightenment did not eliminate archaic or superstitious

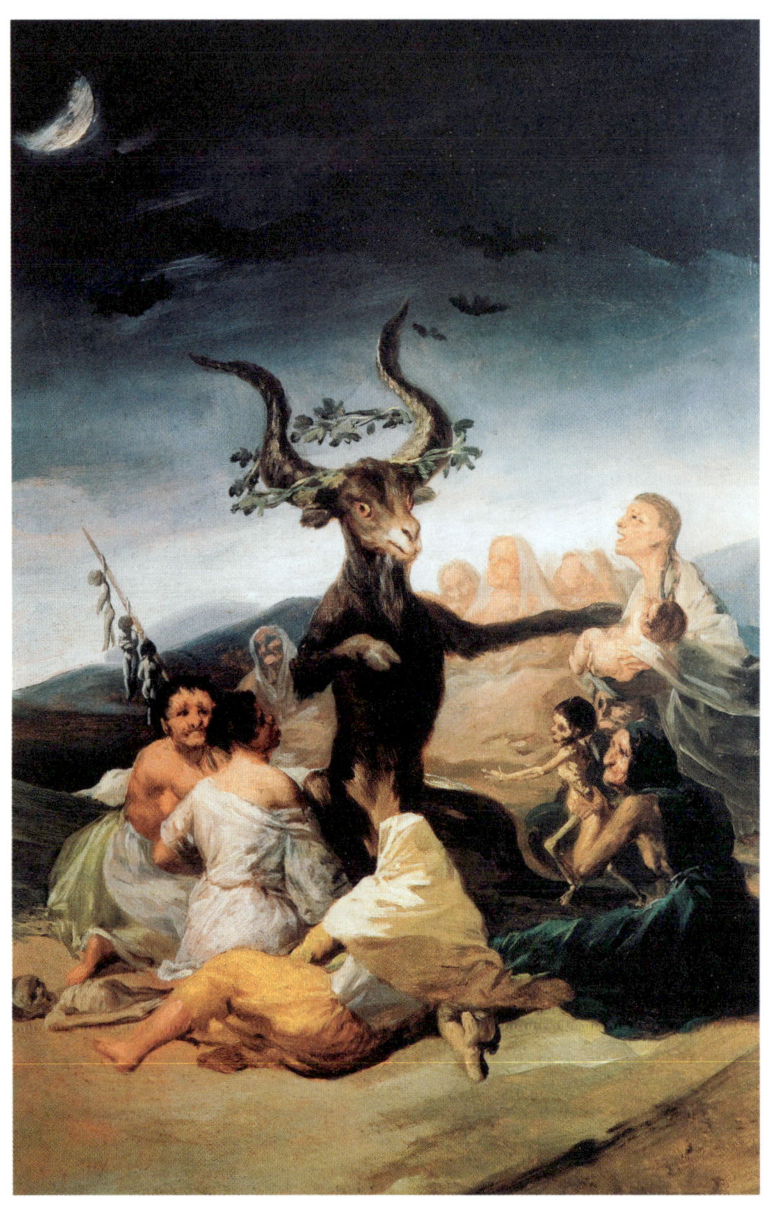

Figure 5.13.
The Witches' Sabbath, 1797–98. Oil on canvas, 43×30 cm.
Museo Lázaro Galdiano, Madrid.

beliefs, thereby allowing the free exercise of the rational will; rather, archaism persists and leads to thralldom.

As in the carnivalesque *Burial of the Sardine* (Figure 5.14), that archaism remains always ready to pierce through the otherwise homogeneous surface of mass cultural life and present itself with a smile.[38] This is hardly to suggest that Enlightenment thinkers were oblivious to the importance of feeling and desire in human life. On the contrary, Rousseau built his theory of the public will on the very basis of feeling. For others, ranging from Shaftesbury to Goethe and Kant, sympathy was one basis on which human beings could temper the proclivity to allow self-interest to displace our regard for others. I will take up the role of sympathy in greater detail in Chapter 8. Here, it may be sufficient to note that one solution to the difficulty that feelings pose is an aesthetic one that involves the sublimation of feelings, together with the effects of corporeality and materiality that the concept of feeling takes in train, such that they could form the basis for universalizable judgments. This was Kant's approach. As is made abundantly clear in Kant's aesthetics that is, in the *Critique of Judgment*, judgments of beauty are best characterized by the "disinterested" quality of the pleasures that attach to it. Indeed, it is through the sublimation of feeling that art could be justified as a cultural sphere consistent with the principles of reason. In Goya, however, any response to the ethical problems the Enlightenment confronted in reckoning with the persistence of feelings would have to recognize the limitations of the universal framing power of judgment. It would indeed have to recognize that the attempt to impose that power might well fail and that it was at best likely to reproduce a set of conflicts in which the power of the frame stands in conflict with elements both internal and external to the work in question. As suggested by the drawing of *The Woman Viper* (Figure 5.15), held in the Prado which shows a woman reflected in a mirror as a serpent on a scythe, the power of the frame is able to show, but not always able to correct, the distortions of the images it attempts to contain.[39] Insofar as the authority of the frame was conceived as supporting

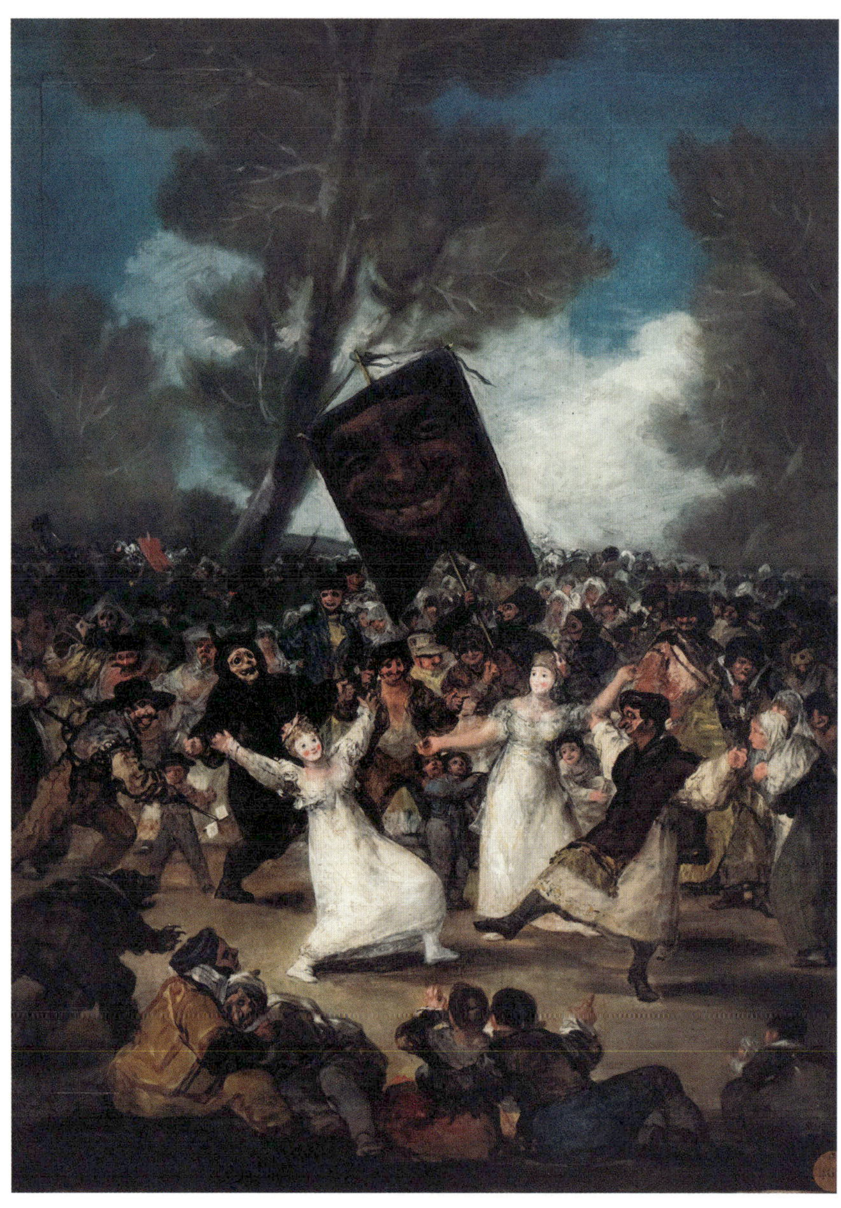

Figure 5.14.
Burial of the Sardine, 1812–19. Oil on wood, 82.5×62 cm.
Real Academia de Bellas Artes de San Fernando, Madrid.

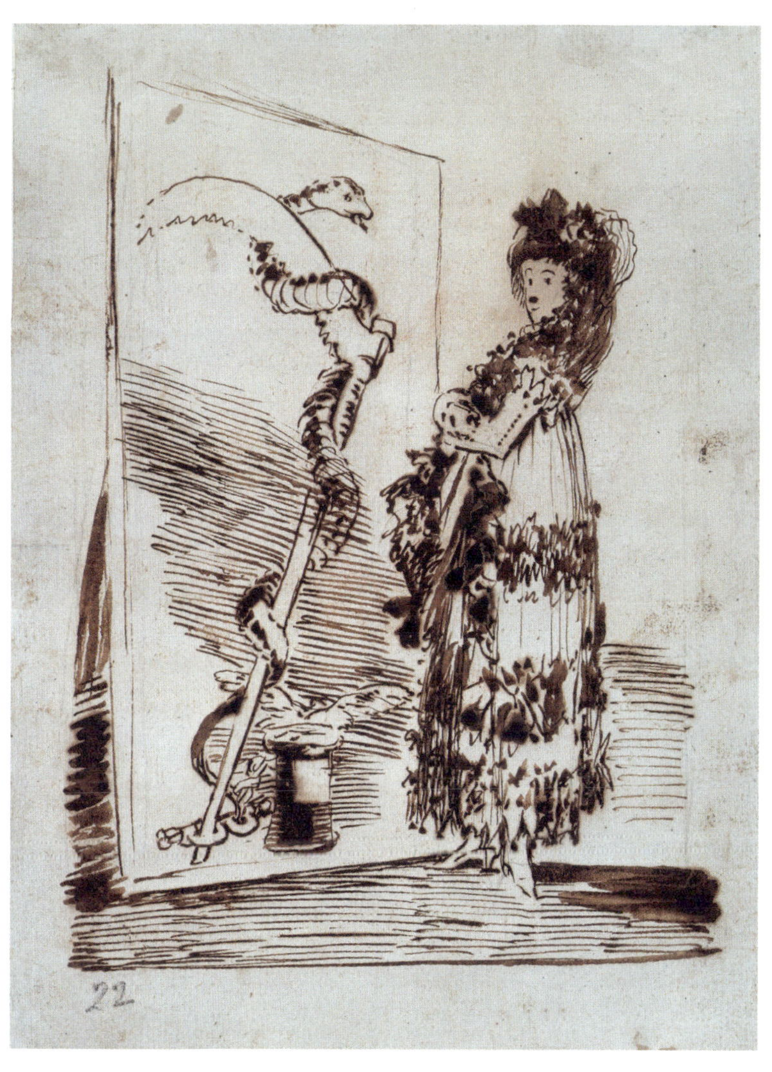

Figure 5.15.
The Woman Viper, 1797–98. Bougainvillea ink over black pencil, 21.1 × 14.7 cm.
Museo del Prado, Madrid.

the construction of art as an autonomous cultural domain, it was precisely the autonomy of art that Goya sought to resist. The project of critique required it.

These are among the reasons why Goya may be described not as the first modern artist, but as an artist engaged in refusing to adopt an independent ethics for painting or, indeed, for art in general. Yet here, paradoxically, is where the ethical import of Goya's work lies. The ambition of his work is to draw us consistently outside the frame of art (that is, outside "art itself") toward a critical reflection on history, society, religion, and desire as the fields in terms of which the obligations bearing on the subject of enlightened modernity were experienced. A certain self-consciousness is of course integral to this effort. But in sharp contrast to a "painterly" artist such as Velásquez, whose work reflects on and thus regulates its own status as a mere resemblance or similitude of the real, there is no singular "ethics of painting" that emerges from Goya's work. In Goya's self-portrait, the *Self-Portrait at an Easel* (see Figure 3.27, above), the self-reflective elements prominent in Velásquez's *Las Meninas* have been eliminated in favor of the artist's confrontation with a canvas that is itself directly exposed to the source of light but whose painted surface remains nonetheless hidden from the spectator's view. The source of the image being painted on the canvas must lie in the mirror into which Goya is gazing but whose presence we can only impute. And rather than show the artist bathed in the light of truth, Goya positions himself obliquely with respect both to the canvas and to the principal source of light coming from the window, as if to suggest that any questioning of the powers of representation — here, a consequence of the blinding and potentially destructive, power of light — would necessarily have consequences for the artist's stance vis-à-vis the practice of painting itself.[40]

This is also to say that Goya's stance with respect to the traditions of art illuminates the ethical situation of the modern, Enlightened subject as one for which an aesthetic solution is both the locus of hope and the site of a refusal, the reflex of a potentially sublime encounter with things that seem to be nearly impossible to represent, as in the "*Gran coloso dormido*," but also with insufficiencies that lead to a recovery of hope in art itself, as even a work such as the *Semisunken Dog* (see Figure 3.7, above) might suggest. In this respect, as in others, Goya's work marks an important moment in relation to the beginning of "modern art." On the one hand, as noted earlier, modernism points to the autonomy of art, to its independence from all other practices and their rules. But at the same time, the significance of modernism in the arts is also located in its rejection of the idea that painting (or any other activity) is a practice with internally consistent and coherent rules. Modernism is iconoclastic. It leads to a practice in which, as Arthur Danto has said, "anything goes."[41] Goya offers a different possibility from either of these, which has consequences not just for art itself, but for ethics. It is one that sees art as standing in relation to a series of competing ambitions and constraints, such that the ethical "subject" can be constructed from the partial and particular obligations that bear upon it, each one of which is nonetheless aware of its inability to comprehend the whole. Goya's work reflects this awareness. The great hope of the Enlightenment's project to establish an ethics and to justify morality on the basis of reason was to synthesize these perspectives through the adoption of a neutral or anonymous third-person point of view coincident with a liberal public space. But in Goya, the incommensurability of the frameworks under which ethical obligations present themselves instead reveals a series of differential shifts, such that no one field may be identified as the source of obligations that can underpin all the others. The ethical ground of action lies no more "outside" the sphere of art than it can be located within it. In this regard, Goya's work reveals not just a questioning or undermining of the subject whose constructive powers might be reflected in art, but a more thorough and complex confrontation between the demand for an ethics that reflection on those powers creates and the impossibility of locating a singular category through which the responsibility of that reflection and a response to it can be located. When dealing with Goya, it is essential to regard works of art as the material examples of forms of consciousness that do not themselves belong to an autonomous cultural domain, but that challenge the idea that any single framework of principles can underwrite the whole of cultural life.

Extremities

There is nothing like a traumatic experience to shake up one's thinking.
—Joel Whitebook, "The Marriage of Marx and Freud"

Among the undergirding principles of the project of critique is one that we have seen at work in Goya's art at virtually every turn: that there can be no adequate reckoning with the "truth" that does not also take into account the fact that any given form of representation is bound to play a role in shaping the truth—whether in distorting or obscuring, in concealing, or in framing it through some prevailing normative lens. Whereas the hope for an "objective representation" of things would seem to be well aligned with the enlightened modern hope that we can see the truth by shining the light of reason through a through a neutral window into the black box of the world, it turns out that the standard Enlightenment view of things is at best incomplete; the window through which we peer inevitably plays a role in shaping whatever we see inside the box. This is the case both for the work of *visual* representation that Goya inherited through a history that goes back to the early Renaissance and also for the construction of reality in the social world, that is, for the way in which various forms of self-representation helped sustain distorted behaviors and beliefs.

Among the most challenging questions that Goya's work raises is how to locate a stance from which such distortions can be recognized. An answer that might suggest itself in relation to the *Caprichos* might be that the captions step outside the images to provide that stance. The captions can of course be linked to the stance of the observer pictured in the frontispiece, offering an oblique and "knowing" perspective on the represented scenes they accompany. But we have already seen how this answer leaves a further difficulty unresolved, namely, that locating such a stance is not enough to provide an opening onto the world of action. While Goya's work is wholly consistent with the aims of critique (as opposed to criticism and also to what Horkheimer characterized as the aims supported by "traditional theory"),[1] it also brings to light a gap between the work of theory and the demands of practice. It leaves us with the question: What is to be done — what can art do — once the frames of representation are brought into view and social contradictions are exposed? Are there situations in which showing the truth is sufficient as a form of efficacious action?

The work of showing the truth to a world that is reluctant to accept it and doing so under conditions where the conventions of representation conspire to make the lack of transparency systemic is rendered all the more fraught where the truth at hand is as atrocious as what Goya presents in the *Disasters of War*. The *Disasters* are linked to the *Caprichos* in a number of ways: by virtue of the fact that they share a medium (etching and aquatint), by the fact that the images in both series bear captions, and because the full title of the *Disasters* describes them as incorporating a series of *caprichos enfáticos* (emphatic *caprichos*): *Fatales consequencias de la sangrienta guerra en España con Buonaparte [sic], Y otros caprichos enfáticos* ("Fatal consequences of the war of Spain with Bounaparte [*sic*]. And other emphatic caprichos"). But the differences between the *Disasters* and the *Caprichos* are substantial, and the things they discover in confronting the limits of representation offer very different insights into the critical role of art with respect to the truth. The *Disasters* respond to historical events, not social ones. While the prints were made between 1810 and 1820, they were not published during Goya's lifetime, but only posthumously, in 1863. The captions, constructed from Goya's notes, were likely written by his friend Ceán Bermúdez. And perhaps most important of all, many of them (especially plates 1 through 47) deal with subject matter that is so horribly violent that it is nearly too difficult to witness. They show us things from which we would wish to avert our eyes, and in so doing, they raise the question of what it means to bear witness to unbearable things. In showing us humanly inflicted horrors from which we cannot avert our gaze, they call on us to think about how we can face things that seem to outstrip what sight can bear. The *Disasters* thus further challenge the notion that the ends of critique can be met by acknowledging the conditions and the contingencies surrounding the representation of the truth. Showing the truth, no matter how unwelcome, is of course important for any form of art engaged in a critical enterprise. But the *Disasters* do something different in presenting the truth as not masked at all, but shown with full frontal force and in a way that may be too awful to bear. In this way, they expose the painful restrictions of the position of the spectator when confronted with circumstances that overwhelm any possibility of action.

One of the claims that has consistently been made about the *Disasters* — and more specifically one of the claims often made about their role in the history of modern visual culture — is that they present the naked, unvarnished truth about the horrors of war. Fred Licht linked them directly to modern wartime photojournalism as part of an argument about the relationship between Goya's work and the origins of the "modern temper" in art. Both the *Disasters* and photojournalism, he argued, have their basis in the portrayal of "ascertainable reality," and both demonstrate an urgent sense of immediacy: "All of the pages [of the *Disasters*] have an inevitability and an impetuousness that give them the double impact of being at once truthful testimony of all that is vulnerable, vile, insane, and cruel in man, and an urgent exorcism of such knowledge."[2] Following Jakob Rosenberg, he argued that they record the events of war directly and without mediation, as a seismograph might record an earthquake or as if produced by "an impassive camera shutter."[3] To his mind, this is what explains the fact that the images were left unpublished until some fifty years after Goya's death. But this may not be entirely right.

First, the *Disasters* do have a precedent in the etchings of Jacques Callot, *Les misères et les malheurs de la guerre* (1633) and in Allesandro Magnasco's paintings of interrogations in jail (Figure 6.1), which Goya may well have seen during his time in Italy.[4] Second, and more important, is the fact that Goya's *Disasters* raise questions about what it means to bear witness to extreme violence, even if the images in the series do not count as records of matters of fact. Licht also argues that the *Disasters* are devoid of any hope for human justice or the consolation of divine order, from which it seems reasonable to conclude that their role as art is not to point toward transcendence or even toward meaning (which can also be a form of transcendence), but to show the truth of war in all its brutal horror and to do so as directly as possible. This bears further inquiry.

The question of whether art can or cannot transcend the awfulness of war is not readily answered by saying that Goya presents the violence of war as something true "in itself." Moreover, the question of transcendence — literally, of going beyond — is a crucial one, since nearly every image shows something that goes beyond what we might possibly be able to imagine. That indeed is one aim of the *Disasters*: to show things that are beyond the imagination, not because they are too fanciful to conjure or too wild to believe but because they are so brutally, awfully, unimaginably horrible. Indeed, the reversal of the expected relationship between art, the imagination, and the real is crucial to understanding the *Disasters* and their place within Goya's work. In the Black Paintings, Goya set out to show imagined things as having a visible reality, but in the *Disasters*, he shows the reality of war as exceeding the powers of the imagination. As I will discuss below, these issues are knitted together in Goya's engagement with the aesthetics of the sublime.

An ancient category of rhetoric with roots traceable to Longinus, the sublime was reinvigorated and substantially transformed

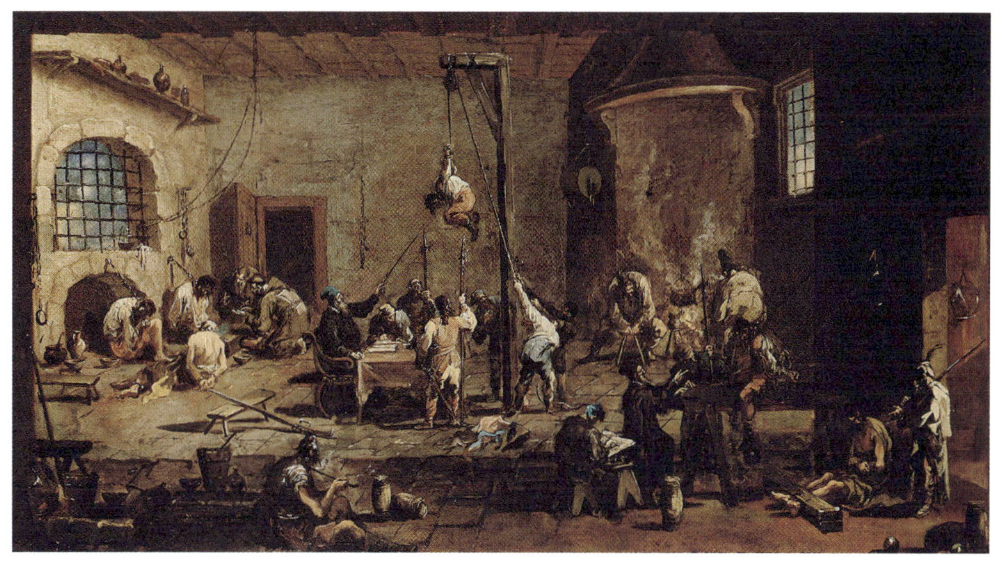

Figure 6.1.
Alessandro Magnasco, *Interrogations in Jail*, ca. 1710–20. Oil on canvas,
44.5×82.5 cm. Kunsthistorisches Museum, Vienna.

in the late eighteenth century by figures such as Edmund Burke and Kant, not least because of their awareness of the violence associated with revolutions (the French Revolution, in particular). But no less important than the aesthetics of the sublime for an understanding of the *Disasters* are questions about the ethics of the spectator in the face of extreme violence. First, however, turning to the relationship between the *Disasters* and modern wartime photojournalism can help guide us to some insights into these questions of ethics and aesthetics in the *Disasters*.

The cover of Susan Sontag's book, *Regarding the Pain of Others* features plate no. 36 of the *Disasters* ("*Tampoco*" ["Nor him"], Figure 6.2). On her account, Goya introduces "a new responsiveness to suffering in art … the account of war's cruelties is fashioned as an assault on

233

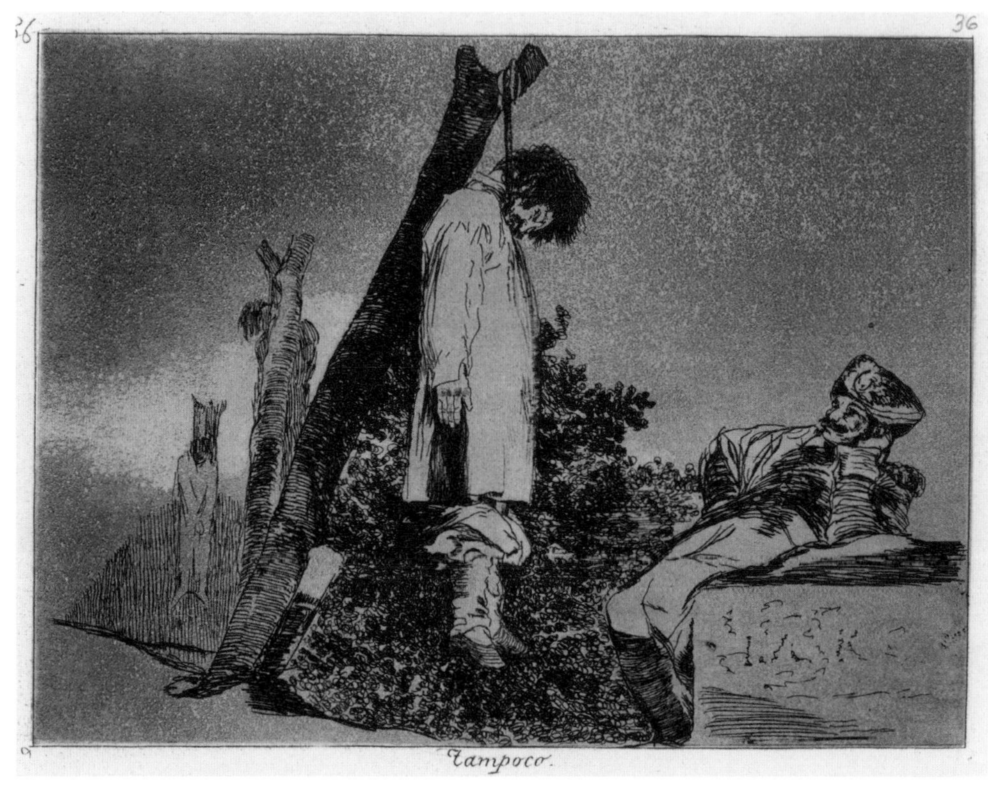

Figure 6.2.

"*Tampoco*" ("Nor him"), *Disasters of War*, no. 36, ca. 1810–15, published 1863. Etching and burin, 15×21.6 cm.

the sensibility of the viewer. The expressive phrases in script below each image comment on the provocation."[5] The issue of the viewer's responsiveness to suffering places questions of ethics squarely alongside issues of aesthetics. There is an ethics of photography rooted in the fact that every photograph is in some measure chosen, not determined, in spite of the fact that a photograph is a record of reflected light,[6] but photographs can count as evidence in ways that the *Disasters of War* cannot. This is not to say that photographs are inherently more veracious than etchings or paintings, but that they respond to a different set of norms; specifically, they respond to norms for the presentation of what is available to be seen and can be accepted as evidence.[7] These are hardly neutral norms. And in fact all photographs are, as Sontag recognizes, a species of rhetoric. As such, they are never merely representations of facts. They can provoke an ethical response though in order to do so, they must invariably do more than shock the viewer with the brutal facts, they must also appeal to the sense that one *must act* — that *someone must act* — in the face of such brutality. In presenting visual evidence that outrages our sense of humanity, they make a claim on us, issuing an implicit demand that *something must be done*. But the questions *who* must act, and how are not easily answered. Photojournalistic images are designed for public viewing and so call for a public response; often the nature of this response is intended to be political. Yet paradoxically, some of the outrage provoked by photographic images of war comes from the awareness that we may be powerless to act even while acknowledging that something must be done.

This same kind of outrage pervades the *Disasters*. We are directed toward the unimaginable violence of the horrors of a war whose political lines are well known, and at the same time, we are faced with our inability to do much, if anything, about it. These are the twin routes of the suffering that the *Disasters* provoke — the suffering experienced by the victims of the violence of war and its aftermath (most importantly, the famine that swept Madrid across the years 1811–12) and the suffering of those who witnesses that violence, whose position as "passive" viewers is directly at odds with the urgency that the images convey. In viewing the *Disasters*, we inevitably find ourselves in that predicament. Why? One reason may lie in the fact that Goya does not identify individual perpetrators of the violence of war. The violence is best attributable to the state and so confounds the prospect of individual response. Moreover, the decontextualization of these images, that is, the absence of contextualizing frames, contributes to the illusion that the responsibility for the atrocities of war is so generalized that it lies beyond the reach of any conventional form of ethical response. And yet they clearly produce an affective response in the viewer.

What are the connections between those responses and the ethical position in which the *Disasters* place the viewer, and where does politics come into play? Indeed, there is no doubt that the *Disasters* have a historical and a political dimension, which can be limned in the three groups by which critics often classify them. Plates 1 through 47 show the ravages of a war in which the civilian Spanish population was a victim of horrific French aggression. Plates 48 through 64 show the devastating effects of the famine that swept Madrid between August 1811 and August 1812, killing some twenty thousand people. The famine was a result of many factors, but Goya is not concerned with parsing the causes. He is far more interested in the claim that the suffering makes on the attention of the viewer. Plates 65 through 82 are the *caprichos enfáticos* and include allegorical scenes that critique postwar Spanish politics and institutions, including the Inquisition and the common judicial practice of torture. Robert Hughes has called this group the "disasters of peace."[8] (If war is the continuation of politics by other means, then these images show politics as the continuation of war.) All these details about the series are important to bear in mind when it comes to assessing the failed promises of the Enlightenment. They mirror what Goya took to be a historically unresolvable predicament that presented two equally unacceptable alternatives—a choice between the violence inflicted by "enlightened" French culture and the return to practices associated with the Spanish past. Which one is worse, the violence of the French mercenaries, or the practice of judicial torture as enforced under the totalitarian regime of Fernando VII? Indeed, Goya suggests that if anything could in fact be worse than the violence inflicted by the French, it might well be the restitution of Spanish-style justice (as in no. 74, "¡*Esto es lo peor!*" ["This is the worst!"], Figure 6.3). To confront these alternatives and to recognize that they pose an impossible choice contributes to the sense of cultural and historical dislocation in the *Disasters*. They are views seen as if from nowhere, not least because the elements of cultural and historical location have been undone. The distinction between "French" violence and "Spanish" violence is broken down early in the series. A French soldier, possibly a mercenary, carries off a lightly robed woman while an ordinary citizen prepares to knife him in the back (no. 9, "*No quieren*" ["They do not want to"], Figure 6.4).

This is a kind of violence that begets violence, and showing it in such an uncensored way raises questions that go beyond politics, questions that have to do with the relationship between the core activities of art (picturing, viewing) and the call for an ethical response to unambiguously violent situations. And yet the issue of responsibility, one of the basic questions of ethics — the question of who is ultimately responsible for the violence of these images — turns out to be especially fraught. At some level, the answer to that question is "everyone," and the implications of that suggestion are so broad that they reach beyond individuals to the unpictured state sponsors of war and the suffering in its aftermath. The source of the violence is generalized and impersonal, though its effects are all too personal indeed. But one might also say of the *Disasters* what Stan Gontarski said of Beckett — that the focus of injustice is not local, civil, or social, but cosmic ("the injustice of having been born.")[9] The suffering in the period following the Napoleonic wars is different from, but no less than, the suffering brought about by the violence of war. It carries the added burden of having been produced

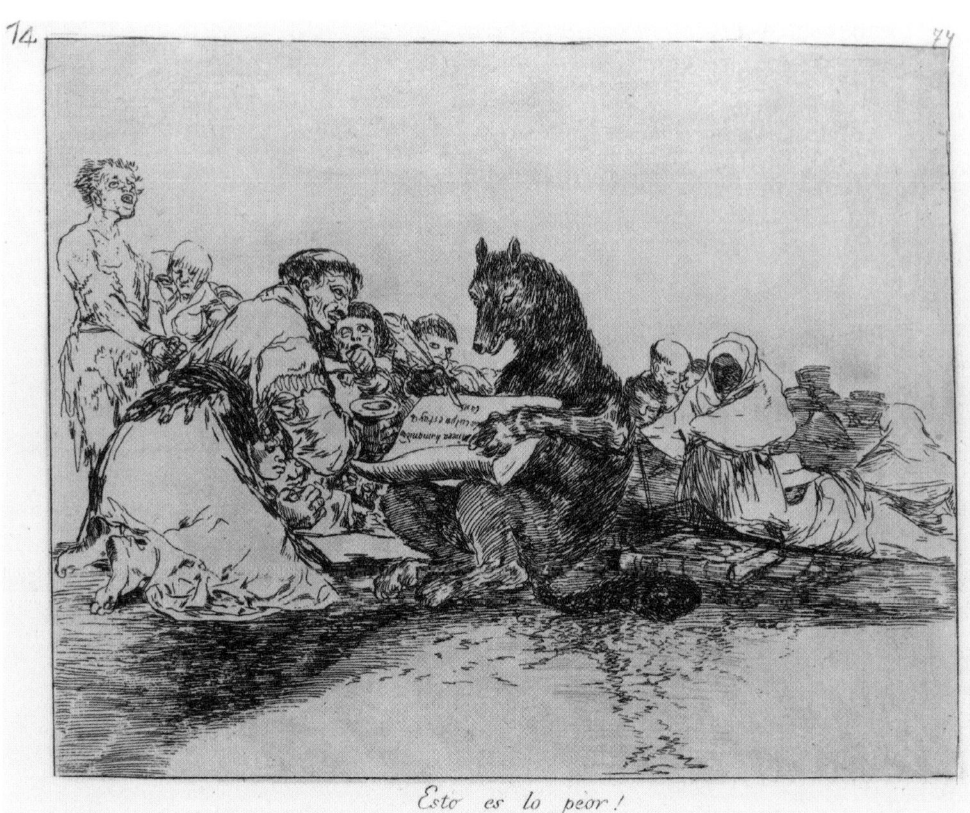

Figure 6.3.
"¡*Esto es lo peor*!" ("This is the worst!"), *Disasters of War*, no. 74, ca. 1814–15, published 1863. Etching and burnisher, 17.9 × 22 cm.

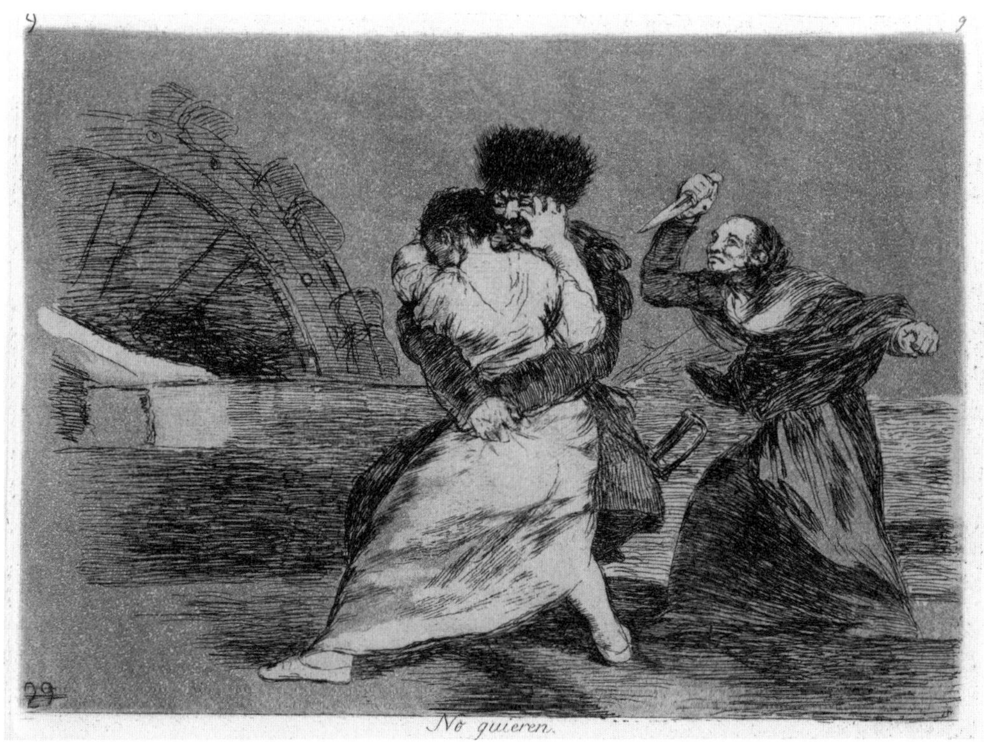

Figure 6.4.
"*No quieren*" ("They do not want to"), *Disasters of War*, no. 9, ca. 1810–15,
published 1863. Etching, burnished aquatint, drypoint, and burnisher, 15.3×20.7 cm.

by institutions dedicated to the public good, to truth, and to justice. But the *Disasters* also implicate the viewer in the suffering they picture. The viewer experiences an ethical responsibility that cannot be met, because the images cry out for something to be done, and there is nothing that can be done. The viewer of these plates is hardly in the position of cool neutrality that Kant famously identified as the ideal way to deal with the violence of the French Revolution (more about which below). On the contrary, the *Disasters* position the spectator as a witness to atrocities that he or she is powerless to avert. Here, the gap between theory and practice, as between seeing and doing, points well beyond the limits of art to expose the suffering that attaches to an ethical demand that we cannot meet.

To pursue this argument further, it is important to consider again what it means for questions of ethics to be raised through a set of images rather than through the discursive means by which ethical matters are typically addressed (for example, in philosophy). The difference is hardly a minor one and goes to the heart of some of the central differences between the discursive medium of philosophy and the visual language of art. For one thing, the two adopt very different stances with respect to the role of the medium in such matters: whereas the ideal in philosophy is for the medium (language as a vehicle of thought) to disappear and for the moral law to be transcendental, an etching counts every element of the medium in all its materiality — every line and tonal gradation, along with the composition and the framing of the image as a whole — as contributing to its ethical outlook. But the differences do not stop there. In the *Disasters*, questions of ethics are inseparable from affect, which is to say both that they communicate by appeal to the emotions and also that they regard the emotions as integral to ethical life. This is in stark contrast to Enlightenment (Kantian) notions of ethics, which rest on rational foundations and are intended to have a universal scope. Those foundations rest on transcendental arguments, that is, arguments that begin from some putatively undeniable facet of experience and that go on to conclude that this experience must have a certain set of features or be of a particular type if it is to be possible at all.[10] Indeed, the tension between an ethics that is shaped by reliance on the universality of a moral law and an ethics that is rooted in the particularities of a given situation, conveyed by images of overwhelming power such as any of the ones Goya shows in the *Disasters*, is reflective of one of the prevailing differences between the interests of philosophy and of art as they approach the central questions that ethics requires us to ask: What ought to be done? What must I do? To recognize that in the *Disasters*, Goya approaches ethics by forcing us to face the particulars — the horrible and unavoidable particulars of wartime violence as rendered in a material medium — is also to recognize their resistance to ethical constructs that are built upon necessarily abstract principles of rationality that can appeal to the notion of a universal moral law. Kant thought just the opposite.

This distinction is at its sharpest with regard to the philosophical framework that Kant advanced in the *Critique of Practical Reason*. Having already completed a critique of pure reason, Kant extended his enterprise to the domain of pure *practical* reason, that is, to the rational principles that determine the will and lead to action. The chief goal of his second *Critique*, he says, is "to prevent the empirically conditioned reason from claiming exclusively to furnish the ground of determination of the will."[11] Indeed, Kant recognizes that we can identify all manner of reasons that might determine the will. There are many things that present themselves as imperatives for action. But many are conditioned by particulars, and especially by desired outcomes, and so are not general enough to qualify as rational laws for determining the will. They are merely precepts. As Kant says toward the very beginning of the second *Critique*, "Imperatives themselves . . . when they are conditional (i.e., do not determine the will simply as will, but only in respect to a desired effect, that is, when they are hypothetical imperatives), are practical precepts but not laws. Laws must be sufficient to determine the will as will, even before I ask whether I have power sufficient for a desired effect, or the means necessary to produce it; hence they are categorical."[12] The kinds of rules Kant wants must be objectively and universally valid, and this can happen only when they hold "without any contingent subjective conditions, which distinguish one rational being from another."[13] They cannot be based on feelings (for example, of pleasure or pain, preference or dislike), even if we could agree on such things, as for instance might be the case with something like the feeling of self-love: "even supposing, however, that all finite rational beings were thoroughly agreed as to what were the objects of their feelings of pleasure and pain, and also as to the means which they must employ to attain the one and avoid the other; still, they could by no means set up the principle of self-love as a practical law, for this unanimity itself would be only contingent."[14] These remarks give a good sense of the considerations Kant takes into account in formulating what he describes as the Fundamental Law of pure practical reason: "Act so that the maxim of thy will can always at the same time hold good as a principle of universal legislation."[15]

Among the most remarkable things to note about the direction Kant takes here is the extraordinary level of generality he expects in these matters, all the while upholding the ideal that each individual, qua moral agent, has the obligation to act such that whatever may direct his or her will could also be binding on all others. For Kant, this is validation of the claim that we all share something by virtue of our reason, which brightens the world of the will, just as it illuminates the external world. It is one of the grounds for Kant's extraordinary optimism about human nature; it provides the basis on which we can feel elevated, even where we might be overwhelmed by the vastness of the universe around us:

> Two things fill the mind with ever new and increasing admiration and awe, the oftener and the more steadily we reflect on them: the starry heavens above and the moral law within. I have not to search for them and conjecture them as though they were veiled in darkness or were in the transcendent region beyond my horizon; I see them before me and connect them directly with the

consciousness of my existence. The former begins from the place I occupy in the external world of sense, and enlarges my connection therein to an unbounded extent with worlds upon worlds and systems of systems, and moreover into limitless times of their periodic motion, its beginning and continuance. The second begins from my invisible self, my personality, and exhibits in me a world which has true infinity, but which is traceable only by the understanding, and with which I discern that I am not in a merely contingent but in a universal and necessary connection, as I am also thereby with all those visible worlds. The former view of a countless multitude of worlds annihilates as it were my importance as an animal creature, which after it has been for a short time provided with vital power, one knows not how, must again give back the matter of which it was formed to the planet it inhabits (a mere speck in the universe). The second, on the contrary, infinitely elevates my worth as an intelligence by my personality, in which the moral law reveals to me a life independent of animality and even of the whole sensible world, at least so far as may be inferred from the destination assigned to my existence by this law, a destination not restricted to conditions and limits of this life, but reaching into the infinite.[16]

I cite this passage for its own value in shedding a contrastive light on Goya's *Disasters*, but also because it proves to be important for what Kant later writes about the aesthetics of the sublime in the *Critique of Judgment*, where he talks about how we can succeed in dealing with experiences that make us feel utterly overwhelmed. But here, in what Kant writes about the moral law, he approaches such matters with a more austere sense of discipline, philosophical and otherwise. His claim toward the very end of the passage, that the moral law separates us not only from "animality," but also from the whole sensible world, is shocking to any sensibility that regards humanity as intimately connected to both. Certainly it is shocking to a sensibility such as Goya's in the *Disasters*, which demonstrate that human beings have the potential to be as vicious as any animal, but also to an aesthetic sensibility that refuses to separate questions about how we should act from questions about how we belong to the sensible world. Indeed, the fact that we are part of the sensible world is one of the reasons Goya will not let us turn away from the awful things he shows in the *Disasters*. It is one of the reasons he insists on showing the fact that human beings are capable of atrocious violence. Our capacity for atrocity is paradoxically one of the grounds of our moral nature and does not depend for that fact on the prospect of redemption—whether by reason, by religion, or by art itself. Questions about ethical action have to be raised in direct view of these things, not from a position above or beyond them.

While there may be no prospect for transcendence in any of these terms, there is an extreme quality about what the *Disasters* show that goes beyond what might ordinarily be captured in assertions about our participation in the sensible world. To be sure, the sensuous world is nothing new to Goya's pictures. The tapestry cartoons are replete with images of pleasure and pain—picnics and play, seductions, brawls, and much more. But, as discussed above, these images revolve largely around social life. Likewise, a number of the *Caprichos* engage questions about bare human life, though clearly for the purpose of exposing the human capacity for contradiction and self-deception (for example, as an old hag looks in a mirror, but does not recognize how aged and ugly she has become). The sensuous world of the *Disasters* is quite different. In it, we see mutilated and dismembered bodies; (for example, no. 39, "*Grande hazaña. Con muertos*" ["A great deed. Against the dead"], Figure 6.5); tortured bodies (no. 32), bodies rendered unrecognizable by acts of unspeakable violence (for example, no. 28, "*Populacho*" ["Rabble"], Figure 6.6); corpses piled in heaps (for example, no. 63, "*Muertos recogidos*" ["A collection of dead men"], Figure 6.7). We are shown the sensuous world through physical suffering *in the extreme*, and we are shown that it makes no sense. One is reminded of the question that Vladimir asks in Beckett's *Waiting for Godot*: "Where are all these corpses from?"[17]

The extremity of Goya's images in the *Disasters* is in fact a key to understanding their role in representing the limits of reason. The actions they show us completely overwhelm notions of the "unreasonable" or "irrationality," both of which assume some concept of

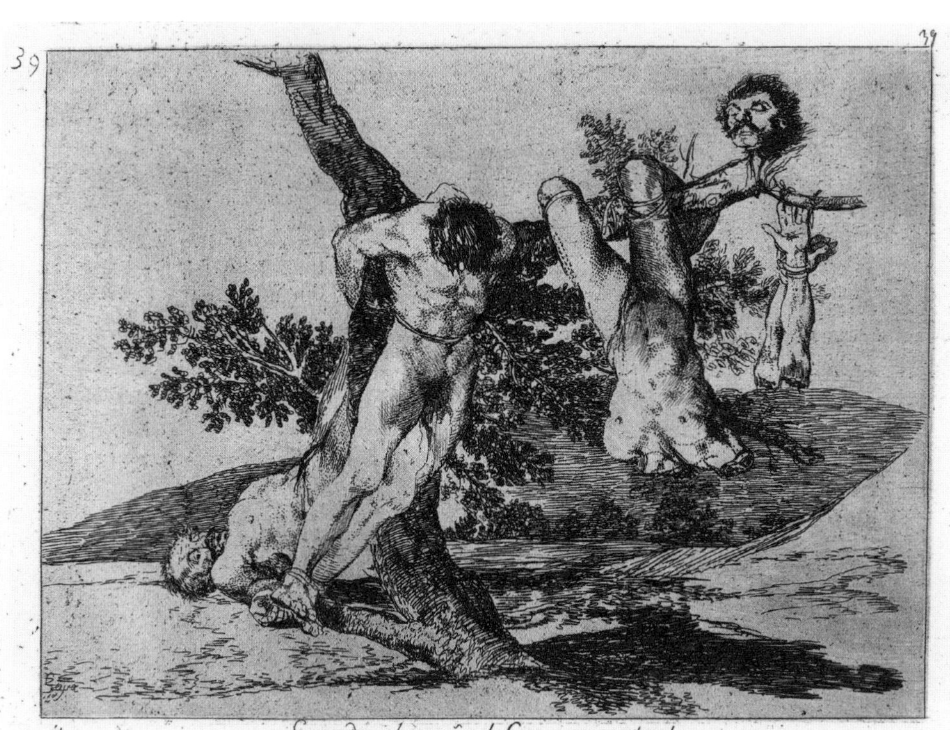

Figure 6.5.
"*Grande hazaña. Con muertos*" ("A great deed. Against the dead"), *Disasters of War*, no. 39, ca. 1812–15, published 1863. Etching, lavis, and drypoint, 15.6 × 20.8 cm.

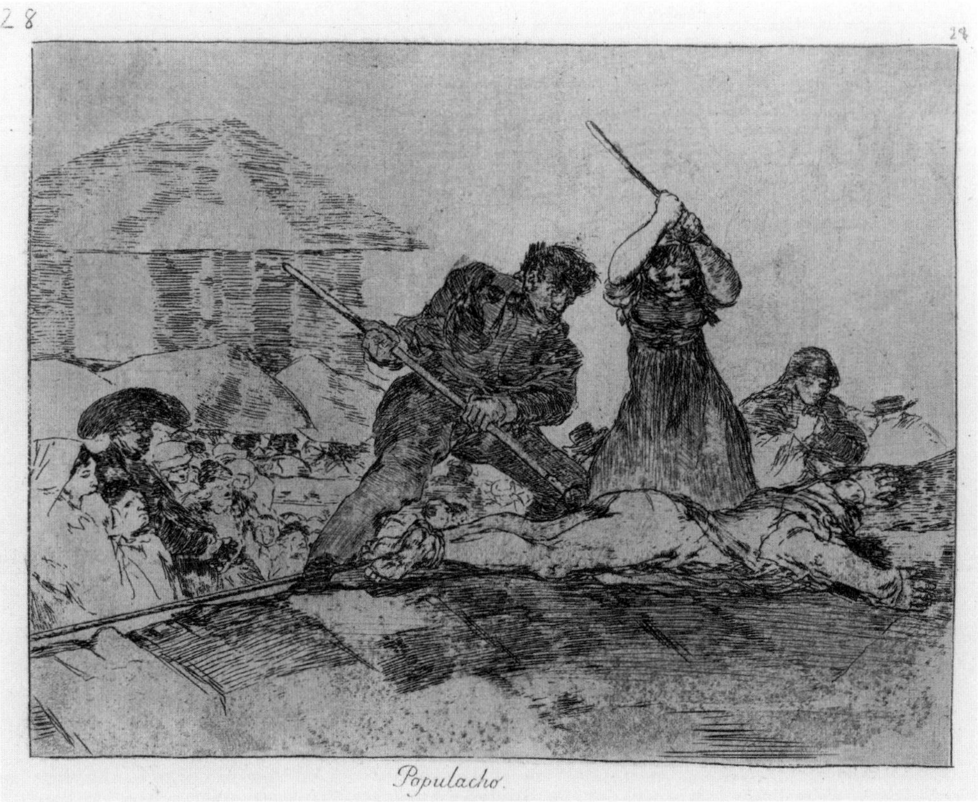

Figure 6.6.
"*Populacho*" ("Rabble"), *Disasters of War*, no. 28, ca. 1810–12,
published 1863. Etching, aquatint, burin, drypoint, and burnisher, 17.7×22 cm.

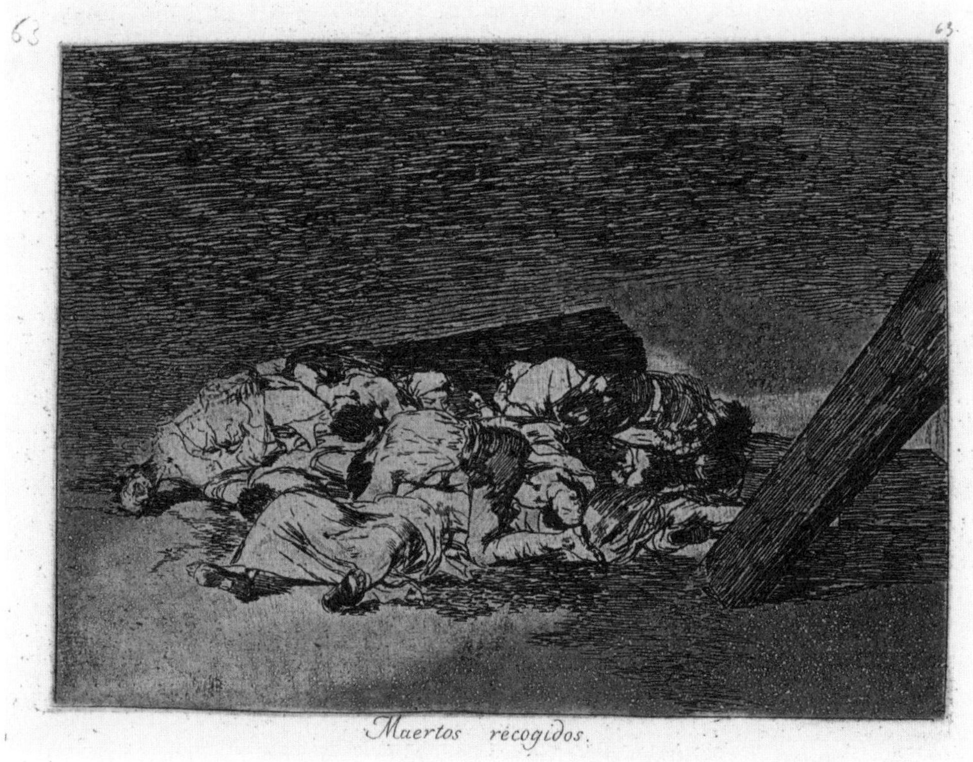

Figure 6.7.
"*Muertos recogidos*" ("A collection of dead men"), *Disasters of War*, no. 63, ca. 1812–15, published 1863. Etching and burnished aquatint, 15.5×20.8 cm.

reason as a reference. They take us to a place where reason simply does not apply. One of the first plates (no. 2) bears the caption "*Con razon ó sin ella*" ("With or without reason"); the following image (no. 3) shows bodies being hacked apart by swords and axes and bears the caption "*Lo mismo*" ("The same thing," Figure 3.23, above). It seems to matter little who is right or wrong in these things (which is one way to understand the caption accompanying plate no. 2, which can also be translated as "Rightly or wrongly"). In one image (no. 4), women inspire courage, fighting off their attackers ("*Las mujeres dan valor*" ["The women give courage"], Figure 6.8), but in the very next plate, they act like beasts ("*Y son fieras*" ["And are like wild beasts"], Figure 6.9). The question "Why?" that accompanies one of the most horrific images of torture (no. 28, "*Populacho*" ["Rabble:], Figure 6.6) has no answer. Or as the caption of no. 35 says, "*No se puede saber por qué*" ("Nobody can know why," Figure 6.10). The lack of any reason behind the violence shown in these images is also reflected in the way Goya blocks any attempt to extract a meaning that might be drawn from them by reading them sequentially. Indeed, if there is a logic to their ordering, it is only to show the arbitrariness of violence. One plate (no. 42) says "*Todo va revuelto*" ("Everything is topsy-turvy," Figure 6.11). The one immediately following adds "*Tambien esto*" ("This too"). This is a blunt and brutal logic that defies the sense-making power of syntactical ordering.

What is nonetheless surprising in light of the senselessness of the violence in the *Disasters* is the fact that the very first plate of the series raises some questions about how we are to interpret them. (It may have been the last one Goya made.) The image shows a figure in prayer or supplication, and the caption reads "*Tristes presentimientos de lo que ha de acontecer*" ("Sad premonitions of what must come to pass"). What is it that this figure sees — or perhaps better put, what is it that this figure sees *into*? Knowing the images that follow, what is "bound to come" is a revelation of the horrific violence of which human beings are capable. If this figure sees *into* anything, it is the utter darkness of the human soul, reflected in the background

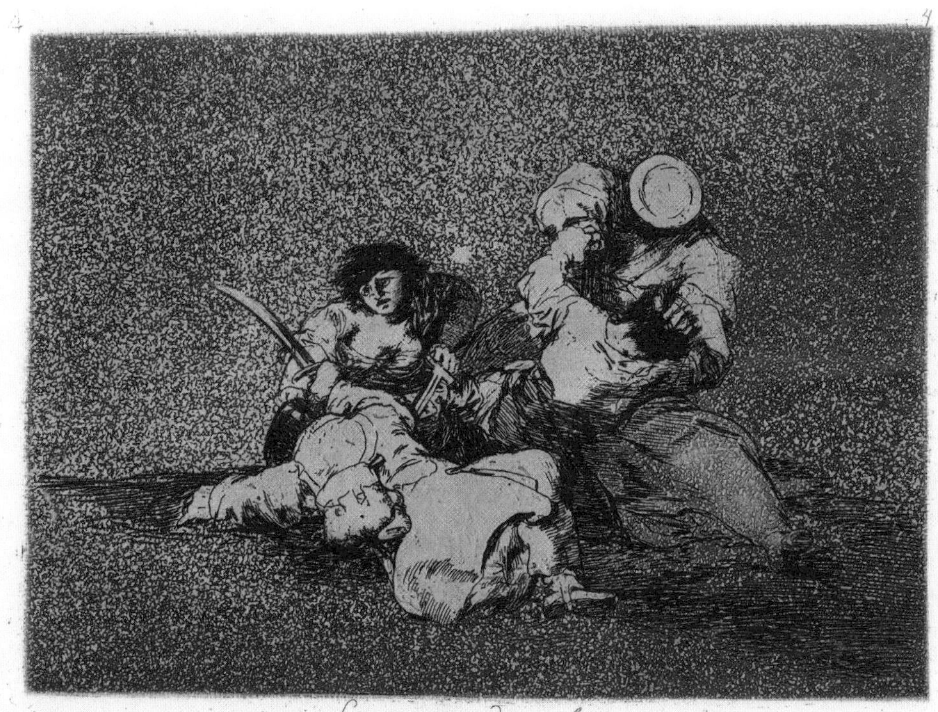

Figure 6.8.

"*Las mujeres dan valor*" ("The women give courage"), *Disasters of War*, no. 4, ca. 1810–15, published 1863. Etching, lavis, drypoint, burin, and burnisher, 15.5×20.6 cm.

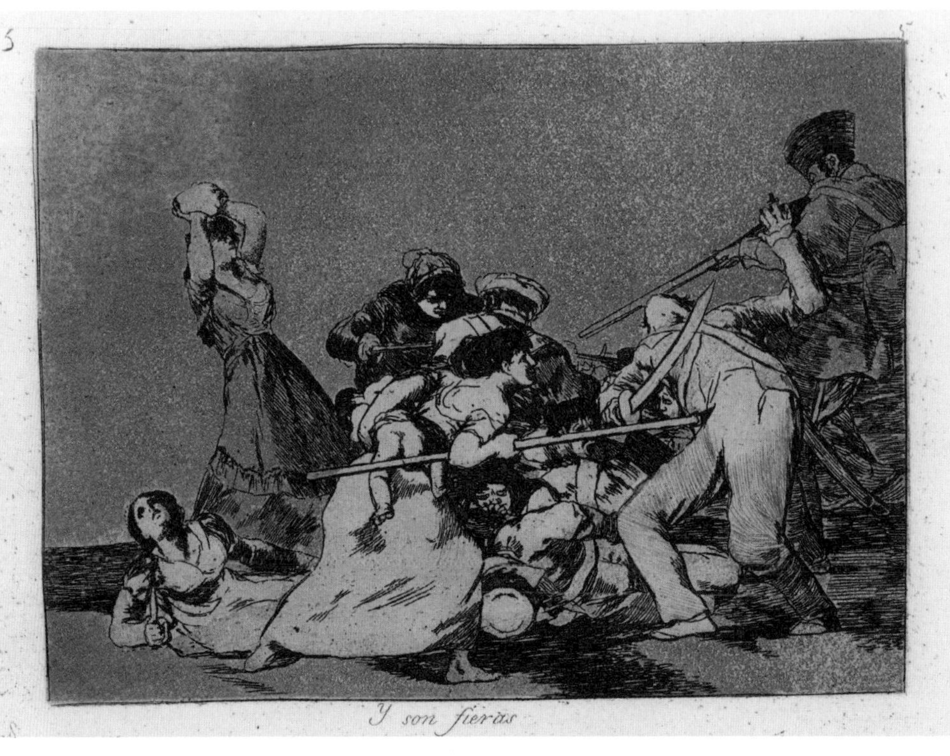

Figure 6.9.

"*Y son fieras*" ("And are like wild beasts"), *Disasters of War*, no. 5, ca. 1812–15, published 1863. Etching, burnished aquatint, and drypoint, 15.6×20.8 cm.

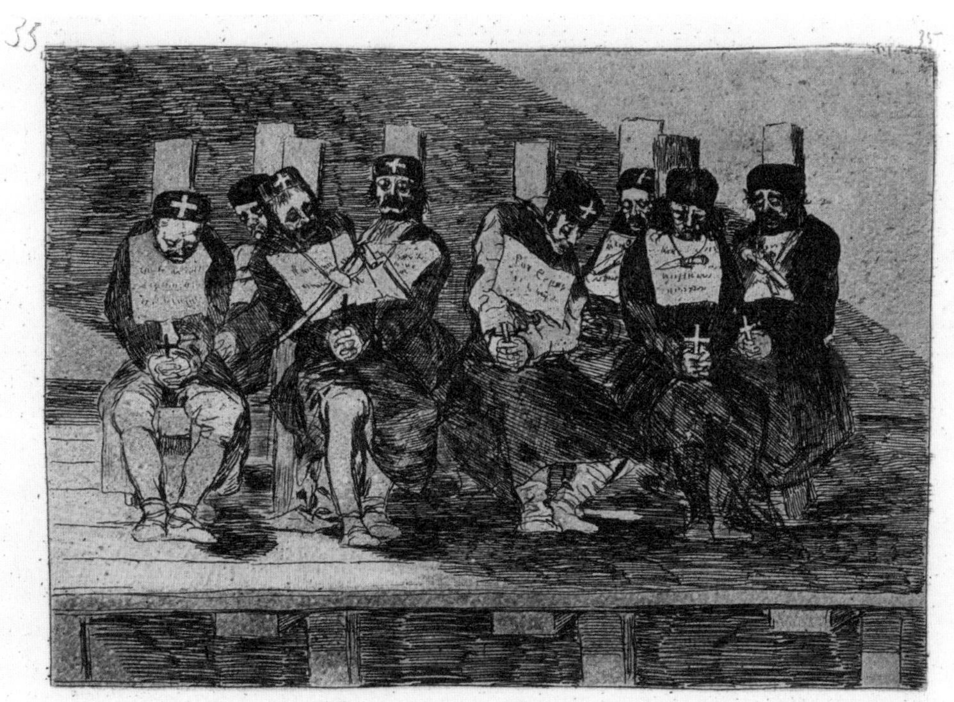

Figure 6.10.
"*No se puodo sabor por qué*" ("Nobody can know why"), *Disasters of War*, no. 35,
ca. 1812–15, published 1863. Etching, burnished lavis, drypoint, and burin, 15.4×25.6 cm.

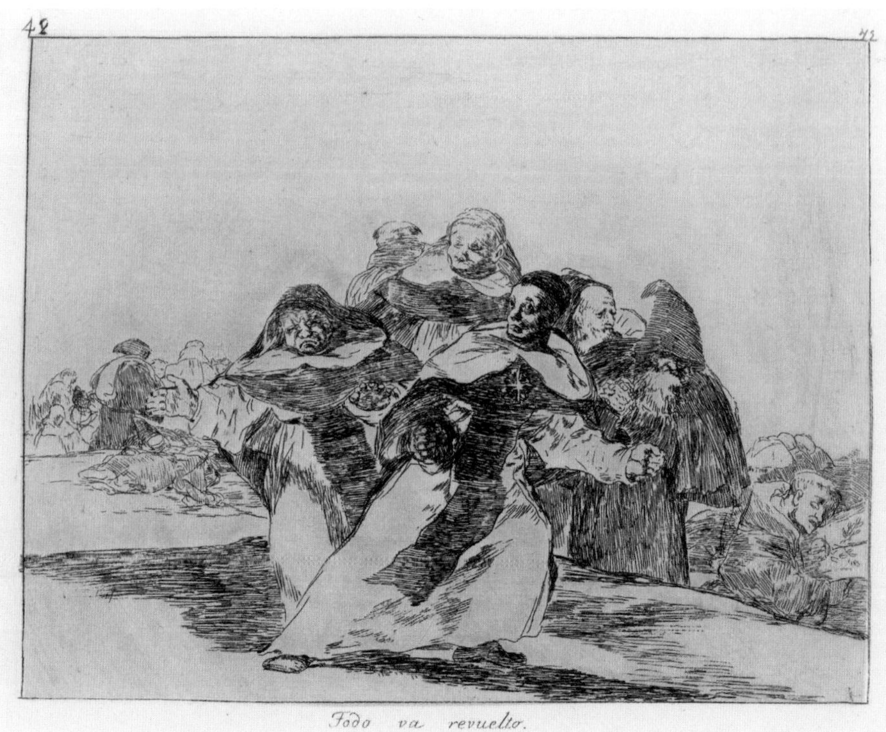

Figure 6.11.

"*Todo va revuelto*" ("Everything is topsy-turvy"), *Disasters of War*, no. 42, ca. 1810–15, published 1863. Etching and burin, 17.8×22 cm.

surrounding him. That enveloping darkness is a major factor in the *Disasters*, including in this plate, where the darkness of the sky contravenes any hope for divine illumination. Darkness is propagated throughout the series and shows up not only in the blackness that provides the backdrop for images such as no. 30, *"Estragos de la guerra"* ("Ravages of war," Figure 6.12), but also in the graves where so many bodies are dumped (for example, no. 27, *"Caridad"* ["Charity"], Figure 6.13). What Goya's particular handling of darkness seems to suggest is that these graves are bottomless — that there is no measure by which the earth can contain the suffering of those who have been killed by the violence of war. There is no consolation in burial.

Any attempt to show that there is no measure of the violence of war and its consequences places special burdens on art. This is because traditional conventions of perspective and composition are in fact built around principles of measure and order. Those conventions range from the geometric grid by which point of view and vanishing point are constructed to the principle of thirds that guides the compositional elements of the kinds of images that had become normative. Indeed, the very framing of an image, both literally in its placement on the page in the case of prints and in the way its figural borders are established, is an act that involves establishing measure and order; it also determines questions of scale by virtue of the relationship between the physical size of the image and the size of things pictured in it. Taken in the broadest sense, it helps make the image intelligible. But where the subjects of the images in question are so extreme that they lie beyond any measure is where these conventional resources fail. In fact, this is why the relationship between the suffering figures in Goya's prints and their surroundings are often so distressing. To be sure, there are hints of some recognizable landscape backgrounds in some of the plates — the outlines of what may be a countryside house, as in no. 28 (*"Populacho"* ["Rabble"], see Figure 6.6), a hillock in the distance (no. 7, *"¡Qué valor!"* ["What courage!"], Figure. 6.14), or a small cluster of buildings (no. 24, *"Aún podrán servir"* ["They will still be able to serve"], Figure 6.15). But

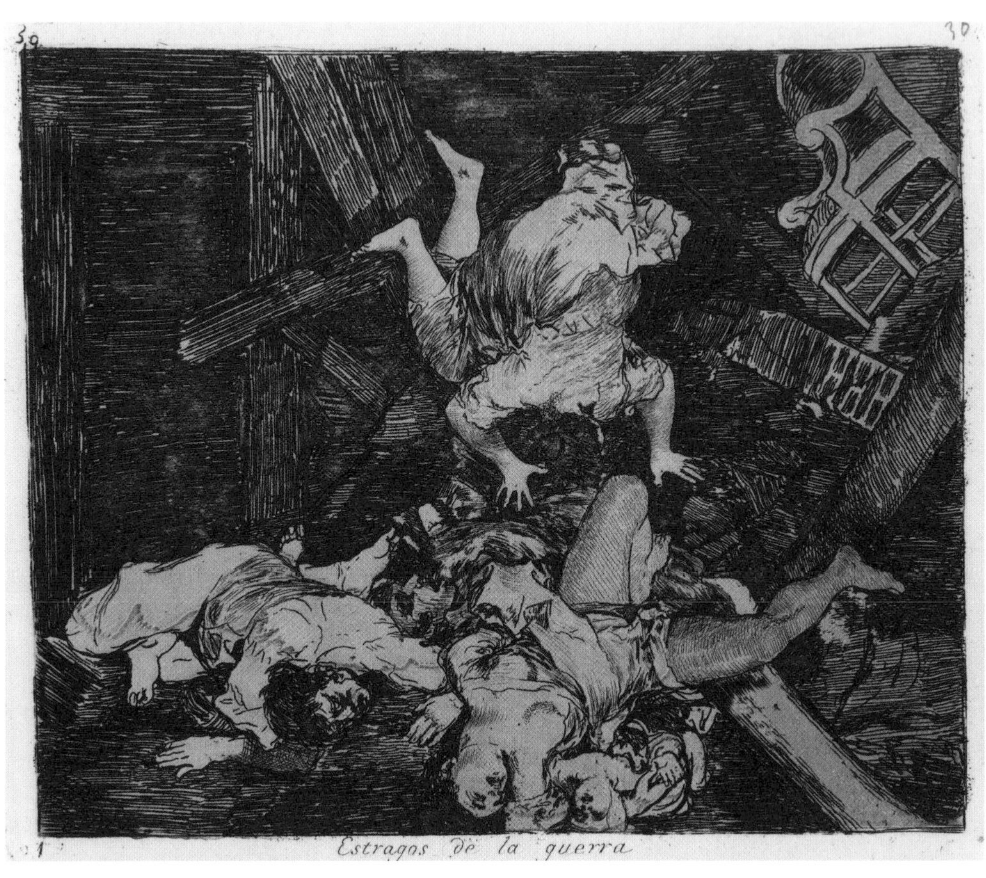

Figure 6.12.
"*Estragos de la guerra*" ("Ravages of war"), *Disasters of War*, no. 30, ca. 1810–12, published 1863. Etching, burin, drypoint, and burnisher, 14.1 × 17 cm.

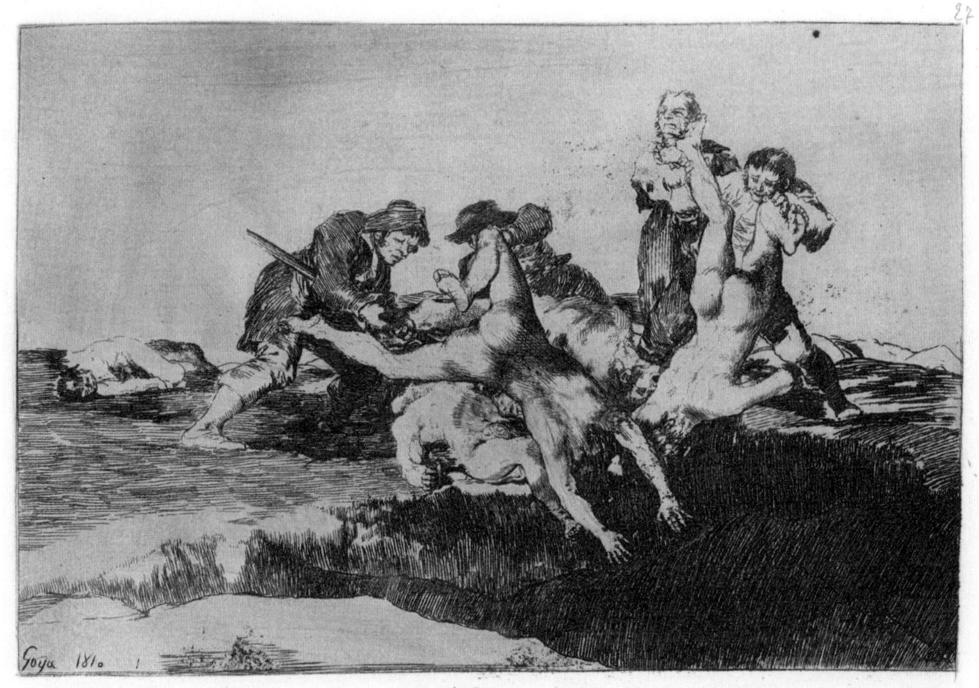

Figure 6.13.
"*Caridad*" ("Charity"), *Disasters of War*, no. 27, 1810, published 1863.
Etching, aquatint, burin, drypoint, and burnisher, 16.3×23.6 cm.

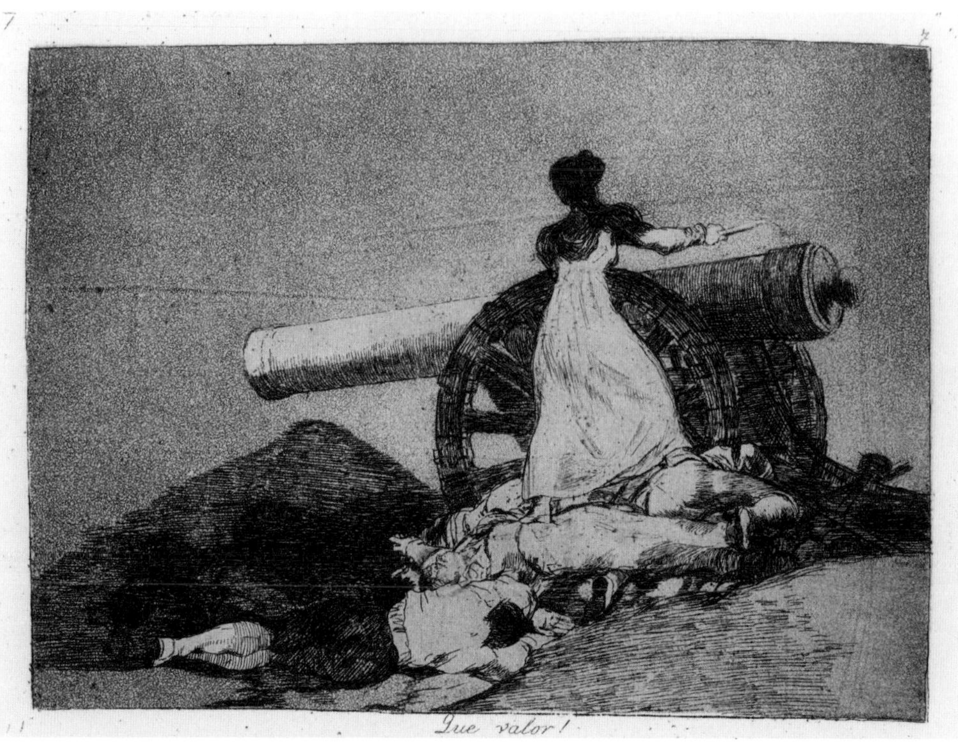

Figure 6.14.
"*¡Que valor!*" ("What courage!"), *Disasters of War*, no. 7, ca. 1810–15,
published 1863. Etching, aquatint, burin, drypoint, and burnisher, 11.5×20.8 cm.

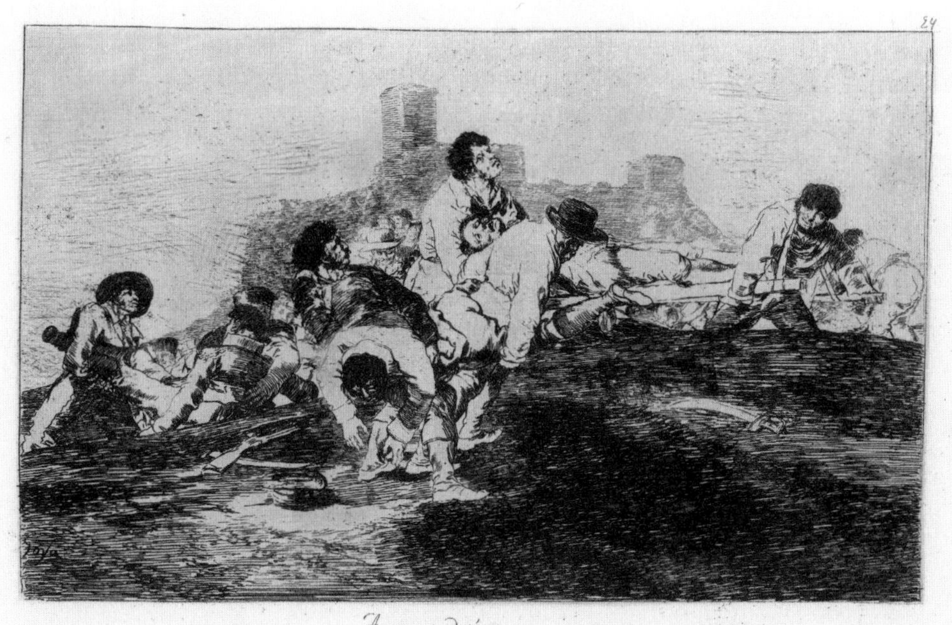

Figure 6.15.

"*Aún podrán servir*" ("They will still be able to serve"), *Disasters of War*, no. 24, ca. 1810–12, published 1863. Etching and burnisher, 16.3×26 cm.

the backgrounds of most of the *Disasters* are devoid of any figural forms. They are monochrome versions of the kind of nothingness discussed above in relation to the *Semisunken Dog* (Chapter 3, Figure 3.7). This gives heightened emphasis to the figures in the foreground of the image, but it also isolates them, detaching them from context and frame. Consequently, we are asked to confront them without reliance on context for reference. We are in fact led to understand that there is no context for these images because what they show is so extreme.

Though Burke's *Philosophical Enquiry into the Origin of Our Ideas of the Sublime and Beautiful* was more widely known in Spain than Kant's *Critique of Judgment*,[18] to broach the idea of an image "without measure" in the early nineteenth-century context and not make reference to Kant's theory of the sublime is virtually impossible. Indeed, one of the main roots of the sublime as Kant conceives it, derived in no small measure from Burke, lies in those things that are characterized as "absolutely great," that is, without measure. (Burke associates the sublime with pain, which is "always inflicted by a power in some way superior, because we never submit to pain willingly"; Kant says that the sublime conversely relates to things "in comparison with which all else is small.")[19] When such things present themselves to us, we find that the ordinary powers of our intellect are defeated. Our cognitive abilities are overwhelmed by them. These things require aesthetic judgment. ("What is indicated [as absolutely great] is not a pure concept of understanding, still less an intuition of sense; and just as little is it a concept of reason, for it does not import any principle of cognition. It must, therefore, be a concept of judgment.")[20] Kant exemplifies this in the experience of seeing the great pyramids in Egypt or St. Peter's in Rome. We cannot visually take in the pyramids as a whole: "it takes the eye some time to complete the apprehension from the base to the summit; but in this interval the first tiers always in part disappear before the imagination has taken in the last, and so the comprehension is never complete." Likewise, Kant suggests, we experience a sense of bewilderment upon first entering St. Peter's: "here a feeling comes home to him of the inadequacy of his imagination for presenting the idea of a whole within which that imagination can attain its maximum, and, in its fruitless efforts to extend this limit, recoils upon itself."[21] In instances such as these, we experience the inadequacy of our ability to form representations, and that awareness in turn precipitates the need for aesthetic judgment, in this case, precipitating a judgment of the sublime. The sublime is complex because it involves an effort toward the comprehension of something that outstrips the power of cognition to grasp it. This generates a similarly complex cascade of feelings:

> The feeling of the sublime is a pleasure that only arises indirectly, being brought about by the feeling of a momentary check to the vital forces followed at once by a discharge all the more powerful, and so it is an emotion that seems to be no sport, but dead earnest in the affairs of the imagination. Hence charms are repugnant to it; and, since the mind is not simply attracted by the object, but is also alternately repelled thereby, the delight in the sublime does not so much involve positive pleasure as admiration or respect, i.e. merits the name of a negative pleasure.[22]

Since the "absolutely great" has principally to do with questions of magnitude, Kant calls it the "mathematically sublime." But the sublime has a second root, lying in things that are so powerful as to appear threatening. This is the form of the "dynamical sublime," which Burke had associated with "vastness," "infinity," and "magnitude": "*Might* is a power which is superior to great hindrances. It is termed *dominion* if it is also superior to the resistance of that which possesses might. Nature considered in an aesthetic judgment as might that has no dominion over us, is *dynamically sublime*. If we are to estimate nature as dynamically sublime, it must be represented as a source of fear."[23] But as Kant goes on to say, this is a *faux* fear, since to experience nature as sublime and ultimately to derive some pleasure from the experience requires that our position be secure. We must be physically protected, yet in the process of confronting the might of nature and withstanding its apparent threat, we are in turn ennobled. "We readily call these objects sublime, because they raise the forces of the soul above the height of the vulgar commonplace, and discover within us a power of resistance of quite another kind, which gives us courage to be able to measure ourselves against the seeming omnipotence of nature"; this reveals a sphere of the mind that "altogether exceeds the realm of nature."[24] The sublime is thus a way of representing the final (moral) good; it arouses a feeling that is best characterized as respect (*Achtung*).

Kant's idea of the sublime is ultimately redemptive, which is one of the reasons why it can serve as such a useful contrast to Goya's handling of extremity in the *Disasters*. Just as Kant's conception of the beautiful relies on the idea that we can communicate universally about certain things that are grounded in feeling, so, too, his idea of the sublime relies on the idea that certain feelings are the basis on which we — that is, everyone — can place ourselves in relation to a higher power. These are complex feelings, to be sure, but the important thing is that they allow us to arrive at a universally acknowledged relationship to the moral law. (Kant's sublime is redemptive in just this sense.) Insofar as the French Revolution was in the background of his thinking, he wanted to believe that even the most violent upheavals could yield respect for moral principles.

Reflecting directly on the revolution toward the very end of his life, Kant directed his focus beyond the violence of the events to the position from which it allows us to find confidence in the morality of the human race. This is the equivalent of an aesthetic perspective (Kant describes it as the position of the neutral spectator). It closely resembles the experience of the sublime insofar as it is close enough to the violence of the revolution to inspire powerful feelings but distanced safely enough away to afford an engagement of a shared enthusiasm for the cause. It reveals a moral disposition, regardless of whether or not history bears out the hopes of the revolution in the short run. Kant's argument that human beings have a moral disposition, offered in his advocacy for the role of spectators in response to the French Revolution (cited in the previous chapter) are particularly illustrative here.

As that passage and similar ones make clear, one of the keys to Kant's thinking about our relationship to the violence of revolution lies in the establishment of an aesthetic position from which to regard it. To repeat, it lies in "the mode of thinking of the spectators which reveals itself publicly in this game of great revolutions, and manifests such a universal yet disinterested sympathy for the players on one side against those on the other, even at the risk that this partiality could become very disadvantageous for them if discovered."[25]

This discussion of Kant is hardly intended to suggest that Goya's work can fit into preestablished aesthetic categories or that he knew of and sought directly to challenge a particular Enlightenment aesthetics. Nor is it meant to suggest a comparison between the French Revolution and the bloody conflicts between Spanish citizens and Napoleon's French forces on the Iberian Peninsula. To be sure, Goya was aware of the grim irony of a situation in which the forces of "Enlightened" France were the perpetrators of bestial violence, just as he was in the *Second of May, 1808* and *The Third of May, 1808*. But what shocks most about the *Disasters of War* is the fact that Goya does not allow for the kind of safeguards that Kant imagines in the aesthetic of the sublime and that Kant likewise affords to the spectators of historical revolutions. Goya's vision of war is brutally raw in aesthetic terms, and he is far less reassuring than Kant when it comes to questions of morality. The exposure to unfathomable violence in the *Disasters* is unbuffered and opens the viewer to a kind of suffering that refuses to be "aestheticized" at all. And that in turn is one element of what renders the *Disasters* so deeply troubling as works of art — the fact that they refuse the conventional principles by which art enables us to relate to the world, for example, by establishing the visual frameworks through which we can view and interpret it, transforming it into something that is at least at one remove from raw reality. Those same conventions of art are the ones that enable us to make sense of the world, and in Kant's analysis of the sublime, they do more than this. They also enable us to appreciate the role that our mental powers play in that very process. That appreciation is part of the ennobling effect of the sublime and is among the metaphysical comforts the *Disasters* deny.

In attempting to explain further how and why Goya does this, two interlinked answers present themselves. The first revolves around the fact that the Kantian sublime is evidenced mostly in nature. The majority of Kant's examples, whether of the mathematical or of the dynamical sublime, are not drawn from the human world, although the great pyramids and Saint Peter's in Rome are clearly important exceptions to this rule. Goya's *Disasters of War* are by contrast depictions of unbounded violence that reduce human beings to their animal nature and yet that is the result of human factors. The violence of war as seen in the *Disasters* is entirely man-made. Moreover, that violence is profoundly destructive. It involves a powerful unmaking of the world that runs painfully contrary to the constructive impetus of art.[26]

The second answer, related to the first, has to do with the particular nature of the Napoleonic wars and with the effect they had on the populace as a whole. The Napoleonic wars were among the first conflicts in history to introduce the techniques of "total war" as we have since come to know it. These techniques included mass conscription, the marshaling of all available resources, and the establishment of armies of unprecedented proportions, reaching over a million for the first time in history. The tactics of total war are extreme. They disregard bounds in ways that are analogous to the disregard for boundaries in the *Disasters*. As characterized by one of its most influential historians, David A. Bell, "total war" is war "involving the complete mobilization of a society's resources to achieve the absolute destruction of an enemy, with all distinction erased between combatants and noncombatants." What marked the conflicts that began in 1792 was a process that drove participants toward what Bell described as "a condition of total engagement and the abandonment of restraints."[27] In such circumstances, war itself becomes *absolute* — absolute in such a way that there is no standing "outside" it. It cannot be gauged by any reasonable measure. Before 1790, relatively few battles involved more than one hundred thousand troops, while France alone suffered more than *one million losses* during the Napoleonic period.[28]

The affinities between Goya's *Disasters* and the concept of "total war" has been the subject of an especially insightful volume by Nil Santiáñez that establishes convincing links between two improbable figures, Goya and Clausewitz. The conditions of "total war" produce a profound challenge to the sense-making abilities of reason, which Clausewitz explained in *On War* by means of a new conceptual paradigm and to which Goya responds by shattering the norms of art: "Goya transposed the violence, the irrationality, and the incomprehensibility of war into a new language, which was employed to represent it. For the Spanish artist, war was a formal and semantic absurdity. By using art to interiorize the shattering of limits characteristic of absolute war, Goya pursued a multiple destruction."[29] Contemporary art, made in response to the violence of war, must find a new language, and in the *Disasters* that is a language that runs contrary to the principles of art.[30]

This involves, first, the destruction of physical bodies, and along with that destruction, a destruction of classical ideals of beauty. Consider plates nos. 33, 37, and 39. Torsos and limbs are displayed like broken pieces of classical statuary, which once upon a time had been modeled according to norms of integrity, proportion, and balance as ways to give expression to the qualities of inner beauty and strength. The neoclassical aesthetic ideals promulgated by thinkers like such as Johann Joachim Winckelmann are subjected to active destruction in these particular plates, and with them, the idea that art in the postclassical age can be great by imitating the works of the ancients is utterly destroyed. (A copy of Winckelmann's *Geschichte der Kunst des Altertums* in a 1779 Italian translation had been acquired by Francisco Cerdá y Rico for the Royal Library at El Escorial, where Goya might well have encountered it.)[31] Greek beauty, he suggested, depends upon the representation of an ideal as much as on the representation of physical form. In Goya's *Disasters*, it is the underpinnings of such an ideal, and not just the physical human form, that are subjected to ruination, and in these particular plates explicitly so.

Second, it involves a destruction of the logic of spatial organization and with that, a destruction of compositional principles. Figures in many of the *Disasters* refuse the logic of relationship by which the effect of an ensemble is created. But they are not randomly placed. Rather, they are positioned so as to show the destruction of spatial logic. Third, a number of the *Disasters* have at their center what can best be described as an essential nothingness. This nothingness is essential in the sense that it is not mere blank space or the site of a neutral invisibility, but something that must be shown and seen in spite of the fact that it may be unfathomable (for example, plates no. 17, "*No se convienen*" ["They do not agree"] and no. 29, "*Lo merecía*" ["He deserved it"], Figure 6.16).

The encounter with the emphatic nothingness that Goya associates with the violence of war again raises the question of meaning in the *Disasters*. In plate no. 71 (Figure 6.17), a grotesque winged creature is in the process of writing pages of a book that are appear as illegible scribbles. In plate no. 74 (see Figure 6.3), one can make out an upside-down inscription whose sense goes beyond all irony: "*Misera humanidad, la culpa es tuya*" ("Miserable humanity, the fault is yours"). And in plate no. 69, the central skeletal figure issues but a single word, echoed in the caption: "*Nada. Ello dirá*" ("Nothing. Time will tell," Figure 6.18).

In all these instance, Goya works against the common belief that language is the medium of reason and offers our best chance for making sense out of a sometimes chaotic world. One of the upshots of the *Disasters* is that neither language nor art can make sense of something that is as destructive as absolute war. But in fact, they also make the stronger and more direct point that the destructiveness of war is equally a violation of the powers of language and of art. That

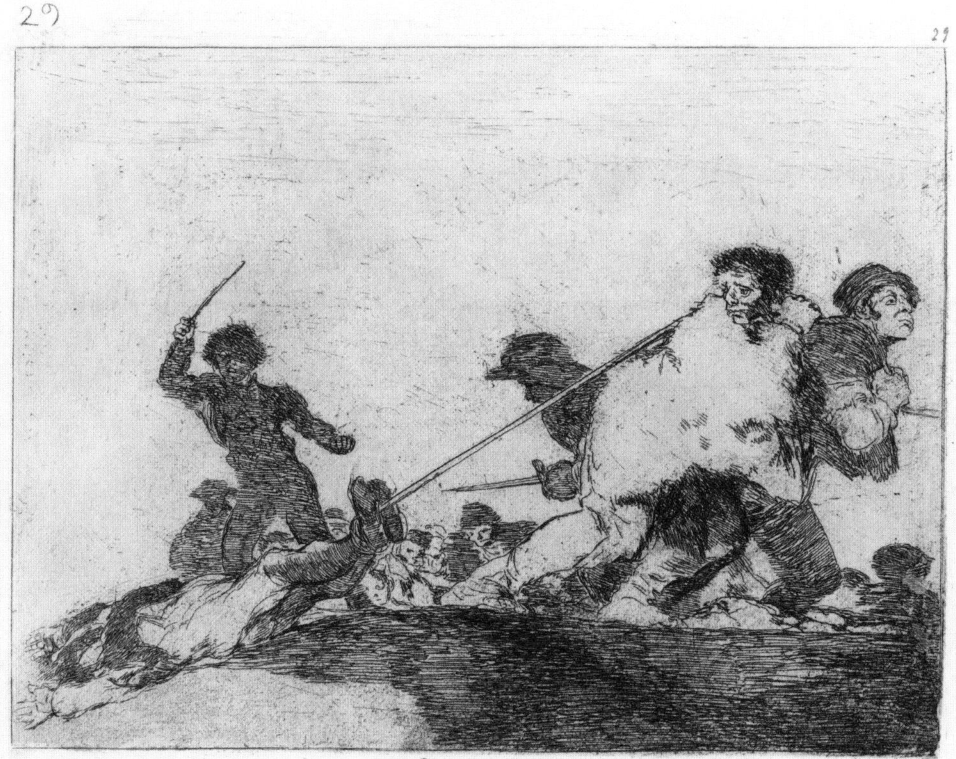

Figure 6.16.
"*Lo merecía*" ("He deserved it"), *Disasters of War*, no. 29, ca. 1810–12, published 1863. Etching and burnisher, 18×22 cm.

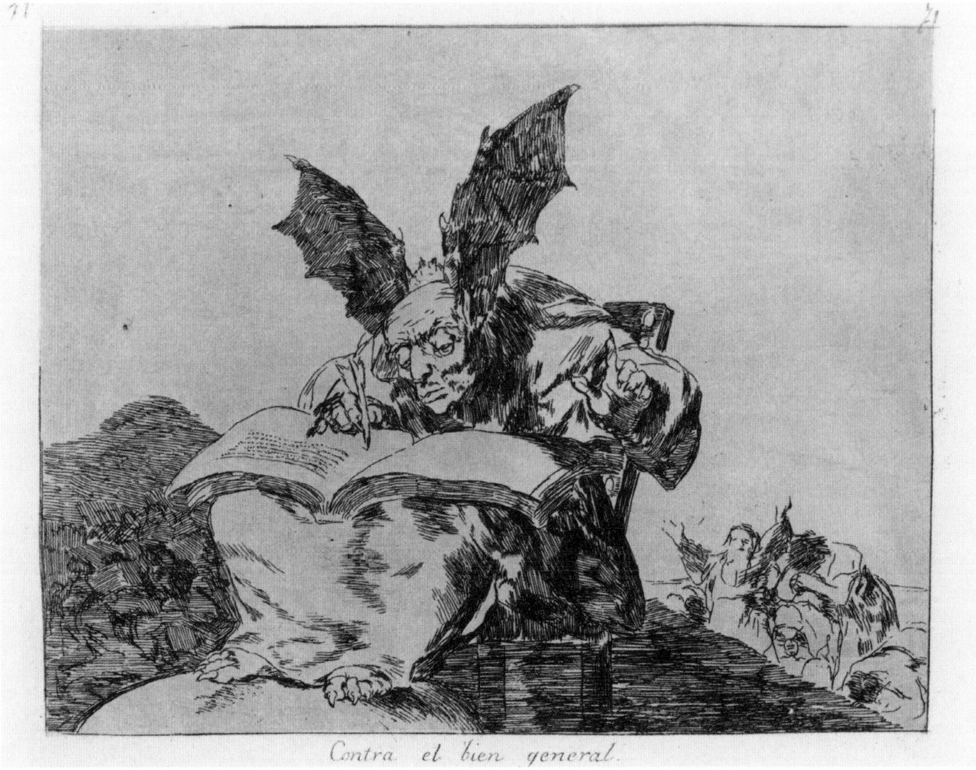

Figure 6.17.
"*Contra el bien general*" ("Against the common good"), *Disasters of War*, no. 71, 1820–23, published 1863. Etching and burnisher, 17.7 × 22.1 cm.

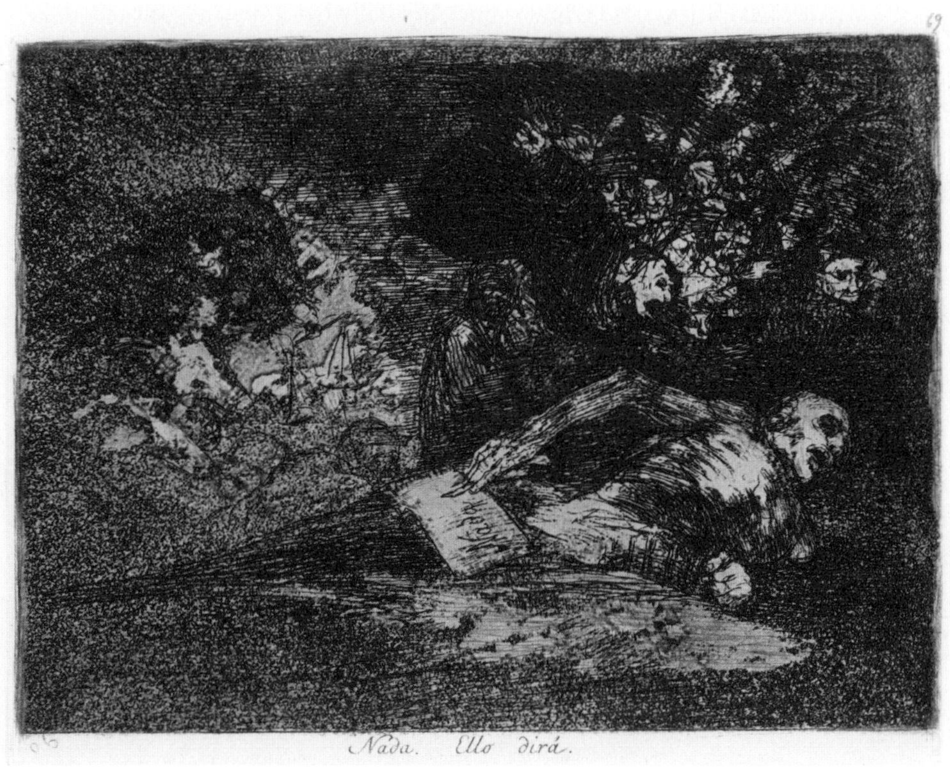

Figure 6.18.
"*Nada. Ello dirá*" ("Nothing. Time will tell"), *Disasters of War*, no. 69, ca. 1820–23,
published 1863. Etching, drypoint, burin, and burnisher, 15.5×20.1 cm.

is to say, its destructiveness goes beyond what it does to embodied human beings. It destroys the very powers by which human beings raise themselves up out of the mere physical world to a place where they can avail themselves of speaking and showing the meaning of the world. It is enormously challenging to marshal the powers of art for the purpose of demonstrating the destruction of those very powers, but having done just that in the *Disasters*, Goya's example in turn came to serve as a model for some of the greatest works of art — the example of Picasso's *Guernica* would be hard to avoid — in which the encounter with the absolute destruction of war again provides the impetus for the development of a new visual language.

CHAPTER SEVEN

Freedom and the Face

of Darkness

Our soul does most of its work in the dark, and has its greatest treasure in the dark as well. . . . We are partly a play of dark conceptions (sympathy, disgust, fear, hate, none of which we can offer a reason for), and we partly play with dark conceptions, in order to stimulate someone through something without him knowing how it happens.

— Kant, *Anthropology from a Pragmatic Point of View*

There is perhaps no better group of works to exemplify the challenges that Goya presents for interpretation than the so-called "Black Paintings." These are the set of fourteen images that Goya made on the walls of his small estate on the outskirts of Madrid — the Quinta del Sordo (Deaf Man's Country Home) — during the period from 1819, when he purchased the property, until his exile to France in 1824.[1] The name of the estate derives from an adjacent property, which had previously been owned by a deaf man, but was quickly applied to Goya's house when he acquired it, given the fact that Goya, too, was deaf. The darkness of this group of paintings — dominantly dark not only in their coloring, but also in the subjects they depict — has sometimes been explained as a reflection of Goya's inner turmoil, one root of which was no doubt physical and lay in the fact that his deafness had greatly altered his sensory connection to the external world. His situation has been compared to Beethoven's, who died only a year before Goya,[2] and the Black Paintings can be likened to Beethoven's later quartets. Add to this the fact that Goya suffered severe bouts of illness during him time at the Quinta and it is no surprise that critics have been drawn to regard the Black Paintings as symptomatic of deep physical and mental distress that is in turn the source of the greatness of these works.

Forensic experts and critics alike have long speculated about the causes of Goya's physical illness. Viral encephalitis, Ménière's disease, paranoid dementia, a series of miniature strokes, Vogt-Koyanagi-Harada syndrome, and lead poisoning (possibly caused by his use of white paint), have all been suggested.[3] We are unlikely ever to be certain about the precise nature and cause of his illness. But the truth is that Goya had gone deaf in 1793 and that his physical and mental downturn seems to have coincided roughly with the French declaration of war on Spain—a period well in advance of the time when he made the Black Paintings on the walls of the Quinta del Sordo. In a letter to Goya's friend Martín Zapater, Sebastián Martínez notes that "the noises in his head and deafness aren't improving, yet his vision is much better and he is back in control of his balance."[4] Additionally, the Black Paintings were hardly the first time Goya made nightmarish images. While convalescing during the years 1793–94, he painted a set of eleven small pictures, including the well-known "*Yard with Lunatics*," that seem to tap directly into "the darkest reaches of fantasy and nightmares." Goya himself said of these small paintings that they reflected his self-doubt, anxiety, and an imagination "tormented . . . by contemplation of my sufferings."[5]

Moreover, the sense that the Black Paintings may reflect Goya's inner torment is at odds with the fact that the Goya who moved into the Quinta del Sordo was perhaps freer than he had ever been in his career. He was financially comfortable, if no longer as prosperous as he had once been, and his purchase of the Quinta afforded him a place to live across the river Manzanares and away from the tumult of public life in Madrid. No less important, the years in which he owned and lived in the Quinta coincided with the signing of the

Constitution of 1820 and the establishment of a liberal government, albeit a short-lived one — a period referred to as the "trienio liberal." (Goya's advocacy of a constitutional government had been clear since the *Allegory of the Adoption of the Constitution of 1812*.) Alas, the restored constitutional government collapsed under the power of Spanish monarchists, who were strongly supported by French armed forces. Though political liberty had been lost at the national level, and while Goya's allegiance to the constitution and the liberal cause placed him at personal risk once monarchical rule was reinstated, the fact is that Goya was as free during his years at the Quinta as he ever was, free to make images that did not need to gain public favor: free of the obligation to satisfy a paying patron, and free of any need to adhere to aesthetic norms, to respect decorum, or to advance any particular cause. In the words of one critic, this is the culmination of an art "that, for the first time in some three centuries, owed nothing to nobility, harmony or beauty, and which, despite the eighteenth century's firmly established belief that the essential purpose of art was to please, dared to do otherwise."[6] The Black Paintings were made on the walls of Goya's private space, in which he was the primary viewer. For these reasons, no doubt, critics have also regarded them as some of his most personal works.

And yet out of this freedom there emerged some of the darkest and most difficult images in the history of Western art — images that seem designed to resist whatever illumination interpretation might shed upon them. This is not wholly surprising. Goya's freedom was tinged by melancholy, poignantly visible in the image associated with his beautiful maid and caretaker Leocadia Weiss (*La Leocadia*, Figure 7.1) and terrifyingly expressed in the image of Saturn devouring his son (Figure 7.2).[7]

The years following Goya's acquisition of the Quinta were those of his old age and of political tensions that ultimately led to his exile to Bordeaux in 1824. Whether because or in spite of all this, the Black Paintings have drawn the attention of critics in the ways that enigmas often do. Indeed, the subject of their resistance to interpretation

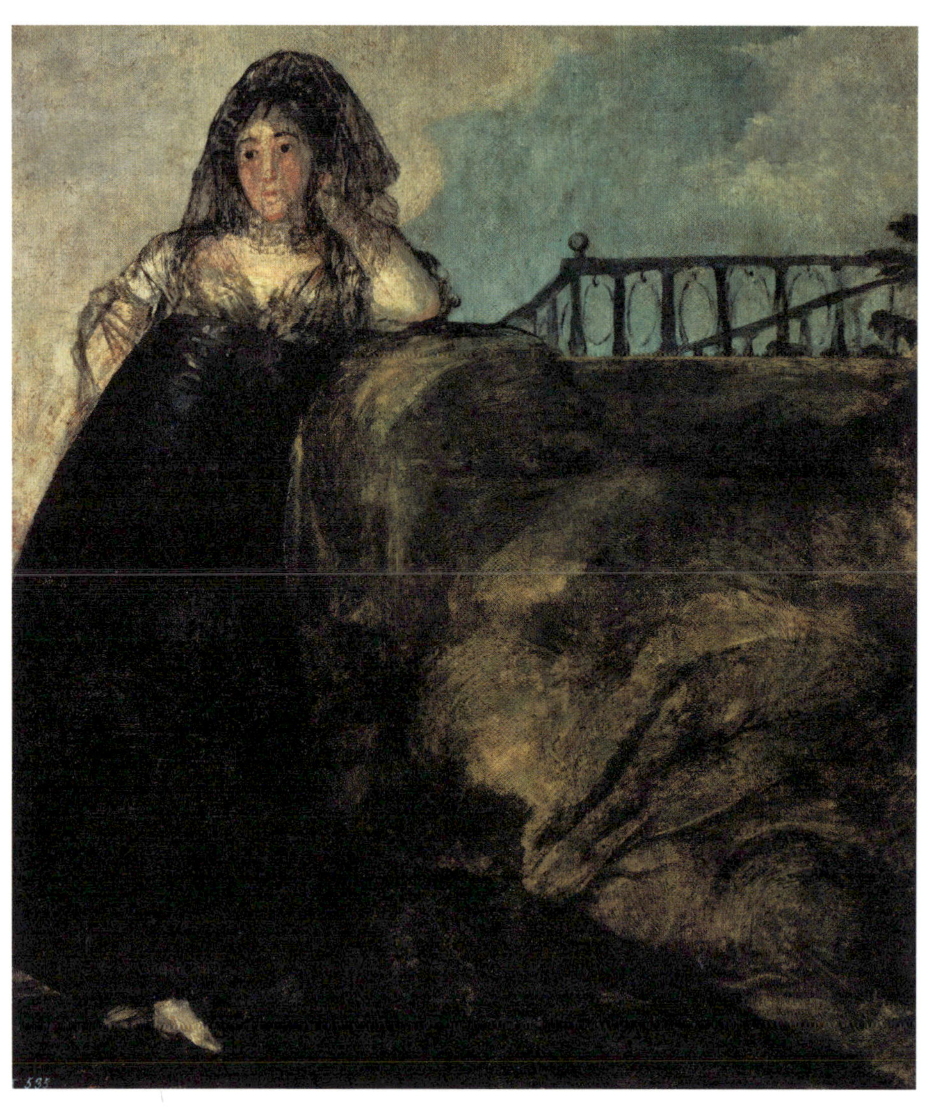

Figure 7.1.
La Leocadia, 1819–23. Oil mural transferred to canvas, 145.7 × 129.4 cm.
Museo del Prado, Madrid.

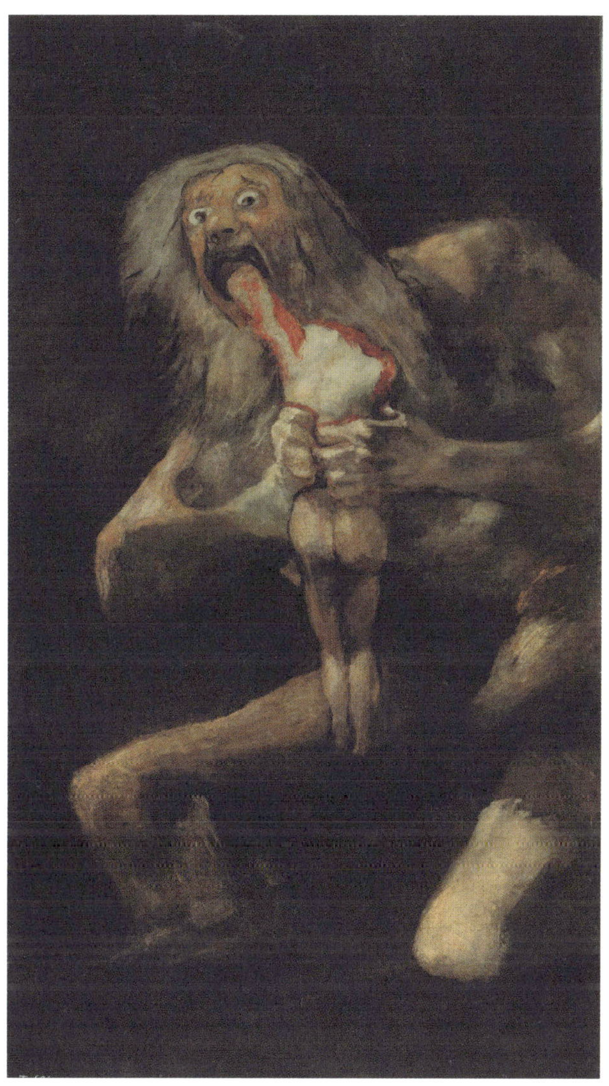

Figure 7.2.
Saturn Devouring His Son, 1820–23. Mixed media mural
transferred to canvas, 43.5×81.4 cm. Museo del Prado, Madrid.

has run throughout critical commentary on them for many years,[8] and all the while, critics have struggled unsuccessfully to find a set of terms, typically political and psychological, by which to render their meanings transparent and their purpose relevant to contemporaneous events. The impression that they are indecipherable has only been strengthened by that fact that some of the paintings are unfinished and that we have no real certainty regarding why Goya chose to place them precisely where he did in the house.[9] This is no doubt an additional reason why the appeal to Goya's inner turmoil as a way of explaining the Black Paintings may be so attractive, since that interior life is as opaque as the paintings themselves seem to be.

How ironic, then, that their opacity has been taken as a reason to find them "universally" meaningful.[10] Goya's particular suffering has been taken as a proxy for suffering *tout court*, because the difficulty of the Black Paintings seems to underscore the fact that there is something unfathomable to the outsider in any form of suffering. And while there is more to be said about the ways in which this dark, enigmatic, and disturbing set of images may reflect Goya's suffering, the fact remains that they have long seemed resistant to interpretive decoding, including the kinds of decoding that an investigation of personal psychology can provide.

If they are not psychologized in personal terms, it is tempting to see the Black Paintings as psychological allegorizations of the turbulent political realities of early nineteenth-century Spain. Roland Paulson, for example, takes *Saturn Devouring His Son* as representing the backlash against revolution. Paulson's influential study of revolution and its representation in the eighteenth and nineteenth centuries displays Goya's *Saturn* proudly on its cover and traces the counter-revolutionary genealogy of Goya's image back to writings about the French Revolution by Pierre Verignaud.[11] Similarly, Robert Hughes has written about *Saturn* that

> what Goya painted is the combination of uncontrollable appetite and over-whelming shame that comes with addiction — Saturn goggle-eyed and gaping, tormented by his lust for human meat, for an unthinkable incest. . . . In what sort of society would the fathers eat the young? Surely, one in which the old perceive the new as a deadly threat: a society so reactionary that "tradition," imagined as the absolute reign of total authority, is worth murdering for.[12]

And yet, compelling though this interpretation may be, Hughes also recognizes that it remains entirely speculative. Moreover, to take a painting such as *Saturn* as fundamentally political misses what may be one of the most disturbing things about it, as about all the Black Paintings, that is, the fact that while its violence seems frighteningly real, it cannot be tied directly to anything particular in the world. These issues can help illuminate why the Black Paintings heighten some of the central questions that have been raised throughout this book. Whereas in other works Goya establishes a relationship between artworks and the world that places art in critical engage-ment with some specific domain of life (for example, religion, soci-ety, politics, and so on), the Black Paintings bear a connection to the world that is especially difficult to pin down.

The Black Paintings are troubling not just because of some of the terrifying things they show, but also because they challenge the means by which interpretation helps make sense of things: they seem to defy efforts to make articulate statements about what an image "means," to offer coherent explanations of how and why a painting came about or to define the relationship of a given image to its social, political, historical, and personal contexts. But as I hope to explain over the course of what follows, there is good reason to doubt the claim that the Black Paintings are entirely uninterpretable, though they may well be uninterpretable in the conventional terms just men-tioned. It may be more useful to see the Black Paintings not as mani-festations of Goya's inner turmoil or of contemporary politics, but rather as visual engagements with the elemental roots of fear and vio-lence and as strangely reflective of the darkness that absolute freedom may invite. For Fred Licht, who has written about a similar question, the roots of the Black Paintings lie in pure evil: "The infectious nature of evil is the beginning and end of Goya's Black Paintings. The fear of being killed turns us into killers. The fear of a totally vacant universe turns us into vacant mechanisms who react only under the stimulus of terror."[13] Yet it is important to say that the Black Paintings challenge the ways in which psychology tends to make sense of the roots of such fear, which is to say that they are terrifying in part because they ask us to confront a kind of violence that has no discernible source. It is for this reason that some of the most haunting images among the group — for example, *Saturn Devouring His Son* and *Atropos, or the Fates* — draw on the archaic resources of myth.

I will turn to the question of Goya's engagement with myth below. But before proceeding, a few words of caution ought to be introduced in relation to the tendency, noted above, to believe that these paintings seem unfathomable because they represent "all the wild imaginings that consumed the brain of an aged, presumably isolated artist."[14] In a sweeping study of artistic creation from antiquity until through the eighteenth century entitled *Born under Saturn*, Margot and Rudolf Wittkower in fact take Goya's *Saturn* as exemplary of this particular understanding of artistic production.[15] Similarly, Folke Nordström placed Goya squarely in the line of melancholy Romantic artists and writers, partly on the basis of iconographic visual evidence and partly by association with the writings of José Cadalso, whose *Noches lúgubres* had in turn been inspired by Edward Young's *Night Thoughts*.[16] (I would note that while these interpretations place Goya within an iconographic tradition, well documented by Nordström, they ignore the fact that Goya was iconoclastic with regard to his use of myth.) To understand the Black Paintings as dependent on their relationship to Goya's interior creative life also speaks to the broader temptation, prevalent within modern society, to regard private life as inscrutable while accepting a notion about public life that revolves around a commitment to individual freedom, self-determination, autonomy, and a conception of the public good that depends on the will of individuals.[17] Without directly broaching questions regarding the public domain, the Black Paintings press us to consider that the lines between freedom and its antitheses call some of these modern assumptions into question. What happens if individuals are not free or if radical freedom leads to violence? Moreover, interpretation of the Black Paintings in relation to the interior life cannot avoid engagement with the set of shared archaic myths that have often been invoked in order to provide a common understanding of how the shared contours of psychic life are determined and that modern conceptions of the individual did not wholly displace.[18] Part of what holds interest about the Black Paintings lies in the fact which Goya turned to these archaic sources of understanding just when it would seem that he was committed to fighting superstition and all other forms of false belief.[19] But perhaps Goya knew that if Enlightenment meant the complete rejection of myth, then one immensely important resource for understanding the human condition would go missing.

With this in mind, a central thesis of this chapter can be brought into focus: that the critical power of these works is linked to their active refusal of the particular "worldly" frames through which interpretation customarily proceeds, in relation to which what may seem like the most plausible alternative — the appeal to individual psychology and mysterious creative powers — can be regarded as a last, but quite insufficient resort. At the same time, to understand the way in which the Black Paintings resist conventional interpretation is to see them as dialectically engaged with the very things they would appear to resist — the principles of sense-making, articulate discourse, and rationality on which interpretation relies. This is why their use of myth is important, since myth is one of the most ancient ways of making sense of things that seem otherwise to be unintelligible. As stories, myths have their own rationality — a rationality that incorporates and makes sense of things that might otherwise seem contrary to reason and impossible to understand. This is one way in which Goya understood in his terms something that Horkheimer and Adorno much later stated explicitly as part of their interpretation of the "dialectic of enlightenment," that is, that myth and enlightenment are in fact twins and that myth presents us with a form of interpretation that was already a species of enlightenment.

As noted above, the Black Paintings have long provoked reflection on the limits of interpretation. The question was raised most directly in Priscilla Muller's 1984 volume, *Goya's 'Black' Paintings: Truth and Reason in Light and Liberty*. In her case, however, she proposed to resolve the interpretive difficulties presented by the Black Paintings by suggesting that Goya himself intended to write an accompanying explanation of the paintings, an account that was never realized. She goes so far as to speculate that Goya "perhaps planned a commentary of some sort, quite possibly a 'verbal enclave,' which would furnish his guests with the key needed to unlock the mysteries of the 'black' paintings . . . extra-pictorial assistance [that] would permit proper unfolding of the true content and meaning of elements that might act as visual metaphors."[20] In spite of the lack of evidence for any such commentary, she insists that Goya had a "program" in mind for the paintings and argues that ordinary viewers and professional critics alike have proceeded to interpret the paintings as if by a process of free association, leaping "from image to metaphor, from actualities to analogies." As she goes on to assert, "Goya may . . . have planned a verbal and aural, as well as perhaps a supplementary visual, complement for the 'black' paintings to assist his visitors in discovering the ideas and themes prudently obscured in his program."[21] But since no such written account has ever materialized, she argues that Goya choose not to complete his program in view of the hope that the images might one day not be constrained by the need for circumspection. That is, he was deterred by

> the inexpediency of clearly illustrating subjects and themes that might one day not only cease to be urgent but could in fact become highly censurable, as they indeed did when monarchy and Church regained control of Spain in 1823. The Quinta program could then be allowed to lapse into obscurity, and

remain unheeded and hence unintimidating after Goya gave the property to his grandson and some months later moved to France.[22]

Of what might that program have consisted? The answer she gives is not implausible, however speculative it might be: to present a vision of the world that would exist should reason be allowed to fail.[23] This suggestion is guided by a reading of plate 43 of the *Caprichos* ("*El sueño de la razon produce monstruos*" ["The sleep/dream of reason produces monsters"]), that is, however, inconsistent with the ambiguity of the caption that plate bears. Instead, she sees that image as a brief in favor of the Enlightenment, presented in the simple guise of a warning against any lapse in the watchfulness of reason. Her interpretation of the Black Paintings follows directly from this view:

> Once again, and for a last time, Goya, the philosopher-painter, here [in the Quinta del Sordo] pictorially synthesized the appalling effects of unreason, bringing to his Quinta audiences a most vivid realization of life-threatening forces manifested when Reason, Truth and Light faltered. Drawing upon a life-experience shared by many of his contemporaries, and upon his unequaled artistic imagination, he didactically as well as compellingly presented in his Quinta rooms the evils endangering an unalert and ill-informed people. On regarding this re-created world of which they were now free, invited guests could ponder upon such embarrassments in their nation's history as now came to view, embarrassments they too had suffered . . . many would sympathize with their host's critiques of morally censurable, as well as psychologically and physically harmful, beliefs and practices which had been fostered by lamentably stupid superstition, a Catholicism twisted awry, war, and a reign that had denied the freedoms which many in Spain, as elsewhere, at last had come to cherish.[24]

It is not implausible to relate the paintings in the Quinta to these social and political issues in some way. But it is limiting and ultimately reductive to understand them as repeating the work that Goya had accomplished elsewhere, and it is limiting to ground that interpretation on a relatively flat view of Goya's relationship to Enlightenment rationality. Similarly, to regard the Black Paintings as warnings about the dangers associated with "unreason" requires believing that Goya took the opportunity to produce a set of works on the walls of his personal dwelling in order to lecture any would-be viewer, when his long career had shown that art could do so much more. There are, moreover, images j among the Black Paintings, such as the small figure of the semi-sunken dog (see Figure 3.7, above), that have little to do with reason or unreason in any direct way. Their enigmas are unresolved by the notion that the purpose of the paintings in the Quinta was to show a dystopian image of the world.

This said, there is no doubt that the Black Paintings point us toward the persistence of irrational and destructive impulses, impulses that have the power to undermine the very principles of freedom and autonomy that were among the central premises associated with the ideals of rational enlightenment. As a measure of just how troubling the Black Paintings are to those ideals, the images also undermine the hope for an unambiguous attribution of those impulses, much less for a resolution of them. We might of course regard those impulses as evidence of the irreducibly irrational roots that persist in any of the domains considered in earlier chapters of this book — religion, society, politics, and so on. Given the relatively "free" conditions in which Goya made the Black Paintings, this is not implausible. More importantly, to see the Black Paintings simply as exercising the freedom to expose the irreducible irrationality that runs through all human conduct raises the question of the relationship between these paintings and Goya's reflection on the condition of freedom itself, including his reflection on the things that might most seriously undermine it and whether absolute freedom is in fact an unalloyed good.

This is also to say that the Black Paintings can't readily be grasped by answering questions about freedom or its absence or antithesis within any particular context. "Freedom," in the way I would suggest Goya engages it, is something other than what any of its flawed or limited or idealized manifestations might lead us to understand. To be sure, freedom would be an empty notion, devoid of the content necessary for its realization, were it not to have the possibility of being exercised in the world. Denials of freedom likewise take root within the context of human experience as it is shaped through the institutions that govern individual and collective life. My suggestion about the Black Paintings, however, is that they do something other than what we have seen in the *Caprichos* or the *Disasters of War*. Those images engage directly with the many particular actions, institutions, and beliefs that render human beings less than free, sometimes painfully so. But the Black Paintings engage the question of freedom from within and in itself, that is, as something that depends upon a set of internal conditions and underlying beliefs and not just on its worldly contexts. Among those is a confidence in the existence, autonomy, and value of the individual. To this confidence in the individual there corresponds the belief that while external conditions may limit particular freedoms, there are no forces inherent within the individual to limit what he or she may freely will to do. (Goya's aristocratic portraits are perhaps the finest example within the body of his work of a confidence in the individual, albeit a confidence that seems limited to a particular class of individuals.) One prong of my argument is that Goya's residence in the Quinta afforded him the freedom to reflect on and to question these basic beliefs. Indeed, the Black Paintings suggest views about freedom that stand in stark opposition to a core Enlightenment idea, expressed by many, but perhaps best captured by Hegel, who held that autonomy is basically "self-determining universality" and that freedom is "the unity of thought with itself," such that the will is only truly free as the "thinking will."[25] Everything that comes from the fleshly nature of human beings, from the passions, the desires, and the affects, is perforce a limitation of freedom. (The Quinta's enigmatic painting of the masterless dog suggests a being wholly mired in affect and hence unable to act.) From Goya, one might indeed draw the conclusion that the will has much in common with nature, and from this it may be inferred that human nature is not, cannot be, morally free.[26]

Self-Reflection and Technique

Not surprisingly given the fact that they were made so late in his career, there is a considerable amount of self-reflection involved in the paintings of the Quinta, and before proceeding further to pursue their involvement with myth and their critique of freedom, it is important to address this issue. In invoking the term "self-reflection," I mean to say that in making these paintings, Goya was taking stock of his own career as an artist: that he was reengaging with works he had made earlier in his career, revisiting and extending the implications of techniques he had previously employed, and considering expanded versions of questions he had raised earlier about the relationship between art and the world around it, which included questions about the extent to which art could be an enterprise with a separate and autonomous purpose.

The fact that the Black Paintings were made directly on the walls of the Quinta and in such a large format speaks to three particular elements in their genealogy in relation to Goya's earlier work and the methods of reversal they involved. It speaks, first, to the work of the tapestry cartoons, which, as mentioned in Chapter 2, were made as the basis for wall decorations that would be woven from behind. Second, it speaks to the frescoes on the dome of San Antonio de la Florida, which, as noted in Chapter 1, resemble a "resolved" anamorphosis. And it speaks, third, to the *Caprichos* and other etchings, in which the original copper plates were reversed, both in their manner of inscription and orientation (left-right) in relation to the prints that would be struck from them.[27] But there is more to say. With reference to the first of these genealogical strands (their relationship with the tapestry cartoons), the Black Paintings show a refusal of any decorative purpose and likewise a refusal of the association of art with pleasure in any conventional sense.[28] And in relation to the San Antonio frescoes and the *Caprichos*, Goya chose in the Black Paintings to work directly on the flat walls of the Quinta, without the technical mediation required by the process of etching and likewise without the need to resolve as seemingly flat an image that was created on a surface that was curved. The fact that they were made in oil directly on the walls speaks likewise to the wish to set the apparatus of canvas and stretcher aside. (It should also be said that, in contrast to the San Antonio frescoes, the Black Paintings are emphatically secular and might well be regarded as instances of what Susan Buck-Morss called "profane illumination.")[29] Their relationship to the *Caprichos* revolves principally around the fact that those images — especially the plates in the first half of the series — were designed for the purpose of critical mirroring, that is, to reflect back to the viewers the things that they were unable to recognize about themselves or the world around them. The Black Paintings are hardly involved in the work of mirroring; rather, they project images of things that have nothing to resemble or that are unspeakable, as in the case of *Saturn Devouring His Son*. (I will turn to the issue of projection in more detail below.) The effort to work obliquely, characteristic of the *Caprichos* and of the work of social critique operative in them, seems inadequate and beside the point when faced with the roots of horror.

At the same time, the Black Paintings offer *thematic* reflections on Goya's earlier works. A number of the Black Paintings involve the dark inversion of images that Goya made earlier in his career, making fully visible things that were merely hinted at, for example, in the tapestry cartoons. To take one example, *Duel with Cudgels* renders terribly prominent the violence lurking in the seemingly innocent game of blind man's buff. (See Figure 2.5, above.) Similarly, *The Pilgrimage to San Isidro* casts the crowd that was so brilliantly bathed in light in *The Meadow of San Isidro* under the pall of a menacing darkness (see Figures 5.8 and 5.7, above). And whereas Goya's earlier works engaged issues of society, politics, religion, and history, the Black Paintings raise questions about the role of art when it refuses such direct engagement with the world. What results in the Black Paintings is not just the repetition of earlier themes, but an effort to probe to the very bottom of issues that were merely hinted at in his previous works.

Consider the two examples just mentioned. The *Duel with Cudgels* can be regarded as a reprise of one of Goya's earlier works, the cartoon for the tapestry *Blind Man's Buff*. As mentioned in Chapter 2 above, *Blind Man's Buff* shows a dimension of play that skirts on the edge of violence. But it represents socially sanctioned play, or rather play as socially sanctioned violence, in which the violence is subliminal and kept under control. The game is, moreover, a convention that counts upon the implicit agreement of all the participants not to allow themselves fully to be overtaken by whatever violent impulses they might have and likewise not to be overtaken by the forces of nature that are so visible in the centripetal motion of the figures in the image. The figures in the game flirt with violence and with the raw forces of nature. *Blind Man's Buff* was also likely a reference to the relations between the sexes and to the formalities of courtship and by connotation a reference to the blind forces of love that society somehow finds a way to make conventional and to normalize. By contrast, *Duel with Cudgels* represents a vastly different engagement with related issues, that is, with what happens when there are no restraints on the impulses that might drive us to violence as a way to prevail in even basic social situations such as the relationship between two seemingly independent individuals. The image is yet another view into what absolute freedom might look like where no restraints are in place — no social conventions, no norms, no rules or laws to bind us. In philosophical terms, this is freedom as "freedom from" — freedom from restraints.

The image has been interpreted as an indirect critique of the politics of Fernando VII's monarchy, suggesting that rulers sow discord so that they themselves might be regarded as the source of peace.[30] This is a plausible dynamic but an unconvincing interpretation of the image. Far more significant is the fact that these two figures are situated in a landscape that is scarcely able to hold them and against which they appear to be disproportionately large. It is yet another instance in which Goya exaggerates perspectives for some deeper reason. The outskirts of a town, perhaps nothing more than a village, are visible in the distance, but this fight takes place in a space from which all the markings of civilization are absent. The two figures,

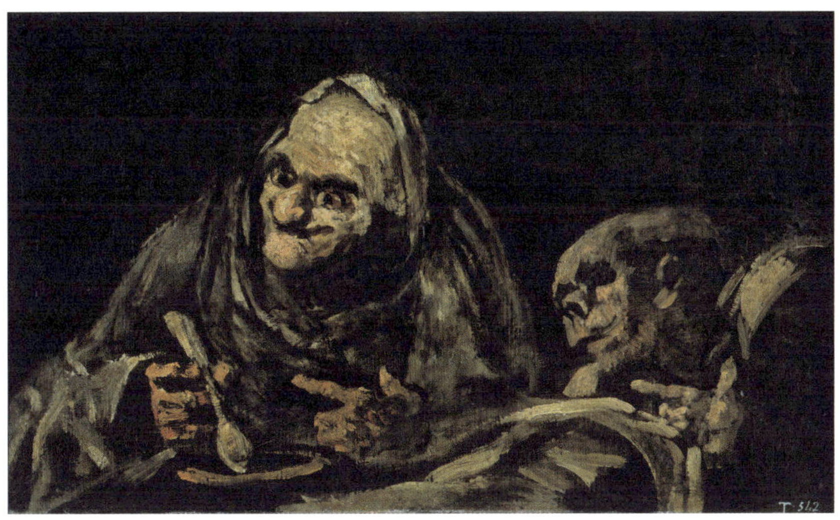

Figure 7.3.
Two Old Ones Eating Soup, 1823. Mixed media mural transferred to canvas,
83.4×49.3 cm. Museo del Prado, Madrid.

nearly indistinguishable from one another, have been identified as
cowherds, which is reasonable enough given the fact that we see live-
stock in the distance, but we know nothing about what they might
be fighting over. That they are herders rather than farmers — and
that the development of agriculture required far greater organization
than herding — may well suggest something fundamentally primitive
about them. Their weapons are nothing more than crudely fashioned
clubs, and these are all they have to use as instruments of attack or
defense. But these clubs might also be taken for giant spoons; they
bear a resemblance both to the spoon in *Blind Man's Buff* and to the
spoon with which the old man feeds himself in another of the images
in the Quinta, *Two Old Ones Eating Soup* (Figure 7.3). If there are
resemblances among these images, then the point of the echoes would
seem to be that the distance between nourishment and destruction is

slight. Moreover, the brutishness of the fight suggests that it does not take the firearms that "modern" civilization was beginning to produce in order to bring the human penchant toward violence to light. Perhaps all that is needed to expose violence, Goya darkly suggests, is sufficient freedom and any implement that may be to hand.

As for another of the Quinta images, *The Pilgrimage to San Isidro*, one of the principal differences between it and its precursor, *The Meadow of San Isidro*, lies in the way in which the individuals that make up the crowds in them are rendered, not to mention the enormous difference in light and in tonality between the two. In *The Meadow of San Isidro*, individuals are socially situated by virtue of their dress and their shared activity; they are members of a social group. Better said, perhaps, society gives definition to individuals, as manifested in their activity and dress. The image is, moreover, organized by a symmetry that suggests balance and in which perspective, exaggerated though it is, lends a sense of orientation to a landscape that is also made to appear vast. Seen through the lens of Goya's social critique, the *Meadow* is also a superb example of "naturalization," that is, a situation where, in Norman Bryson's words, "those who live within the social formation have *no awareness* of the conventional nature of the montage of values, beliefs, conventions, maxims, rituals and myths which constitute their reality."[31] The denotative dimension of the image — its function as the representation of a picnic by the river — serves as a convenient support for the process of naturalization; indeed, the image scarcely provides an opening by which to see that process for what it is.

All these things are reversed in *The Pilgrimage to San Isidro*, which we can regard as Goya's critical reflection on the *Meadow*. It bears noting, first, that the *Pilgrimage* takes place on the side of the Manzanares toward which the spectator of the *Meadow* looks. (This was the side of the river where the Quinta was in fact located.) To say that in the *Pilgrimage* society no longer plays a role in supporting the identity of the individual is true but insufficient. The figures in this painting merge into a swirling mass of pigment. In it, Goya seems intent on manifesting the fear of disindividuation, as is also true of a number of the other Black Paintings. Everything that served to support the process of naturalization in the *Meadow* is gone. Moreover, the denotative dimension of the image is pressed to its limit: the picture is barely recognizable as being of a pilgrimage at all.[32] In place of the nearly perfect symmetries of *The Meadow of San Isidro*, we find a purposeful distortion that can be understood as a manifestation of what happens when the forces that help sustain social identity — forces that allow social identities to appear as if natural — are no longer in place. The result is indeed a form of freedom, to wit, the freedom we experience when all social constraints are removed, a freedom that lays bare the impulsive and uncontrollable elements of human nature.

There is, moreover, an enormous difference in scale between the two works — a difference that has implications for many of the other Black Paintings as well. *The Meadow of San Isidro* is a work of relatively modest size (44 x 94 cm), and certainly small when one considers that it depicts such a large-scale landscape. The *Pilgrimage* (140 x 438 cm) is more than three times its height and more than four times its width. Its aspect ratio (height to width) is also far more exaggerated than the *Meadow*'s. Finally, its scale — by which I mean its size relative both to the figures depicted in it and relative to the viewer, is far greater. The image is only slightly less tall than an average person and many times wider. The figures pictured in it are of a size vastly greater than those of the *Meadow*. This means, in part, that while the scene pictured in the *Meadow* is one that could have been seen from the perspective of the implicit viewer, the image represented in the *Pilgrimage* could not. This impossibility stems from the fact that while we can get far enough away from a scene to make the figures in it seem smaller than us (as in fact they must), we cannot get close enough to others to make them seem bigger than we are — unless of course they are painted larger than life. The manipulation of scale is a technique that Goya used directly and indirectly in other images, as for example in *Duel with Cudgels* and in the figure of the bogeyman in plate 52

of the *Caprichos* ("*Lo que puede un sastre!*" ["What a tailor can do!"],
Figure 7.4). In both images, the exaggerations of scale suggest an
inscrutable and irrational fear.

The literal magnification of scale in the *Pilgrimage* and other
images is a way that Goya gets us close to the overwhelming quality of fear itself at the base of which lies the dread of a loss of indi-
viduation. But in order to describe how Goya exposes that fear in
the Quinta, we need a term other than the conventional ones such
as "representation" and "expression," notwithstanding the fact that
the Black Paintings have been pointed to anachronistically as having
affinities with expressionist art. That term is *projection*.

Projection

I use the term "projection" advisedly, referring not so much to the
psychoanalytic sense associated with Freud — where thoughts and
desires that cannot be accepted as one's own are ascribed to, that is,
projected onto, someone else; but rather in the technical way we have
come to understand in relation to the cinema, that is, where an image
is cast against a screen by means of a source of light and where a combination of distance and optics is able to render that image larger than
life. In addition to appearing as if they were projections, the works in
the Quinta are a collection of juxtaposed images, which together create a montagelike effect.[33] They are Goya's phantasmagoria — itself
a term implying projection. As Muller has suggested, they bear a
connection to the ways in which the theatre in the early nineteenth
century had adopted newly invented lighting effects to make those
projections possible. At this time, elaborate equipment was devised
to allow illuminated images to appear on walls, as if to move through
corridors, and to seem as if they were composed of multiple planes.

These effects went considerably beyond what could be achieved by
the magic lantern referred to in Chapter 4. At the same time, the so-
called "*teatro pintoresco*" that was staged in the inns of Goya's Madrid
often included painted images enhanced by the addition of sound
and lighting.[34] Both were forms of phantasmagoria, that is, a type of

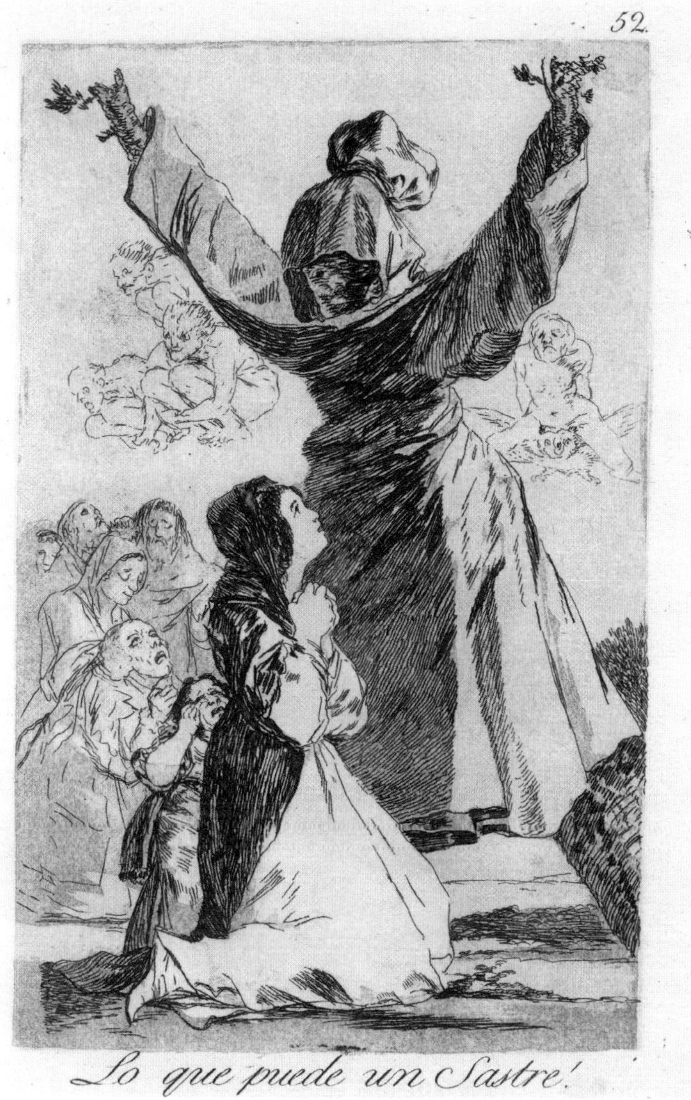

Figure 7.4.
"*Lo que puede un sastre!*" ("What a tailor can do!"), *Caprichos*, no. 52, 1797–98, published 1899. Etching, burnished aquatint, drypoint, and burin, 21.8×15.1 cm.

horror theatre that incorporated illusionistic techniques in order to project images of skeletons, demons, and ghosts onto walls, screens, and sometimes even onto smoke, often using rear projection as a way to conceal the lantern. In certain instances, mobile or portable projectors were used, which allowed the projected image to move and change size; multiple projecting devices allowed for quick switching of different images. One prominent exponent of these techniques, a Belgian named Étienne-Gaspard Robert, published a detailed account of how they worked, and it seems likely that Goya may have seen Robert's phantasmagoria performances in Madrid, which were presented at the Teatro Príncipe.[35] Well documented and summarized by Muller, they included presentations of witches and demons, with titles such as *The Witches' Dance*, *Preparations for the Sabbat*, and *The Saint Nicholas Pilgrimage*. Goya's exposure to such projections may indeed have led him to think of the Quinta as a space for the presentation of scenes drawn from the underworld and from myth. Among the Black Paintings, the use of light and the silhouetting in *The Witches' Sabbath* is clearly reminiscent of the techniques of the phantasmagoria. But perhaps what matters even more is that Goya's exposure to the mechanistic projection of horrific images served as a constant reminder of the fact that all such images were in fact human artifacts. This insight has further implications for Goya's use of myth, since it serves to underscore the fact that myth is likewise a human creation and moreover that the truths of myth when seen from an enlightened perspective reflect an understanding that human beings have created of themselves rather than truths commended from any external source.

Saturn, Self-Reflection, and Myth

There is no question that one of the most striking myth-driven images in Goya's entire corpus, *Saturn Devouring His Son*, depicts one of the most unspeakable things imaginable. The painting shows a monstrous human figure tearing tender flesh from the body of what may be either a small child or a fetus, often identified as female.[36] The uncertainties are significant, and though the mythological allusion is clear, the possible interpretations are numerous. Saturn is time, devouring youth. An echo of Goya's *Truth, Time, and History* would not be impossible to imagine, but the picture may also be taken as a reference to Goya's own old age and the loss of his sons. Goya's earlier drawing of *Saturn* placed clear emphasis on the advanced age of the male figure, which could potentially be a reference to Goya himself.[37] But this Saturn is at the same time a colossus, and the disproportion between Saturn and the child is reminiscent of some of the tapestry cartoons and other images in which there are also manifest disproportions among the principal figures. For those who are inclined to pursue a political reading of the painting in relation to the question of its scale, Saturn the colossus may also be Napoleon, whose aggression attempted to "devour" Europe (and Spain in particular). Finally, this Saturn is also a satanic figure, an allusion to the persistence of the Inquisition and its satanic powers in Spain.[38]

All of these associations are plausible, but each one is in some measure overdetermined, depending on a reading of the image as an allegory for something other than what it depicts—for example, Goya's personal life, the political history of Spain, the Inquisition. In the process, something basic about the myth of Saturn is overlooked. Saturn stands at the root of the Saturnalia, which in ancient times were celebrations of liberation and freedom associated with productivity, abundance, and feasting.[39] This was a festive time when slaves enjoyed the same the freedoms as citizens, could imbibe in public, gamble, and flout the principles of decorum they were bound to respect during the rest of the year.[40] There was a structure to this abandonment, which involved the reversal of ordinary social relations, just as in the related carnival traditions and in the earlier celebrations of Kronos.[41] Each Saturnalia was presided over by a quasi-king, selected for the occasion, known as the *Saturnalicius princeps*. Sometimes referred to as the "Lord of Misrule" the *Saturnalicius princeps* was selected from the lowliest members of a household and was given the right to impose a reign of mischief, albeit on a temporary basis. Saturnalia were also associated with mob pleasure. This was one in fact a longstanding complaint about these celebrations, namely, that, in Seneca's words, during the Saturnalia, the "whole mob has let itself go in pleasures."[42]

The celebration of Saturn was tied intimately to agriculture and fecundity, which no doubt accounts for its association with feasting. Indeed, the Roman Saturnalia typically opened with a public meal.[43] The gluttony of Goya's voracious Saturn devouring a fleshy child sheds a grimly ironic light on this tradition; it also illuminates a double-edged relationship with *The Witchy Brew*. The bulging eyes of the figure on the left in *The Witchy Brew* echo Saturn's, but the figure on the right, in direct contrast to it, is withered and wan. The two figures in this image are antithetical twins — gluttony and starvation, positioned side by side as if to suggest that they are two faces of the same unfathomable coin. The logic that binds them points to the domination of human beings by appetite and desire.

But Goya's *Saturn* is also the image of a sacrifice. Better said, it is an antifable about the impossibility of escaping sacrifice. This Saturn is a cannibal god, echoing Goya's earlier painting of cannibals living on the outskirts of civilization. By showing sacrifice, Goya's painting suggests an unspoken truth about modern individuals, that is, that they are not free, and emphatically not free from sacrificial behavior. As Horkheimer and Adorno suggested in *Dialectic of Enlightenment*, the modern subject came into being not from the elimination of sacrificial rites, but through "the introversion of sacrifice," that is, from the direction of sacrifice inwardly.[44] Goya's image of Saturn and the affinity with the Saturnalia are rebukes to the bargain by which the unruliness of brute nature is brought under control by a unitary and purpose-driven ego, an ego that requires repressing unconscious, instinctual life. As Joel Whitebook has said in commenting on *Dialectic of Enlightenment*, the ego gains strength as the demands to renounce instinctual nature increase, but instinct is never fully tamed: "Every additional act of renunciation adds to the reality of ego's consolidation and strength, further transforming it into a rational *qua* strategic subject who can manipulate the external world. And to the extent that external nature is reified, it is transformed into appropriate material for domination."[45]

The association of Saturn with the Saturnalia says something about the fact that Goya's image is one of grotesque (albeit individual) feasting, but it can help also make sense of some of the other images in the Quinta. The *Pilgrimage to San Isidro* also shows a Saturnalia-like scene in which the crowd gathers under the cover of darkness, rather than during the day. (As for the ostensible freedom of the crowd, one might best describe it by invoking the words of Horkheimer and Adorno: "the liberated finally themselves become the 'herd.'")[46] So too Saturn has relevance for *The Witches' Sabbath* (Chapter 5, Figure 5.13, above). Though the latter is conventionally interpreted as a convening of witches presided over by a he-goat — a witches' Sabbath, in other words, though one painted in a very different manner from the one Goya made on the same theme in 1797 — the image in fact shows a crowd of ordinary individuals held in thrall by yet another devilish "Lord of Misrule." Both *The Witches' Sabbath* and *Saturn Devouring His Son* could be regarded as examples of the thralldom that comes about when the ego is set free.[47]

In this regard, the image stands in stark contrast to Enlightenment notions of freedom as autonomy. Elsewhere in this book I have contrasted Goya with Kant, but in this case, Hegel may serve as a better counterpoint. As Charles Taylor put it, referring to Hegel, "autonomy expresses the demand of Spirit to deduce its whole content out of itself, not to accept as binding anything which is merely taken up from the outside."[48] This reinforces the view that the achievement of autonomy requires the domination of inner nature, but it fails to recognize that the project of freedom falters if forces operating inside the individual cannot be reconciled with this demand. Ironically, it may have required some degree of freedom for Goya to have come to terms with this fact, but it would certainly help account for some of the horror of the Black Paintings. Adorno said that "there is horror because there is no freedom yet."[49] Whether or not Goya sees the achievement of true freedom as a future possibility of some sort is a question that two additional images can help answer. These are *Atropos, or the Fates* and *Asmodea*.

Atropos (Figure 7.5) presents a notable contrast to the way freedom is imagined in the images discussed in this chapter so far. I turn to it both for what it has to say about freedom and for what is says about how Goya regards the ability of myth to make sense of things that may otherwise be unfathomable. It binds those two questions together quite closely. Though this title, as with all the other titles given to the Black Paintings, was not Goya's, there is no doubt about what the image shows, nor is there any uncertainty about how Goya inflects the basic myth of the fates. The figures in the image are Clotho, pictured holding what may be either a doll or a newborn child; Lachesis, who is shown spinning the thread of life and measuring its length; and Atropos, the goddess of death, who carries a pair of scissors with which to cut the thread of life. To these mythical figures Goya adds a fourth one, possibly male, whose hands are bound behind his back, as if he were captive. This figure is doubly unfree: he is bound physically, and he is also bound figuratively by the power of the mythological drama into which he is cast. He is, in other words, the subject of a story whose outcome he is unable to influence, and his presence adds an important dimension to how we are to understand myth. Myths are generally understood to be stories about the worlds of gods and archetypes, including their relationships to one another (for example, Mars, Prometheus, Icarus, Echo, and Narcissus). What this conventional understanding is liable to forget is the fact that myths are about *us*, that's is, that *we* are the subjects of myth, even when we fail to recognize that fact. Such is precisely the point of one of the most influential of all myths, that of Oedipus — a figure who, until far too late, spectacularly fails to see that he himself is the murderous subject for whom he is searching.

The figure of the captive who is introduced into Goya's interpretation of the myth of the fates allows the spectator the opportunity to

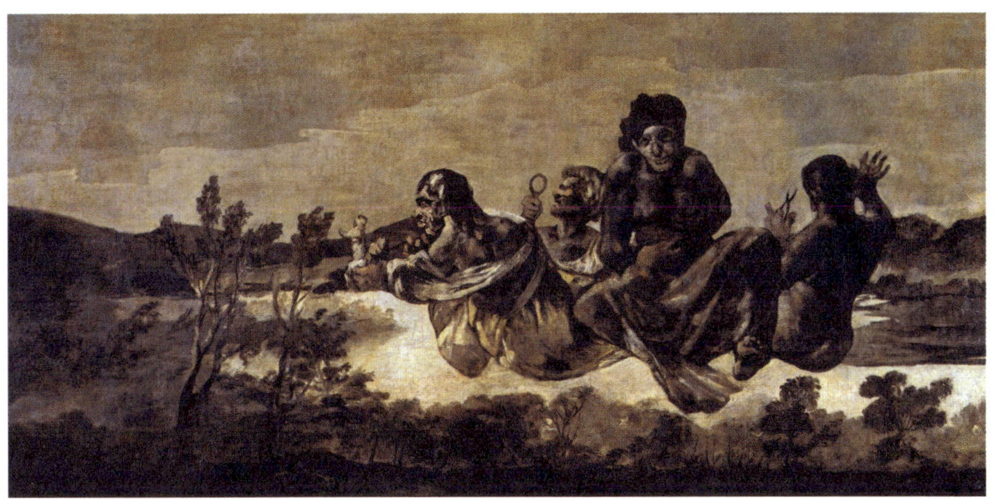

Figure 7.5.
Atropos, or the Fates, 1820–23. Mixed media mural transferred to canvas,
123×266 cm. Museo del Prado, Madrid.

see things (specifically, the captive's situation vis-à-vis his own fate) of which the captive himself is not fully aware. More broadly conceived, his situation illustrates the unwitting incorporation of figures or subjects into framing situations. Moreover, his presence suggests that the very same myths that can explain things to us play a role in determining who we are, even though we may remain unaware of that fact. The situation is similar to what in postmodern theoretical terminology would be called interpellation, that is, the incorporation of subjects into a structure that is present in advance, that constructs the reality of the subject, and over which he or she has no say.[50] Goya's *Atropos* provides the viewer with an enlightened understanding of this situation. The captive figure is deprived of the power by which to liberate himself; his particular fate is something he cannot know. But the truth of his unfreedom is something that Goya's representation of the myth clearly understands and makes plain for us to see.

There is, to be sure, a significant difference between the critical work that a term such as interpellation is designed to accomplish and an understanding of the shaping power of myth. This is in part because the critical power of interpellation, unlike myth, is rooted in a critique of ideology. It posits structured sets of beliefs that operate within particular social domains (for example, class structures) in which individuals are less then fully free. Indeed, the very notion of ideology would be vacuous without the social structures and institutions through which it operates and is perpetuated. And yet in Goya's hands, what interpellation enables us to understand is an appreciation of how myths work are surprisingly similar. A thoroughgoing critique of ideology must recognize that even if there is no ground outside of ideology on which one might stand in order to grasp its full extent (a significant *if*, to be sure), the work of critique remains the most powerful and important example of how far one must go in unmasking the impediments to freedom. Similarly Goya, late in his career, seems to suggest in *Atropos* that even while there may be no place outside of myth, the task of art, in the service of critique, is to bring that very fact to light.

Atropos offers an especially powerful view of the conditions of unfreedom that the resources of critical reflection are called upon to address. It is a view that stands at the opposite pole from what we see in the equally distressing images, such as *Duel with Cudgels*, where absolute freedom begets absolute violence. These images and many others like them are nonetheless bound together by the fact that they refuse utopian prospects — they refuse to envision any condition in which freedom might operate as an ideal. And while one would hardly expect to find anything resembling a utopian vision among the Black Paintings, there is nonetheless one work that alludes to such a prospect, however distant and problematic it may seem. It occurs in an unlikely painting, *Asmodea* (Figure 7.6). I turn to it in concluding both as a way of completing the discussion of freedom and as a way of introducing the subject of the chapter to follow, which revolves around the relationship between ideology and utopia.

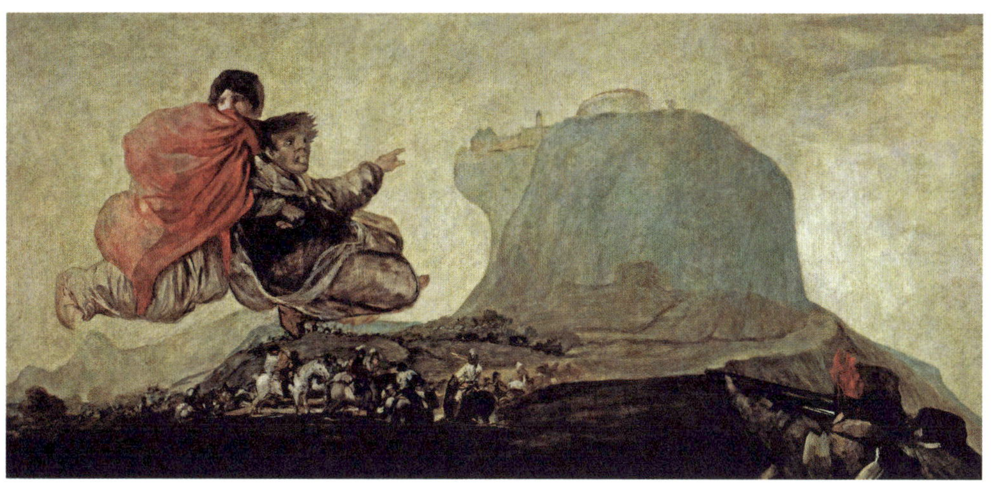

Figure 7.6.
Asmodea, 1820–23. Mixed media mural transferred to canvas,
127×263 cm. Museo del Prado, Madrid.

Asmodea is, no doubt, the image that gave rise to the suggestively utopian painting *City on a Rock*, now in the Metropolitan Museum of Art but no longer attributed to Goya. A good deal of research has been done on *Asmodea* that helps interpret much of the image. We know for instance that Asmodea is the female form of Asmodeus, a demon king mentioned in the Book of Tobias in the Hebrew Bible, as well as in other Hebrew and Islamic sources. He is identified variously as a prince of demons, the king of earthly spirits, and an icon of abandon. Asmodeus figures in *El diablo cojuelo* (1614) — a satirical work by Luis Vélez de Guevara — as a devil who shows the insides of houses. In Goya's painting, Asmodea is depicted flying through the air, pointing to a castle atop a distant hill and clutching with her a female figure who is garbed in flowing robes. It seems impossible to say whether the pair are escaping to safe ground and Asmodea is escorting the female figure to freedom, or whether this is a scene of abduction, such as we see in a number of Goya's other works; for example, *Capricho* no. 68, *"Linda maestra!"* ["Pretty teacher!"]. As for the rest of the image, a political interpretation is certainly possible. Critic Evan Connell, for instance, notes that the shape of the mountain in the distance resembles Gibraltar, which was a refuge for Spanish liberals during the aftermath of the Peninsular War. Moreover, the lower right foreground shows a line of French soldiers, not unlike those shown in *The Third of May, 1808* (Figure 3.9, above), taking aim at what appears to be a group of civilians passing in the distance. Traveling with horses and wagons, these may well be refugees from the war. They resemble the stream of civilians depicted in the lower portion of the formerly attributed *Gran coloso* (1808–12). What remains largely ignored in these accounts, however, is the castle atop the hill.

The castle has nonetheless drawn the attention of some other critics, including Muller, who speculates that it might be an allusion to the Sermon on the Mount, to Mount Purgatory in Dante's *Inferno*, or to the house on a rock referred to in the Gospel of Matthew (5:5–14 and 7:24–25). However, in the way Goya paints it, it is in fact barely the outline of a castle; attached to it (or adjacent to it — we cannot tell) is a suite of buildings that may suggest a city. Moreover, the castle-like structure in Goya's painting is round, and while round castles were certainly known, they were hardly the norm. Of those in Europe, the Minčeta Tower in Dubrovnik and the Castel Sant'Angelo in Rome are by far the most prominent, and the latter the more relevant, given Goya's travels to Rome. What interests about the Castel Sant'Angelo in relation to Goya's painting is that it served as a fortress, a residence, and a prison; it provided safe refuge, a dwelling place, and a space of forced confinement. To regard the castle in Goya's image as alluding to the Castel Sant'Angelo and its multiple valences makes sense, not least because of its contradictory purposes. Moreover, recognizing the image of the castle in *Asmodea* as multivalent rather than indecipherable helps underscore the fact that a number of the Black Paintings deal in contradictions more than in unintelligibility. In the Black Paintings, we are often in a world where the difference between freedom and confinement seems unfathomable, where a house may be both a refuge and a psychological prison, where eating may be a horrible thing to consider, and so on.

And yet, there is a quality to the way in which the castle is represented that goes beyond what these contradictions encapsulate. The castle is an attraction, an object of desire. Indeed, it condenses desire because it is represented so sketchily, one might say alluringly. It stands off in the distance, seemingly attainable only by magical means. (Can the ordinary citizens possibly ever get there?) It stands above the politically driven conflicts that operate on the ground, and offers a hint — a glimpse — of a place where everything might be resolved. Indeed, this may be key to resolving the puzzle about what Asmodea is doing in taking a female companion by the hand and flying off with her to the castle. The answer might well be that whatever the castle represents is powerful enough, and good enough, to draw a demon to flee worldly conflict and take refuge. It is, I would suggest, an icon of utopia and of a kind that, while hardly common, in Goya's works, is not entirely absent.

CHAPTER EIGHT

Beauty and Sympathy

In every chapter thus far, I have been exploring the ways in which Goya's work involves a penetrating, critical reflection on the world. That critical enterprise engages religion, society, politics, history, ethics, and of course, the conventions of art making themselves. In assessing this work, we have seen how the very terms that are commonly invoked in order to explain Goya's multifaceted output are in fact the very domains of the world to which he was responding. Politics does not *explain* Goya: Goya responds to it. War does not *explain* Goya: Goya responds to it. The social relations among classes and genders do not *explain* Goya: he responds to them. Neither does history *explain* Goya: he responds to the assumption that history is a guided course of affairs that is bound to turn out for the better or doomed to yield the worst. Moreover, he puts art in a place of being able to see critically the things that otherwise go ignored in each of these domains. But we have also seen Goya explore the limits of art in its role as a form of critique on two fronts. First, art must recognize that it is not a form of direct action in the world: the artist is, for better or worse, a critical observer of the world, able to see things as they are, able to see how others fail to recognize them, and of course able to show those things. The work of seeing and showing can create pathways for action, not least in its consciousness-raising role, but as a form of action, it is indirect. Second, if we recognize Goya's commitment to art as a form of critique, we must also recognize the complex nature of art as a particular form of practice: art can and does have much to say in its critical engagement with history, society, politics, and so on, but this means that its distinctiveness as a domain of practice must be constructed dialectically — constructed, that is, on the basis of its relationship to and difference from all the things that it is not, rather than determined on the basis of anything essential about it.

But the matter does not end there. When a critical project is as thoroughgoing as Goya's, a further question arises. This is the question of whether art can offer any positive or constructive ideals, ideals that can survive the rigors of critical reflection with some measure of intactness and be brought to bear on our thinking about how we might want the world to be. One line of argument is that a world in which critical reflection flourishes is itself the best possible world to be hoped for and that the promise of a heightened self-awareness ought to preempt the demand for an ideal of any different kind. Indeed, such an argument would likely suggest that to believe otherwise would be to succumb to the allure of false utopias, which a critique of some kind will inevitably unmask. According to this line of thought, the primary function of critique is just this: to expose utopias as false, to identify in a particular way the false basis on which they rest, and ultimately to dismantle the very grounds for the construction of false utopian ideals.

There is, however, a different view of utopian thought and likewise a different view of the critical project that ought to be considered. On this view, there can be no sense at all to a project of critique if there is no view of what truth might look like, no sense to the notion of ideology if there is no idea of what utopia might be, and no reason for a critique of those things that make us unfree if we have no view of what freedom might truly be.[1] The premise of this final chapter is that Goya does in fact make space for a set of ideals, though in a way that remains consistent with the project of critique. This is where Goya creates room for beauty to do its work; though not surprisingly, he incorporates a critique of beauty as an abstract ideal, and he finds ways to valorize some of the very elements that contemporaneous theories of beauty thought it necessary to exclude.

In taking up this line of argument, I should nonetheless warn against the temptation to regard this chapter as offering a "happy ending" to a story that has all along been about the relentless power of Goya's art to serve as a vehicle of critique, one that seems almost systematically to refuse the claims of Enlightenment reason to provide access to a better world. But this chapter is not a happy ending, not least because it is not about the ending of Goya's career. The examples at hand, which demonstrate ideals of beauty grounded in sympathy for particular individuals and a respect for the public good, do not all mark the final phase of Goya's work as an artist, nor do they align with his biography in any other particular way. While it would be tempting to see Goya as moving from a fiercely critical practice to one that is more readily open to hopeful prospects, this is not the case. He admits of both darkness and light on a continuing basis, sometimes simultaneously. Consider how, even among the "Black Paintings," Goya finds a place for beauty and dignity in the midst of darkness (to wit, in *La Leocadia*, Figure 7.1, above). *La Leocadia* is hardly an uncomplicated image: a formal resonance of the background with *Asmodea* and an echo of Goya's 1797 portrait of the Duquesa de Alba (with the famous inscription "Solo Goya") are both present, however incompatible those two other images may be with one another. But *La Leocadia* has also convincingly been seen as an image of melancholy, as noted briefly above.[2] As described in the previous chapter, many of the Black Paintings, including this one, involve reflections on Goya's own prior work. Among those reflections are not just the revisiting of prominent themes, forms, and techniques drawn from the earlier work, but a much more significant reflection on the relationship between the project of critique and the prospects for hope, however tempered — prospects for something that points beyond what critique identifies as deficient, ignorant, blind, self-deceiving, malicious, and irrational, to something that is at once generous and vulnerable. Such is the case with *La Leocadia*, where beauty holds a promise of happiness, even though the face of beauty is veiled.[3] (See Figure 7.1, above).

To find a place for hope amid the darkness of the Black Paintings — where a figure such as the wistful *La Leocadia* seems to deflect that darkness with her feminine nonchalance or buffer it with a poignant disinterest that distances her from the world — prompts first a consideration of the place of beauty in relation to its antithesis, ugliness, in Goya's work. The issue extends well beyond the Black Paintings, which are hardly alone in bringing to light the nature of ugliness as born of superstitions, ignorance, and evil and which draw us to question what that "truth" might be. Ugliness in Goya has deep roots, and those roots are often social and ethical: ugliness is a malformation that manifests itself in those who act in bad faith or who fail to understand the true sense of their actions. Such is overwhelmingly the role of ugliness in the *Caprichos* and the *Disparates*, as well as in many of the drawings in the late Bordeaux albums. Ugliness may well be a reflection of character (for example in some of the figures in the portrait of the family of Charles IV, Figure 8.1, or still more strikingly in Goya's portrait of Ferdinand VII, Figure 8.2). It is remarkable how these images register superficiality as a character flaw that displays itself in the very physiognomy of the person in question.

Far more emphatic is the ugliness that shows itself in Goya's renderings of the true horrors of the world — horrors not limited to those shown in the *Disasters of War* — horrors that one critic vividly described as "the sick, the insane, victims of hangings, the skeleton-man, the half-man half-chicken, men sawn in two, flagellants, the courts of the Inquisition, nightmares, flying men and bulls, brigands, rapes, tortures, the stake, murders, executions, children abandoned, human sacrifice, cannibals, fetuses."[4] It is hard to disagree with André Malraux that the most striking feature of Goya's horrific etchings and the Black Paintings, along with works such as *The Madhouse* and *The Third of May, 1808*, is not, as often claimed, the caustic social commentary but rather their radical departure from

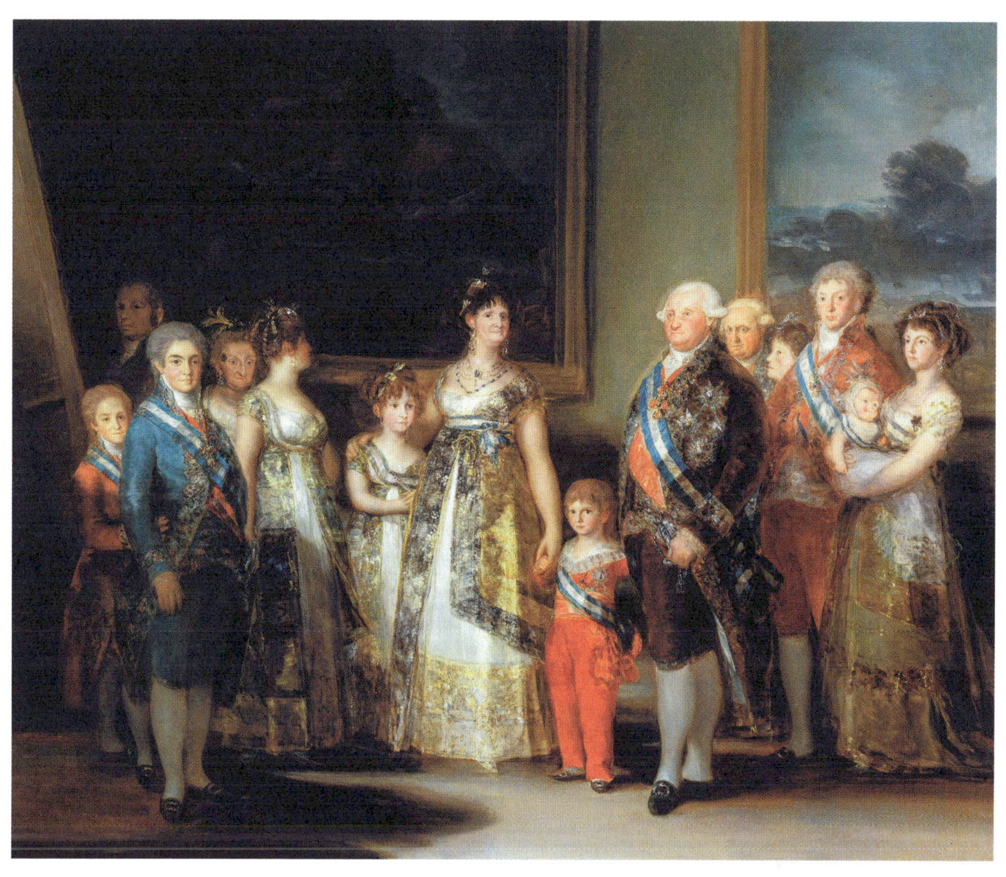

Figure 8.1.
Charles IV of Spain and His Family, 1800. Oil on canvas, 280×336 cm.
Museo del Prado, Madrid.

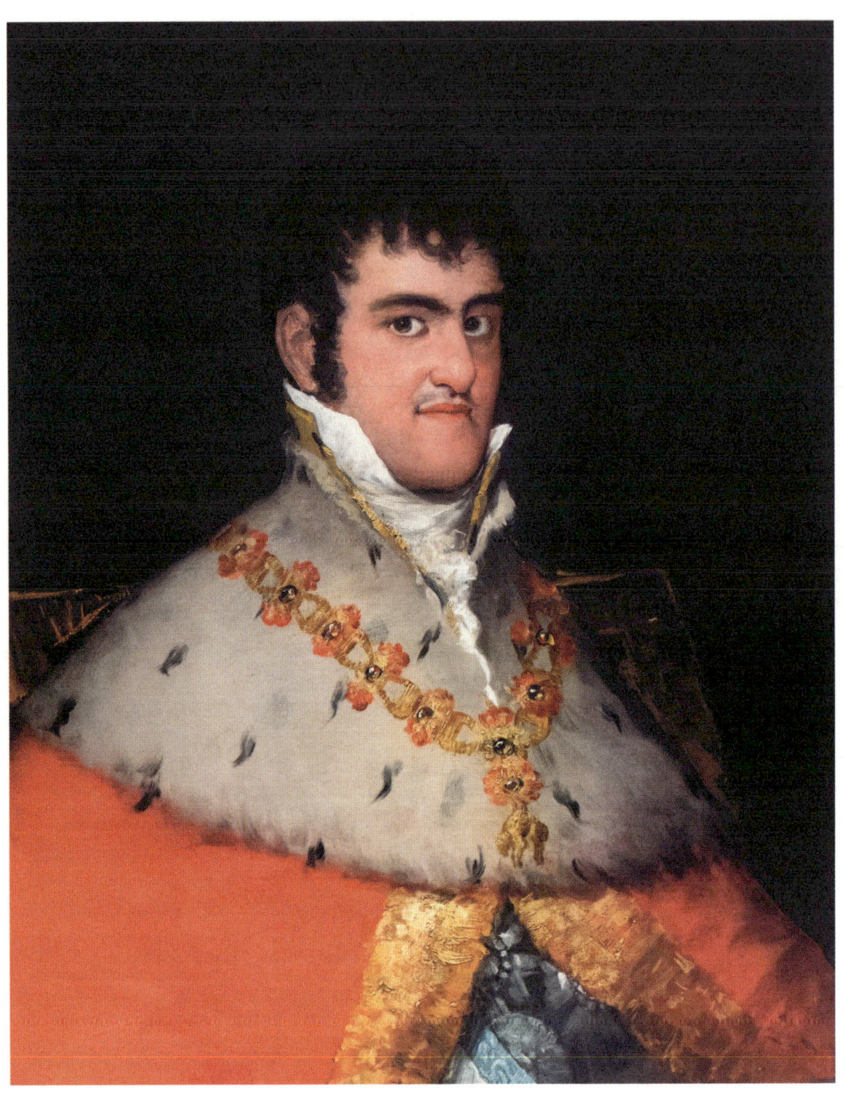

Figure 8.2.
Portrait of Ferdinand VII, ca. 1814–15. Oil on canvas, 84 × 63.5 cm.
Museo Nacional Thyssen-Bornemisza, Madrid.

the governing ideals of beauty, nobility, and harmony in favor of an ugliness that their subjects all but require.

Indeed, the departure from those ideals is hardly a matter of aesthetics alone. In this tormented world, Malraux writes, "There is no love, nor above all motherhood. In the *Disasters* [Goya] only draws children snatched from their mothers; and there are no women among the weeping onlookers of the *Third of May*. His patriots vanquish or die almost alone, and his crowds are only ever there as onlookers."[5] We might of course like to think that even the greatest horrors can find some source of redemption, a prospect that we might well expect to see presented under the guise of beauty. But whether beauty can serve as a redemptive agent or as a counterforce to everything that ugliness may encompass remains to be seen. Some actions may in fact be so horrible that they leave the individual desouled, that is, beyond any hope of redemption by secular means, of which of course beauty is one.

But what if beauty *could be* a source of hope? What form might it take? This is an important question to address, because much of Goya's work is devoted to a rejection of whatever is shallow and facile about beauty, which is just how beauty often appears when it masks the actions and beliefs that keep people from recognizing their potential for freedom. Those shallow and facile forms of beauty include the things we would associate with the aesthetic category of the picturesque, which was much in vogue during the late eighteenth and early nineteenth centuries and which Goya had engaged from a critical perspective at a relatively early stage in his career in the tapestry cartoons. Beauty in its most facile and shallow forms is apt to support the process of naturalization, discussed earlier, which makes things look as if naturally and pleasantly created for us. It gives us images of nature and society as both happy and well-ordered so as to suppress what is ugly, to disguise what is true, and to impede the project of critical reflection.

Neoclassical aesthetic ideals calling for the artist to strive for order amid variety — ideals of just the kind described in Ignacio de

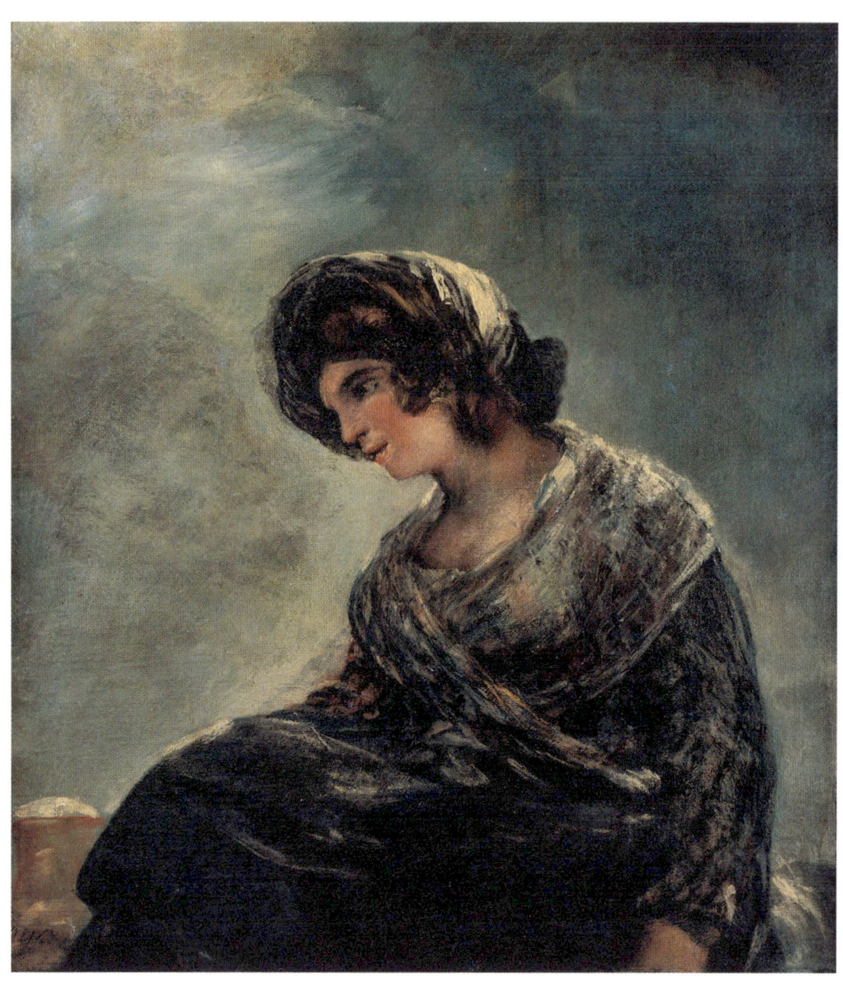

Figure 8.3.
The Milkmaid of Bordeaux, 1825–27. Oil on canvas, 74×68 cm.
Museo del Prado, Madrid.

Luzán's *Poética* of 1737 — provided a convenient theoretical support for this very process. These aesthetic ideals are associated with unreflective kinds of pleasure, that is to say, with forms that are meant to please the eye by giving it what it wants to see without challenging the mind, forms that satisfy the appetite for pleasure by inviting the eye to take delight in what is depicted and to stop there, looking through the surface of the work as if through a transparent window onto a pleasant world beyond, but paying little attention to the work itself and to its role in reframing the world. It is hardly surprising, given his critical bent, that Goya would bristle at neoclassical principles and the ideals of beauty they imply. But it does not imply a rejection of beauty *tout court*.

One of his most alluring images, *The Milkmaid of Bordeaux* (Figure 8.3), puts natural beauty in a very different, human light.[6] Though sometimes considered a genre painting, the image devotes remarkable attention to an anonymous figure who might otherwise have merely been playing a role. Goya imagines her as an individual worthy of the sympathy that he, as an artist, seems able and willing to express. The image is furthermore remarkable for the way in which it captures the value of the individual while showing us someone who bears no name but whose individuality nonetheless supersedes her identity as a type.

To be sure, later eighteenth-century thinkers and some in the early nineteenth associated beauty with much higher, but also more abstract, ideals. Those ideals and the discussions surrounding them are worth bearing in mind, because Goya was addressing some of the same questions they raised in visual, rather than explicitly philosophical terms and because his stance on questions of beauty was quite different from some of those that became dominant in the European philosophical traditions that were developing around him. For Kant, in particular, beauty was grounded in a particular type of pleasure, a pleasure that is pure and dissociated from all interest in whether the object in question is itself something agreeable or good for some purpose. Such a kind of beauty ought to have nothing to do with utility. Because it is pure and because our relationship to it is free of interest, to say that something is beautiful for Kant does not mean just that *I* find it pleasing or useful for my purposes, but that *everyone* should find it beautiful. This is beauty conceived as a universal category, and it involves a claim in which the *I*, the *you*, and the *we* are in principle convergent in our judgments. In making a claim of beauty, I must imagine myself to be in the position of *everyone else* (even though perhaps speaking just to you). Beauty so conceived offers the promise of universal agreement about something that is rooted in a subjective experience because it depends upon a form of sympathy that Kant calls "common (aesthetic) sense," the *sensus aestheticus communis*.[7] Its universality is in turn one of the reasons why Kant believes that beauty offers a "symbol of morality." As he says, "the beautiful is the symbol of the morally good, and only in this light . . . does it give us pleasure with an attendant claim to the agreement of every one [*sic*] else, whereupon the mind becomes conscious of a certain ennoblement and elevation about mere sensibility to pleasure from impressions of sense."[8]

I will turn to discuss the matter of sympathy further in connection with Goya below. Here, I simply aver that the way Kant has interpreted beauty leaves much to be desired because it is abstract. In order to be truly disinterested, judgments of beauty must limit their concern to matters of form (to things such as shape, symmetry, arrangement, and so on); they cannot engage with the things available to the senses such as color, hue, and contrast, much less with anything of a thematic nature. Moreover, placing myself in the position of everyone else only means that I imagine their *possible* judgments, but do not necessarily have to contend with their *actual* ones, even if I must be able to communicate my judgments in a way that all could accept.[9] The result is an elevated and universal but entirely formal notion of beauty, one that leads us to ask whether it is worth the price. Moreover, it is founded on a notion of sympathy that does not, in the end, make room for concrete others.[10] Indeed, if one stakes the hope of a countercritical aesthetics on the promise of beauty regarded in such a way, and if beauty is the promise of happiness, then one might wish to be similarly skeptical of whatever happiness it may offer.

A different argument about beauty can nonetheless be made, one that takes this ideal into account and rather than reject it, asks how it can be made more amenable to the full range of human experience. There is indeed much more to be said about beauty from a human perspective than that it is a matter of form or a symbol of morality, and my argument is that this is in fact what Goya does in some of his most striking works. Sympathy is one of the keys to it, as we will see further below. But alongside a more human conception of beauty grounded in sympathy, utility also plays a significant and perhaps surprising role in Goya's works.

This runs quite contrary to the fact that the very notion of utility was thought to be anathema to the category of the beautiful by a thinker such as Kant, even though it was hardly without support elsewhere in Enlightenment thought. More specifically, Goya rejects an idealized notion of beauty for something more human while also embracing the value of constructive activity with a social purpose as a way of imagining a more humane world. The latter has little in common with instrumentalist thinking, that is, with utilitarian*ism* of the kind one might associate with Goya's near contemporary Jeremy Bentham. Goya's appreciation for utility as a value that is both practical and aesthetic is significant on its own but is especially important in the context of an artist whose work also involves a thoroughgoing critique of Enlightenment principles and ideals. That critique, or any other, is relatively easy to mount from a position in which one holds the objects of one's scrutiny at a safe distance, but to return to terms introduced much earlier in this study, such an effort is better described as a form of criticism rather than as critique. The project of critique requires instead a proximate relationship to its object, because it is only in this way that the object can be encountered fully enough for critique to be meaningful. It ought not to go unnoticed that Hegel identified utility as the specific domain where the Enlightenment could overcome its alienation from the object sphere and finally see itself *in* its object: "it is in utility that pure insight achieves its realization and has itself for its *object*, an object which it now no longer repudiates and which, too, no longer has for it the value of the void or the pure beyond."[11] Goya's appreciation for the value of utility does even more, however, insofar as it provides an opportunity to conjoin — perhaps better said, rejoin — utility with beauty.

Goya's approach bears further comparison with philosophical ideas about the relationship between beauty and utility that were circulating widely in the late eighteenth century, perhaps most importantly Edmund Burke's *A Philosophical Enquiry into the Origin of Our Ideas of the Sublime and Beautiful*, which was translated into Spanish in 1807 by Juan de la Dehesa as *Indagación filosófica sobre el origen de nuestras ideas acerca de lo sublime y lo bello*.[12] Burke argued forcefully against the notion that something could be called beautiful *because* it is useful. For, as he wrote,

> on that principle, the wedgelike snout of a swine, with its tough cartilage at the end, the little sunk eyes, and the whole make of the head, so well adapted to its offices of digging, and rooting, would be extremely beautiful. The great bag hanging to the bill of a pelican, a thing highly useful to this animal, would be likewise as beautiful in our eyes. The hedgehog, so well secured against all assaults by his prickly hide, and the porcupine with his missile quills, would be then considered as creatures of no small elegance.[13]

Burke notwithstanding, the period leading up to Kant saw a number of prominent thinkers struggle to make a place for utility in relation to beauty — as Goya would — while not making beauty merely a utilitarian affair. This was not easy to accomplish, as the following examples will suggest. On Francis Hutcheson's account, for example, the response to beauty, though a sensory one, precludes any connection with the utility of the object.[14] Shaftesbury insisted on the independence of beauty from the possession of the object in question and therefore from its use. But even Shaftesbury did not think that beauty and utility are wholly unrelated. In the *Characteristics of Men,*

Manners, Opinions, Times (1711), he acknowledged that some qualities that make objects beautiful — proportions, shapes, symmetries, and the like — also make them well suited to use, and hence that beauty and utility "are plainly joined" and are a reflection of Nature. The contrary can be said about ill-proportioned things:

> 'Tis impossible we can advance the least in any relish or taste of outward symmetry and order, without acknowledging that the proportionate and regular state is the truly prosperous and natural in every subject. The same features which make deformity create incommodiousness and disease. And the same shapes and proportions which make beauty afford advantage by adapting to activity and use. Even in the imitative or designing arts . . . the truth or beauty of every figure is measured from the perfection of Nature in the just adapting of every limb and proportion to the activity, strength, dexterity, life and vigour of the particular species or animal designed.[15]

Rather than position himself on one side or the other in the controversy about beauty versus utility, David Hume — great skeptic though he was — tried to resolve it by recognizing two varieties of beauty. In *A Treatise of Human Nature* (1739-40), he maintained that the distinctive kind of feeling we associate with beauty can be produced in two different ways, one that depends upon utility or appearance and another that hinges on the crucial category of sympathy and its link to the imagination. His explanation includes the examples of a well-designed artifact or well-endowed piece of nature that are useful, but that can be used only by a particular proprietor: the rest of us can enjoy it because of our sympathy with the pleasure of that proprietor, which requires the work of the imagination: a beautiful house that is not our own, for example, can delight us "by communication, and by our sympathizing with the proprietor of the lodging. We enter into his interest by the force of the imagination, and feel the same satisfaction, that the objects naturally occasion in him."[16] One thinks again of Goya's *Milkmaid of Bordeaux*, who exists only in the imagination and is treated with remarkable sympathy. Not surprisingly, the conjuncture of sympathy and imagination opens a path to morality.[17]

Though this sampling of views might appear digressive, it can help contextualize and establish what is distinctive about Goya's engagement with the intersections of beauty and utility. Goya offers a humanized and dignified appreciation of the value — including the aesthetic value — of truly useful endeavors, of projects designed to improve the world for human beings, that is, projects that aim to make the world a better place *for ourselves and for others*. But more importantly, he concentrates less on useful objects than on useful civic projects and above all on the character qualities of those who undertake them. The focus on character establishes a link, through utility, to a beauty of the person, one that resonates with early modern conceptions of "moral beauty," which I turn to below in connection with Goya's portrait of Bartolomé Sureda.

Goya's deep admiration for those who pursue useful projects — and especially projects that are of benefit to the public good — is abundantly visible in his 1783 painting of the Count of Floridablanca, mentioned earlier (see Figure 1.9, above). There is no doubt that Goya — who also depicts himself in the painting — was hoping for recognition from the count and for his patronage, as well, but the admiration of the young Goya for Floridablanca is genuine, all the same. The count stands at the center of the work, with a portrait of Charles III hanging on the wall behind him, looking down benevolently on his prime minister. Overseeing the drawings for the Aragón Canal on the table is the military engineer and architect, Julián Sánchez Bort, whose work on the canal (ca. 1771), had been carried out some twelve years before Goya made this painting. That the canal was of important public benefit for Goya's native province perhaps goes without saying. Less obvious from the picture are the many other, related accomplishments of Floridablanca in his role as a public administrator — with involvement in projects including hydraulic works, dams, the creation of an observatory, a cabinet of natural history, an academy of science, and the Academy of Fine Arts. Indeed, the canal can be thought of as standing in for the many other works that he directed. (Floridablanca was also the founder and financier of the National Bank of San Carlos, the predecessor to the Bank of Spain.) These projects were evidence of genuine progress in Spain and specifically of a kind of progress that benefitted civil society. The deployment of such administrative talent to achieve valuable practical ends would never have been possible in Hapsburg Spain, in which the style of monarchical rule was deeply rooted in personal power and ultimately did little to advance large-scale projects organized for the greater good.[18] Alas, there were many forces still at play in post-Hapsburg (that is, Bourbon) Spain working directly against any sense of the common, public good. The issue is the direct source of one of the images of the *Disasters of War* (no. 71 "*Contra el bien general*" ["Against the common good"], Figure 6.17, above).

This said, Floridablanca's long career was scarcely unflawed, a fact that Goya does not leave unnoticed in other works. By the time Charles IV retained Floridablanca in his position as prime minister upon his accession to the throne (1789), the terrible reality of the French Revolution had transformed the count from an enlightened and progressive leader into an authoritarian figure who resuscitated the Inquisition and imposed severe censorship rules. Such reversals of character and fortune were hardly uncommon among enlightened figures across Europe. To take but one of the most notorious examples, the widely admired Marquis de Lafayette and supporter of the revolution eventually abandoned his command of a French army and ended up spending five years in Prussian and Austrian prisons. Napoleon himself was an institution builder and founder of the Bank of France and the Legion of Honor, but met a legendarily ignominious end on the island of St. Helena.[19] Among Floridablanca's more dubious successes was the founding of the Philippines Company, which was created at the urging of the French-born adventurer and financier Francisco Cabarrús. In a large-scale work — nearly the largest of all his canvases — painted relatively late in his career (*Sessions of the Junta of the Royal Company of the Philippines*, Figure 8.4) that now hangs in the Goya Museum in Castres, France, Goya depicts this as a severe and ponderous body of largely faceless individuals.

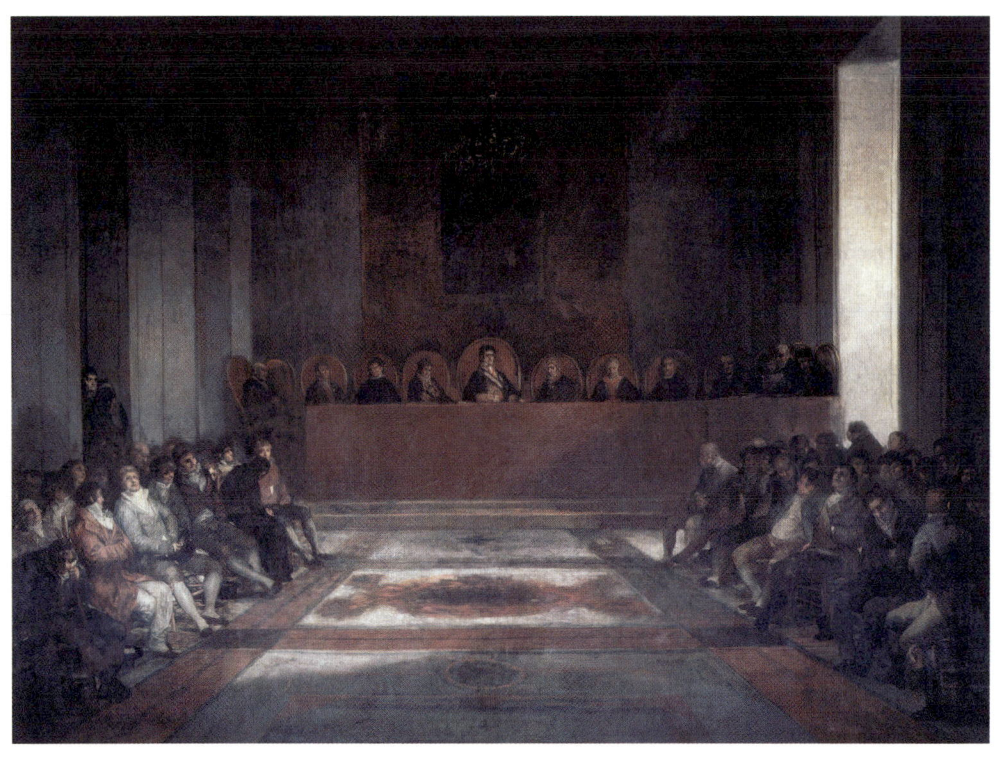

Figure 8.4.
Sessions of the Junta of the Royal Company of the Philippines, ca. 1815.
Oil on canvas, 320×433 cm. Musée Goya, Castres, France.

The painting shows a meeting of the junta that Ferdinand VII attended as a show of his support for Spain's imperial mission. However, the Spanish economy and empire were in tatters after the Peninsular War, and the Royal Company of the Philippines was by that time so unprofitable and ineffective as to be inconsequential, despite its massive scale. There is no doubt an ironic relationship between the grand size of the painting, the bureaucratic seriousness of the meeting, and the hollow accomplishments of the Philippines Company. The one individualized figure in the image appears entering or exiting from the side: Miguel de Lardizábal, minister of the Indies and president of the Company of the Philippines until he was dismissed and imprisoned following accusations of favoritism toward his native Mexico. The vacuous reality of the junta is captured in the vast, open, empty central expanse of the painting. Robert Hughes has suggested that the painting echoes Velásquez's *Las Meninas*,[20] which is no doubt true, except for the fact that Goya's play with light, structure, and reflection takes the magic by which Velásquez produced the illusion of volume as an opportunity to demonstrate the emptiness of the endeavors about which the junta convenes. The contrast between Floridablanca, the once successful and pragmatic administrator, and the anonymous, deindividuated members of the junta he helped establish could not be more pronounced.

It is indeed a respect for the individual and for qualities of character that characterizes Goya's most striking portraits of accomplished figures whose practical works made a contribution to the public good. Two stand out. The first is the portrait of Brigadier Ignacio Garcini y Queralt (Figure 8.5); the second is the portrait of the civilian engineer Bartolomé Sureda y Miserol from roughly the same era (Figure 8.6). An official in the War Department, Brigadier Garcini wears the distinguished uniform of the Corps of Engineers. (The embroidered red cross on his coat and the badge of the Order of Santiago are distinctions he received in 1806 and so must have been added after the painting was finished.)[21] Garcini is shown against a neutral, blank background, which lends prominence and dignity to

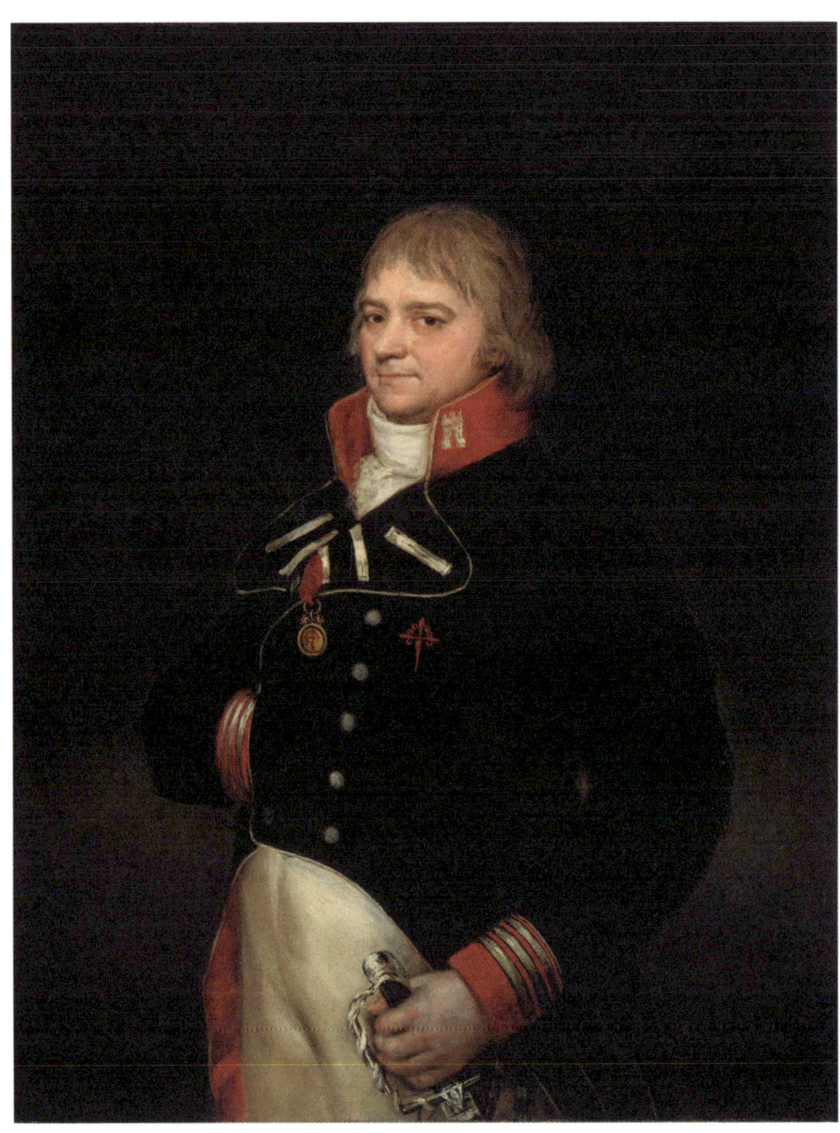

Figure 8.5.
Ignacio Garcini y Queralt, 1804. Oil on canvas, 104×83 cm.
Metropolitan Museum of Art, New York.

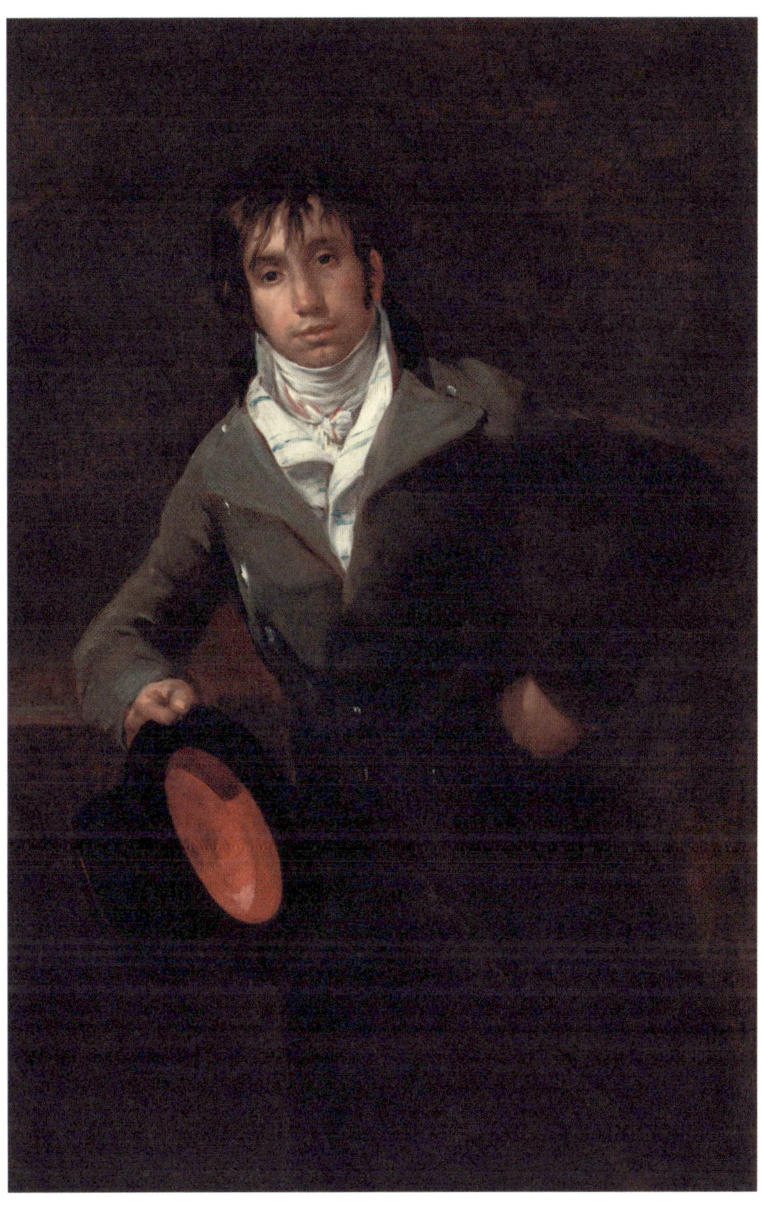

Figure 8.6.
Bartolomé Sureda y Miserol, ca. 1804–1806. Oil on canvas, 119 × 79 cm.
National Gallery of Art, Washington, DC.

the subject. One might compare the image with that of the highly decorated Charles IV in the well-known portrait of the royal family (1800–1801).

The Sureda portrait is quite different. Sureda's career was dedicated to science, fine arts, and industry. He was a protégé of Agustín de Betancourt, the internationally known engineer who traveled the world in order to bring the most modern machinery to Spain. But unlike the image of Garcini, the portrait of Sureda makes no direct allusion to his practical accomplishments. He is dressed in a proper frock coat, which is to say in outdoor, city attire. Goya shows him as a pensive man, lost in thoughts, as if to suggest the inner qualities that underlie his achievements, but that also threaten to draw him away from the world of action. Indeed, the pose is reminiscent of Jovellanos at his desk (1798) and of the melancholy of *La Leocadia* in the Quinta. In tilting the balance between thought and action clearly toward thought, Goya's portrait of Sureda stands in the line of Velásquez's images of Aesop and Menippus and looks forward to Manet's *Absinthe Drinker* (1859) and *Philosopher* (Figure 8.7).

Several implications follow from this aspect of the Sureda portrait, if we bear in mind his professional career. One is the recognition that a life of action stands in a dynamic relationship with thought and reflection. The *vita activa* and the *vita contemplativa* have been held in contrast since classical antiquity, but in fact, they are both necessary components of a fully lived life.[22] The second is that Sureda's contemplative demeanor also demonstrates some of the liabilities associated with an increasingly common figure in the late eighteenth and early nineteenth centuries in Europe, the so-called "beautiful soul." The conceptual profile of such a figure was outlined well before Hegel gave the term the currency it subsequently came to have. For many continental thinkers — especially Goethe, whose *Werther* was translated into Spanish in 1803 and then retranslated in 1819 and again in 1820 — the pursuit of inner moral beauty was a necessary and valuable response to the horrors of the French Revolution and the Terror of the 1790s. Though with no guarantee of success

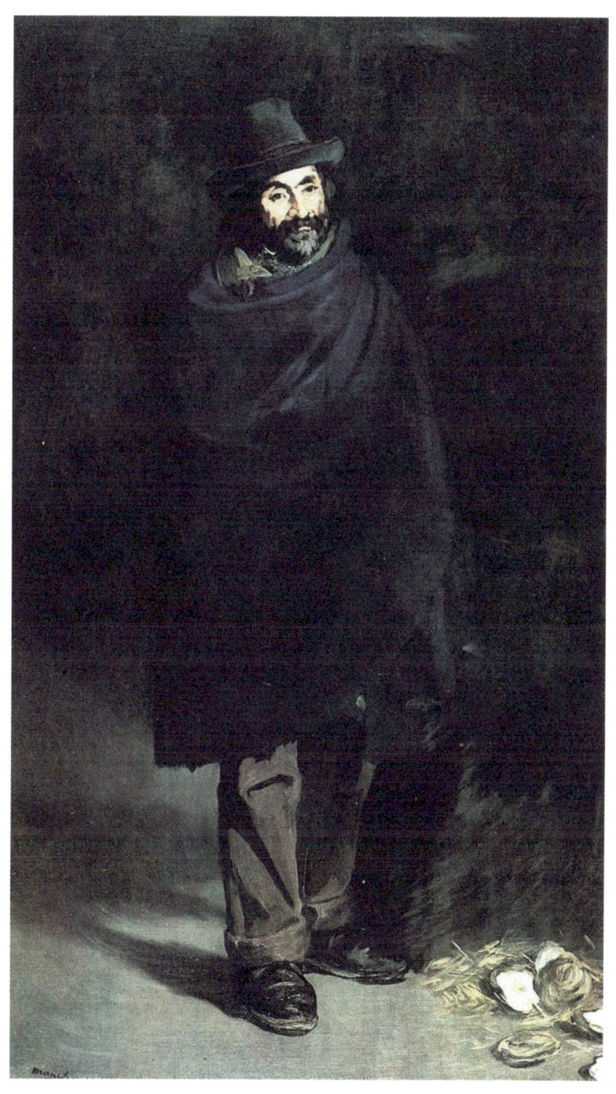

Figure 8.7.

Édouard Manet, *Philosopher*, 1865–67. Oil on canvas, 188×111 cm.
Art Institute of Chicago.

or happiness, at its core was the idea that each individual possesses an inherent potential and along with it the potential for good. In the proper environment and with the right education, this potential could be developed to yield a more perfect state of morality, character, and conduct. (Goya's picture of inbred ugliness in *Capricho* no. 25, "*Si quebró el cantaro*" ["For he broke the pitcher"], gives us a close-up look at the inverse circumstances, a portrait of maleducation and the creation of the "ugly soul"; see Figure 4.9, above). The beautiful soul is virtuous, possesses a sense of justice, acts to achieve the highest ends, and is able to feel compassion for others and thereby contributes to the well-being of society. Inspired originally by ancient Greek philosophy, the beautiful soul fuses aesthetics and morality. Plotinus's words were an abiding inspiration:

> Withdraw within yourself, and examine yourself. If you do not yet therein discover beauty, do as the artist, who cuts off, polishes, purifies until he has adorned his statue with all the marks of beauty. Remove from your soul, therefore, all that is superfluous, straighten out all that is crooked, purify and illuminate what is obscure, and do not cease perfecting your statue until the divine resplendence of virtue shines forth upon your sight.[23]

But as this passage suggests, the "beautiful soul" also runs a risk, namely, of losing sight of actions that contribute to the social good. As the case of the character Werther so vividly demonstrates, the early modern concept of the beautiful soul is easily transformed into a practice of aesthetic self-cultivation that sees no need to look beyond the aims of self-perfection.[24]

Goya likewise sees those limitations and exposes them visually in the portrait of Sureda, all the while demonstrating a remarkable sympathy for his subject. Moreover, the affirmation of value as manifested in a respect for the individual demonstrates itself in Goya's ability to regard his subject not just critically, but also sympathetically. In the case of the Sureda portrait, this means exposing a potential weakness in the subject (if melancholy and the self-absorption associated with it are indeed a weakness), without allowing a recognition of that weakness to undermine the integrity of the character or his other virtuous attributes. I would underscore that this is not just a matter of the artist reflecting something virtuous about his sitter; indeed, the greater accomplishment is to see weakness amid virtue in a sympathetic way. It requires a generosity of the spirit that may well have been sharpened by the critical gaze but finally not undermined by it. Seeing in this way can rightfully be characterized as an aesthetic ideal, an ideal of beauty underpinned by sympathy. Indeed, sympathy can be regarded as the hopeful face of critique.

As the mentions of Burke, Shaftesbury, and Hume above may have suggested, there was a substantial history of thinking about sympathy in this and related ways throughout the eighteenth century—ways that run contrary to the abstract understanding of sympathy characteristic of Kant's aesthetics. (Kant's aesthetics was probably known in Spain via the Latin translation.)[25] It was well represented in the conceptual landscape in Spain via Dehesa's translation of Burke, which described sympathy as a kind of substitution "by which we place ourselves in the position of another human being and have the same feelings as he."[26] That said, it was hardly a novel idea. For Sebastián de Covarrubias in the *Tesoro de la lengua castellana o española* 1611) "simpatía" is the "friendship and conformity that one thing naturally has for another";[27] it is directly related to "codolencia" (*sic*) and "compasión." As a form of fellow feeling, it is the sine qua non of social peace and harmony. Its antitheses are "antipatía" and the relationship to one's "natural enemies."

A richly human sense of sympathy permeates one of Goya's most moving paintings—the portrait of himself being treated by Doctor Arrieta (Figure 8.8). That it presents a *human* ideal is underscored by the fact that the image suggests a vision of secular salvation. It is, as critics have noted, visually akin to a secular *pietà* in which the physician-minister takes the place of the Virgin Mary.[28] It is an image that inverts the temper of a much earlier image of ministry to the sick, *St. Francis Borgia at the Deathbed of an Impenitent* (Figure 5.1, above).

The physician in question, to whom the painting is dedicated

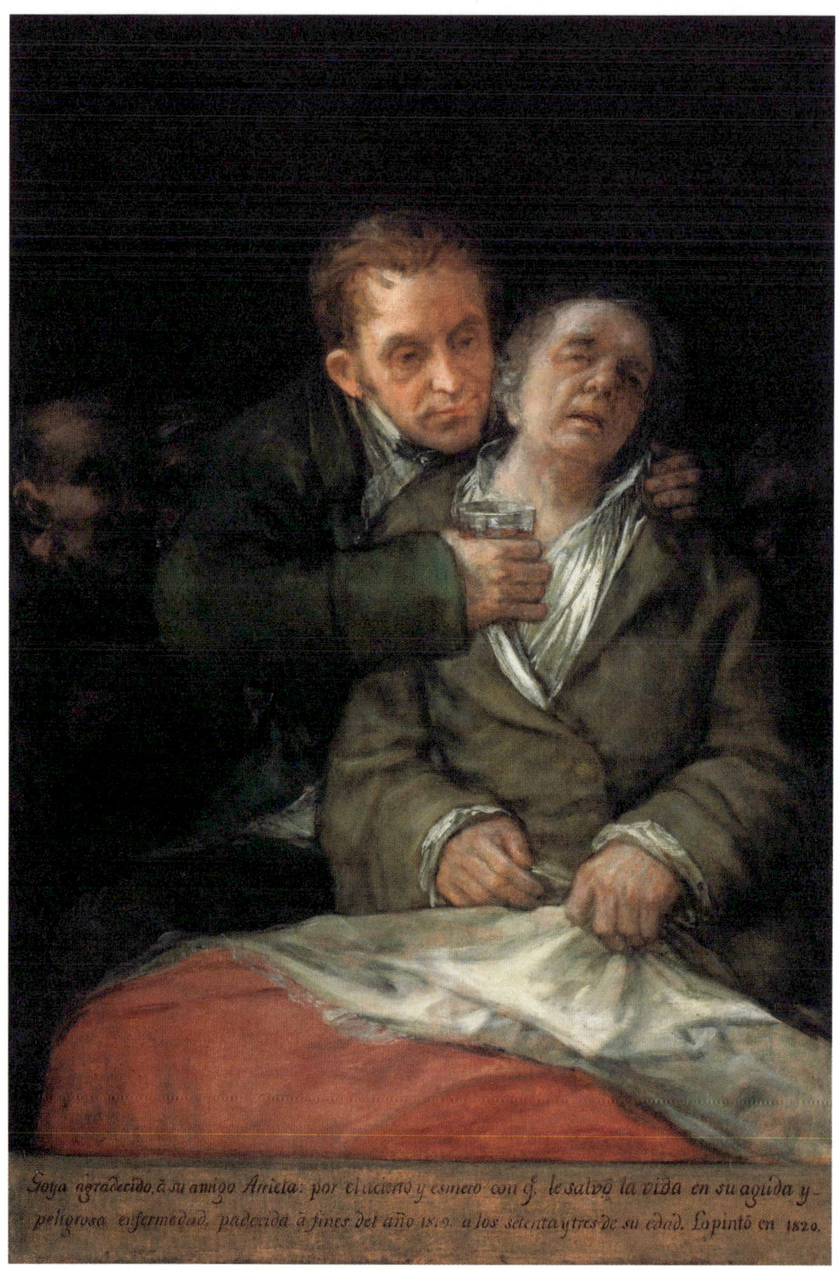

Figure 8.8.
Self-Portrait with Dr. Arrieta, 1829. Oil on canvas, 114.62 × 76.52 cm.
Minneapolis Institute of Art, Minneapolis, Minnesota.

in gratitude, is Eugenio García Arrieta. Arrieta was born in 1770 to an enlightened family. He practiced medicine in Madrid, and his brother, Eugenio García Arrieta, served as the inaugural director of the Library of the University of Madrid. Shortly after he treated Goya, in 1820, Arrieta was commissioned by the Spanish government to travel to Africa to study the plague, where it is likely that he perished. Goya's image of the doctor reverses the brutal satire of doctors in the *Caprichos* (no. 40, "*¿De qué mal morirá?*" ["From what illness will he die?"]; see Figure 4.13, above) and in the drawings related to the *Caprichos* known as the *Sueños* (no. 27, "*Brujas disfrazadas en físicos comunes*" ["Witches disguised as common doctors"], Figure 8.9).

And it goes far beyond his earlier, innocuous genre scene from in the tapestry cartoons (*El médico* ["The doctor"], 1799) that shows a country doctor warming his hands over a fire alongside some open books and two young men, possibly students. That image is as much about winter as it is about medicine, if not more so. Whether the caustic depictions of doctors in the *Caprichos* and the *Sueños* are meant to reflect on the physicians who had treated Goya prior to Arrieta would be difficult to say, though as is so often the case with interpretations of Goya, biographical theories abound. The images certainly are representative of Goya's critique of Spain's backwardness with respect to the science and practice of medicine. Indeed, *¿De qué mal morirá?* and *Brujas disfrazadas en físicos comunes* show Goya's critique of the ignorance and superstitions that were thriving in Spanish popular culture and contributing to Spain's isolation and backwardness with respect to the medical advancements happening elsewhere in Europe.

Some of these things did nonetheless begin to change during the reign of Charles III. New medical schools were founded, and older ones improved under him, even as the Inquisition kept its watchful eye over them. More important for Goya, no doubt, were the progressive ideas promoted by Father Jerónimo Feijóo. A principal objective of the essays gathered in the volumes of his *Teatro crítico universal* was to advance the value of empirical science and to undermine superstition. Feijóo had a particular interest in medicine, and

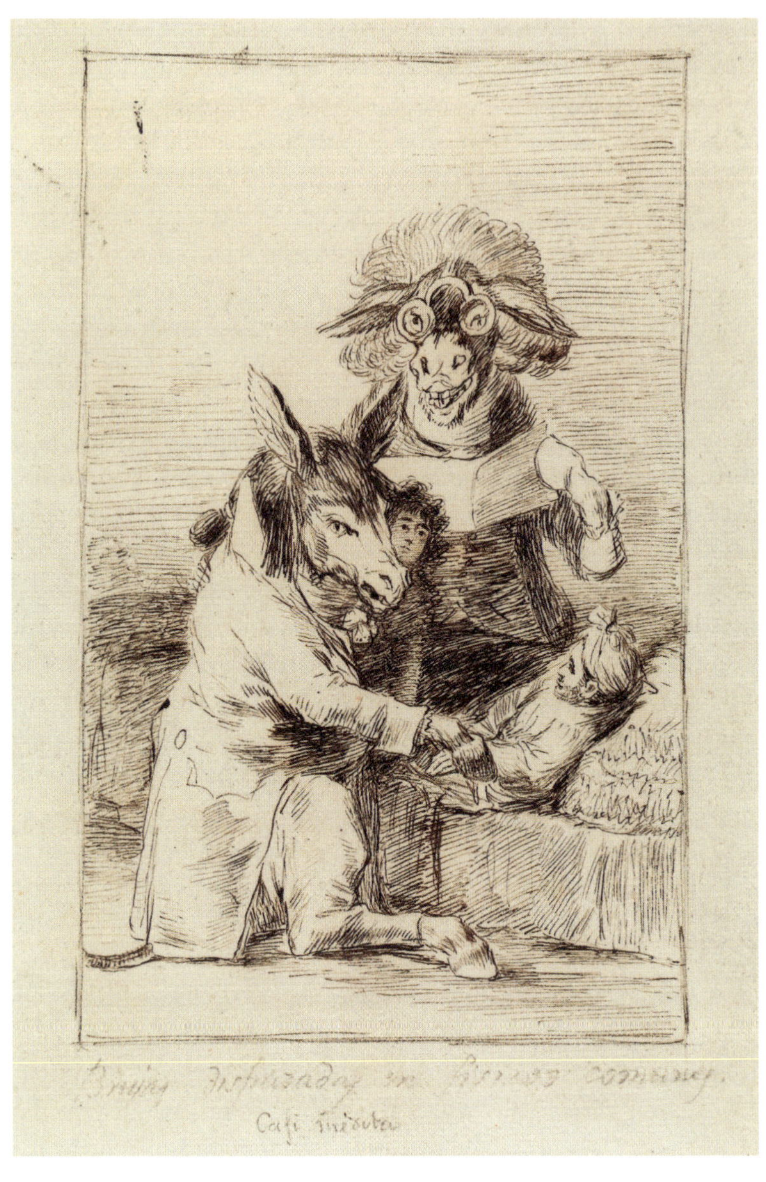

Figure 8.9.
"*Brujas disfrazadas en fisicos comunes*" ("Witches disguised as common doctors"), 1796–97.
Bougainvillea ink over black pencil, 24.6×18.4 cm. Museo del Prado, Madrid.

his texts were so widely read — including by Goya and his coterie of enlightened acquaintances — that his followers in the practice of medicine finally began questioning the validity of many inherited medical ideas, a good number of which had remained in force since antiquity and the Middle Ages. This shift in views about medicine enabled what one critic has called "the emergence of medicine from the shadows of the Church and the Inquisition."[29] It corresponds to the change from the images showing doctors as asses to Goya's portrait with Dr. Arrieta.

But a critique of Spain's resistance to science, or alternatively an embrace of the values of truth and transparency, is not quite enough to produce the kind of sympathy on which beauty can rely. And indeed, Goya's eloquent portrait of himself being treated by Dr. Arrieta implies much more than a changed vision of medicine. The image is among those few self-depictions that are neither a self-portrait of Goya as artist nor a self-portrait of himself as critical observer. The former include the many instances in which Goya either inserts himself obliquely into an image (such as in the portrait of the royal family or the painting for the altarpiece in San Francisco el Grande) or paints himself in full control of his identity as an artist. The latter include the frontispiece of the *Caprichos*, and the portrait in front of the easel, in which Goya turns aside, presumably to glance at himself reflected in a mirror that we cannot see. The self-portrait with Dr. Arrieta is rather more like the mature self-portrait of 1815. In both instances, Goya presents himself as vulnerable and exposed, revealing a degree of sympathy that stands out against the backdrop of his fiercely critical oeuvre. But the portrait with Dr. Arrieta exhibits an even more distinct vulnerability, one that derives from an acknowledgment of the fragility of the body, of human mortality, and of one's dependence on the kindness of others. Goya faces this vulnerability and does so quite literally, that is, by presenting himself frontally, allowing the viewer to see his face in a completely unguarded way.

To do so requires a form of sympathy that transcends pity (on the part of Arrieta), but it also requires the courage to confront the truth about one's own weakness in a way that transcends self-pity (on the part of Goya). The image shows a remarkable humility and can serve as a fitting conclusion and counterweight to the knowing and guarded self-portrait that prefaces the *Caprichos*. As John J. Ciofalo noted, "There is not the faintest allusion to his greatness [in the inscription], and where is the hallmark enigma, the innuendo, the irony and satirical acid for which he was s renowned? In the vicinity of death, he seems — in image and word — to have stripped himself stark naked of myth."[30]

Humility, the avoidance of self-pity, and sympathy are, I would suggest, are among the specific moral qualities that inform beauty in Goya's work. They are not mere symbols of morality, and they offer us significant insights into a human ideal that can counterbalance the potentially destructive consequences of the project of critique. It may well be true that one can recognize and express generosity of spirit only if one has also seen the worst in human beings, but a critique of the baseness of humanity is apt to bring despair if it is not coupled with some more sympathetic view of things. Indeed, it is all too likely to end in self-destruction. Goodness can be found in the capacity to feel compassion for others, which in turn may contribute to the betterment of society and to a sense of self-worth. Whether beauty is predicated on or is necessary for these things is not something Goya allows us to conclude. But that they are aligned is something that he certainly lets us see. Given the thoroughness of his critical project, this is a vision in which we might well be inclined to place our trust.

Acknowledgments

This book has been long in the making. Its genesis reaches back a few decades when I first attempted to teach Goya alongside Velásquez and Picasso and found myself stumped by the apparent discontinuities and contradictions in his work when viewed as a whole. It was only much later, in the context of a graduate seminar, that some answers to the apparent enigmas presented by Goya's work began to come clear and when the basic shape of the arguments presented in this book cane into focus. Two published pieces emerged during this evolutionary period, and traces of those are, to a greater or lesser extent, reflected in some of the pages that come before. They are "The Ethics of Enlightenment: Goya and Kant," *Philosophy and Literature*, 15 (October, 1991), pp. 189–211; "Goya: La dialéctica entre la Ilustración y el arte," in Francisco La Rubia Prado and Jesús Torrecillas, eds., *Razón, tradición y modernidad: Re-visión de la ilustración hispánica* (Madrid: Tecnos, 1996), pp. 53–85, and "Goya: Secularization and the Aesthetics of Belief," in Paul Kottman, ed., *The Insistence of Art* (New York: Fordham University Press, 2017), pp. 227–56.

I am especially grateful for the opportunity to have presented some earlier versions of these ideas in various public contexts: at NYU, Carleton College, Columbia University, UCLA, the University of South Carolina, as the Keniston Lecture at the University of Michigan, at my home institution of UC Berkeley, and in Barcelona at the kind invitation of Joan Sureda and Anna María Guasch. Francisco

Ros was extraordinarily generous to me in gaining access to see a number of Goya's works held in the offices of the Bank of Spain in Madrid. The Committee on Research of the Academic Senate at UC Berkeley long ago provided initial support funds that allowed me to make bridges from the worlds of literature and aesthetics to art history. In those same early years, Matthew and Elisa listened to me talk about many of the images included in this book as they were projected on the walls at home.

For assistance with the preparation of the manuscript and the detailed work of securing permissions to reproduce the images included here, I thank my nonpareil research assistant, Jason de Stefano. Darcy Grigsby shared valuable advice about the process for securing permissions that helped greatly streamline that work. For the support and encouragement of Zone Books, I am especially grateful to Ramona Naddaff, Jonathan Crary, and Meighan Gale. Julie Fry has been a superb designer. Bud Bynack has made the copyediting process a learning experience and a joy.

Finally, I wish to thank my wife, Jennifer Howard, for sharing the pleasures and perplexities of looking at many of Goya's works with me and for engaging in seemingly endless conversations about the notion of "critique."

Notes

INTRODUCTION

1. See, for example, Fred Licht, *Goya: The Origins of the Modern Temper in Art* (New York: Universe Books, 1979), and Valeriano Bozal, *Goya y el gusto moderno*, 2nd. ed. (Madrid: Alianza, 2002).

CHAPTER ONE: SECULARIZATION
AND THE AESTHETICS OF BELIEF

1. I follow the translation of Goya's speech as included in the Appendix to Janis Tomlinson, *Francisco Goya y Lucientes, 1746–1828* (London: Phaidon, 1994), p. 306. The term "inventadas," which is not uncommon in printmaking, is meant to suggest that the images are not copied or otherwise derived from prior ones, but are instead originally conceived. The term was prominent in Antonio Palomino de Castro y Velasco's treatise the *Museo pictórico, y escala óptica* (Madrid, 1715–27; 2nd ed. 1795–97), where it carries the sense of rhetorical invention, that is, of finding or uncovering the topic to be treated (see especially vol. 2, pp. 122–26: "Qué cosa sea inventar.") Already in making some of the tapestry cartoons Goya would assert that they were of his "own invention" ("de invención mía"). See Valentín de Sambricio, *Tapices de Goya* (Madrid: Patrimonio Nacional, 1946), doc. 22, where Goya refers to *The Meadow of San Isidro*. For more on the sense and the implications of invention in Goya, see Janis Tomlinson, *Francisco Goya: The Tapestry Cartoons and Early Career at the Court of Madrid* (Cambridge: Cambridge University Press, 1989), especially ch. 2, "Of My Own Invention," and the epilogue, "Invention into Metaphor." Tomlinson links the importance of invention in Goya in part to the development of a tradition of national painting in Spain.

2. Bozal, *Goya y el gusto moderno*, p. 67. Joseph Addison's *The Spectator* (1712) was translated

into Spanish from the French and was a direct influence on Clavijo y Fajardo's influential text (in Goya's time) *El pensador*. Bozal goes on to note that Spain had virtually no native tradition of picturesque painting. The picturesque painters who held greatest sway in the decades before Goya's ascendancy were foreigners such as Miguel Ange Houasse.

3. Norman Bryson, *Vision and Painting: The Logic of the Gaze* (New Haven: Yale University Press, 1983).

4. The writer/translator was José Francisco de Isla, whose *Año cristiano* drew on a text by Jean Croiset, in the *Année chrétienne*. See Enrique Lafuente-Ferrari, *Goya and the Frescoes in San Antonio de la Florida*, trans. Stuart Gilbert (New York: Skira, 1955), p. 23. The story is cited in Hans Rothe, *Las pinturas del panteón de Goya*, trans. Manuel Gutiérrez Marín (Barcelona: Orbis, 1944).

5. Fred Licht, *Goya: The Origins of the Modern Temper in Art* (New York: Universe Books, 1979), pp. 65–66.

6. Rothe, *Las pinturas del panteón de Goya*, p. 12.

7. Robert Hughes, *Goya* (New York: Knopf, 2006), p. 213.

8. Roberto Calasso, *Tiepolo Pink* (New York: Knopf, 2009), p. 197.

9. Tiepolo (Giovanni Battista) was assisted by his son Domenico on this project.

10. Giorgio Vasari, *Lives of the Artists: Volume 1*, trans. George Bull (1971; London: Penguin, 1987), p. 96.

11. Calasso, *Tiepolo Pink*, p. 198.

12. Svetlana Alpers and Michael Baxandall, *Tiepolo and the Pictorial Intelligence* (New Haven: Yale University Press, 1994), pp. 93–94.

13. Édouard Manet on Tiepolo, as recorded by Charles Toché, winter, 1874–75: "They're so boring, these Italians, with their allegories, their characters from *Jerusalem Delivered* and *Orlando Furioso*, with all that showy bric-à-brac," in *Manet by Himself*, ed. Juliet Wilson-Bareau (1991; Edison: Chartwell Books, 2001), p. 172.

14. Michael Fried, "The Structure of Beholding in Courbet's 'Burial at Ornans'," *Critical Inquiry* 9.4 (June 1983), pp. 635–83.

15. The issue of what it means for a work to refuse or to invite the presence of the beholder is one that Michael Fried has discussed at length over the course of many works, beginning with *Absorption and Theatricality* (Berkeley: University of California Press, 1980). Tomlinson notes that as with the tapestry cartoons, Goya attempts to mitigate the fact that the works were to be placed high on a wall by compressing the figures against the background. Tomlinson, *Francisco Goya y Lucientes*, p. 22.

16. See Tomlinson, *Francisco Goya y Lucientes*, pp. 25–37.

17. See, for example, ibid., pp. 21–22.

18. See ibid., p. 18.

19. Tomlinson notes that the *Adoration* refuses baroque ebullience and avoids rococo complexity. *Francisco Goya y Lucientes*, p. 18. And yet the work does recall the rococo painting of Giaquinto.

20. Tomlinson, *Francisco Goya y Lucientes*, p. 54.

21. Hughes, *Goya*, p. 99.

22. Goya was fascinated by Velásquez's techniques, as the etchings show, but also determined to displace their unique sense of space in the process of transposing them to the far more resistant medium of etching.

23. The portraits of St. Ambrose and St. Gregory bear substantial resemblance to Murillo's portraits of St. Isidore and St. Leander in the Cathedral of Seville.

24. For this sense of the "sculptural," see Clement Greenberg, "Modernist Painting." I cite the version published in *Art and Literature* 4 (1965), pp. 193–201. This highly influential essay has also met with serious objections. Among the sources of resistance to Greenberg's focus on flatness is his emphasis on the autonomy of modernist art, that is, its separation from the social and political worlds. Insofar as Goya's engagement with the physical grounds of art is positioned at the intersection of the sacred and secular worlds, it would be difficult to align it fully with Greenberg's ideas.

25. Janis Tomlinson, *Goya in the Twilight of Enlightenment* (New Haven: Yale University Press, 1992), p. 11.

26. For a discussion of this work in the context of the others in San Francisco el Grande, see ibid., especially p. 28–38. The image offers what Tomlinson describes as a warning to anyone who would interpret it as a mimetic recording of the scene (p. 12).

27. Antonio Palomino de Castro y Velasco, *Museo pictórico, y escala óptica*, 2nd ed., 3 vols. (Madrid: Sancha, 1795–97), vol. 2, pp. 177–79.

28. See Santiago Alcolea Blanch, "Aníbal, máscaras y anamorfosis en el *Cuaderno italiano* de Goya," (Barcelona: Fundación Instituto Amatller de Arte Hispánico, 1998, pp. 1–18, https://www.academia.edu/24759108/An%C3%ADbal_m%C3%A1scaras_y_anamorfosis_en_el_Cuaderno_Italiano_de_Goya. These figures — Goya's sketch and Alcolea Blanch's computer projections — reproduce the images in his essay.

29. Quoted in Tomlinson, *Francisco Goya y Lucientes*, p. 306.

30. Greenberg, "Modernist Painting," p. 196.

CHAPTER TWO: A PROMISE OF HAPPINESS?

1. See Janis Tomlinson's discussion of their influence on Goya's tapestries in *Francisco Goya: The Tapestry Cartoons and Early Career at the Court of Madrid* (Cambridge: Cambridge University Press, 1989), p. 187.

2. Though he might have wished to follow them in choice of subject matter, his royal patron asked specifically for images that would reflect Spanish life. Tomlinson discusses this issue in *Francisco Goya: The Tapestry Cartoons*.

3. The tapestry works were established in 1721, after Spain lost its ties to Flanders and its source of imported tapestries. So-called "high-warp" looms were introduced in 1744 in order to improve production capacity and quality. See Real Fábrica de Tapices, "History," https://realfabricadetapices.com/en/history.

4. There are many examples. To take but one, *La acerolera* ("The Haw Seller") depicts a scene that ordinarily would have been painted in a format with a much wider ground in order to provide greater visual context. The tapestry for which it was painted was intended for the bedroom of the Prince and Princess of Asturias (the future Charles IV and Maria Luisa de Parma) in El Pardo Palace. Given its shape, it was in all likelihood meant to be placed beside a door or between two windows. Tomlinson reconstructs the possible (though by no means certain) placement of the tapestries for El Pardo in *Francisco Goya: The Tapestry Cartoons*, pp. 69 and 96.

5. Fred Licht, *Goya: The Origins of the Modern Temper in Art* (New York: Universe Books, 1979), pp. 24–25.

6. The discussion of these factors in Norman Bryson, *Vision and Painting: The Logic of the Gaze* (New Haven: Yale University Press, 1983), pp. 134–35, is illuminating.

7. This is one reason why it matters that the *Caprichos* were undertaken independent of patronage or commission. See Andrew Shulz, *Goya's Caprichos: Aesthetics, Perception, and the Body* (Cambridge: Cambridge University press, 2005), pp. 77–119.

8. F. D. Klingender, *Goya in the Democratic Tradition* (London: Sidgwick and Jackson, 1948), p. 41.

9. Tomlinson discusses both in *Francisco Goya: The Tapestry Cartoons*. Other examples include *Las floreras o La Primavera*, which features a rabbit as a symbol of fecundity.

10. See Valentín de Sambricio, *Tapices de Goya* (Madrid: Patrimonio Nacional, 1946), doc. no. 129, p. 93.

11. See Yvonne Fuentes, "British Aesthetics and the Picturesque in Spain: Jovellanos's Affinity with England," *Hispania* 87 (2004), pp. 210–19. At the core of the aes-

thetics of the picturesque for Jovellanos was the intent to please the eye and move the heart.

12. Edith Helman discusses this relationship in *Jovellanos y Goya* (Madrid: Taurus, 1970), pp. 257–71.

13. Roland Barthes, *Camera Lucida*, trans. Richard Howard (New York: Hill and Wang, 1981).

14. Theodor Hetzer, "Francisco Goya and the Crisis in Art around 1800," in Fred Licht, ed., *Goya in Perspective* (Englewood Cliffs: Prentice Hall, 1973), p. 109.

15. Quoted in Edith Helman, *Trasmundo de Goya* (Madrid: Revista de Occidente, 1963), pp. 30–33, referring to José Ortega y Gasset, *Papeles sobre Velázquez y Goya* (Madrid: Revista de Occidente, 1950).

16. "Más vivaces y verosímiles, más pintorescos, más convincentes en todo aquello que hace referencia a la representación de la vida cotidiana, tipos y lugares." Valeriano Bozal, *Goya y el gusto moderno*, 2nd. ed. (Madrid: Alianza, 2002), pp. 109–110. He nonetheless gives a nod to some of the connections between the tapestry cartoons and the later works: "El Goya de la noche, el Goya de los *Disparates* y las *Pinturas Negras* arroja luz sobre el Goya más luminoso . . . aquél no debe ensombrecer a éste, pero la luminosidad de éste tampoco puede hacernos ignorer lo que en ella se oculta" (p. 131).

17. The question of what kinds of religious images should and should not be represented was a subject of formal discussion in Spain, particularly in Juan Interián de Ayala's *El pintor christiano y erudito* (1782).

18. Leon Battista Alberti, *On Painting*, trans. Martin Kemp (London: Penguin, 1991), p. 72.

19. Bryson's *Vision and Painting* is a crucial text in the development of a theory of art that departs from Gombrich. See especially pp. 18–35 and, for the critique of perceptualism, pp. 37–66. The "natural attitude" is a phrase that Bryson adopts from the work of the phenomenologist Edmund Husserl.

20. See above, Chapter 1, note 2. The phrase believed to have been written by Goya's friend Juan Agustín Ceán Bermúdez. See also the discussion in Tomlinson, *Francisco Goya: The Tapestry Cartoons*, pp. 26–64.

21. The Rubens painting was acquired after the artist's death, by Philip IV. See Manuela B. Mena Marqués and Gudrun Mauer, *Goya en Madrid: Cartones para tapices, 1775–1794* (Madrid: Museo del Prado, 2014), p. 179. Another important work, *Saturn Devouring His Son*, is related to a Rubens painting on the same theme, also in the royal collection.

22. On the social context of this game in Spain and Europe, see ibid., p. 174. This is not to say that Goya found mythology wholly uninteresting. A relatively early work, *The Rape of Europa* (1772), makes that clear, as does *Saturn Devouring His Son* (1820–23).

23. In 1776, Mengs proposed that fees for original artworks for tapestries be assessed independent of the regular salary. See Tomlinson, *Francsico de Goya: The Tapestry* Cartoons, p. 28.

24. Quoted in Margherita Abruzzese, *Goya: The Life and Work of the Artist* (London: Thames and Hudson, 1967), p. 20.

25. Pamela H. Smith, *The Body of the Artisan: Art and Experience in the Scientific Revolution* (Chicago: University of Chicago Press, 2004), p. 9.

26. Robert Hughes offers an illuminating discussion of this image in *Goya* (New York: Knopf, 2003), pp. 87–88.

27. Goya's painted sketch for the cartoon was of a fight outside the *Mesón del gallo* (Cock Inn). The sketch is of interest because it shows Goya attempting to decide where the center of focus for the image might possibly be. The sketch is available at https://es.wikipedia.org/wiki/Ri%C3%B1a_en_el_Mes%C3%B3n_del_Gallo#/media/File:Ri%C3%B1a_en_el_Mes%C3%B3n_del_Gallo_de_Goya.jpg.

28. See Museo del Prado, "*A Fight at the Venta Nueva*," https://www.museo-delprado.es/en/the-collection/art-work/a-fight-at-the-venta-nueva/d08c4091-331b-4678-b91d-08df66d0dec8.

29. Goya paints other card games in the cartoons, for example, *Jugadores de naipes* (*The Card Players*, 1777–78). Even though there are some rough types in the background of that image, the game does not get out of control. This suggests that violence is not connected with card playing in any regular or necessary way.

30. "El ser humano sacando lo peor de sí, convertido en un salvaje, peor aún que las bestias, como nos indican los dos perros de la composición, que observan la escena sin intervenir, uno tranquilo y otro ladrando nervioso." Museo del Prado, "El cuadro del día," August 13, 2015, http://www.elcuadrodeldia.com/post/128021721758/francisco-de-goya-ri%C3%B1a-en-la-venta-nueva.

31. Rousseau was known in Spain among Goya's enlightened friends. The Duquesa de Alba was educated according to his principles, and Goya himself suggested liberal teaching along Rousseauean lines in his 1792 address to the Royal Academy of San Fernando. See J. R. Spell, *Rousseau in the Spanish World Before 1833* (Austin: University of Texas Press, 1938); J. Ezquerra del Bayo, *La Duquesa de Alba y Goya. Estudio biográfico y crítico* (Madrid: Aguilar,

1959); and Jutta Held, "Goyas Akademiekritik," *Münchner Jahrbuch der bildenden Kunst*, n.s., 17 (1966), pp. 214–24. The best study of his understanding of human beings in relation to nature and society remains that of Judith Shklar, *Men and Citizens: A Study of Rousseau's Social Theory*, 2nd. ed. (Cambridge: Cambridge University Press, 1985). The bestiality of human beings is on clear display in the *Caprichos*, in many of which human beings take on animal forms. See José Lópe-Rey, *Goya's Caprichos: Beauty, Reason, and Caricature*, 2 vols. (Princeton: Princeton University Press, 1953), vol. 1, p. 68.

32. This is laid out clearly in Tomlinson, *Francisco Goya: The Tapestry Cartoons*, pp. 200–203.

33. See Michael Kubovy, "Goya Breaks Alberti's Window to Send a Message," *Rivista di Estetica* 43 (2003), pp. 89–95, https://pdfs.semanticscholar.org/3b18/183ec398efb475eaf6 ae75a66204d71b8ac0.pdf?_ga=2.151905147.378435685.1499180179-9645571.1499180179. This is an expanded version of an addendum written for the Spanish translation of Kubovy, *The Psychology of Perspective and Renaissance Art* (New York: Cambridge University Press, 1986), *Psicología de la perspectiva y el arte del Renacimiento* (Madrid: Trotta, 1996).

34. Tomlinson sees the bride in this image as a "mercenary precursor" of many of the women we see in the *Caprichos*. *Francisco Goya: The Tapestry Cartoons*, p. 201.

35. He is one of Goya's many cynics, comparable to the etching made after Velásquez's painting of the ancient Greek cynic Menippus.

36. The relationship to Moratín's play on this theme, *El sí de las niñas*, is well known.

37. Manuela B. Mena Marqués, "El matrimonio desigual," in Manuela B. Mena Marqués, and Gudrun Maurer, *Goya en Madrid* (Madrid: Museo del Prado, 2014), pp. 150–61. The prints were published in *Colección de trajes de España, tanto antiguos como modernos*, vol. 1 (Madrid, 1777; facsimile, Madrid: Turner, 1988), nos. 62 and 63.

38. Tomlinson, *Goya: The Tapestry Cartoons*, p. 202.

39. Jean Starobinski, *1789, The Emblems of Reason*, trans. Barbara Bray (Charlottesville: University Press of Virginia, 1982), p. 187.

40. And not only the Black Paintings, but other works as well, for example, the way in which the tapestry cartoon *El pelele* (*The Sstraw Manikin*) anticipates one of the *Dispartes*, the *Disparate femenino*.

41. There is no complete agreement about the attribution of this image.

42. See Mena Marqués and Mauer, *Goya en Madrid*, pp. 200–202.

43. The image is related to *Niño montando un carnero* (*Boy Riding a Ram*).

44. See also *El pelele* (*The Straw Manikin*, 1791). The labor involved in carrying is of

relevance to the pair of images *El albañil borracho* (*The Drunken Mason*, 1786) and *El albañil herido* (*The Injured Mason*, 1786–87).

45. In addition, there are two images that allude to the structural support that was necessary both for the making of an oil painting (stretcher, easel, and so on) and for the work of tapestry weaving itself (loom and so on): *El albañil borracho* and *El albañil herido*. That Goya was interested in the structures and mechanisms of support is something not accounted for in what otherwise is said and undoubtedly true about these images; for example, that they reflect the desire of the monarchy to portray its change in attitude and policy toward workers and that Goya displays particular compassion for the wounded mason. In both images, the ground surrounding the principal figures displays the brick-layer's scaffolding, but scarcely shows anything of the built structure itself. In the case of the injured mason, it may well be that the scaffolding was faulty. We cannot say for sure. But it is also conceivable that this scaffolding is an allusion to the material support that was a necessary part of the work of painting and of weaving.

46. See Tomlinson, *Goya: The Tapestry Cartoons*, p. 146, and also Thomas P. Campbell, "How Medieval and Renaissance Tapestries Were Made," Metropolitan Museum of Art, http://www.metmuseum.org/toah/hd/tapm/hd_tapm.htm. The commonly used "low-warp" technique was one in which the warp threads were stretched horizontally rather than vertically.

CHAPTER THREE: GOYA, MODERNITY, AESTHETIC CRITIQUE

1. These reactions to the painting from the Paris Salon of 1864 are all cited in Theodore Reff, *Manet's 'Incident in a Bullfight'* (New York: The Frick Collection, 2005), pp. 10–11.

2. Theodor W. Adorno, *Aesthetic Theory*, eds. Gretel Adorno and Rolf Tiedemann, trans. Robert Hullot-Kentor (London: Continuum, 1997), p. 436.

3. "De insertar un papel o libro noticias algunas favorable o adversas de las cosas pertenecientes al reino de Francia." Mardid, Real Orden, June 7, 1793. I owe the reference to Lioba Simon Schuhmacher, "Burke's Political and Aesthetic Ideas in Spain: A View from the Right?," in Martin Fitzpatrick and Peter Jones, eds., *The Reception of Edmund Burke in Europe* (London: Bloomsbury, 2017), p. 236.

4. Neil Larsen, *Hegemony and Modernity* (Minneapolis: University of Minnesota Press, 1990), p. 39.

5. "Les sciences ouvrent chaque jour une nouvelle carrière. . . . Au milieu de ces arts

nouveaux et consolateurs, aurons-nous la férocité de ces siècles barbares que nôtre raison flétrit?" Louis-Sébastien Mercier, *L'an deux mille quatre cent quarante*, 2 vols. (London, 1785), vol. 2, pp. 18–19. On the revolutionary aspect tensed against rationalism, see Jean Starobinski's study of light and other symbolic structures at this time: *1798: Les emblèmes de la raison* (Paris: Flammarion, 1979), which includes a chapter on Goya and the roles of shadow, disorder, etc. (pp. 123–35). Most recently, Ronald Paulson devotes an extensive chapter to Goya's perception of regression and failed revolution, calling Spain's "paradoxical progress/regress" at the same time "a personal psychomachia." *Representations of Revolution, 1789–1820* (New Haven: Yale University Press, 1983), pp. 386–87. On the subject of light, Paulson follows the emblematic interpretation of sleep and dream, in which the cat is a lynx, "the supernatural penetration of the moral eye of *fantasia*" (p. 327). Paul Ilie, "Goya's Teratology and the Critique of Reason," *Eighteenth-Century Studies* 18.1 (Autumn 1984), p. 41 note 9.

6. Georg Wilhelm Friedrich Hegel, *Phenomenology of Spirit*, trans. A. V. Miller (Oxford: Oxford University Press, 1977), sec. 545, p. 331.

7. The notion of a "simple abstraction" derives from Marx. On its elaboration for dialectical criticism, see Michael McKeon, *The Origins of the English Novel, 1600–1740* (Baltimore: Johns Hopkins University Press, 1987), pp. 17–18.

8. Alfonso E. Pérez Sánchez and Julián Gallego, *Goya: The Complete Etchings and Lithographs* (New York: Prestel, 1995), p. 146.

9. See Enrique Lafuente Ferrari, "Ilustración y elaboración en la 'Tauromaquia' de Goya," *Archivo Espanol de Arte*, 19. 75 (1946), pp. 177–82, and Frank I. Heckes, "Goya's 'Tauromaquia': A Criticism of Bullfighting?," *Print Quarterly* 18.1 (March, 2001), pp. 41–63.

10. Janis Tomlinson, *Graphic Evolutions: The Print Series of Francisco Goya* (New York: Columbia University Press, 1989), pp. 35–36. Previously, in an exhibition catalogue of 1983, she considered the series "an intentionally ambiguous satire on the national pastime, the '*bábara diversión*.'" She relates these prints to a subject common to all of Goya's other series, namely, "the follies of mankind." See Tomlinson, *Francisco Goya y Lucientes: The 'Disasters of War', 'La Tauromaquia', Spanish Entertainment and Other Prints from the Collection of the Arthur Ross Foundation* (Philadelphia: The University of Pennsylvania Publications Office, 1983), p. 39.

11. Max Horkheimer and Theodor Adorno, *Dialectic of Enlightenment*, trans. Edmund Jephcott (Stanford: Stanford University Press, 2002), p. 18.

12. The best discussion of the differences between the three versions of the image is Ilie, "Goya's Teratology and the Critique of Reason."

13. Hegel, *Phenomenology of Spirit*, sec. 549, p. 334.

CHAPTER FOUR: THE LIMITS OF REPRESENTATION

The epigraph is from André Malraux, *Saturn: An Essay on Goya*, trans. C. W. Chiltern (New York: Phaidon, 1957), p. 82.

1. See Whitney Davis, *Visuality and Virtuality: Images and Pictures from Prehistory to Perspective* (Princeton: Princeton University Press, 2017), p. 264.

2. Michael Kubovy, *The Psychology of Perspective and Renaissance Art* (Cambridge: Cambridge University Press, 1986), p. 89.

3. This conforms to Alberti's description of the painter as a kind of god. Davis provides one account of how the painter's perspective came to be associated with this kind of certainty in the work of Brunelleschi in *Virtuality and Visuality*, p. 309.

4. Peter Sloterdijk, *In the Interior World of Capital*, trans. Wieland Hoban (Cambridge: Polity, 2017), p. 57.

5. Ibid.

6. Cf. the argument made by Norbert Elias in *The Civilizing Process*, trans. Edmund Jephcott (New York: Pantheon, 1982).

7. Sloterdijk, *In the Interior World of Capital*, p. 57.

8. Goya kept the original copper plates until he struck a deal with the crown in 1803, trading the plates and 240 copies of unsold prints for a lifetime annuity for his son.

9. Cf. plate no. 74, *"No grites, tonta"* ("Don't shout, you foolish girl"), which shows a similar mixture of fear and avoidance in response to something phantasmatic. The juxtaposition raises the question of whether or not there is an absolute difference between the first and second half of the *Caprichos*.

10. The development of the science of optics and still-life painting in the Dutch seventeenth century was of particular importance in this history.

11. Interpretations of the captions have relied heavily on manuscript sources, of which the so-called "Prado" and "Ayala" (Adelardo López de Ayala y Herrera) manuscripts are the best, the former in the collection of the Museo del Prado and the latter in the Biblioteca Nacional. These are gathered in Edith Helman, *Trasmundo de Goya* (Madrid: Revista de Occidente, 1963), pp. 219–41. To be sure, Goya is not the first artist to have coupled images with enigmatic texts. But the examples that precede him work in vastly different ways. The tradition of the emblem (*emblema*) is a case in point. Interpreting the *emblema* is a matter of deciphering signs and symbols — some visual and some verbal — and appreciating

their distilled wisdom. Moreover, text and image do not confront divergent perspectives in the emblem.

12. For complete details on all these, several in multiple states, see the *Catálogo de las estampas de Goya en la Biblioteca Nacional* (Madrid: Biblioteca Nacional, 1996), pp. 27–50.

13. The need was first noted by Antonio Ponz in 1776, in *Viaje de España*, vol. 4. See the *Catálogo de las estampas de Goya*, p. 25.

14. To be clear, Goya's work as a colorist inspired by Velasquez is amply evident in certain paintings such as *The Knife Grinder*.

15. See William Stirling-Maxwell, *Velásquez and His Works* (London: J. W. Parker and Son, 1855), p. 243.

16. Giorgio Vasari, *Vasari on Technique, Being the Introduction to the Three Arts of Design, Architecture, Sculpture and Painting, Prefixed to the Loves of the Most Excellent Painters, Sculptors and Architects*, trans. Louisa S. Maclehose (1907; New York: Dover, 1960), pp. 263–64.

17. The *lanterna magica* technique had long been in use, and was the subject of discussion among Goya's contemporaries. See Francisco Javier Frutos, "Media Archaeology in Spain," *Media History* 22.1 (2016), pp. 1–12, http://www.tandfonline.com/doi/full/10.1080 /13688804.2015.1102631. On Goya and the magic lantern see also Isabelle van den Broeke, "Visual Anti-Tales: The Phantasmagoric Prints of Francisco Goya and William Blake," in Catriona McAra and David Calvin, eds., *Anti-Tales: The Uses of Disenchantment* (Cambridge: Cambridge Scholars Publishing, 2011), pp. 142–51.

18. On the image of the black box, see Peter Sloterdijk, The *Aesthetic Imperative: Writings on Art*, trans. Karen Margolis (Cambridge: Polity, 2017), pp. 66–67.

19. Immanuel Kant, *Critique of Pure Reason*, trans. J. M. D. Meiklejohn (London: George Bell and Sons, 1890), Preface to the first (1781) edition, p. xvii.

20. Ibid., Preface to the first edition, p. xix.

21. Ibid., Introduction, p. 17.

22. Ibid., Kant "The Discipline of Pure Reason," p. 459.

23. Leon Battista Alberti, *On Painting*, trans. Martin Kemp (London: Penguin, 1991), p. 54, italics mine. James Elkins has argued that the metaphor of perspective in the West depended less in its Renaissance origins on the notion of a "window" that has often been supposed. But he nonetheless affirms its central place in the way in which perspective came to be understood over the course of subsequent centuries. See Elkins, *The Poetics of Perspective* (Ithaca: Cornell University Press, 1994).

24. See Victor Stoichita and Anna María Coderch, *Goya: The Last Carnival* (London: Reaktion Books, 1999).

25. See James Christen Steward, "Masks and Meanings in Tiepolo's Venice," *The Masks of Venice: Masking, Theater and Identity in the Art of Tiepolo And His Time* (Berkeley: University of California Berkeley Art Museum, 1996), pp. 15–33.

26. This interpretation is clearly supported by the Prado, Ayala, and Biblioteca Nacional commentaries.

27. Nigel Glendenning gives a good account of the English translations of the commentaries on the *Caprichos* in "Goya and England in the Nineteenth Century," *Burlington Magazine* 106.730 (January 1964), pp. 4–14; see especially pp. 8–9.

28. Here the manuscript tradition suggests that she has been sacrificed to support her hungry family, but there is little visual evidence that they are destitute or in need.

29. Miguel Adellac y González de Agüero, ed., *Plan para la educación de la nobleza y clases pudientes españolas: Trabaxado de orden del Rey en 1798* (Gijón: Sangenís, 1915).

30. See Glendinning, "Goya and England in the Nineteenth Century."

31. For a related discussion, see Tzvetan Todorov, *Goya à l'ombre des lumières* (Paris: Flammarion, 2011).

32. "Luego que amanece huyen, cada cual para su lado, Brujas, Duendes, visiones y fantasmas. ¡Buena cosa es que esta gente no se deje ver sino de noche y a oscuras! Nadie ha podido averiguar en donde se encierran y ocultan durante el día." The text is available at Fundación Goya en Aragón, "*Ya es hora*," https://fundaciongoyaenaragon.es/obra/ya-es-hora/951. Quoted in Helman, *Trasmundo de Goya*, p. 241.

33. "La última estampa de la colección representa a un grupo de gente de lo más variado—monjes, aristócratas, etc. —, despertándose de un profundo letargo. Bostezan de manera terrible y gritan Ya es hora." Museo del Prado, "*Ya es hora*," https://www.museodelprado.es/coleccion/obra-de-arte/ya-es-hora/a751ccae-e90a-4068-ba5c-b131c621e2f0.

CHAPTER FIVE: CONFLICTS OF THE FACULTIES: GOYA AND KANT

1. Alfonso E. Pérez Sánchez and Eleanor A. Sayre, et al., *Goya and the Spirit of Enlightenment* exh. cat. (Boston: Museum of Fine Arts, 1989); Arthur Danto, *Encounters and Reflections: Art in the Historical Present* (New York: Farrar, Straus & Giroux, 1990), p. 254.

2. More recent studies have suggested that Goya's work may be realigned with Enlightenment values and goals. See *Goya and the Spirit of Enlightenment*. For a critical view of that

position, see Jonathan Brown, "The Unliberal Imagination," *New Republic*, May 15, 1989, pp. 30–35.

3. "Sa pensée trouve son point de départ dans l'esprit des Lumières qu'il découvre autour de lui; mais, très rapidement, il en repousse les limites et en découvre les taches aveugles . . . Eduqué dans leur esprit, il a su explorer et révéler ce que les Lumières laissent dans l'ombre. Les puissances nocturnes qui dirigent la conduit des humains non moins que leur volonté et leur raison." Tzvetan Todorov, *Goya à l'ombre des lumières* (Paris: Flammarion, 2011), p. 291.

4. See Dick Howard, *The Politics of Critique* (Minneapolis: University of Minnesota Press, 1988), and Gillian Rose, *Dialectics of Nihilism* (Oxford: Blackwell, 1984).

5. Howard, *The Politics of Critique*; Rose, *Dialectics of Nihilism*.

6. Virtually the only critic to recognize the ambivalence in Goya's *Capricho* no. 43 is Paul Ilie. He writes, "but what of the reasoner who no longer merely sleeps but who dreams? Since his reason exceeds its normal function by performing irrationally, he requires a portrait of corresponding excess and absurdity." Ilie, "Goya's Teratology and the Critique of Reason," *Eighteenth-Century Studies* 18.1 (Autumn, 1984), p. 53. The entire essay is relevant to this point.

7. Immanuel Kant, *Critique of Pure Reason*, trans. J. M. D. Mieklejohn (London: George Bell and Sons, 1869), preface to the second edition, p. xxxvi.

8. Immanuel Kant, *Religion within the Limits of Reason Alone*, trans. Theodore M. Greene and Hoyt M. Hudson (New York: Harper and Row, 1960), p. 48.

9. Kant, *Critique of Pure Reason*, B xxxiv; p. 32.

10. Kant, *Religion within the Limits of Reason Alone*, pp. 48–49.

11. Kant, *Critique of Pure Reason*, B xxx, p. 29.

12. See Hans Blumenberg's critical discussion of this view in *The Legitimacy of the Modern Age*, trans. Robert M. Wallace (Cambridge: MIT Press, 1983).

13. Fred Licht, *Goya: The Origins of the Modern Temper in Art* (New York: Universe Books, 1979), p. 46.

14. Ibid., p. 63.

15. For a more sustained discussion of the differences between the two, see ibid., pp. 52–53.

16. In Goya's sketch for *The Death of Saint Joseph*, the figures hovering over the dying man may be angels but with a decidedly secular look; in the painted version of the work (1787), those figures have been eliminated.

17. Kant, *Religion within the Limits of Reason Alone*, p. 39.

18. Cf. Tobin Siebers, "Kant and the Origins of Totalitarianism," *Philosophy and Literature* 15.1 (1991), pp. 19–39. Siebers argues that on the one hand, the modern age has rejected the belief that clear-cut codes, rules, or imperatives can regulate the disorder and unpredictability of social life. On the other hand, the adherence to such codes makes the social life of modernity impossible.

19. Immanuel Kant, *The Conflict of the Faculties*, trans. Mary J. Gregor (Lincoln: University of Nebraskka Press, 1979), p. 35.

20. Kant, *Critique of Pure Reason*, B xiii, p. 20.

21. Jacques Derrida, "Parergon," in *The Truth in Painting and Other Essays*, trans. Geoff Bennington and Ian McLeod (Chicago: University of Chicago Press, 1987), pp. 15–147.

22. Cf. Annibale Caracci, *Allegory of Truth and Time*, Royal Collection Trust, https://www.rct.uk/collection/404770/an-allegory-of-truth-and-time; and Sebastiano Ricci, *Allegory with Figures of Hope, Time, and Death*, Metropolitan Museum of Art, https://www.metmuseum.org/art/collection/search/339893.

23. "La Pradera de San Isidro, en el mismo día del Santo con todo el bullicio que en esta Corte acostumbra haber." *Diplomatario de Goya*, ed. Ángel Canellas López (Zaragoza: Librería General, 1981), March 31, 1788, p. 289.

24. "The depictions of the *romerías* and folk festivals by Goya and his contemporaries involved a simplification, idealization of characters, and grouping of figures which reflected the idea of the dignity of the humble people invoked by Rousseau. The circularity of the central group shows the characteristic demand for the neoclassical order and it also reflects the rococo mood of a pleasant moment in which the dance acts as a unifying element of the composition. This fact provides a new reading of this image as an idealized depiction." Ruth Piquer Sanclemente and Gorka Rubiales Zabarte, "Music Representation and Ideology in the Paintings of Francisco de Goya and His Contemporaries," *Music in Art*.34.1–2 (Spring–Fall 2009), p. 187.

25. Goya's words to Zapater show his quandary about the representation of the customs and music of the Spanish lower classes: "You will find it very satisfying to listen to them. [But] I have not listened to them yet, and I certainly will never listen to them because I am not used to going to the places where they are performed. I am convinced that I must maintain a certain idea and keep a certain dignity that one has to have. About which, believe me, I am not very happy." Letter to Martín Zapater, March, n.d., 1790, *Diplomatario*, p. 304, translation mine.

26. See Renato Composto, *La cuarta crítica kantiana* (Palermo: Biblioteca di Cultura Moderna, 1954), p. xviii, and also Kurt Borries, *Kant als Politiker: Zur Staats- und Gesellschaftslehre des Kritizismus* (Leipzig: F. Meiner, 1928). For a dissenting view, see Hannah Arendt, *Lectures on Kant's Political Philosophy*, ed. Ronald Beiner (Chicago: University of Chicago Press, 1982).

27. "Ethics," as I understand it, carries the Aristotelian sense of the settled or characteristic ways human beings have of comporting themselves in the world.

28. Immanuel Kant, "What Is Enlightenment?," in *Kant on History*, ed. Lewis White Beck (Indianapolis: Bobbs-Merrill, 1957), p. 3.

29. Hegel had a dialectical solution to the problem posed by the Kantian division of the spheres that from the perspective of postmodernism may seem indistinguishable from Kant's: both incorporate the "unpresentable" within the framework of a totality that ultimately makes reference to the category of subjectivity. In Kant, the principle of the aesthetic judgment refers us back to the totality of rational agents; in Hegel, the totality is a projection or emanation of the collective Spirit of historical subject-selves. Even this schematic account is enough to suggest that the ethics of postmodernism depends not only on its ability to call into question the internal limits of a system like Kant's, but also on a rejection of the Hegelian solution to the problems posed by Kant.

30. Though Hegel does claim that cultural awareness of *Geist* originated in ancient Judaism, he links the history of *Geist* to a narrative of disenchantment and a decline in pagan polytheism. See Jason Josephson-Storm, *The Myth of Disenchantment: Magic, Modernity, and the Birth of the Human Sciences* (Chicago: University of Chicago Press, 2017), pp. 85–86.

31. Immanuel Kant, "An Old Question Raised Again: Is the Human Race Constantly Progressing?," in *Kant on History*, p. 144.

32. Ibid., p. 143.

33. See Eleanor Sayre's commentaries on the *Allegory* in *Goya and the Spirit of Enlightenment*, pp. 167–70.

34. The painting is now in the Museo Municipal de Madrid.

35. Cf. the interpretation of the Boston image by in Manuela B. Mena Marqués in *Goya and the Spirit of Enlightenment*, p. 65.

36. Immanuel Kant, *Foundations of the Metaphysics of Morals*, ed. Robert Paul Wolff, trans. Lewis White Beck (Indianapolis: Bobbs-Merrill, 1969), p. 23.

37. See the essay by Nigel Glendenning, "Goya's Circle," in *Goya and the Spirit of Enlightenment*, pp. lxiv–lxxvi.

38. See Victor Stoichita and Anna María Coderch, *Goya: The Last Carnival* (London: Reaktion Books, 1999).

39. The distortion is quite specific and reveals the "split subject" — the one she is and the one she sees herself to be.

40. See André Malraux, *Saturn: An Essay on Goya*, trans. C. W. Chiltern (London: Phaidon, 1957); Malraux, *Le triangle noir: Laclos, Goya, Saint-Just* (Paris: Gallimard, 1970); and Georges Bataille, *Manet*, trans. Austryn Wainhouse and James Emmons (New York: Skira/Rizzoli, 1983).

41. Cf. Arthur Danto, Charles Altieri, Anthony J. Cascardi, and Anne Wagner, *Anything Goes: The Work of Arts and the Historical Future* (Berkeley: Doreen B. Townsend Center for the Humanities, 1998).

CHAPTER SIX: EXTREMITIES

The epigraph is from Joel Whitebook, "The Marriage of Marx and Freud: Critical Theory and Psychoanalysis," in Fred Rush, ed., *The Cambridge Companion to Critical Theory* (Cambridge: Cambridge University Press, 2004), p. 75.

1. Max Horkheimer, "Traditional and Critical Theory," in *Critical Theory: Selected Essays*, trans. Matthew J. O'Connell et al. (New York: Continuum, 1972), pp. 188–243.

2. Fred Licht, *Goya: The Origins of the Modern Temper in Art* (New York: Universe Books, 1979), p. 128.

3. Ibid., p. 132. Rosenberg is quoted by Philip Hofer in *The Disasters of War by Francisco Goya y Lucientes* (New York: Dover, 1967), p. 1.

4. For the comparison with Magnasco, see André Malraux, *Saturn; An Essay on Goya*, trans. C. W. Chilton (New York: Phaidon, 1957), pp. 9–11.

5. Susan Sontag, *Regarding the Pain of Others* (New York: Farrar, Straus and Giroux, 2003), p. 45.

6. Ibid., p. 154.

7. Commenting on Sontag, Judith Butler describes the photograph in relation to "a structuring scene of interpretation." Butler, *Frames of War: When Is Life Grievable?* (London: Verso, 2009), p. 67.

8. Robert Hughes, *Goya* (New York: Knopf, 2004), p. 273.

9. Stan Gontarski, introduction to *The Complete Short Prose of Samuel Beckett, 1929–1989* (New York: Grove Press, 1995), p. xxiii. It is needless to say, perhaps, that the genealogy of the phrase lies in Segismundo's complaint in Calderón de la Barca's *La vida es sueño*.

10. This formulation follows the language of one of Charles Taylor's essays on Hegel, "The Opening Arguments of the 'Phenomenology'," in Alasdair MacIntyre, ed., *Hegel: A Collection of Critical Essays* (Garden City: Doubleday, 1972), p. 151.

11. Immanuel Kant, *Critique of Practical Reason*, trans. Thimas Kingsmill Abbott (London: Longmans, 1909), p. 102.

12. Ibid., p. 106.

13. Ibid., p. 102.

14. Ibid., p. 106.

15. Ibid., p. 119.

16. Ibid., p. 260.

17. Samuel Beckett, *Waiting for Godot* (New York: Grove Press, 1954), p. 41b.

18. I treat Burke at greater length in Chapter 8. His *Philosophical Enquiry into the Origin of our Ideas of the Sublime and Beautiful* had been translated into Spanish in 1807; Kant's third *Critique* would have been known through the German version or Latin translation (1796–98).

19. Edmund Burke, *Philosophical Enquiry into the Origin of our Ideas of the Sublime and Beautiful* (1757), in T. O. McLoughlin and James T. Boulton. eds., *The Writings and Speeches of Edmund Burke, Volume 1: The Early Writings* (Oxford: Clarendon Press of Oxford University Press, 1999), p 185; Immanuel Kant, *Critique of Judgment*, trans. James Creed Meredith (Oxford: Oxford University Press, 1952), p. 97.

20. Kant, *Critique of Judgment*, pp. 94–95.

21. Ibid., pp. 99–100.

22. Ibid., p. 91. In arguing along these lines, Kant builds consciously on the work of Burke, who identified the roots of the sublime in the instinct of self-preservation and even more importantly in a form of fear from which we eventually derive some sort of pleasure. To be sure, this is not pleasure in the ordinary sense; it is precipitated by something that involves risk—by allowing the imagination to subject itself to a feeling of great insufficiency, it yields "a sort of tranquility shadowed with horror." Burke, *A Philosophical Enquiry*, p. 213. Kant refers to Burke directly in the *Critique of Judgment*, p. 131.

23. Kant, *Critique of Judgment*, p. 109.

24. Ibid., pp. 11 and 120.

25. Ibid., p. 143.

26. See Elaine Scarry, *The Body in Pain* (Oxford: Oxford University Press, 1987).

27. David A. Bell, *The First Total War: Napoleon's Europe and the Birth of Warfare as We Know It* (New York: Houghton Mifflin, 2007), pp. 7 and 8.

28. The figures are from ibid., p. 7.

29. "Goya traspuso la violencia, la irracionalidad y la incomprensibilidad de la guerra al lenguaje artístico empleada para representarla. Para el artista español, la guerra es una absurdidad semántica y formal. Al interiorizar a través del arte la ruptura del límite característica de la guerra absoluta, Goya procedió a una multiple destrucción." Nil Santiáñez, *Goya/Clausewutz: Paradigmas de la guerra absoluta* (Barcelona: Alpha Decay, 2009), p. 84.

30. See Malraux, *Saturn*, and Derek Allan, "The Death of Beauty: Goya's Etchings and Black Paintings through the Eyes of André Malraux," *Journal of the History of European Ideas* 42 (2016), pp. 965–80.

31. Johann Joachim Winkelmann, *Storia delle arti del disegno presso gli antichi*, 1779. In the Royal Library, procedence from Francisco Cerdá y Rico.

CHAPTER SEVEN: FREEDOM AND THE FACE OF DARKNESS

The epigraph is from Immanuel Kant, *Anthropologie in pragmatische Hinsicht*, in *Gesammelte Schriften*, ed. Preussiche Akademie der Wissenschaft (Berlin: Georg Reimer, 1907) vol. 7, p. 665. The translation is by Victor Lyle Dowdell, Kant, *Anthropology from a Pragmatic Point of View*, ed. Hans H. Rudnick (Carbondale: Southern Illinois University Press, 1978).

1. As to the exact number of the paintings, fourteen corresponds to those exhibited in 1878. Contemporary accounts differ. There are just two published firsthand accounts of the paintings by contemporaries of Goya. The first is the so-called Brugada inventory, compiled by Goya's friend Antonio de Brugada. Brugada accounted for fifteen paintings, not fourteen. The second contemporary record is in an 1838 article by Valentín Carderera, who wrote that in Goya's country retreat, "'there is hardly a wall that is not full of caricatures and works of fantasy, including the walls of the staircase.'" Quoted in Arthur Lubow, "The Secret of the Black Paintings," *New York Times*, July, 27, 2003. See also Priscilla Muller, *Goya's 'Black' Paintings: Truth and Reason in Light and Liberty* (New York: The Hispanic Society of America, 1984), p. 67.

2. See Augusto L. Mayer, *Historia de la pintura española* (Madrid: Espasa-Calpe, 1928), p. 469. The irony of Beethoven's situation was no doubt greater, given the fact that he, a composer, was deaf, while Goya, an artist, was not blind.

3. In "Goya y los médicos," *Gaceta médica de México* 145.5 (2009), pp. 443–45, Dr. Arturo Vargas Origel suggests that bipolar disorder, schizophrenia, lateral sclerosis, and Kogan syndrome are also considered suitable diagnoses. Other authors, such as Felisati and Sperati even suggest that the correct diagnosis of Goya involves a combination of more than one disease. See D. Felisati and G. Sperati, "Francisco Goya and His Illness," *Acta otorhinolaryngologica Italica* 30.5 (October 5, 2010), pp. 264–70.

4. Francisco de Goya, *Diplomatario*, ed. Ángel Canellas López (Zaragoza: Librería General, 1981), March 29, 1793, p. 455.

5. See Robert Hughes, "The Unflinching Eye," *Guardian*, October 4, 2003.

6. See Derek Allan, "The Death of Beauty: Goya's Etchings and Black Paintings through the Eyes of André Malraux," *History of European Ideas.* 42.7 (2016), pp. 965–80.

7. See Folke Nordstrom, *Goya, Saturn, and Melancholy: Studies in the Art of Goya* (Stockholm: Almqvist & Wiksell, 1962).

8. To take two examples, see Valeriano Bozal, who describes them as "hermetic": *Goya y el gusto moderno*, 2nd. ed. (Madrid: Alianza, 2002), p. 298, and Fred Licht, *Goya: The Origins of the Modern Temper in Art* (New York: Universe Books, 1979), p. 172.

9. For virtual reconstructions of the placement of images in the Quinta del Sordo see http://www.artchive.com/galleries/goya/notes.html#paintings and https://commons.wikimedia.org/wiki/Pinturas_negras#/media/File:Quintasordo.svg.

10. The argument has been made specifically about Goya as part of the larger case that "great art" can provide therapeutic benefits. See Paul Williams, ed., *The Psychoanalytic Therapy of Severe Disturbance* (London: Karnac Books, 2010), p. 238.

11. See Ronald Paulson, *Representations of Revolution, 1789–1820* (New Haven: Yale University Press, 1983), pp. 24 and 367. Verignaud compares the revolution to Saturn devouring his son.

12. Robert Hughes, *Goya* (New York: Knopf, 2006), p. 383. There is a long line of political interpretations of this image. See, for example, Paulson, *Representations of Revolution*. But *if* the image is political, then there may be a reason why it is so utterly negative. In the words of Charles Taylor regarding Hegel, "the drive to absolute freedom is . . . incapable of rebuilding; it can only destroy an *ancién regime*, not construct a new one. It is in fact fixed permanently in its negative, destructive phase." Taylor, *Hegel and Modern Society* (Cambridge: Cambridge University Press, 1979), p. 103.

13. Fred Licht, *Goya: The Origins of the Modern Temper in Art* (New York: Universe Books, 1979), p. 166.

14. Muller, *Goya's 'Black' Paintings*, pp. 27-28.

15. Rudolf and Margot Wittkower, *Born under Saturn: The Character and Conduct of Artists, a Documented History from Antiquity to the French Revolution* (New York: Norton, 1969).

16. Nordstrom, *Goya, Saturn, and Melancholy.*

17. See Charles Taylor, *Hegel* (Cambridge: Cambridge University Press, 1975). Taylor also observes that "Modern society . . . is Romantic in its private and imaginative life and utilitarian or instrumentalist in its public, effective life" (p. 541). This is why, Taylor argues, thinkers who stand in a Romantic or expressivist tradition of whatever kind are all "estranged" from modern Western society (p. 542). What can be said about the political domain, and in particular about revolution, is no less true of most areas of human activity — namely, that it is easier to destroy than to (re-)create. Re-creation requires differentiated structures, and (as Taylor put it) "no particular differentiated structure can be tolerated" in modern/postrevolutionary society, "for it would stand on the supposedly unconditioned freedom of rational will to remake the world according to its dictates." Taylor, *Hegel and Modern Society*, p. 103.

18. For the fullest treatment of this topic, see Hans Blumenberg, *Work on Myth*, trans. Robert M. Wallace (Cambridge, MA: MIT Press, 1985).

19. I refer to Muller, *Goya's 'Black' Paintings.*

20. The puzzling phrase "verbal enclave" is one that Muller strangely relates to an episode from Cervantes, *Don Quixote*, part 2, chapter 3, though without sufficiently accounting for the fact that the story in Cervantes about a painter from the town of Úbeda — a painter who needs to put labels on his images because they are so poorly drawn as to be unrecognizable — is part of a joke. Muller's line of thinking is soundly contradicted by Licht, who writes that Goya "never composed 'program notes' for them as he did for the *Caprichos* and *Disasters of War*, and, lacking even the slightest trace of his having explained the paintings to his friends and family, it seems highly probable that he never spoke about them with anyone." Licht, *Goya*, pp. 159-60.

21. Muller, *Goya's "Black" Paintings*, p. 207.

22. Ibid., pp. 208–209.

23. Ibid., p. 237.

24. Ibid., p. 209.

25. Georg Wilhelm Friedrich Hegel, *Vorlesungenüber die Gesischte der Philosophie*, in *Sämtliche Werke*, ed. Hermann Glockner, 26 vols. (Stuttgart: F. Frommanns, 1928–41), vol. 19, pp. 528–29. See also Taylor, *Hegel*, p. 370.

26. This is why Hegel concluded that in order to be truly free human beings must remake their own nature. See Taylor, *Hegel and Modern Society*, p. 156.

27. It is worth noting that in the years following his residence at the Quinta, Goya eventually turned to lithography, a technique in which a positive image was made with a waxy crayon directly on the stone from which the print would be struck.

28. As one critic wrote of the Black Paintings and of *Saturn Devouring His Son*, in particular, linking Goya's renunciation of the decorative function of art with an inward turn: "Goya suddenly unleashes his art, covering over the colorful landscapes, refusing himself the bland pleasures of the merely picturesque, recognizing in every surface a new opportunity, until the Quinta mirrors his internal world, the meanings personal, all sense of decoration dismissed. Only truth remains." Jay Scott Morgan, "The Mystery of Goya's 'Saturn'," *New England Review* 22.3 (Summer, 2001), p. 42.

29. See Susan Buck-Morss, *The Origin of Negative Dialectics* (New York: Free Press, 1977), p. 125.

30. Xavier de Salas, *Goya*, trans. G. T. Culverwell (New York: Mayflower Books, 1978), p. 151. The interpretation is based on the suggestion that Goya may have been recalling Saavedra Fajardo's seventy-fifth "emblem," *Bellum colligit qui discordias seminat*. See Jesús María González de Zárate, "Las empresas políticas de Saavedra Fajardo: Antecedentes gráficos y trascendencia artística," in Saavedra Fajardo, *Idea de un príncipe político-cristiano representada en cien empresas* (Murcia: Real Academia Alfonso X el Sabio, 1994), pp. 71–72.

31. Norman Bryson, *Vision and Painting: The Logic of the Gaze* (New Haven: Yale University Press, 1983), p. 69.

32. Here it bears emphasizing that this and all the titles of the Black Paintings were given by later critics intent on making sense of the images, not by Goya.

33. Susan Buck-Morss provides a clear statement of the differences, along with an insightful comment on the relationship to conventional printed matter intended for reading: "montage [was] the technique developed in the new film medium using single frames rather than scenes as the basic unit of construction. Film montage made possible the rapid succession of seemingly disconnected images. And its inner logic was radically different from the conceptual, linear logic of the traditional print medium." Susan Buck-Morss, *The Origin of Negative Dialectics*, p. 126.

34. See Muller, *Goya's "Black" Paintings*, p. 213.

35. Robert provides rich documentation of his experiments, methods, and apparatus

in his *Mémoires Récréatifs scientifiques et anecdotiques* (1831; London: Forgotten Books, 2017).

36. If this is the case, then there is an important relationship to the painting of Judith and Holofernes, where it is a young woman who kills an old man by cutting off his head. Valeriano Bozal points out this reversal in *Goya y el gusto moderno*, 2nd ed. (Madrid: Alianza Editorial, 2002), p. 284. So, too, Robert Hughes in *Goya*, p. 384.

37. Morgan makes this suggestion in "The Mystery of Goya's 'Saturn.'"

38. The figure is also reminiscent of the Satan of Dante's *Inferno* (canto 34), whose three mouths tear up and devour Judas, Brutus, and Cassius. Dante Alighieri, *Inferno*, trans. Henry F. Cary (New York: Bartleby.com, 2001):

If he were beautiful

As he is hideous now, and yet did dare

To scowl upon his Maker, well from him

May all our misery flow. Oh what a sight!   35

How passing strange it seem'd, when I did spy

Upon his head three faces: one in front

Of hue vermilion, the other two with this

Midway each shoulder join'd and at the crest;

The right 'twixt wan and yellow seem'd; the left   40

To look on, such as come from whence old Nile

Stoops to the lowlands. Under each shot forth

Two mighty wings, enormous as became

A bird so vast. Sails never such I saw

Outstretch'd on the wide sea. No plumes had they,   45

But were in texture like a bat; and these

He flapp'd i' th' air, that from him issued still

Three winds, wherewith Cocytus to its depth

Was frozen. At six eyes he wept: the tears

Adown three chins distill'd with bloody foam.   50

At every mouth his teeth a sinner champ'd,

Bruised as with ponderous engine; so that three

Were in this guise tormented. But far more

Than from that gnawing, was the foremost pang'd

By the fierce rending, whence oft-times the back   55

Was stript of all its skin. "That upper spirit,

Who hath worst punishment," so spake my guide,

"Is Judas, he that hath his head within

And plies the feet without. Of th' other two,

Whose heads are under, from the murky jaw   60

Who hangs, is Brutus: lo! how he doth writhe

And speaks not. The other, Cassius, that appears

So large of limb. But night now reascends;

And it is time for parting. All is seen."

39. "For Homer, the definition of barbarism coincides with that of a state in which no systematic agriculture, and therefore no systematic, time-managing organization of work and society, has yet been achieved." Max Horkheimer and Theodor Adorno, *Dialectic of Enlightenment*, trans. Edmund Jephcott (New York: Continuum, 1999), p. 50.

40. Mark Cartwright, s.v. "Saturnalia," *World History Encyclopedia*, https://www.world history.org/Saturnalia/.

41. For significant details of the Saturnaila in this regard, see H. S. Versnel, *Inconsistencies in Greek and Roman Religion, Volume 2: Transition and Reversal in Myth and Ritual* (Leiden: Brill, 1993), pp. 149–50.

42. Lucius Annaeus Seneca, *The Moral Epistles to Lucilius*, trans. Richard Gummere (London: W. Heinemann, Loeb Classical Library, 1917), vol. I, Letter XVIII, "On festivals and Fasting," p. 117.

43. See Versnel, *Transition and Reversal*, p. 147.

44. Horkheimer and Adorno, *Dialectic of Enlightenment*, p. 55. As Joel Whitebook wrote in relation to *Dialectic of Enlightenment*, "Sacrificial practices derive from a central principal of mythical thinking.... Every piece of good fortune, every advance [including, in this case, freedom]... must be paid for with something of comparable value." Joel Whitebook, "The Marriage of Marx and Freud: Critical Theory and Psychoanalysis," in Fred Leland Rush, ed., *The Cambridge Companion to Critical Theory* (Cambridge: Cambridge University Press, 2004), pp. 76–77.

45. Whitebook, "The Marriage of Marx and Freud," p. 77.

46. Horkheimer and Adorno, *Dialectic of Enlightenment*, p. 9.

47. See Whitebook "The Marriage of Marx and Freud," p. 78.

48. Taylor, *Hegel*, p. 369.

49. Theodor Adorno, *Negative Dialectics*, trans. E. B. Ashton (New York: Continuum, 1973), p. 218.

50. See Louis Althusser, "Ideology and Ideological State Apparatuses (Notes towards an Investigation)," in Althusser, *Lenin and Philosophy and Other Essays* (1971; New York: Monthly Review Press, 2001).

CHAPTER EIGHT: BEAUTY AND SYMPATHY

1. See Karl Mannheim, *Ideology and Utopia* (New York: Harcourt, Brace, 1946).

2. See Juan José Junquera, *The Black Paintings of Goya* (London: Scala, 2008), p. 27.

3. Cf. Alexander Nehamas, *Only a Promise of Happiness: The Place of Beauty in a World of Art* (Princeton: Princeton University Press, 2007).

4. André Malraux, *Saturn: An Essay on Goya*, trans. C. W. Chiltern (New York: Phaidon, 1957), p. 137. See also Derek Allan, "The Death of Beauty: Goya's Etchings and Black Paintings through the Eyes of André Malraux," *History of European Ideas* 42.7 (2016), p. 973.

5. Malraux, *Saturn: An Essay on Goya*, p. 158.

6. Some critics have doubted that this work is in fact by Goya. While many continue to believe it is by Goya, Manuela B. Mena Marqués of the Prado confirms those doubts and, writing in 2011, suggests that the work may be by Asensio Juliá. See Museo del Prado, Estudio técnico y restauración, *"El coloso y su atribución a Goya,"* https://www .museodelprado.es/recurso/el-coloso-y-su-atribucion-a-goya/661a409d-72c2-48dd-9247 -34a241f81f43. See also Nigel Glendinning, "El problema de las atribuciones desde la Exposición Goya de 1900," in *Goya 1900: Catálogo ilustrado y estudio de la exposición en el Ministerio de Instrucción Pública y Bellas Artes*, vol. 1 (Madrid: Dirección General de Bellas Artes y Bienes Culturales-Instituto de Patrimonio Histórico Español, 2002), pp. 29–32.

7. Immanuel Kant, *Critique of Judgment*, trans. James Creed Meredith (Oxford: Clarendon Press of Oxford University Press, 1952), pp. 83–84.

8. Ibid., pp. 223–24.

9. See Karin Schutjer, "The Persistence of Sympathy in Kant's Aesthetics," *Monatshefte* 91.2 (Summer 1999), pp. 170–87.

10. Ibid.

11. Georg Wilhelm Friedrich Hegel, *Phenomenology of Spirit*, trans. A. V. Miller (Oxford: Oxford University Press, 1977), sec. 580, p. 353.

12. *Indagación filosófica sobre el orígen de nuestras Ideas acerca de lo Sublime y lo Bello, escrita*

en inglés por Edmundo Burke y traducida a castellano por Don Juan de la Dehesa (Alcalá: Oficina de la Real Universitatd, 1807).

13. Edmund Burke, *Philosophical Enquiry into the Origin of Our Ideas of the Sublime and Beautiful*, in T. O. McLoughlin and James T. Boulton. eds., *The Writings and Speeches of Edmund Burke: Volume 1: The Early Writings* (Oxford: Clarendon Press of Oxford University Press, 1999), p. 266. In the Dehesa translation, pp. 136–37.

14. See Francis Hutcheson, *An Inquiry into the Original of Our Ideas of Beauty and Virtue*, 4th ed. (London: D. Midwinter, 1738).

15. Anthony Ashley Cooper, Third Earl of Shaftesbury, *Characteristics of Men, Manners, Opinions, Times*, ed. Lawrence E. Klein (Cambridge: Cambridge University Press, 1999), p. 267.

16. David Hume, *A Treatise of Human Nature*, ed. David Fate Norton andf Mary J. Norton (Oxford: Oxford University Press, 2000), p. 235.

17. While differences in taste may be the topic announced in his most famous work on aesthetics ("Of the Standard of Taste"), his more major work, the *Treatise on Human Understanding*, takes up questions of aesthetics in the context of moral judgment.

18. This point is made illustratively in Antonio Rumeu de Armas, *El testamento político del Conde de Floridablanca* (Madrid: CSIC, 1962), pp. 13–14.

19. See Lynn Hunt, "More Fraternité than Liberté," *New York Review of Books* 67.5, March 26, 2020, p. 42.

20. Robert Hughes, *Goya* (New York: Knopf, 2006), p. 346.

21. His longer career was inglorious. After the French invasion of Spain in 1808, Garcini became a collaborator, and in 1811, he wrote a book chronicling his alleged persecution and suffering, *Chronicle of Spain since the Reign of Charles IV: Account of the Persecution Suffered by Colonel D. Ignacio Garcini*. The discussion in the Metropolitan Museum online resource is informative. See "Ignacio Garcini y Queralt (1752–1825), Brigadier of Engineers," https://www.metmuseum.org/art/collection/search/436542.

22. This is true quite apart from any moral or ethical dialectic of which a given action may be a part. That dialectic is of tremendous interest to Goya, though in images other than the ones at issue here. Bullfighting, of which Goya made many images, would be a good example of the latter: for all the bravado and panache, there is no escaping the violence of the sport. No. 14, *El diestrisimo estudiante de Falces*, no. 20, *Ligereza y atrevimiento de Juanito Apiñani*, and no. 21: *Desgracias acaecidas en el tendido de la plaza de Madrid, y muerte del alcalde de Torrejón* from the *Tauromaquia* (1816) are good examples.

23. See Justine Kolata, "The Revolutionary Figure of the Beautiful, Self-Improved Soul," *Ordinary Philosophy*, https://ordinaryphilosophy.com/tag/beautiful-soul. See also Drew Milne, "The Beautiful Soul: From Hegel to Beckett," *Diacritics* 32.1 (Spring, 2002), pp. 63–82.

24. It was most famously Hegel who recognized the potential limitations of the beautiful soul both as prone to the "self-deceptive delusion of its own virtue" and as unable to recognize itself in another moral consciousness or see the need for action. This is Hegel speaking of Jacobi's novel *Woldemar* in Georg Wilhelm Friedrich Hegel, *Lectures on Aesthetics, Volume 1*, trans. T. M. Knox (Oxford: Clarendon Press of Oxford University Press, 1998), pp. 241–42.

25. The Latin version of the *Critique of Judgment* was made in 1796–98. It is possible that a French translation was made in 1796. See Kant in the Classroom, "Kant in Translation," https://users.manchester.edu/FacStaff/SSNaragon/Kant/Helps/KantsWritings Translations.htm#CritiqueJudgment.

26. "Por la cual nos ponemos en lugar de otro hombre y tenemos los mismos afectos que él." *Indagación*, sec. 13, p. 44.

27. "[La] amistad y conformidad que naturalmente suele tener una cosa a otra."

28. See John J. Ciofalo, *The Self-Portraits of Francisco Goya* (Cambridge: Cambridge University Press, 2000), pp. 106–10.

29. See Mónica Salazar, "Goya's Doctors: An Insight into the Spanish Enlightenment," *SMU Pony Express(ions)*, https://smuponyexpressions.wordpress.com/2013/06/11 /goyas doctors an insight into the spanish-enlightenment-by-monica-salazar.

30. Ciofalo, *The Self-Portraits of Francisco Goya*, pp. 102–103.

Index

Unless otherwise noted, all works of art are by Francisco de Goya.

"ABOUTNESS," 12, 120–23.
Abstraction, 10, 24, 89, 96, 97.
Addison, Joseph, 331–32 n.2.
Adoration of the Name of God by the Angels (1772), 37, 39; Tomlinson on, 37, 333 n.19.
Adorno, Theodor W.: *Aesthetic Theory*, 98; *Dialectic of Enlightenment*, 110, 126, 277–78, 292, 293, 353 n.44; on freedom, 293.
Aesthetics: as critique, 10; Enlightenment principles, 60; of Kant, 213, 243, 323; neoclassical, 307–309; picturesque, 307; of the sublime, 213, 232–33, 243, 261.
Agility and Audacity of Juanito Apiñani in the Ring at Madrid (*Tauromaquia*, no. 20, 1816), *121*, 123, 355 n.22.
Alba, Duquesa de, 303, 336 n.31.
Albañil borracho, El (*The Drunken Mason*, 1786), 338 nn.44–45.
Albañil herido, El (*The Injured Mason*, 1786–87), 338 nn.44–45.
Alberti, Leon Battista: *De pictura*, 66; *historia*, 67; orientation toward nature, 67–68; painter as god, 340 n.3; theory of artificial perspective, 18, 27, 50, 66–67, 68, 138, 154.
Alciati, Andrea, 157.
Alfonso V, King, of Aragón, 32, 42–44.
Allegory of the Adoption of the Constitution of 1812, 271.
Allegory of the City of Madrid (1810), 214, *215*, 216–17.
Alpers, Svetlana, 30.

Altamira, Count, portrait of, 57.
Altarpieces, 40, 42–44, 191, 327.
Anamorphosis: in ceiling frescoes of San Antonio, 47, 51, 282; defined, 46; in Goya's Italian sketches, 47, *48–49*.
Another Madness of His in the Same Ring (*Tauromaquia*, no. 19, 1816), *122*.
Anthony of Padua. See *Miracle of St. Anthony*; San Antonio de la Florida church.
Aquatint, 46, 87, 88, 150–51. *See also* Etchings.
Aragón Canal, 44, 314.
Archaism, 187, 213, 221–23, 276–77.
Aristotle, 345 n.27.
Arrieta, Eugenio García, 323–25, *324*, 327–28.
Art as critique, 68, 107, 301–303. *See also* Critique.
Art criticism, 13.
Artificial perspective: Alberti's theory of, 27, 50, 66–67, 68, 154; conventions built on measure, 253; exaggeration of, 206–207, 284; Kubovy on, 138; and the limits of representation, 138–39, 140, 144, 172; and "naturalness," 18, 67–68; radical foreshortening, 206–207; and secular art, 11–12; and use of color, 149–50. *See also* Alberti, Leon Battista; Perspective.
Asmodea (1820–23), 294, 296–99, *297*, 303
Asmodeus, 297.
Atropos, or the Fates (1820–23), 276, 294–96, *295*
Attack on a Coach (1793), 75.
Aula Dei paintings, 32, 35–36; *Betrothal of the Virgin* (1774), 35, *36*, 47.
Autonomous art and decorative art, 56.

BANDERILLAS IN THE COUNTRYSIDE (1793), *118*, 119.

Bank of San Carlos, 145, 315.

Baroque illusionism, 17, 21, 26.

Barthes, Roland, *studium*, 64.

Basilica of the Virgen del Pilar (Zaragoza), 32, 37; *Adoration of the Name of God by the Angels* (1772), 37, 39, 333 n.19; *Mary, Queen of Martyrs* (1780–81), 37–39, *38*.

Bataille, Georges, 107, 126.

Baxandall, Michael, 30.

Bayeu, Francisco, 15, 39.

Bayeu, Ramón, 30, 39, 65.

Beauty: "beautiful soul," 320–22, 356 n.24; Goya's critique of, 302–303; Kant on, 309–10, 311; neoclassical, 307–309; in philosophy, 309–311, 312; as prospect for hope, 303–304, 307; and sympathy, 310–11, 313, 328; and ugliness, 304, 307; and utility, 311–14.

Beckett, Samuel, 237; *Waiting for Godot*, 244.

Beethoven, Ludwig van, 269–70, 348 n.2.

Beholder, presence of the, 31–32, 35, 332 n.15.

Bell, David A., 262–63.

Bentham, Jeremy, 311.

Bermúdez, Juan Agustín Ceán, 231, 335 n.20.

Bernardino of Siena, 32, *34*, 42–44.

Betancourt, Agustín de, 320.

Betrothal of the Virgin (1774), 35, 47; detail, *36*.

"Black box," 151–53, 155, 173, 229.

Black Paintings (1819–24): affinities with expressionist art, 9, 288; *Asmodea*, 294, 296–99, *297*, 303; *Atropos, or the Fates*, 276, 294–96, *295*; beauty and dignity in, 303–304; and *Bulls of Bordeaux*, 123–24; contradiction in, 298–99; creation and placement at Quinta del Sordo, 269, 274, 282–83; darkness of, 55–56, 152, 193, 269–70, 271, 275–76; *Duel with Cudgels*, 81, *82*, 283–86, 287, 296; engagement with myth, 276 77, 290 91, 294–96; and Enlightenment culture, 188, 279–81; Goya's state of mind, 269–70, 274, 276–77, 351 n.28; imagination and reality in, 10, 232; interpretation and critical commentary, 274–79, 284, 298, 349 nn.8,12, 351 nn.28,30; *Leocadia*, 271, *272*, 303–304, 320; number of, 348 n.1; *Pilgrimage to San Isidro*, 207, *208–209*, 221, 283, 286–87, 293; political interpretation, 274–75, 284, 291, 298; as

projections, 288–90; as reflection on freedom, 280–81, 284, 287, 293–96; relationship to earlier works, 81, 124, 282–83; renunciation of decorative function of art, 282, 351 n.28; self-reflection in, 282, 303; *Semisunken Dog*, 100–102, *101*, 227, 258, 280; size and scale, 287–88, 291; titles of, 294, 351 n.32; *Two Old Ones Eating Soup*, 285, *285*. See also *Saturn Devouring His Son*.

Blind Man's Buff (1788), 68, *69*, 81, 284, 285.

Bonaparte, Joseph, 216.

Bonaparte, Napoleon, 105, 291, 315.

Borbón, Infante Don Luis de, family portrait, 114.

Bordeaux albums, 203, 304; "*Gran coloso dormido*," *202*, 203, 227.

Bort, Julián Sánchez, 314.

Boy Riding a Ram (1786–87), 81, *83*, 337 n.43.

Boys Picking Fruit (1778), 84.

Boys with Mastiffs (1786–87), 84, *85*.

Bozal, Valeriano, 17, 65, 332 n.2, 335 n.16, 349 n.8, 352 n.36.

Bravo de Rivero, Tadeo, 216.

Brugada, Antonio de, 348 n.1.

"*Brujas disfrazadas en fisicos comunes*" (1796–97), *325*, 326.

Brunelleschi, Filippo, 340 n.3.

Bryson, Norman, 68, 286, 335 n.19; *Vision and Painting*, 18, 335 n.19.

Buck-Morss, Susan, 351 n.33; "profane illumination," 283.

Bullfight, Suerte de Varas (1824), 116, *117*.

Bullfight images, 11, 24, 79, 90, 116–26, 355 n.22. See also *Bulls of Bordeaux*; *Tauromaquia* series.

Bulls of Bordeaux (1824–25), 119; connection with Black Paintings, 123–24; no. 11, *Andalusian Dance*, 124; no. 12, *Modern Duel*, 124; no. 14, "*El famoso Americano, Mariano Ceballos*," 124; no. 16, "*Diversión de España*," 124, *125*; no. 18, *Bullfight*, 124.

Burial of Christ (1771–72), 32, *33*, 39–40.

Burial of the Sardine (1812–19), 223, *224*.

Burke, Edmund, 233, 259, 347 n.22; Dehesa's translation, 312, 323; *Philosophical Enquiry into the Origin of Our Ideas of the Sublime and Beautiful*, 258, 312, 347 n.18.

Butler, Judith, 346 n.7.

CABARRÚS, FRANCISCO, 315–16.

Cadalso, José, *Noches lúgubres*, 276.

Cádiz constitution of 1812, 214.

Calasso, Roberto, 30; *Tiepolo Pink*, 26–27.

Callot, Jacques, *Les misères et les malheurs de la guerre* (1633), 232.

Cano y Olmedilla, Juan de la Cruz, 77.

Caprichos (1799): announcement for, in *Diario de Madrid*, 16; background, 150–51, 178; bestiality of human beings, 337 n.31; captions, 140, 145, 146, 155–59, 169, 178, 185, 189, 229–30, 340 n.11; commentaries, 178, 185; copper plates and image-making process, 66, 340 n.8; as criticism and critique, 88, 128, 134, 145, 154–55, 283; darkness in, 31, 55, 172–85, 178; dating of, 19; distortions, 66, 140; and Enlightenment values, 131, 134, 173, 187, 213; as inventions, 16, 201; isolation of central figure, 64; precursors, 64, 79, 337 n.34; relationship to Black Paintings, 282–83; as social criticism, 11, 16, 145, 162–69, 283; and subjectivity, 139, 221; two sections of, 154–55, 169–73, 178–85; ugliness in, 159, 162–64, 244, 304; undertaken without patronage, 140, 334 n.7, 340 n.8; unmasking of self-deception, 79–81, 146, 154–57, 159, 162, 169–72, 244; violation of conventions of representation, 138, 140–44, 201; withdrawn from sale, 185. See also *Caprichos*, plates.

Caprichos, plates: "*Bien tirada está,*" 140; frontispiece "*Francisco Goya y Lucientes, Pintor,*" *132*, 134–35, 154, 189, 230, 327, 328; no. 4, "*El de la rollona,*" 164, *166*; no 5, "*Tal para qual,*" 159; no. 6, "*Nadie se conoce,*" 155–57, *156*; no. 7, "*Ni así la distingue,*" 140, *141*, 157; no. 12, "*A caza de dientes,*" 140, *142*; no. 14, "*¡Que sacrificio!*" 159–62, *160*, 342 n.28; no. 15, 164; no. 23, "*Aquellos polbos,*" 197, *198*; no. 25, "*Si quebró el cantaro,*" 162–64, *163*, 221, 322; no. 26, "*Ya tienen asiento,*" 157, *158*; no. 27, "*¿Quien más rendido?*" 159, *161*; no. 37, "*¿Si sabrá más el discípulo?*" 164, *167*; no. 38, "*Bravísimo,*" 169; no. 39, "*Asta su abuelo,*" 169, *170*; no. 40, "*¿De qué mal morirá?*" 164–69, *168*, 325; no. 41 "*Ni más ni menos,*" 169, *171*; no. 42, "*Tú que no puedes,*" *78*, 79, 178; no. 43, "*El sueño de la razón produce monstruos,*" 131–34, *133*, 155, 189, 279, 343 n.6; no. 46,

"*Corrección,*" 164, *165*; no 47, "*Obsequio al maestro,*" 173, *177*; no. 49, "*Duendecitos,*" 140, *143*; no. 51, "*Se repulen,*" 140, 173, *174*; no. 52, "*Lo que puede un sastre!*" 287–88, *289*; no. 59, "*Y aún no se van,*" 173, *175*; no. 62, "*¿Quién lo creyera?*" 178, *180*; no. 63, "*Miren que grabes,*" 173, *176*; no. 64, "*Buen viaje,*" 131; no. 68, "*Linda maestra!*" 298; no. 70, 173; no. 71, "*Si amanece, nos vamos,*" 140, *183*, 185; no. 72, "*No te escaparás,*" 217, *219*; no. 75, "*¿No hay quién nos desate?*" 173–78, *179*; no. 76, "*¿Está Vmd . . . pues, Como digo . . . eh!*" 178, *181*; no. 77, "*Unos a otros,*" 178; no. 78, "*Despacha, que dispiertan,*" *184*, 185; no. 79, "*Nadie nos ha visto,*" 185; no. 80, "*Ya es hora,*" 178, *182*, 185.

Captions. See under *Caprichos*; *Disasters of War.*

Caravaggio, Michelangelo Merisi da, *Supper at Emmaus,* 50.

Carderera, Valentín, 348 n.1.

Carracci, Annibale: *Dead Christ,* 50–51, *51*; Goya on, 50–51.

Castel Sant'Angelo, 298.

Castro y Velasco, Antonio Palomino, *Museo pictórico, y escala óptica,* 331 n.1.

Celestinas, 24, 52, 73.

Cerdá y Rico, Francisco, 263.

Cervantes, Miguel de, 350 n.20.

Charles III, King, 314, 325.

Charles IV, King, 57, 315; and his family, 304, *305*, 320.

Charterhouse of the Carthusian Monks (Aula Dei), 32, 35–36; *Betrothal of the Virgin* (1774), 35, *36*, 47.

Children, 59, 81, *83*, *84*, 307.

Christ Crucified (1780), 40, *41*, 333 n.23.

Churriguera, José Benito de, 23.

Ciofalo, John J., 328.

City on a Rock (prev. attrib. Goya), 297.

Civil society, 70, 75, 199, 212, 315.

Clausewitz, Carl von, *On War,* 263.

Clavijo y Fajardo, *El pensador,* 332 n.2.

Colonialism and race, 77.

Color, 42, 55, 100, 149–50, 341 n.14; Manet's use of, 96, *93*; in tapestries, 56, 88; Velásquez's use of, 148–50, 341 n.14.

Colossus (attrib. Goya), 201, *203*. See also "*Gran coloso dormido.*"

Connell, Evan, 298.

Constitutional government, 271; constitution of 1812, 214; constitution of 1820, 271.

Courbet, Gustave, 52; *Burial at Ornans*, 32.

Covarrubias, Sebastián de, *Tesoro de la lengua castellana o española*, 323.

Critique: *Caprichos* as, 88, 128, 134, 145, 154–55, 283; critical function of art, 68, 107; and criticism, 10, 134, 145, 230, 311; of Enlightenment ideals, 112, 134, 311; Goya's project of, 10–13, 112, 116, 128–29, 135, 145, 226, 230, 296, 301–303; Kant and, 152; of Spain's backwardness, 112, 162–69, 325–27; of subjectivity, 139; and sympathy, 323, 328; in the tapestry cartoons, 63–66, 75. *See also* Kant, Immanuel.

DANCE ON THE BANKS OF THE MANZANARES (1777), *60, 62, 70.*

Dante Alighieri, *Inferno*, 298, 352–53 n.38.

Danto, Arthur, 187, 227.

Daring of Martincho in the Ring at Zaragoza, The (*Tauromaquia*, no. 18, 1816), *121, 123.*

Darkness: in *Caprichos*, 31, 55, 172–85, 178; in *Disasters of War*, 193, 248–53; and reason, 187, 203; in tapestry cartoons, 55, 66. *See also* Black Paintings.

David, Jacques-Louis, 35.

Death of Pepe Hilo, The (*Tauromaquia*, no. 38, 1816), 123.

Death of Saint Joseph, The (1787), 343 n.16.

Deception and self-deception, 11, 145, 220. *See also* under *Caprichos*.

De-composition and dis-figuration, 95–100.

Decorative art, 56, 63, 70, 282, 351n28. *See also* Tapestry cartoons.

Delacroix, Ferdinand Victor Eugène, *Lamentation*, 191.

Derrida, Jacques, "Paregon," 201.

Desastres de la Guerra, Los. See Disasters of War.

Descartes, René, 200.

Diario de Madrid, 16.

Disasters of War (*Los Desastres de la guerra,* 1810–20): aesthetics of the sublime, 232–33; backgrounds, 253–58; *caprichos enfáticos*, 236; captions, 230–31; classification and ordering, 236, 248; compared to *Caprichos*, 172, 230; and conventions of representation, 140, 145, 203, 261, 263–64; creation and publication, 230, 232; darkness in, 193, 248–53; discursive supplements, 146; and the Enlightenment, 187, 188, 236; ethics of the spectator, 233, 236, 240–41; historical and political dimension, 236; horrific images in, 126–28, 232, 244; and the limits of reason, 244–48; as model, 268; precedents for, 232; presaging of photojournalism, 9, 231–32, 233, 235; and the truth function of art, 10, 230–31; Sontag on, 233–35; violence of, 232–33, 235–36, 237, 244, 248–53, 261–62, 263; vision of war, 231, 261–68. *See also Disasters of War*, plates.

Disasters of War, plates: no. 1, *"Tristes presentimientos de lo que ha de acontecer,"* 248; no. 2, *"Con razon ó sin ella,"* 248; no. 3, *"Lo mismo,"* 126, 127, 248; no. 4, *"Las mujeres dan valor,"* 248, 249; no. 5, *"Y son fieras,"* 248, 250; no. 7, *"¡Qué valor!"* 253, 256; no. 9, *"No quieren,"* 237, 239; no. 15, *"Y no hai remedio,"* 128; no. 17, *"No se convienen,"* 264; no. 24, *"Aún podrán servir,"* 253, 257; no. 26, *"No se puede mirar,"* 208–209, 209; no. 27, *"Caridad,"* 253, 255; no. 28, *"Populacho,"* 244, 246, 248, 253; no. 29, *"Lo merecía,"* 264, 265; no. 30, *"Estragos de la guerra,"* 253, 254; no. 33, 263; no. 35, *"No se puede saber por qué,"* 248, 251; no. 36, *"Tampoco,"* 233, 234; no 37, 263; no. 39, *"Grande hazaña. Con muertos,"* 244, 245, 263; no. 42, *"Todo va revuelto,"* 248, 252; no. 43, *"Tambien esto,"* 248; no. 44, *"Yo lo vi,"* 126, 129; no. 63, *"Muertos recogidos,"* 244, 247; no. 69, *"Nada. Ello dirá,"* 264, 267; no. 71, *"Contra el bien general,"* 264, 266, 315; no. 74, *"¡Esto es lo peor!"* 237, 238, 264.

"Disinhibition," 140–44, 162.

Disparates, Los, 123, 140, 146, 193, 304; *The Simpleton* (1815–19), 84, 87.

Dogs and Hunting Equipment (1775), 56.

Dragging the Bull Away (*El arrastre,* 1793), 116.

Duel with Cudgels (ca. 1820–23), 81, 82, 283–86, 287, 296.

Dürer, Albrecht, *Melancholia I* and *Saint Jerome*, 102.

EDUCATION, 162–64, 173, 322, 336 n.31.

El Greco, 44.

Elkins, James, 341 n.23.

Emblem (*emblema*), 157–59, 340–41 n.11, 351 n.30.

Enlightenment: aesthetics, 60; "black box" notion, 151–53, 155, 173, 229; and the Black Paintings, 188, 279–81; and *Caprichos*, 131, 134, 173, 187, 213; complexities and contradictions, 188–89, 203; critique of religion, 190–91, 197, 220; "dialectic of" (Horkheimer and Adorno), 110, 277–78; ethics and morality, 207–211, 216, 217, 227, 240–41; failed promises, 236; and the French Revolution, 221, 237; and Goya's critique, 10, 13, 110–14, 187–89, 193–99, 220–23, 311; Hegel's critique of, 112, 134, 311; and history, 203, 213–14; Kant's thought, 139, 152–53, 197, 212–13, 220, 311; and myth, 277, 278; and reason, 152, 173, 187, 199, 213, 229; and representation, 200; and Spanish backwardness, 9, 13, 112, 162–69; thinkers, 200, 223, 336 n.31; values of good breeding and learning, 114.

Ensemble painting, 52, 67, 264.

Etchings: process of, 88, 282; after Velásquez, 42, 146–50, 333 n.22. See also *Caprichos*; *Disasters of War*; *Tauromaquia* series.

Ethics: and affect, 240; Aristotelian sense, 345 n.27; in art versus philosophy, 240–41; bourgeois, 221; in Goya's works, 203–205, 226, 227–28; issue of responsibility, 237–40; Kant on, 200, 205, 208, 210–12, 241; and morality, 207–211, 217–20, 241; photography and, 235; of postmodernism, 345 n.29; and representation, 201; of the spectator, 205, 233, 236, 240–41.

FAJARDO, SAAVEDRA, 351 n.30.

Famine of 1811–12, 100, 235, 236.

Feelings, 214, 223, 242. *See also* Sympathy.

Feijóo, Father Jerónimo, *Teatro crítico universal*, 325–27.

Ferdinand VII, 237, 284, 317; portrait of, 114, 216–17, 304, *306*.

Ferrari, Enrique Lafuente, 120.

Fight at the New Inn (1777), 59, *59*, 74–75, 336 n.27.

Figuration, 10, 12, 89–90, 97–98, 105, 107.

"First Bordeaux Album" (1824–28), 203; "*Gran coloso dormido*," 202, 203, 227.

Flatness, 12, 42, 46, 50, 52, 333 n.24.

Floridablanca, Count of, 32, 44, 314–15, 317; portrait, 44–46, *45*.

Flying Witches, 40.

Fragonard, Jean-Honoré, 55.

Framing, 129–31, 138, 149, 200, 207, 253, 295, 309. *See also* Representation.

Francis Borgia, St., 44. See also *St. Francis Borgia at the Deathbed of an Impenitent* (1788).

Freedom, 280–81, 284, 287, 302.

French occupation, 105, 216–17, 236. See also *Disasters of War*; French Revolution; Napoleonic wars; *Second of May, 1808 (1814), The*; *Third of May, 1808, The* (1814).

French Revolution, 105, 213–14, 221, 237, 240, 260–61, 274, 315, 320.

Frescoes. *See* San Antonio frescoes; *Miracle of Saint Anthony*; Tiepolo, Giovanni Battista.

Freud, Sigmund, 193.

Fried, Michael, 32, 332 n.15.

GAME OF HORSE AND RIDER, THE (1791–92), 84, *86*.

Garcini y Queralt, Ignacio, 355 n.21; portrait of, 317–20, *318*.

Gaspar Melchor de Jovellanos at his Desk (1798), 114, *115*, 320.

Genealogy, 169.

Giaquinto, Corrado, 333 n.19.

Glendenning, Nigel, 342 n.27.

Godoy, Manuel, 105.

Goethe, Johann Wolfgang von, *Werther*, 320, 322.

Gombrich, Ernst, *Art and Illusion*, 68, 335 n.19.

Gontarski, Stan, 238.

Goya, Francisco de: career as artist, 15, 40, 145; commissions, 15, 19, 40, 57, 60, 145, 216; darkening view of the world, 15, 269–74, 351 n.28; deafness and illness, 269–70, 348 n.2, 349 n.3; early years, 15; exile in Bordeaux, 100, 271; on "invention" in art, 16, 46, 68, 331 n.1; as painter to the king and court painter, 30–31, 56–57, 216; political stance, 63, 124, 271; prestige and appointments, 145; project of critique, 10–13, 112, 116, 128–29, 135, 145, 226, 230, 296, 301–303; relationship to modern art, 9–10, 12, 52–53, 68, 227; sources of inspiration, 68–70. See also Goya, Francisco de, works.

Goya, Francisco de, works: bullfight images, 11, 24, 79, 90, 116–26, 355 n.22; contradictions in, 10, 124, 192, 203, 298–99; ethical force of, 203–205, 226, 227–28; folk customs and festivals, 205–206, 344 n.24, 344 n.25; historical paintings, 102–107, 109–112, 236; images of violence, 126–28, 209–10, 232; Italian sketchbook, 15, 47, *48–49*; light and dark in, 31, 42–44, 55, 84, 110, 114–16, 172–73, 185, 253, 339 n.5; negation in, 102, 107, 116, 126; relationship to external factors, 12–13, 124; religious painting, 17–23, 32–35, 42, 53; scenes of bourgeois life, 10; self-incorporation in, 44, 314; self-reflection in, 131, 282; standard views of, 10, 12; still lifes, 98–100, *99*; subjectless, 12. *See also* Black Paintings; *Caprichos*; *Disasters of War*; Portraits; Self-portraits; San Antonio frescoes; Tapestry cartoons; *Tauromaquia* series; *and titles of specific works*.
Goya and the Spirit of Enlightenment (catalogue), 187–88.
Gran coloso (formerly attrib., 1808–12), 298.
"*Gran coloso dormido*" (1824–28), *202*, 203, 227.
Greenberg, Clement, 52–53, 95–96, 333 n.24.
Guevara, Luis Vélez de, *El diablo cojuelo*, 297.

HANNIBAL CROSSING THE ALPS (ca. 1771), 47, *48*, *49*.
Hegel, Georg Wilhelm Friedrich, 13, 213, 345 nn.29–30; "beautiful soul," 320, 356 n.24; critique of Enlightenment, 112, 134, 311; on freedom, 281, 293, 349 n.12, 351 n.26; on utility, 311–12.
Heidegger, Martin, "The Age of the World View," 137–38.
Hetzer, Theodor, 64.
Highwaymen Attacking a Coach (*Asalto de la diligencia*, 1786–87), *75*
History, 200, 203, 213–17, 301.
Hogarth, William, 134.
Horkheimer, Max, 230; *Dialectic of Enlightenment*, 126, 277, 292, 293, 353 n.44.
Houasse, Miguel Ange, 332 n.2.
Hughes, Robert, 24, 40, 236, 274–75, 317, 336 n.26.
Human savagery, 75, 81, 126, 337 n.31. *See also Disasters of War*.

Hume, David, 313, 323, 355 n.17.
Hunt with Birdcall (1775), 56, *57*.
Husserl, Edmund, 335 n.19.
Hutcheson, Francis, 312.

IBARRA, JOSÉ DE, *De mestizo y española, castizo*, 77.
Ideology, 296, 302.
Ilie, Paul, 343 n.6.
Inquisition, 197, 237, 291, 304, 315, 325–27.
Interpellation, 295–96.
Invention, 16, 46, 68, 201; term "inventadas" for, 331 n.1.
Italian sketchbook, 15, 47, *48–49*.

JACOBI, FRIEDRICH HEINRICH, *Woldemar*, 356 n.24.
Jovellanos, Gaspar Melchor de, 19, 162, 221, 334–35 n.11; portrait of, 114, *115*, 320.
Juliá, Asensio, 354 n.6.

KANT, IMMANUEL: on aesthetics, 213, 243, 323; on autonomy, 139; on beauty, 309–310, 311; *The Conflict of the Faculties*, 199–200, 203; *Critique of Judgment*, 212, 223, 243, 258, 347 n.18, 356 n.25; *Critique of Practical Reason*, 210, 241–43; *Critique of Pure Reason*, 152, 189–90, 200–201, 211; critique of religion, 190–91, 197, 220; on ethics, 13, 190, 200, 205, 208, 210–12, 241; on the French Revolution, 213–14, 240, 260–61; on moral law, 153, 242–43; priority of philosophy, 199–200; on reason and history, 213, 217–20; *Religion within the Limits of Reason Alone*, 153, 190–91; on representation, 201; theory of the sublime, 201, 213, 233, 243, 258–60, 262, 347 n.22; "What Is Enlightenment?" 212. *See also* Enlightenment; Hegel, Georg Wilhelm Friedrich.
Kirchner, Ludwig, 9.
Klingender, F. D., 59.
Knife Grinder, The, 341 n.14.
Kubovy, Michael, 138.

LAFAYETTE, MARQUIS DE, 315.
Lanterna magica, 151, 288, 341 n.17.
Lardizábal, Miguel de, 317.
Larsen, Neil, "Modernism, Manet, and the 'Maximilian,'" 107–110.

Las Meninas (Goya after Velásquez, ca. 1778–85), 146, *147*, 149. *See also* Velásquez, Diego: *Las Meninas.*

Last Supper (1796–97): detail, *50*; oblique perspective of, 47–50.

Leocadia, La (1819–23), 271, *272*, 303–304, 320.

Licht, Fred: on the Black Paintings, 276, 350 n.20; on *Disasters of War*, 231–32; on religious art, 191; on the San Antonio frescoes, 21, 192; on the tapestry cartoons, 57–58.

Light, 31, 42–44, 55, 84, 114–16; of reason, 152, 173, 229; in Tiepolo's works, 27–30; and truth, 110, 172, 226.

Lithography, 351 n.27.

Luzán, Ignacio de, *Poética*, 307–309.

Luzán, José, 15.

MADHOUSE, THE, 304.

Madrid, 15; *Allegory of the City of Madrid* (1810), 214, *215*, 216–17; bullfighting images of, 24, *121*, *123*, 355 n.22; celebration of, 206–207; famine year, 100, 235, 236; riots, 59, 105; San Antonio de la Florida church, 23; San Francisco el Grande church, 32, *34*, 40, 42–44; Tiepolo's Royal Palace frescoes, 27, *28–29*, 30–31. See also *Caprichos*; Quinta del Sordo; San Antonio frescoes; Tapestry cartoons.

Magnasco, Allesandro, *Interrogations in Jail* (1710–20), 232, *233*.

Majos and *majas*, 24, 51, 59.

Malraux, André, 107, 126, 304–307.

Manet, Édouard: *Absinthe Drinker* (1859), 135, 320; *Asparagus* (1880), 98, *99*, 102; *The Bullfight* (1864), 116–19; *Dead Toreador* (ca. 1864), 90–95, *91*, *92*, 96–97, 98; *Execution of Emperor Maximilian* (1868–69), 107–10, *108*; *The Fifer* (1866), *94*, 95; *Incident in a Bullfight* (ca. 1864), 90–93, *91*, *92*, 96, 97, *97*, 116; and modernism, 95, 96–97, 107, 126; *Philosopher*, 135, 320, *321*; portraits of lone individuals, 95; on Tiepolo, 31, 332 n.13.

Marqués, Manuela B. Mena, 77, 354 n.6.

Martínez y Pérez, Sebastián, 221, 270; portrait of, *113*, 114.

Mary, Queen of Martyrs (1780–81), 37–39, *38*.

Material support, 37, 52, 338 n.45; canvas, 42, 46, 52.

Meadow of San Isidro (1788), 205–207, 221, 283, 286–87, 331 n.1; detail, *205*.

Medicine, 325–27; *El médico* (1799), *325*.

Mena, Luis de, *Castas o escenas de mestizaje*, 77.

Mengs, Antón Raphael, 15, 336 n.23.

Mercier, Louis-Sébastien, 110–12.

Metaphysics of modernity, 137, 138–39.

Milkmaid of Bordeaux, The (1825–27), *308*, 309, 313, 354 n.6.

Miracle of St. Anthony (1798), 19–23, *20*; anamorphosis, 46–47, 51, 282; architectural element of railing, 24, *25*, 26, 31, 35; details, *22*, *25*; as ensemble painting, 51–52, 67; figures, 24, 44, 51–52; landscape and sky, 24–26, 36; perspective and composition, 31, 36–37, 52, 192; presaging of modernism, 52–53; presentation to painting's beholder, 31–32; secular imagery, 23–26, 46, 192; and Tiepolo's throne room ceiling, 30. *See also* San Antonio frescoes.

"Mirroring effect" (Ortega y Gasset), 65.

Modernism, 52–53, 93, 96, 109, 227; and "modern," 12, 137–38. *See also* Modernist art; Postmodernism.

Modernist art: as aesthetic self-reflection, 95–96; and Goya's work, 12, 52–53, 98–100, 226, 227; Greenberg on, 95, 333 n.24; Manet and, 95, 96–97, 98, 107; as move from figuration toward abstraction, 12, 89, 97–98, 107. *See also* Abstraction.

Modernity, 10, 138–39.

Monnet, Charles, 155.

Moral beauty, 314, 320–22.

Morality: and ethics, 207–211, 217–20, 241; and sympathy, 313, 328.

Moratín, Leandro Fernández de, 64, 221; *Carta histórica sobre el origen y progresos de las fiestas de toros en España*, 119–20; *El sí de las niñas*, 337 n.36.

Muller, Priscilla, 288, 290, 298; *Goya's 'Black' Paintings*, 278–79, 350 n.20.

Munch, Edvard, 9.

Murat, Joachim, 105.

Murillo, Bartolomé Esteban, 40, 333 n.23.

Myth, 276–78, 290–93, 294–96.

NAPOLEON, 105, 291, 315.

Napoleonic wars, 237, 262, 291. *See also Disasters of War; Second of May, 1808, The* (1814); *Third of May, 1808, The* (1814).

National painting (Spain), 331 n.1.

Naturalization, 286–87, 307.

Negation, 98, 102, 107, 109, 116, 126.

Nordström, Folke, 276.

OEDIPUS, 294.

Optics, 46, 66, 288, 340 n.10. *See also* Perspective.

Ortega y Gasset, José, on the "mirroring effect," 65.

Osuna, Duke and Duchess of, 42; portrait of, 57, 114.

PACHECO, FRANCISCO, 40.

Palomino, Antonio, *Museo pictórico*, 44–46, 47, 66.

Parasol, The (1777), 55, 70, *70*.

Pardo Palace, 56, 60, 334 n.4.

Pascal, Blaise, 191.

Paulson, Ronald, 274, 339 n.5.

Pelele, El (*The Straw Manikin*, 1791), 337 n.44, 337–38 n.45.

Pérez de Castro, Evaristo, 221.

Perspective: Albertian, 18, 27, 50, 66–67, 68, 138, 154; altered for curved surfaces, 46–47, 51; disruption of, by Manet, 95; eighteenth-century conventions, 16–17; oblique, in *Last Supper*, 47–50; in Palomino's *Museo pictórico*, 46, 47; in religious paintings, 27, 31, 32, 37, 47–51; as secular, 31; as a window, 154, 341 n.23. *See also* Artificial perspective.

Phantasmagoria, 288–90.

Philip IV, King, 335 n.21.

Philippines Company, 315.

Philosophy, 199–200.

Photography, Sontag on, 235, 346 n.7.

Photojournalism, 126, 231–32, 233.

Picasso, Pablo: *Guernica*, 52, 268; *Massacre in Korea* (1951), 107, *109*.

Picnic on the Banks of the Manzanares, 70, 73, 336 n.26.

Picturesque naturalism, 17, 18, 71, 307, 332 n.2.

Pilgrimage to San Isidro, The (1820–23), 207, *208–209*, 221, 283, 286–87, 293.

Pliny the Elder, *Historia naturalis*, 67–68.

Plotinus, 322.

Politics, 12, 235–36, 274–75, 284, 291, 298, 301, 349 n.12.

Ponz, Antonio, 341 n.13.

Portrait of Ferdinand VII (1814–15), 114, 304, *306*.

Portraits: of aristocrats, 9, 10, 57, 114–16; for the Bank of San Carlos, 145; of Bartolomé Sureda y Miserol, 314, 317–23, *319*; of Brigadier Ignacio Garcini y Queralt, 317–20, *318*; *The Count of Floridablanca* (1783), 44–46, *45*, 154, 314; of the Duquesa de Alba, 303; family of Charles IV, 304, *305*; family of Infante Don Luis de Borbón, 114; Ferdinand VII, 114, 216–17, 304, *306*; *Gaspar Melchor de Jovellanos at his Desk* (1798), 114, *115*, 320; group, 114; of intellectuals, 10, 112–14, 221; King Joseph I, 216; of the royal family, 146; *Sebastián Martínez y Pérez* (1792), *113*, 114; ugliness in, 304.

Postmodernism, 137, 345 n.29.

Pottery Seller, The (1799), 71–73, *72*.

Projection, 151, 288–90, 341 n.17

Puvis de Chavannes, Pierre, *Legend of St. Genevieve*, 191.

QUEVEDO, FRANCISCO DE, *Sueños*, 155.

Quinta del Sordo, 55, 81, 188, 269, 270, 281, 286. *See also* Black Paintings; *Witches' Sabbath, The*.

RAPE OF EUROPA, THE (1772), 336 n.22.

Reason: Enlightenment and, 152, 173, 187, 199, 213, 229; light of, 152, 173, 203, 229; limits of, 244–48. *See also under* Kant, Immanuel.

Religious painting: aesthetic conventions, 53, architectural elements, 35; Licht on, 191; neoclassical formalism in, 17, 18, 35; presence of the beholder, 31–32, 35; salvation, 192–93; visual effects required by the supernatural, 31–32, 40. See also *Crucified Christ; Miracle of St. Anthony*; San Antonio frescoes; Secular art.

Rembrandt Harmenszoon van Rijn, 44, 68.

Renaissance pictorial tradition, 200, 229.

Representation: conventions of artificial perspective in, 138–39, 144–45, 154; Heidegger on, 137–38; limits of, 138–39, 140, 145, 146, 200–203; nature of, 151–52; reliance on framing, 200, 229; and truth, 146, 162, 172, 229–30, 231; use of radical foreshortening, 206–207.

Ribera, Jusepe de: *Crucifixion*, 40–42.

Ricci, Sebastiano: *Saint Anthony of Padua Healing a Young Man*, 193; *San Gaetano Comforting a Moribund Sinner*, 193.

Robert, Étienne-Gaspard, 290, 351–52 n.35.

Rococo painting, 192, 333 n.19, 344 n.24.

Rosenberg, Jakob, 231.

Rothe, Hans, 23–24.

Rousseau, Jean-Jacques, 75, 336 n.31; invocation of humble people, 206, 344 n.24; *Philosophie*, 155; sympathy, 221, 223.

Royal Academy of Fine Arts (San Fernando): Goya's address to, 16, 336 n.31; Goya's admission to, 40, 46, 50; Goya's directorship of, 145.

Royal Company of the Philippines, 315.

Royal Palace (Madrid), Tiepolo's throne room ceiling fresco, 27, 28–29, 30–31.

Royal Tapestry Works (Santa Bárbara), 30, 55, 56, 65, 87–88, 334 n.3. *See also* Tapestry cartoons.

Rubens, Peter Paul, 68, 335 n.21.

SACRIFICE, 159, 292, 353 n.44.

St. Francis Borgia at the Deathbed of an Impenitent (1788), 193, *194*, 323; preliminary sketch, 193, *195*.

Salvation, 192–93, 197, 217, 323.

San Antonio de la Florida church (Madrid): construction of, 23; fresco ceiling, 19, *20*, 30, 35, 36–37; as ordinary people's place of worship, 23. *See also Miracle of St. Anthony*; San Antonio frescoes.

San Antonio frescoes, 19–23, 25, 27, 35–37, 40, 44, 47, 87, 192, 145, 282, 283, 332; commission, 19; miracle scene, 19, 21–23. *See also Miracle of St. Anthony*.

San Francisco el Grande church (Madrid): altarpiece commission, 40, 42–44; *Sermon of Saint Bernardino of Siena* (1781–83), 32, *34*.

Santa Bárbara Royal Tapestry Factory, 30, 55, 56, 65, 87–88, 334 n.3. *See also* Tapestry cartoons.

Santiáñez, Nil, 263.

Saturnalia, 291–93.

Saturn Devouring His Son (1820–23), 271, *273*, 274–75, 276, 283, 290–91, 335 n.21, 351 n.28; and the myth of Saturn, 291–93, 336 n.22; political interpretation, 275, 349 n.12.

Sebastián Martínez y Pérez (1792), 113, *114*.

Second of May, 1808, The (1814), 102–107, *103*, 124, 126, 261; detail, *106*.

Second of May uprisings, 102, 105, 216.

Secular art, 17–18, 31; Alberti and, 67; secularization, 11–12, 18–23, 31, 191–92, 193.

See-Saw, The (1780), 84.

Self-consciousness, 18, 114, 128, 134, 137, 203, 221, 226; and self-incorporation, 44.

Self-portraits, 44, 314; "*Francisco Goya y Lucientes, Pintor*" (1797–98), 131, *132*, 134–35, 154, 189, 327, 328; *Self-Portrait at an Easel* (1790–95), 129–31, *130*, 146, 226, 327; *Self-Portrait with Dr. Arrieta* (1829), 323–25, *324*, 327–28.

Self-reflection, 95–96, 102, 107, 131, 226, 282.

Semisunken Dog (ca. 1820–23), 100–102, *101*, 227, 258, 280.

Seneca, Lucius Annaeus, 292.

Sermon of Saint Bernardino of Siena (1781–83), 32, *34*.

Sessions of the Junta of the Royal Company of the Philippines (ca. 1815), 315–17, *316*.

Shaftesbury (Lord Ashley), 312–13, 323.

Siebers, Tobin, 344 n.18.

Simpleton, The ("*Bobalicón*," 1815–19), 84, *87*.

Sleep, 172–73.

Sloterdijk, Peter, 139.

Smith, Pamela H., 71.

Sobradiel, Count of, 39. See also *Burial of Christ*.

Social criticism, 11, 16, 75, 77, 134, 145, 157, 162–69, 283.

Social relations, 11, 64, 81, 144, 162, 173, 291, 301.

Sontag, Susan: on photography, 235, 346 n.7; *Regarding the Pain of Others*, 233–35.

Spanish Golden Age painters, 40–42.

Starobinski, Jean, 79.

Still Life of a Lamb's Head and Flanks (1806–12), 98, *99*, 102.

Still life painting, 98–100, 340 n.10.

Stiltwalkers, The (1797–92), 79, *80*.

Studium (Barthes), 64.

Subjectivity, 139, 221, 334 n.29.

Sublime, the, 201, 212–13, 232, 232–33, 258–60, 262, 347 n.22; aesthetics of, 213, 232–33, 243, 261.

Sueños, no. 27, "*Brujas disfrazadas en físicos comunes*" (1796–97), 325, 326.

Superstition, 11, 40, 123, 153, 325; and Enlightenment thought, 13, 112, 152, 187, 191, 197, 199, 220, 221, 277, 279; portrayed in *Caprichos*, 134, 144, 173, 221; and ugliness in the Black Paintings, 304.

Sureda y Miserol, Bartolomé, portrait of, *319, 320–23*.

Swing, The (1779), 60, *61*.

Sympathy, 223, 310–11, 313, 322–23, 327–28.

TAKING OF CHRIST, THE (1798), 42, *43*.

Tapestries, 56–58; fees for artworks, 336 n.23; technique for making, 56, 65, 87–88, 338 nn.45–46. *See also* Tapestry cartoons.

Tapestry cartoons, 15–16; anticipation of *Caprichos*, 79–81, 337 n.34; and the Black Paintings, 81, 282, 283–84, 291; and conventional visual principles, 64–65; creation of tapestries, 56, 65–66, 87–88; critical work, 58, 63–65, 75–79, 88; darkness and tension in, 55, 66, 153; early, schematic works, 56; images of children, 81–87, *83*; images of human aggression, 81, 124, 244; images of hunting, 81; as images of Spanish life, 9, 55, 58–63, 199, 334 n.2; influences, 64–65, 334 n.1; as invention, 331 n.1; modernity of, 65; as narratives, 35, 63, 70–71, 73–74; naturalism, 17, 18, 68–71, 307; normative view of world, 17, 58–59, 63; payment for, 56; placement of, 35, 56, 60, 334 nn.4,9; rediscovery of, 56; royal patronage, 55, 56–57, 58; tree, 24–26; two periods of, 55, 64. *See also* Tapestry cartoons, by title.

Tapestry cartoons, by title: *La acerolera*, 334 n.4; *The Ball Game*, 60; *Blind Man's Buff* (1788), 68, *69*, 81, 284, *285*; *Boy Riding a Ram* (1786–87), 81, *83*, 337 n.43; *Boys Picking Fruit* (1778), 84; *Boys with Mastiffs* (1786–87), 84, *85*; *Dance on the Banks of the Manzanares* (1777), 60, *62*, 70; *Dogs and Hunting Equipment* (1775), 56; *Fight at the New Inn* (1777), 59, *59*, 74–75, 336 n.27; *Las floreras o La*

Primavera, 334 n.9; *The Game of Horse and Rider* (1791–92), 84, *86*; *Hunt with Birdcall* (1775), 56, *57*; *Jugadores de naipes* (*The Card Players*, 1777–78), 336 n.29; *El médico* (1799), 325; *The Parasol* (1777), 55, 70, *70*; *El Pelele*, 337 n.44, 337–38 n.45; *Picnic on the Banks of the Manzanares*, 70, 73, 336 n.26; *The Pottery Seller* (1799), 71–73, *72*; *The Stiltwalkers* (1797–92), 79, *80*; *The Swing* (1779), 60, *61*; *Two Cats Fighting* (1786), 81, *82*; *The Wedding* (1791–92), 75–77, *76*, 159, 337 n.34.

Tauromaquia series (1816), 119–20; affinities with *Caprichos* and *Disparates*, 123; no. 14, "*El diestrisimo estudiante de Falces*," 355 n.22; no. 18, *The Daring of Martincho in the Ring at Zaragoza, 121, 123*; no. 19, *Another Madness of His in the Same Ring, 122*; no. 20, *The Agility and Audacity of Juanito Apiñani in the Ring at Madrid, 121, 123*, 355 n.22; no. 21, "*Desgracias acaecidas en el tendido de la plaza de Madrid*," 355 n.22; no. 38, *The Death of Pepe Hilo*, 123; Unpublished print "A" (1814–15), *122, 123*.

Taylor, Charles, 293, 349 n.12, 350 n.17.

Teatro pintoresco, 288–90.

Third of May, 1808, The (1814), *104*; as aesthetic self-reflection, 102, 107; as critique, 107, 110–12; and *Disasters of War*, 126, 208, 261; and Enlightenment, 13, 110–12, 187; ethical challenges of, 208–210; horrors of, 304–307; influence on Manet and Picasso, 107–110; line of French soldiers taking aim, 298; Malraux on, 304–307; shooting victim, 74, 110, *111*; traditional views of, 110.

Tiepolo, Domenico, 332 n.9.

Tiepolo, Giovanni Battista: fresco ceilings, 26–27, 30, 332 n.9; *The Glory of Spain*, 30–31; late baroque illusionism, 17; management of natural light, 27–30; religious aesthetic and secularity, 27; Treppenhaus ceiling of the Würzburger Residenz, 27, *28*, 30; Venetian carnival images, 157; *Wealth and Benefits of the Spanish Monarchy under Charles III, 28–29*.

Todorov, Tzvetan, 188.

Tomlinson, Janis: on Aula Dei paintings, 332 n.15; on bullfighting images, 120, 339 n.10; on frescoes for the Basilica of

the Virgen del Pilar (Zaragoza), 37, 39,
333 n.19; on invention in Goya, 331 n.1;
on San Francisco el Grande altarpiece,
44, 333 n.26; on the tapestry cartoons, 79,
332 n.15, 334 nn.1–2, 4, 9, 337 n.34.
Torture, 236–37, 248, 304.
Truth, 31, 214–16, 229, 302, 304; and light, 110,
172, 226; and myth, 290; and role of art,
10, 230–31. See also *Truth Rescued by Time,
Witnessed by History*.
Truth Rescued by Time, Witnessed by History
(1812), 203, *204*, 214–16, 217, 291; preliminary
sketch, 217, *218*.
Two Cats Fighting (1786), 81, *82*.
Two Old Ones Eating Soup (1823), 285, *285*.

UCCELLO, PAOLO, 27.
Ugliness, 75, 77, 159, 162–64, 244, 304–307, 322.
Utility, 311–14.
Utopia, 296–97, 299; false, 302.

VARGAS ORIGEL, DR. ARTURO, 349 n.3.
Vasari, Giorgio, *Lives of the Artists*, 27, 149–50.
Velásquez, Diego: Aesop and Menippus, 148,
320, 337 n.35; *Los borrachos* (*The Drunkards*),
146; conventions of artificial perspective
in, 149; *Crucified Christ*, 42; as influence
and model, 42, 68, 146–50, 333 n.22,
341 n.14; *Las Meninas*, 129, 146, 226, 317;
as "painterly," 226; representation
and framing, 200; self-consciousness,
44; *The Surrender at Breda*, 150; use of color,
149–50, 341 n.14.
Ventas del Espíritu Santo, 74.

Verignaud, Pierre, 274.
Villabriga, María Teresa de, 114.
Vita activa and *vita contemplativa*, 320.

WAR: GOYA'S VISION OF, 231, 261–68; images
of, 235, 268; response to, 301; total, 262–63;
violence of, 235, 248–53. See also *Disasters
of War*; Napoleonic wars.
Watteau, Antoine, 55.
Wedding, The (1791–92), 76; architectural
elements in, 75; arranged marriage, 76–77,
337 n.34; composition and perspective,
75; as narrative of colonialism and race,
77; as social critique, 75.
Weiss, Leocadia, 271.
Whitebook, Joel, 292–93, 353 n.44.
Wilson-Bareau, Juliet, 120.
Winckelmann, Johann Joachim, 263–64.
Witches' Sabbath, The (1797–98), 116, 221, *222*,
290, 293.
Witchy Brew, The, 292.
Wittkower, Margot and Rudolf, *Born under
Saturn*, 276.
Woman Viper, The (1797–98), 223, *225*, 346 n.39.

YARD WITH LUNATICS (ca. 1794), 193, *196*,
270.
Young, Edward, *Night Thoughts*, 276.

ZAPATER, MARTÍN, letters to, 206, 270,
344 n.25.
Zaragoza: bullring, *121*, 123; religious works,
32–40.
Zurbarán, Francisco de, 40.

Image Credits

Agefotostock/Alamy: 4.11, 5.1, 6.12.

AIFA Visuals/Alamy: 3.21.

Album/Alamy: 1.1, 1.2, 1.3, 1.4, 1.18, 2.2, 2.15, 2.16, 3.23, 5.2, 5.3, 5.6, 5.7, 5.8, 5.15, 8.4, 8.6, 8.9.

Album/Art Resource, NY: 1.3, 1.4, 1.5, 2.1.

Album/Scala, Florence: 1.11, 1.12.

Antiquarian Images/Alamy: 3.9, 3.10, 3.11, 3.14, 8.3.

Archivart/Alamy: 2.4, 2.8, 2.10, 2.14, 7.5.

Artefact/Alamy: 1.14, 2.3, 3.16, 8.8.

Artokoloro/Alamy: 2.17, 3.17, 3.19, 3.20, 3.27, 6.3, 6.6, 6.7, 6.13, 8.5.

Art Explorer/Alamy: 5.14.

Art Heritage/Alamy: 1.19, 8.7.

Darling Archive/Alamy: 2.11.

Hemis/Alamy: 5.13.

Heritage Image Partnership Ltd./Alamy: 2.7, 7.3, 7.6.

ImageBar: 1.10.

Incamerastock/Alamy: 2.13, 3.1, 3.11, 3.15, 8.1.

Institut Amatller d'Art Hispànic: 1.16, 1.17.

Museo del Prado. Photo: MNP/Scala, Florence: 1.13.

Museum of Fine Arts Boston, gift of Mrs. Horatio Greenough Curtis
    in memory of Horatio Greenough Curtis: 5.11.

National Gallery of Art, Washington, D.C., Samuel H. Kress Collection: 1.7.

Picture Art Collection/Alamy: 1.8, 1.9, 1.15, 2.12, 3.2, 3.18, 5.5, 6.1, 6.8, 6.9, 6.10, 6.14, 7.2, 8.2.

Prisma Archivo/Alamy: 3.8, 5.10.

PvE/Alamy: 3.6.

PWB Images/Alamy: 4.4.

Rapp Halour/Alamy: 3.7.

Real Academia de Bellas Artes de San Fernando: 2.9, 3.23–3.26, 3.28, 3.29, 4.1, 4.2, 4.3, 4.5–4.25, 5.4, 5.9, 5.12, 6.2–6.18, 7.4.

RMN-Grand Palais/Art Resource, NY: 3.5, 3.13 (photo: Mathieu Rabeau).

Universal Images Group North America LLC/Alamy: 2.6, 7.1.

Wikimedia Commons: 1.6 (photo: Myriam Thyes), 2.5 (photo: Alonso de Mendoza).

World History Archive/Alamy: 3.4.